LET THE GOOD TIMES ROLL

Let the

PARAGON

HOUSE

NEW YORK

GOOD TIMES ROLL

LIFE AT HOME

IN AMERICA

DURING

WORLD WAR II

PAUL D. CASDORPH

Published in the United States by

Paragon House
90 Fifth Avenue
New York, NY 10011

Library of Congress Cataloging-in-Publication
Data

Casdorph, Paul D.
    Let the good times roll: life at home in
America during World War II / by Paul D.
Casdorph.
        p.   cm.
    Includes index.
    ISBN 1–55778–164–8
    1. United States—History—1933–1945.   2.
United States—Social life and customs—
1918–1945.   3. World War, 1939–1945—
United States.   I. Title.
E806.C387   1989
973.917—dc20   89–34057
                                CIP

Designed by Kathy Kikkert
Manufactured in the United States of America

The paper used in this publication meets the
requirements of American National Standard for
Information Sciences—Permanence of Paper for
Printed Library Materials, ANSI Z39.48–1984.

To the memory of my mother,
Virginia Elizabeth Casdorph

CONTENTS

Preface   ix

1   December 1941:
    The Call to Arms   1

2   January–April 1942:
    Home Front America Discovers the War   20

3   May–August 1942:
    A National Paradox   37

4   September–December 1942:
    In Like Flynn   55

5   January–May 1943:
    Off-Color Shenanigans   77

6   June 1943:
    Days of Protest   98

7   July–December 1943:
    A Subversive Autumn   117

8   January–April 1944:
    War Is Hell   136

9   May–July 1944:
    A Mousey-Looking Little Man from Missouri   156

10 August–December 1944:
    Ballots and Baseball   176

11 January–March 1945:
How to Get Married   197

12 April–July 1945:
Two Dictators and a President Die   216

13 August 1945:
The End: New Bombs and Celebrations   238

Index   259

PREFACE

L ife on the domestic home front during America's forty-five month involvement in World War II was a time of demarcation. For better or worse, traditional relationships of every description underwent sweeping changes. No segment of American society—women, minorities, young, or old—escaped the hurly-burly of the war years. The mass infusion of government funds into the economy to produce the machines of war not only ended the crippling depression of the 1930s, but also put money into the pockets of millions for the first time. Easy money and the remoteness of foreign battlefields caused the good times to roll along, with a general snubbing of the old order. Money and movement brought on by war fostered a what-the-hell attitude that did not vanish with the return of peace in 1945.

Another spinoff of the ready availability of money was the remarkable unanimity of purpose that pervaded wartime America however much the excitement and dislocations of 1941–1945 changed the country. For conservatives the war marked a collapse of traditional values and a commitment to the security of the past; for liberals it marked the beginning of greater democracy and a loosening of those shackles that had bound women and minorities to an antiquated traditionalism. Any shift in the American enterprise was bound up in the saga of individuals, great and small, who stayed behind as millions of men—and women, too—went into uniform for the duration. Here, then, is an attempt to tell their story by portraying serious events in human terms; the lives of numerous common folk and celebrities alike have been woven into the narrative. A chronological rendering of events from newspapers and popular magazines of the period, augmented by various secondary works and biographical materials, gives the present reader much the same information as home-front America absorbed during the war itself.

Besides the legions of librarians across the country who responded to my calls for materials about the war, several people helped in special ways to make this book a reality. My late mother, Virginia Elizabeth Casdorph, with whom I traveled across the country from New York to Seattle during 1944–1945, helped a wide-eyed twelve-year-old first grasp the impact of the war on American society. My wife, Patricia Barker Casdorph, not only lent a helping hand throughout my work, but also waited patiently while I cloistered myself with the business of writing. Carolyn Menello, secretary to the history faculty at West Virginia State College, uncomplainingly found time to type the manuscript amid her other duties. Several members of the WVSC library staff—John Scott, Elizabeth Scobell, Linda Mullins, and Ron Wiley—were always generous with advice and help as was my editor at Paragon House, P J Dempsey. Sue Forrest, Lois McCarthy, and Pam Pratt of the West Virginia College of Graduate Studies went out of their way to assist with library loan materials. In the last measure, however, all evaluation of people and events is my responsibility alone.

Paul D. Casdorph
Charleston, West Virginia

1 DECEMBER 1941: THE CALL TO ARMS

"Good, now we can whip their ass," quipped an Appalachian boy named Carl Hager on first hearing radio reports of the Japanese raid on Pearl Harbor. Although the country was plunged into war when news of the attack hit the airwaves that Sunday afternoon in December 1941, his brand of enthusiasm for a good fight soon swept the entire society. Over the next forty-five months—before the return of peace in August 1945—the giant swirl of activity brought on by the war produced a lightness of spirit that changed a tradition-bound America. As millions of people left the familiarity of home for the first time to enter the military or take jobs in bustling defense plants, old values and taboos were forgotten. The absence of social unrest and political protest—at least among white Americans who had clearly defined enemies in Hitler and Tojo during 1941–1945—produced a cohesive society ready for the good life; and the new lifestyles that emerged from a dislocated population were financed by a sudden avalanche of defense spending that reached every corner of the country.

The outbreak of fighting meant hardship for some in the midst of economic plenty and lessened moral restraint. From the instant those first bombs rained down on Oahu, the country was irretrievably changed. In a Dallas theater where 2,000 people were watching Gary Cooper portray the World War I hero, Sergeant Alvin York, news of the bombing was announced at 1:57 p.m. "There was a pause," reported *Time*, "a pin-point of silence, a prolonged sigh, and then thundering applause. A steelworker said, 'We'll kick their teeth in.' " The day was probably best summed up by a Chinese consular agent at New Orleans, who told questioning reporters: "As far as Japan is concerned, their goose is overheated."

Initial word of the Pearl Harbor tragedy was broadcast to the mainland about an hour and a half after the opening attack; unlike previous wars, in which indeterminable time passed before dispatches from distant battlefields reached the folks at home, Americans knew they were at war while the bombs were still falling. The day of instant journalism had arrived; and throughout the war public perception of the conflict was shaped by quick reporting of foreign and domestic events.

"White House Says Japs Attack Pearl Harbor." Those seven words flashed over the news wires at 2:25 p.m. Eastern Standard Time, although it was 3:00 p.m. in Washington and 12:00 noon in California before radio networks began announcing the Japanese thrust.

Commander Mitsuo Fuchida, airborne over the Pacific, had given the attack order at 7:49 a.m., Hawaii time—an hour and forty-nine minutes after leaving his mid-ocean task force—and the bombs struck minutes later. Because six international time zones separate Honolulu and Washington, President Franklin D. Roosevelt did not know about the intrusion until 1:47 in the afternoon, Washington time. News of the attack was passed to him by Navy Secretary Frank Knox, who had learned of the Pacific fleet's near annihilation seconds earlier through regular navy communication channels. A second bombing wave, launched at 12:15 p.m. Washington time, did not terminate until 3:00 p.m., an hour and fifteen minutes after Roosevelt's Day of Infamy had arrived.

There is no other way to say it: Pearl Harbor threw the country into turmoil. Professional football games and afternoon music broadcasts were saturating the East Coast when the networks began coverage of the attacks around 3:00 p.m. WOR in New York interrupted a Giants game at the Polo Grounds and continued brief announcements of the bombings until regular newscasts commenced later in the day. A torrent of telephone calls poured into the station, reported *Time*, "from people too excited about the game to become excited about anything else."

On the West Coast, where most families were in the middle of their Sunday lunch, the news from Honolulu caused more fear and anxiety than in other parts of the country; its closeness to the Pacific produced a near panic that a Japanese attack would follow along the coast. In the scramble for audiences the National Broadcasting Company got an early jump on other networks when it presented an observer live atop a downtown Honolulu building. "It is real war; it is no joke," he said, while recounting the carnage at Hickam Field, Honolulu, and Pearl Harbor.

Newspapers in every hamlet, eager to get on the band-wagon and not be eclipsed by radio, had put out supplemental editions before nightfall filled with late news from Washington and the Pacific. Although an "extra" is unknown to younger-generation Americans, during World War II each turn in the conflict brought out newsboys hawking the inevitable "extra" that detailed faraway theaters of operation. In West Virginia, the Charleston *Gazette* printed a special edition within hours of the attack with three huge letters—W A R—emblazoned across the front page in brilliant red. Yet the furor of approaching conflict did not produce the hysteria caused a few years earlier when Orson Welles broadcast his sham account of Martian invaders.

As one, the whole country launched into a frenzy of preparation to meet the Axis onslaught. And the fever of activity had an intoxicating effect. Before twenty-four hours had elapsed, Roosevelt appeared before a hastily summoned joint session of Congress to urge a formal statement of war. The president spoke solemnly for a brief six and a half minutes while sizing up the national temper: ". . . no matter how long it may take us to overcome this premeditated invasion, the American people in their righteous might will win through to absolute victory." And, as he asked Congress to commit the nation to war: "With confidence in our armed forces—with unbounding determination of our people—we will win the inevitable triumph—so help us God." With those assurances ringing in their ears, a unified House and Senate, with just one dissenting vote, rammed through a declaration of war against Japan. Japanese fleet admiral Isoroku Yamamoto, who had been schooled in the United States and who knew the American fiber, was correct in his evaluation of Pearl Harbor: a sleeping giant had been aroused.

The good times of World War II became identified with "for the duration," a term thrust upon the home front within days after the Japanese attack as a synonym for the conflict itself. Even the idea of a duration became a license for abandon. Roosevelt told his countrymen one day after the declaration of war: "You have a most grave responsibility to the nation now and for the duration of this war." Speaking during one of his fireside chats, the president was not only cautioning American journalists about their obligation to report the war faithfully, but also warning that the duration would make demands on everyone.

A second congressional mandate eleven days later got the attention of every able-bodied man and his family. Although a draft had been in operation for several months prior to Pearl Harbor, men called to arms under the Burke-Wadsworth Act were limited to time of service and to active duty in the Western Hemisphere only. "For the duration and six months" became the message to thousands of GIs already in uniform under the first peacetime selective service plan when Congress moved quickly to meet the Japanese menace. The plan spawned some initial discontent with United States participation in the war. Understandably, not all of the nearly two million men called up before the outbreak of actual hostilities were happy with the prospect of longer military service. Many figured their debt to Uncle Sam had been paid, while most had never reconciled themselves to duty in a peacetime army.

Before the war ended, qualification for military service was expanded to catch eleven million men in the draft net; it was a rare family indeed with no sons or daughters called into uniform before 1945. Throughout the war living room windows of tenement and mansion alike displayed white silken banners with a blue star or stars to signify the number of loved ones in uniform. As the war dragged on, gold-hued stars began to replace blue ones in homes saddened by casualties on unnamed battlefields—battlefields that are history-book footnotes forty years afterward. The patriotic emblems—they could be seen at every crossroads—purchased at countless five-and-dime stores were constant reminders to stay-at-home civilians of a distant war.

Civilian workers who flocked to defense plants by the millions as American industry geared up to become the "Arsenal of Democracy," soon learned that their lives would also be governed for the duration. Although most defense workers searched for work that would finance the good life, edicts handed down by the War Production Board froze some men in jobs and exempted others from the draft. General Lewis B. Hershey, appointed by FDR to head the selective service system in January 1942, told reporters that "men would be deferred from military service when they are 'necessary men' and are difficult to replace." But, Hershey added, "no industry or activity, no matter how closely identified with national production for war, can ever become a refuge for those wanting to avoid the draft."

Not only workers, but the American labor movement which represented them, was restrained by events. A labor–management conference summoned by Roosevelt in late December imposed a "peace formula" upon all civilian workers. And though complete labor harmony remained a dream, the gathering called for "settlement of all disputes through step-by-step conciliation, mediation, and arbitration"; nor were there to be any "strikes or lockouts for the duration."

The country had always hurried forward in time of crisis, but the rush to arms during the first weeks of hostilities, with men scrambling to sign up, was accelerated by Hitler's declaration of war against the United States on December 11. A German–Italian communiqué goaded Congress to respond quickly with a counterdeclaration five days after Pearl Harbor. Even Montana Representative Jeanette Rankin, who cast the lone vote against war with Japan, joined in the unanimous proclamation against Hitler and Mussolini.

The full force of war had not hit the country before great numbers flocked to the various services. Some enlisted out of a sincere impulse to shoulder a gun in the national defense, but for most it was a means of gaining preferential slots in a service branch besides the regular army. Recruiting posters—the famous "Uncle Sam Needs You"—were everywhere, and the thoughts of every physically fit man were never far from the draft. Five brothers named Sullivan, subjects of a Hollywood melodrama later in the war, joined the navy at one time in Waterloo, Iowa. In Elmira, New York, ninety-five-year-old Edwin Morris, a Civil War survivor and commander of the New York G.A.R., vowed he "was ready to shoulder a gun if necessary." All four sons of President Roosevelt were in uniform before the month was out; so were sports stars Hank Greenberg, the highest paid ($55,000 a year) major leaguer, and ace pitcher Bob Feller of the Cleveland Indians.

The call to arms put a strain on the existing recruiting system that continued straight through the Christmas holidays; in several metropolitan areas recruiting stations were forced to remain open twenty-four hours a day. Other centers even found it necessary to stay open on Sunday to accommodate the tidal wave of recruits. The army, which found its share of volunteers, initially signed up men from eighteen to thirty-six years old. Like the Coast Guard, which accepted men from eighteen to twenty-one, the United States Army allowed older men to enlist with previous service. A married man already in the regular army needed his wife's consent to reenlist. The Marine Corps took volunteers from seventeen to thirty; married men were not permitted in the corps, while some could join for a second hitch up to age thirty-five. The United States Navy accepted older men—even some fifty-year-olds; however, those over thirty-six required special skills to sign up. In the first eight days of the war, more than 11,000 men joined the navy; the army, too, got a high number of enlistments.

Self-appointed moralists, not entirely sympathetic with the war spirit, immediately raised questions about societal and ethical dislocations certain to accompany the mass influx of men into uniform. Aubrey W. Williams, National Youth Administrator and longtime New Dealer, warned during January that mobilization could lead to "the collapse of human and individual values." But Williams, who said he was speaking in a "Cassandra-like mood," expressed confidence that military life would not turn the country's young people into "brutes or beasts." The old social worker called on the nation's youth "to seek a generous reconstruction of the world after the war."

The rally to arms also caused masses of people to start moving from place to place. Everywhere truck convoys and trains could be seen hauling not only new inductees but also men already in service. And railroad depots erupted into beehives of activity as military men and their dependents moved from post to post. Volunteer organizations like the U.S.O., Salvation Army, Red Cross, Knights of Columbus, and Boy Scouts, centered much of their wartime effort at assisting traveling servicemen in countless train stations. During the first week after Pearl Harbor, *Life* featured civilian workers at several rail terminals "with baskets of books, magazines and jigsaw puzzles which they give away, and cartons of cigarettes which they sell at cost." Train depots, large and small, became focal points for numberless men and women who wanted to do their bit for the war, and who continued to bring a measure of cheer to soldiers and sailors far from home.

Something new appeared on the American scene as women by the tens of thousands joined in the mass reshuffling in order to be near husbands and boyfriends. Although the movement of women during the war was part of the larger internal migration, difficulties arose when unattended females began to congregate near military posts and in large urban centers. Besides the problems created by the inevitable rise in prostitution and juvenile deliquency among younger women, social workers who came into contact with women on the move found that simply adjusting to new surroundings was a major problem. A sizable majority of the women away from home immediately went into the labor force to support themselves. They found jobs in every conceivable workplace, and the large number of men in uniform provided women with ample opportunity for employment. Since nothing breeds independence faster than financial stability, World War II thereby served as a catalyst, freeing women from age-old bondages. An estimated seven million women left the county of their birth during the first forty-two months of war.

Other surveys suggest that when the war ended in 1945, more than 15,000,000 civilians were living in counties different from their place of residence at the time of Pearl Harbor. The greatest internal migration took place from the South to other parts of the country, as low-income whites and blacks sought well-paid defense jobs. California and the West Coast received a large influx of migrants from the South and Midwest throughout the war. The sprawling shipyards and aircraft assembly plants, pregnant with orders for war matériel, were a magnet that attracted thousands. Oklahoma alone sent 95,000 of its sons and daughters to the Golden Bay State. Texas, Missouri, and Illinois were not far behind. Americans had always exercised their unique brand of freedom by moving across the land in search of new opportunity, but population shifts during 1941–1945 exceeded anything previously known.

The unparalled movement of people—whether young men going into the services followed by their wives and sweethearts; women going into assembly-line work; or men over draft age moving from one location to another in search of defense jobs—had a major impact on the American family. And the onset of mobilization affected family units in as many ways as there were people.

From the first days of the war, when young people began to leave home, it became clear that new living patterns would replace the security of the extended family. Around Fort Bragg, North Carolina, and countless other army and navy posts, hundreds of young married women scurried to find living quarters at any price and jobs to support themselves so that they could spend time with their soldier husbands. Later, these same women, hundreds of miles from other family members (who more times than not lived in small-town or rural America) had little choice but to return home when their husbands went overseas on completion of basic training.

The general trend of wartime movement was from countryside to city; urban centers such as San Francisco, Los Angeles, San Diego, Baltimore, and Seattle exploded with people in the months following Pearl Harbor. And it was in the large cities that many families ran into difficulty. Some of the problems they encountered would have occurred war or no war. World War II may have precipitated the migration, but crowding and substandard housing fueled the increases in juvenile deliquency and sexual promiscuity that accompanied it. In particular, the lives of the cities' new working women and their children, far away from traditional family moorings, added new words to the national lexicon: "Rosie the Riveter," "eight-to-five children," "latchkey kids." Social workers even speculated that the changed status of women might lead to an abandonment of the family unit; yet the American family managed to survive the war. Millions of people simply did what was necessary to cope with wartime changes they did not seek but had foisted upon them.

Others did not join the move to the cities but, like the Withrow and Tinsley clans this author knew as a boy in rural West Virginia, remained at home on farms and in small hamlets. Over the long haul, many such families across the nation were touched by the war: sons joined the army and navy; fathers found jobs in local defense plants; some daughters also went into war work; only the older generation stayed close to the homestead. Everyday life meant grappling with rationing woes, and a constant watch for overseas mail or furlough visits from soldier sons. But once the war ended and loved ones returned from far-flung battle stations, their lives resumed its customary cohesiveness.

Another trial for the home front early in the war was the "blackout." Although little danger of actual air strikes existed, the war was close enough to kindle fears of enemy thrusts at the U. S. mainland. And it was more than the havoc wreaked on Pearl Harbor that produced panic on both coasts. Even before American entry into the war, German U-boats had molested Allied shipping with impunity along the Eastern Seaboard. Shamefully, the country had allowed the lights of coastal cities like Miami which cast a glow for miles out to sea, to be used by Nazi wolf packs to sink freighters within sight of the Florida shore.

Moreover, Japanese submarines began to harass American merchant shipping in California waters. Two weeks after Pearl Harbor, anxieties heightened when the tanker *Montebello* was torpedoed within sight of the coast. The 8,272-ton ship, the third U. S. merchantman attacked after the start of fighting, was sent to the bottom; and the enemy submarine even surfaced long enough to machine-gun lifeboats carrying the ship's thirty-six man crew. Startled civilians ashore not only watched the naval action, but also pulled surviving seamen to safety. Though military authorities refused comment, the same day brought reports of "terrific explosions, which shook houses as far as twenty miles inland."

A month or so later Japanese submarines shelled industrial plants along the same coast. But the drive to darken seaboard areas speeded rumors that enemy planes were about to swoop down on American cities. An alarm which sounded on the night of December 9 precipitated near panic in Los Angeles; and when "unidentified planes were reported over the California metropolis," the Fourth Interceptor Command ordered a three-hour blackout for all of southern California and parts of Nevada. The mysterious aircraft reportedly flew off toward the San Diego Naval Base, 125 miles away. Although an observer atop the Los Angeles *Times* Building could not detect the engine roar of potential attackers, "the giant searchlights of the army and navy posts in the vicinity of the harbor searched the sky."

Los Angeles Mayor Herbert Brown announced the following day that city fathers wanted no more false alarms. One man, thirty-year-old Dillard Mercer from nearby Long Beach, was killed when his automobile rammed a streetcar in the darkness. Both Mercer and the trolley were traveling without lights. Overzealous onlookers in Los Angeles and several Eastern cities smashed lighted windows of unattended shops and stores; signboards were also crashed by people anxious to help blacken the city.

In New York City, where Rand McNally quickly sold out its supply of maps for the Pacific and European war zones, bogus raids were also reported. One alarm set off at peak rush hour on December 9 produced such a jumble that authorities started a drive to halt unnecessary warnings. Mayor Fiorello LaGuardia, visiting in Seattle, where signboards had also been knocked out by anxious citizens, said he was "embarrassed" at New York's unresponsiveness. Although most schoolchildren were sent home when the sirens began to wail, New Yorkers went about their routines with unconcerned confidence—eating in chic cafes, talking and joyriding among the famed Manhattan canyons, a sure omen that many people in the nation's largest metropolis and Americans in general felt they had little to fear from Axis bombs.

Yet preparations cropped up everywhere along both coasts, and several enflamed an already aroused nation. In Carteret, New Jersey, where New York radio station WOR of the Mutual Broadcasting Company had its transmitting towers, precautions were taken to guard against sabotage as well as air strikes. Fifth-column activity in Europe and fear that it might spread to the United States prompted protective measures at radio stations all over the country. In San Francisco, sandbags, barricades, and like security devices were erected on downtown streets in anticipation of a Japanese stab along the coast. Fast-buck artists cashed in on the panic by offering a variety of gadgets guaranteed to shield against enemy bombs. Finally, a joint statement issued by the War Department, Office of Civilian Defense, and Office of Production Management warned against the con men.

Although real danger to the mainland remained imaginary, reminders of the fighting were always near at hand with newspapers, magazines, radio, and movie newsreels blaring out constant war reports. And a shot-up Pan American clipper that arrived in San Francisco on December 10 was a tangible mark of war. The giant transoceanic plane, which left Wake Island during a Japanese attack on December 7, carried sixteen highly visible bullet holes. Captain John H. Hamilton, who had flown sixteen round trips from California to Hong Kong and Singapore, told reporters his crew had been shaken by the ordeal; Hamilton had escaped injury by jumping headlong into a drainage pipe while enemy planes strafed the island.

Then, a few days after Christmas, a convoy reached the West Coast carrying survivors from Pearl Harbor. Thousands of curious onlookers lined the hills overlooking San Francisco Bay as the somber, heavily laden ships passed under the Golden Gate Bridge. On board were women and children who had lost their homes in the attack on Honolulu, as well as wounded navy personnel. Anxious relatives, sweethearts, and questioning reporters rushed as "close as armed guards would permit to catch a glimpse of the maimed and injured."

These reminders of war and a widespread feeling that America herself could be attacked, led Washington to refurbish a slumbering civil defense program. Mayor LaGuardia, who had reason to be upset with the nation's greatest city and its handling of air raid alarms in the days following Pearl Harbor, had been named to head the Office of Civilian Defense in May 1941 by presidential order. With Eleanor Roosevelt as his first assistant, LaGuardia's job was to organize "councils of defense" in all forty-eight states, designed to help the domestic population in case of enemy attack.

OCD, which functioned for the duration, grew out of an earlier agency that had created defense groups in all but four states. Unfortunately, in an era of national unpreparedness, most of the state defense bodies remained paper organizations. New York City alone had enrolled 64,000 civilian air raid wardens, who were given instruction in government-approved civilian defense techniques. Yet when the alarm sounded, New Yorkers continued their daily activities with abandon. Similiar air raid personnel on the West Coast, where a long practice in grappling with earthquake disasters existed, were unable to lessen the confusion caused by the blackouts.

Another effort to protect the home front was the roundup of enemy aliens whom the FBI and military intelligence agents regarded as potential spies and saboteurs. When news arrived about Pearl Harbor and about the outbreak of war with Germany, the G-men acted swiftly. Japanese, German, and Italian nationals were taken into custody within hours of the start of hostilities. Although a number of Asians were arrested, the systematic incarceration of Japanese-Americans did not commence until early January 1942. Seventy-two hours after the Japanese attack, Attorney General Francis Biddle said that 2,303 foreign nationals had been detained. All, he announced from Washington, had been under surveillance for more than a year. The initial dragnet included 1,291 Japanese, 865 Germans, and 147 Italians. Many of the aliens, Biddle continued, would be paroled shortly, while others would be sent to predetermined detention centers.

Some, like the Austrian Princess Stefanie Hohenlohe-Waldenburg-Schillinsfurst, had been deported previously for questionable activities but had found their way back. Detained with other aliens picked up in the first roundup after an automobile chase from New York to Philadelphia, the highborn princess was interned at the United States Immigration station in Glouchester, New Jersey. A "known international agent," she was arrested, authorities said, because of her association with Captain Fritz Weidemann, German Consul at San Francisco. The detention of German nationals continued for weeks. Karl Vollmoelier, a German playwright, author of "The Miracle," was seized on New Year's Eve in Los Angeles and lodged in the county jail. A writer for several Hollywood studios, Vollmoelier, a German citizen, had been in the United States since 1936.

It was not only high-placed foreigners who interested authorities faced with a mounting war scare. Acting under presidential orders, Biddle issued a mandate on December 31 for all aliens to relinquish cameras, guns, shortwave receivers, and transmitting apparatus. Immediately, metropolitan police stations, like one in New York City which received fifteen cameras within hours after Biddle's order, were inundated with a kaleidoscope of odds and ends. Like other hurriedly drawn-up war measures, the surrender edict had its frivolous, if not comic, consequences. One woman brought into a New York station house a "Kodac brownie camera" that was selling for $1.39 at corner drugstores.

A more serious problem developed when the Justice Department sought warrants for "white men" charged with aiding the Japanese. In San Francisco, a newsman named Frederick Vincent (Wiggy) Williams, was hauled into court for contributing to a pro-Japanese propaganda drive. Williams, who was registered as a correspondent for the *Japan Times and Mail*, was indicted for receiving monthly payments from Japanese consular officials to propagandize in this country for the Rising Sun. At Lake Geneva, Wisconsin, another newspaperman, Ralph Townsend, and his California publisher were taken into custody for publishing a pro-Japanese magazine called *Far Eastern Affairs*. Townsend was also charged with distributing a propaganda pamphlet entitled *America Has No Enemies in Asia*.

Yet the average citizen was more concerned with the continual outpouring of governmental decrees curtailing his daily activities than the roundup of several thousand foreigners with strange-sounding names.

Although actual rationing of foodstuffs and consumer goods—things found in every American household—did not begin until early 1942, politicians and the press had been speculating about rationing and restrictions on personal movement from the moment the attack on Pearl Harbor occurred. While some grumbling took place during the war and political pressures were applied to secure favors for special interest groups, most of the country supported the unprecedented moves when they did come.

The curtailment of personal activities started before the outbreak of fighting. The Federal Communications Commission ordered 65,000 radio amateurs, or "hams," to abandon their hobby on December 1. Done at the request of the Defense Communications Board, the edict caused radio and electronics enthusiasts to cease all shortwave transmissions. These hobbyists had been in the forefront of shortwave communications since the 1890s when the art first developed. Practically every technological advance in the field of radio since the days of Marconi had been accomplished by "hams," and often at their own expense. Although the FCC mandate stopped the radio amateurs, who after all were average citizens, an estimated 2,000 ham stations were allowed to continue transmitting. These included W1AW, the powerful home station of the American Radio Relay League at West Hartford, Connecticut, which regularly sent pertinent news to hams throughout the world. W1AW and the other ham stations were ordered off the air in early January.

Even as the hams were forced off the air, they continued to furnish the country with a reservoir of trained technicians and operators for the armed forces and merchant marine. And the radio buffs went right on helping the government as the war hotted up. In Phoenix, Arizona, Ying Ong, a grocer and radio hobbyist, maintained a governmentally endorsed "listening post." By the use of sensitive receiving equipment, he listened to Chinese language broadcasts from Chungking Radio, which spoke for the Free China government of Chiang Kai-Shek, an ally of the United States. Ong made transcripts of messages from the station "somewhere up the Yangtze River," which he relayed to Washington for distribution to newspapers, magazines, and radio stations.

Bureaucratic warnings started to bombard the country that more serious restrictions were on the way—restrictions that would require belt-tightening in two vital areas: sugar and household items. Next to the likelihood that gasoline for the family automobile would be rationed, people dreaded even a limited future without sugar for daily use. When the first sugar-rationing scheme took effect a few weeks after Pearl Harbor, each man, woman, and child was limited to "one half pound a week for the first eight weeks." Although an extra five pounds was allotted to every household for home canning, and the severity of restrictions eased as the duration progressed, the scarcity of readily available sugar supplies remained a family irritant until 1945.

The first of the famous "ration books" for sugar and other food supplies was handed out to consumers during early March at elementary schools. Before that, however, the War Production Board assumed full control of the entire 1942 raw sugar supply in mid-January. Government edicts designated "the exact minimum amounts of sugar which could be purchased by each of the eighteen largest domestic refiners. No others were allowed to purchase or handle raw sugar." And problems arose immediately for soft drink manufacturers. Pepsi Cola, for instance, owned and operated its own refineries, and when those facilities were omitted from the approved list, company officials complained about the changes required to remain in business. Their chief competitor, Coca Cola, bought raw sugar already refined, and, according to Pepsi management, had an unfair advantage. Since Pepsi had a large supply of usable sugar on hand there was no immediate danger from lopsided competition during the first days of war.

The regulation of sugar usage was only part of the larger food supply problem. "Now as never before," asserted Paul S. Willis, president of the Associated Grocery Manufacturers of America, "food becomes an essential instrument of war." Speaking in early January, Willis declared that American food processors were confronted with a three-fold dilemma: to avoid the wild price spiral which occurred in World War I; to make certain adequate food resources were on hand for civilian and military demands; to educate people about the value of nutrition as food supplies slackened. But as the war continued and scarcities of some food and tobacco products developed, the country made do with what it could get through official channels or clandestinely through black markets.

Equally burdensome were the restrictions placed on the purchase of household goods. The first hint of trouble came when the manufacture of both passenger cars and rubber tires was curtailed. Although a defense production plan had been in operation for a year or so, there had been enough steel, copper, aluminum, rubber, nickel, chrome, brass, and similar raw materials to maintain an uninterrupted flow of domestic consumer products. But in the weeks following Pearl Harbor, a stream of bureaucratic edicts squelched the manufacture for civilian use of virtually everything that contained metal. Like the dairies that had begun making sherbert instead of ice cream because of the limitation on the use of sugar, producers turned to replacement substitutes for domestic items. Almost overnight, for instance, a wholly new industry developed for making toys from wood and processed paper. A generation of youngsters growing up during World War II had cardboard or paper toy trains instead of the elaborate metal ones their fathers and older brothers had had. By early January, production cuts of 50 percent, and in some cases higher, had been ordered for home-use refrigerators, ranges, and washing machines.

The public's greatest annoyance came when it learned that private use of automobiles would be sharply curtailed. Americans had enjoyed a special love affair with the automobile ever since the early 1900s, when native ingenuity had perfected the first practical gasoline-driven motorcar. Spearheaded by the assembly line methods of Henry Ford and his competitors, the nation's industrial output soon made a moderately priced automobile available to every American family. In the intervening years, the man in the street had formed a great sentimental attachment to the private automobile; it had become his status symbol, his chief means of transportation, his passport to social and leisure-time activities. Some even argued that the attachment had sexual overtones. But one thing is certain. The automobile was an integral part of American life in 1941 and the prospect of giving it up was not pleasant.

The first assault on the private car came on December 10, when David Donald, one of FDR's appointees and Director of Priorities, issued a ban on the sale of new automobile tires. The only exceptions to the iron-clad decree were tires "for top defense orders." One national magazine reported "a near panic" as motorists rushed to buy any available tire in anticipation of a long duration. Overnight, "a bootleg market was created for new and retreaded tires with prices zooming to a point where sellers ignore official ceilings and take their chances with the law." Tires more often than not while still rims, were stolen at every turn as the unscrupulous tried to get them however they could. Widely circulated press accounts told about workers at defense plants afraid of being ripped off; some even painted slogans on tires in an appeal to the patriotism of thieves. Leon Henderson, Director of the Office of Price Administration and a man in the home-front news, came down hard on those ignoring restrictions on tire use: "Persons who are not inclined to take the rationing regulations seriously should take notice. A nationwide investigation of tire dealers by government inspectors is now in progress." As a result of OPA's get-tough policy, several firms were hauled into federal court during February. The LaSalle Motor Company at Booneville, Indiana, was the first cited because of "false affidavits concerning the number of tires in stock when rationing began." A federal judge in Norfolk, Virginia, issued an order prohibiting delivery of tires obtained before the rationing ban after a consignment of "truck and passenger car tires" valued at $1,427 had been procured by the Smith Douglas Company of Norfolk from another firm. The restraining order upheld the edict of December 11 that not only implemented tire rationing but also froze delivery of tires already purchased.

Henderson told a worried public that rubber for retreaded tires would not be available "except for a small number of vehicles." Retreaded or rubber recaps on old casings was a cheap but practical method of prolonging tire life in the era before artifically-produced rubber. But their use was hampered by orders requiring inspection of old tires and a certificate of need from local rationing boards. Right from the start, boards were set up to involve citizens at the local level in decisions affecting the home front. With the total moratorium on new tires, one of the first attempts at local handling of priority items was the allocation of retreaded automobile tires. The boards decided who in their communities qualified under two lists of potential tire users: List A included only "essential services," such as health, government service, vital transportation for doctors, and farm and industrial vehicles; List B, on the other hand, covered all other nonessential vehicles.

Automobile owners were informed on December 31 that OPA would authorize 35,000 tires per month for civilian use and no more. Normal usage, according to the super agency headed by Henderson, exceeded four million each month. Henderson and his bureau became household words during the first part of 1942; not only tires, but virtually everything from soup to bolts, if used by civilians, was regulated by OPA. Born in New Jersey, educated at Swarthmore and the University of Pennsylvania, the peppery Henderson was designated to head OPA by Roosevelt's executive order in April 1942. Intended to dovetail with the Office of Production Management (OPM), his group was eventually responsible for all domestic rationing.

Tire rationing was the first OPA undertaking that touched masses of people. And with it came a frantic search to find rubber substitutes by large companies and small-time inventors alike. Before the war ended a host of cockeyed schemes surfaced as would-be inventors worked to find a suitable alternative for rubber tires. The press featured one fellow in the Midwest rolling merrily down the highway with wooden strips curved around the rims of his sedan. The press was to carry many similar clips because of their novelty value, but the rubber problem remained basically unsolved until Washington financed a crash research and production effort to make rubber synthetically from natural gas.

Although limited automobile production continued until early January, civilian purchase of new passenger cars and pickup trucks was halted by February 1942. The average American could not buy a new vehicle until 1946 and the return to peacetime production. Only doctors and a few other essential occupations were exempted from the inevitable ban. FBI Director J. Edgar Hoover issued a warning for motorists to guard against thefts following curtailment of automobile and tire sales. Car owners, he said, were "victims of one-third of all thefts in this country"; he cautioned Christmas shoppers to be careful with their autos "and not park in dark alleys or secluded areas." A more optimistic response came from Thomas F. Henry, president of the American Automobile Association, who explained that "the large reserves of used cars will cushion the impact of cuts in automobile production." But, he added, metal and rubber shortages made the future look bleak. Civilians should work at making their cars last: "Good driving is patriotic driving," he avowed.

The OPA mandate also froze the sale of cars in dealer showrooms. Thousands of car salesmen found themselves in a predicament as the need for their services vanished overnight. In Kansas City alone, more than 4,200 new cars consigned to dealers could not be sold. Harry R. Rice, a Buick dealer and president of the local dealer association, said his group would "rent a farm if necessary" to store the unsalable cars. Dealers wanted to get rid of their new car stock in order to use their showrooms for more than 6,000 used cars on hand. A local Chevrolet dealer, William R. Allen, acted alone and moved his cars to a farm two miles from Kansas City. *Business Week*, which reported developments in the wartime economy, said the cars were "parked in his cow lot, frost- or dew-covered, in rain or snow, and on icy Missouri mornings, the new Chevrolets are—physically as well as commercially—frozen tight to the ground." Like other uprooted civilians, the unemployed Kansas City salesmen found work at nearby defense plants, mostly at a local North American bomber plant and the ammunition works at Lake City, Missouri.

Although confronted with a growing list of bans and restrictions, the country learned that life could go on. The society columns reported that seventeen-year-old Gloria Vanderbilt, had announced her intention in December to marry Pasquale di Cicco, thirty-three-year-old son of a Long

Island truck farmer known as the "Broccoli King." The bride, an heiress to a $4,000,000 fortune, had been in the public eye for months when she appeared at social functions in the company of various actors, including the cowboy hero, Randolph Scott. However, Vanderbilt was only one of thousands trooping to the altar in a war-induced marriage boom. In some communities during the first weeks of war, marriages exceeded 150 percent the normal rate. Milwaukee reported a 100-percent increase in marriage applications over December 1940; and at Lincoln, Nebraska, a county judge said that most of the newlyweds "wore uniforms." Thousands of servicemen rushed to the altar while home on Christmas furlough; areas like Seattle and San Diego, with their huge military installations, reported all-time records in marriages during December 1941. Joining the marriage bonanza were great numbers of defense plant workers who had recently found employment after the lean years of the Depression.

In a country looking for diversions, sports boomed throughout the war. Although many athletes were drafted or joined the service in the first call for men, an undercurrent of resentment ran through the nation when seemingly healthy men were able to engage in organized sports and yet escape military duty. Still, 5,000 spectators flocked to the Miami Open four days after Pearl Harbor to watch the legendary Ben Hogan and twelve other golf pros break par in the opening round. By today's standards the purse was skimpy, a mere $2,500 for the winner, but enough to attract the nation's best golfers and an enthusiastic gallery. Outwardly oblivious to the war, moreover, big league baseball began preparations for the 1942 season by fixing player trades among the sixteen teams in the American and National circuits. In one deal announced on December 11, the St. Louis Cardinals sent Johnny Mize, a twenty-eight-year-old Georgia native who batted a whopping .317 during the 1941 season, to the New York Giants for $50,000.

Later, athletes from nearly every sport joined with actors, singers, and other celebrities to participate in the famed war bond drives. Within a week after Pearl Harbor, Treasury Secretary Henry Morgentau, a New York publisher and New Deal stalwart, announced that every employed civilian would "be asked to make regular investments in U.S. Defense Savings Bonds." Before peace returned, the war bond drive, complete with patriotic fanfare and appearances by showpeople and sports figures, became a fixture in most American cities. Government-sponsored payroll deduction plans became almost mandatory in the workplace and the twenty-five-cent "savings stamp" purchased by schoolchildren, afraid of being embarrassed by patriotic or more affluent classmates, enabled Uncle Sam to gather millions for the war effort.

The rush to arms, begrudging support for rationing plans, and war bond drives, however, were only part of the fervor that seized the country in December 1941. Political dissent and actual opposition to government policy practically vanished for the duration. Although an occasional conscientious objector or outright malingerer might look for a way out of the draft, or a dyed-in-the-wool Republican might lash out at some lingering New Deal policy, a remarkable calmness settled over domestic politics. General Robert E. Wood, acting president of the infamous America First Committee, announced on December 11 that his group would disband. Formed in September 1940, the organization was but one of several isolationist outfits opposed to United States involvement in the European conflict. Wood, chairman of the board at Sears, Roebuck, and Charles Lindbergh, the famed aviator, had used the committee for months to oppose the war; they had also picked up support from most pro-Axis groups in the country, but the Japanese attack on America herself produced a dramatic aboutface. "The time for military action is here," Wood lamented, and "the America First Committee has determined to cease all functions and to disband as soon as that can be legally done." On the same day, furthermore, Joseph W. Martin, Jr., chairman of the Republican National Committee, and his counterpart, Democratic National Chairman Edward J. Flynn, exchanged telegrams agreeing to work for the common cause.

Christmas 1941 brought renewed pledges of support between the United States and Great Britain in the struggle against Hitler and Tojo. Prime Minister Winston Churchill, in this country to confer with Roosevelt, helped the president light a giant Christmas tree on the White House lawn in a symbolic gesture of cooperation between the Anglo-Saxon democracies. The two heads of state took the occasion to ask their countrymen to "become fellow workers in the cause of freedom." Beyond the Christmas celebrations, commented the New York *Times*, "was the unshakable ever-present realization of the job that must be done before the world can laugh again." Pope Pius XII delivered his annual Christmas message before a large throng in Vatican City and condemned all countries with movements "of an anti-Christian nature."

The first wartime Christmas was marred by constant reminders of the war. The Bell Telephone System pleaded with customers not to monopolize long distance lines which might be needed for defense purposes;

and intermingled with carolers on American streets were air raid wardens and other civil defense workers. Yet downtown department stores from one end of the country to the other were packed with yuletide shoppers and most reported record sales; the post office broke a ten-year record in mail volume when families rushed to send packages to servicemen. Every conceivable public conveyance was crowded with holiday travelers who crammed bus terminals, train depots, and airports searching for transportation in order to be with family and friends.

Meanwhile, as December 1941 drew to a close, and news from the battlefronts remained bleak, the country found its first war hero: twenty-six-year-old Captain Colin P. Kelly, Jr., who piloted one of the B-17s sent by General MacArthur to attack the main Japanese landing force in the Philippines. The young West Point graduate from Madison, Florida, was killed in action on December 10, badly crippling the battleship *Haruma* with three well-directed bombs before going down himself in a hail of gunfire. In those weeks after Pearl Harbor when the country had little to celebrate, Kelly's daring exploit caught the public imagination. And President Roosevelt added to the Kelly legend by addressing a letter "to the President of the United States in 1956" which requested that Kelly's young son be admitted to his father's military academy.

2 JANUARY-APRIL 1942: HOME FRONT AMERICA DISCOVERS THE WAR

T he year 1942 was ushered in with the usual round of celebrations, which some observers thought surpassed anything known in peacetime. Amidst the clamor, however, were reminders of the ever-present conflict. In New York City, where 500,000 celebrants crowded into the area around Times Square, police and emergency vehicles remained on the alert to sound air raid warnings should enemy planes appear overhead. But earlier fears of German bombs had already subsided as New Yorkers took up their annual hell-raising with more than usual gusto. With the blackout no longer enforced, the undimmed lights of Broadway glared magnificently for the horn tooters and confetti throwers, whose ranks were swelled with sailors and soldiers from nearby military posts.

In New York's Harlem a different kind of celebration took place on New Year's Day, when seventy-five black leaders led a giant rally commemorating the signing of the Emancipation Proclamation. Penned by Abraham Lincoln at the height of the Civil War, the proclamation freeing slaves in the Confederate South had long been a cherished symbol of pride and freedom for the nation's black population. Although the thermometer stood near the freezing mark, more than 200 individuals joined in a parade through the heart of Harlem, and another 1,600 attended the formal celebration. A 100-member choir sang for a pageant "depicting the Negro struggle for freedom." Numerous fraternal and political figures addressed the gathering, including Adam Clayton Powell, Jr. Recently chosen to represent Harlem's 200,000-plus black population on the New York City Council, Powell was one of the country's few elected black officeholders in 1942.

Elsewhere, New Year's Day 1942 found large sections of the country experiencing rough weather; in the South, however, huge throngs forgot

the war long enough to enjoy the customary bowl games. Pouring rains fell on New Orleans, where a crowd of 73,000 watched the Fordham Rams beat the University of Missouri, 2-0, in the eighth annual Sugar Bowl game. Every seat in Tulane's double-decked stadium was taken when the game's only score came on a Fordham safety; Don Greenwood, a substitute end but the best Tiger kicker for the year, attempted to punt on the Missouri goal line. Fordham got its winning tally when team captain and all-American from Kansas City, Alex Santilli, flattened him in the end zone.

Most prestigious of the New Year's classics, the Rose Bowl, was moved from its home in Pasadena, California, 3,000 miles across the country to Durham, North Carolina. The move to Duke stadium resulted from General John Lessesne DeWitt's order banning all parades and public gatherings of more than 5,000 on the West Coast. DeWitt, in charge of the Western Defense Command, also closed all racing facilities. His command, the closest to the Pacific and the Japanese menace, covered eight western states, Alaska and a civilian population exceeding 12,000,000.

The transplanted Rose Bowl between Oregon State and the Duke Blue Devils resulted in a 20-16 victory for the West Coast team. In Dallas 38,000 enthusiastic fans gathered at the sixth annual Cotton Bowl to watch the Crimson Tide of Alabama roll over the Aggies of Texas A&M, 29-21. And in Miami, where the weather was milder, the war seemed very distant to the 35,505 shirt-sleeved spectators who watched the Georgia Bull Dogs thump the Horned Frogs of TCU, 40-26, in the eighth playing of the Orange Bowl.

As the bowl game hoopla wound down and the first full year of war began, the country's population according to the 1940 census, stood at 131,669,275. Males outnumbered females by a slight margin, 66,061,592 to 65,607,683; and more Americans were living in large urban areas than in rural ones. The population was listed as overwhelmingly "native white," but there were 12,865,518 blacks living in the forty-eight states. The most populous state was New York, with 13,479,142 people, while Nevada was the least populous with a mere 110,247. Heart and circulatory disorders were the leading cause of death, with "cancer and other tumors" far behind in second place. Some 17,102 Americans had died by their own hand in 1941; 3,481 had received an earned doctorate. A thirty-five-year-old white male could look forward to another 33.8 years of life, while a black man of the same age could expect to live only another 26.4 years.

Although the continental United States appeared secure enough after the initial enemy attacks, the war did not go well at first. A constant barrage of war news through radio, newspapers, magazines, and movie newsreels kept the country well informed about the first tragic months of war when everything seemed to be going against the United States and her allies. Not until the dual victories in the Coral Sea and at Midway in May–June 1942 was the Japanese thrust checked.

It was perhaps the newsreel, a now-abandoned art form, that most shaped public perception of the war throughout the duration. Since 1911, when *Pathe's Weekly*—"a film issued every Tuesday, made up of short scenes of great international interest from all over the world"—first appeared, moviegoers worldwide had been able to view major events and leading public figures firsthand. American-produced newsreels, more than those done in Europe, followed the journalistic traditions of newspapers and the printed media.

The newsreel reached its peak influence during the war years, when Americans flocked to movie houses in unprecedented numbers. Surprisingly, many theater owners opposed the showing of war footage and even displayed signs advising patrons that no war news would accompany the usual Hollywood features. The United States' entry into the war brought a reversal of that policy when curious audiences began to seek out news from the fighting fronts. Theaters devoted entirely to newsreels sprang up in large cities to satisfy the demand. Moviegoers—and there were plenty of them in the days before television—viewed the war through the presentations of *Fox Movietone*, *The March of Time*, and *News of the Day*, produced by Hearst newspapers.

The best-distributed and financed of the newsreels, Fox's *Movietone*, featured the resonant voice of Lowell Thomas as chief commentator. Thomas, already well known for his nationwide broadcasts since the early thirties, presented a straightforward rendering of the war. He had edited and produced an early project called the *American Newsreel*, which folded before the war, but he became widely recognized for his work with Fox. His famed radio broadcasts, and after the war, his work in television, shaped the perception of world events for millions. An episode in the early 1930s demonstrated his astounding popularity among the listening public. At the instigation of Western Union, Thomas delivered one of his broadcasts from the company's downtown Manhattan office; in closing, he asked listeners to telegraph a response at company expense. Within three hours a staggering 265,654 telegrams had arrived. The incoming messages cost over half a million dollars, and to complicate matters,

Western Union was obliged to pay its rival, Postal Telegraph, several thousand dollars for telegrams sent over their wires. It remains one of the all-time records in media response.

Along with Hans V. Kaltenborn, Thomas dominated news reporting throughout the war years. At sixty-three, much older than Thomas, the Wisconsin-born Kaltenborn, with his rich, gravely voice, built a faithful following with his wide-ranging war communiqués, as well as regular American broadcasts. But it was the movie newsreel that most caught the public imagination, and the highly patriotic *March of Time,* narrated by Louis de Rochemont, rivaled Thomas's *Movietone* in audience appeal. De Rochemont, Massachusetts-born and Harvard-educated, had been a news cameraman since the twenties and often resorted to portrayals and recreations of news events in his *March of Time* productions. Started in 1935 and "produced by the editors of *Time* and *Life*" magazines, the series attracted a large audience whenever it was shown in movie houses during the war.

The war that reached home-front audiences was not good in the aftermath of Pearl Harbor. The Marine garrison on Guam was forced to surrender on December 11, 1941, and Tokyo radio announced that 300 Americans there, including the governor, Captain G. G. McMillan, had been captured. Twelve hundred miles to the east, Wake Island, a tiny dot in the western Pacific between Guam and Hawaii, fell to the Japanese on December 23 following a period of incessant bombing. Landings were also made in the Philippines as part of the Japanese rampage through the South Pacific; and action off the coast of northern Luzon resulted in the death of young Captain Colin Kelly when he blasted the *Haruma* on December 10.

After repeated bombings and thrusts along the coasts, which resulted in thousands of American and Filipino deaths, the main Japanese invading force of 43,000 stormed ashore at Lingayen Gulf on December 23. General Jonathan Wainwright attempted to hold the Luzon attackers at the Agno River, a natural barrier between Lingayen and Manila as well as the huge American naval base at Cavite. His hopelessly outnumbered forces, however, were powerless to check the Japanese plunder. Manila itself was occupied January 2, and the depleted defenders under MacArthur and Wainwright withdrew to the Bataan Peninsula for the final defense of the Philippines. Isolated and cut off from any possible aid from other United States forces, MacArthur was ordered by President Roosevelt on February 22 to leave for Australia. His remaining forces, placed under the command of Wainwright, retreated slowly down the

Bataan Peninsula, and finally to Corregidor, a tiny rock fortress in the middle of Manila Bay. Here, amid unbelievable hardship and suffering, the American troops held out until May 6, 1942, when the Japanese, under General Homma, stormed the island after a relentless six-hour shelling.

The home front did not immediately learn about the Bataan Death March. But when the last remnants of our defending forces were marched to concentration camps north of Manila, a new perception of Japanese inhumanity to Americans and other Europeans was born in the American public. This idea of Japanese cruelty toward whites was reinforced by the destruction of the old colonial empires in southeast Asia. French holdings in Indochina—(later called Viet Nam)—were quickly overrun in July 1941, following German occupation of France. Then, one hour before the attack on Pearl Harbor, Japanese forces landed in Malaya and started a march down the Kra Peninsula toward the huge British naval base at Singapore. Americans were shaken by the great loss of life that occurred when Japanese planes sank the English battle crusiers *Repulse* and *Prince of Wales* in connection with this fighting. The Dutch empire in the Pacific also collapsed when the enemy overran Amboina, Java, Sumatra, and Borneo—the fabled Spice Islands of earlier centuries—but not before Dutch forces sank a transport ship carrying 4,000 enemy troops. Although the Netherlands itself had been overrun by the Nazis, the Netherlands East Indies government held out until late February. Each of the empires fell in rapid succession; Hong Kong capitulated on Christmas day and even the Portugese were forced to surrender Timor on February 24, although it had been occupied a few weeks earlier by Dutch and Australian forces.

Meanwhile, the United States' effort to subdue Hitler was confined to naval action in the Atlantic during early 1942. Of our major allies in Europe, only England remained free of Nazi panzers, although Goring's Luftwaffe wreaked heavy damage on British cities in the Battle of Britain. Since we had given Churchill a solemn pledge that Hitler's defeat would supercede efforts to destroy Japan, the nation's first priority was ridding the north Atlantic of U-boats; but the German wolf packs roamed at will, interrupting the flow of men and matériel from American factories.

Scarcely a day passed in early 1942 without reports of Allied ships torpedoed by German subs, often within sight of the East Coast. In one short period, February 2–5, at least four ships were lost: a Swedish tanker, the *Amerikaland*, was sunk February 2 with a loss of thirty-eight; and the U.S. merchantman *W.L. Sneed* was lost with thirty-five deaths the same day off the New Jersey coast. A freighter owned by the United Fruit Company, *San Gil*, was destroyed off the Maryland coast; and on February 5, a Socony-Vacuum oil tanker went down 100 miles east of Delaware. Still, effective antisubmarine tactics were organized by the American and British navies, enabling convoys to cross the Atlantic with minimal losses. British Home Secretary Herbert Morrison reported on November 1 that "more than 20,000 convoys had been escorted in which 199 of every 200 vessels reached port."

Nor were United States forces totally ineffective in the Pacific following the initial Japanese avalanche. During the battle for Corregidor, Colonel James H. Doolittle launched his famous raid on Tokyo with Army B-25s from Navy carriers in April 1942. Then, two weeks later, the Japanese stab southward was checked by the United States Navy during a raging battle, May 4–9, off the Bismarck Archipelago in the Coral Sea. Though technically the enemy lost fewer ships and the *U. S. S. Lexington*, a carrier, was destroyed, Japanese failure to capture Port Moresby in New Guinea denied them a staging area for later attacks on Australia; the Coral Sea was nothing short of a major Allied victory. As the Japanese hold on the Philippines tightened and the American home front listened tensely to news reports of fierce battles on the Russian front, a turning point in the whole war came on June 4 in the struggle for Midway Island, 1,200 miles west of Hawaii. Here, in a single day, Admiral Yamamoto and the Japanese imperial navy lost four carriers. Japan had finally reached its highwater mark in the Pacific.

Before the successes at Midway and the Coral Sea, however, enemy thrusts in the Pacific had produced strong anti-Japanese feeling in the United States. It started December 9 when some unknown culprit chopped down several cherry trees in Washington D.C. which had been given to this country by the Japanese in an earlier gesture of friendship. And it culminated in the removal of Japanese-Americans living in California and other Western states to "relocation centers" away from the coast. A spate of violently anti-Japanese cartoons appeared in newspapers and magazines soon after the outbreak of war. One typical drawing by Edmund Duffy in the Baltimore *Sun* depicted a huge and sinister-looking Japanese soldier with glaring teeth jabbing a great flaming torch into the Pacific; airplanes and burning ships were shown in the background with three large letters, W A R, written across the carnage.

This widespread hostility was often transferred to Chinese-Americans and Chinese nationals living in this country. Although Nationalist China remained a staunch ally, some Chinese consulates in the United States prepared identifying labels to distinguished their citizens from other Asians. *Life* ran two large photographs of "representative" Chinese and Japanese males with an accompanying description of their racial make-ups: "The difference between Chinese and Japs is measurable in milli-meters. . . .

"The modern Jap is the descendant of Mongoloids who invaded the Japanese archipelago back in the mists of prehistory, and the native aborigines who possessed the islands before them. Physical anthropology, in consequence, finds Japs and Chinese as closely related as Germans and English. It can, however, set apart the special types of each national group." The Japanese, *Life* continued, have "a squat, long-torsoed build, a broader, more massively boned face and head, flat, often pug, nose, yellow-ocher skin and heavy beards." And, as if passions were not in-flamed enough, a Japanese submarine shelled an oil refinery along the California coast on February 23. Though the attack, near Golata, a few miles west of Santa Barbara, caused almost no damage, the thought that American Japanese might have been flashing signals to enemy raiders was frightening to most Americans.

Five days before the Golata incident, President Roosevelt ended a continuing debate among government and military leaders over the status of Japanese-Americans. Acting under the guise of "military necessity" he signed an executive mandate granting authority for the Secretary of War to select appropriate military areas from which "any or all persons could be excluded." Although Japanese or Japanese-Americans were not spe-cifically mentioned, it was soon obvious that only Asians of Japanese origin were covered by the order. Even before the mass evacuations began, under the direction of General DeWitt, the same man who had moved the Rose Bowl game to North Carolina, the Japanese on the West Coast had begun to feel pressure. For months the American public had been bombarded with news reports of fifth column activity by Nazi collabo-rators throughout Europe that made the takeover of defenseless nations much easier. Apprehensions of the same phenomenon happening in America were focused on the Japanese from the moment of Pearl Harbor.

Japanese-Americans simply found themselves in the wrong place at the wrong time. Before the roundup officially ended on August 7, 1942, a total of 119,803 such individuals—young and old, men and women, even children—were detained behind barbed wire at various camps or relocation centers around the country. Japanese of three categories were ordered into the makeshift jails: the Issei, or immigrants from Japan who had not achieved United States citizenship; Nisei, who were children of the Issei or second-generation Japanese-Americans; and the Sansei, or third-generation Japanese living in this country. The camps, under the supervision of the specially-created WRA, or War Relocation Authority, headed in the beginning by Milton Eisenhower, were often situated in inhospitable and remote places. An installation at Topaz, Utah, although it cost nearly $5 million to erect, was in such rough terrain that not even 7,500 small trees and 10,000 shrubs specially planted to beautify the place would grow in its dry, alkaline soil. Some 5,000 babies were born in these barren camps in California, Idaho, Wyoming, Utah, Arizona, Colorado, and Arkansas before they were finally disbanded in 1946. Forty years later, the issue of compensating the detainees for the loss of livelihood and property they sustained during their internment remains unresolved. While the detention centers could never be equated with the infamous Nazi concentration camps (WRA authorities were pledged to protect their charges and provide the necessities of life, if little else) the wartime detention of Japanese-Americans remains a discomforting episode in the national memory.

German and Italian-Americans, on the other hand, had little to fear from a government anxious to protect itself against enemy aliens. President Roosevelt himself proclaimed that it would "be bad for morale" to interfere with either group at the same time Japanese-Americans were driven into detention centers. These groups, unlike the Nisei living along the West Coast, had by and large been assimilated into the national fabric; the Palatinate Germans who came in sizable numbers during the first decades of the eighteenth century had married into families of British descent; and their countrymen who fled the German uprisings of 1848 had been absorbed into the larger society after one hundred years of citizenship. Italian-Americans—who numbered about 600,000 in 1941, although from Mediterranean backgrounds, had been accepted on these shores without hesitation, particularly after their numbers had been curtailed by the immigration laws of the 1920s which had implemented the quota system.

The European origins of German and Italian peoples in the United States made them much more desirable to Washington officialdom. California Attorney General Earl Warren, future chief justice of the U. S. Supreme Court, summed it up best while testifying before a congressional committee during February 1942: "We believe that when we are dealing with the Caucasian race we have methods that will test the loyalty of them, and we believe we can in dealing with the Germans and Italians, arrive at some fairly sound conclusions because of our knowledge of the way they live in the community and have lived for many years." That was not the case with Japanese-Americans, he added.

While it lamented the animosity toward Japanese citizens, the American Civil Liberties Union in 1943 found "no hostility toward persons of German and Italian origin." General Eisenhower was constantly before the public from the first days of the war as he planned and then led the invasions of North Africa and France; certainly no one ever suspected the popular "Ike" of disloyalty because of his German ancestry. And at least two personalities of Italian parentage played conspicious roles on the domestic scene. Twenty-four-year-old Frank Sinatra became nothing short of a cult figure on stage, screen, and radio during the war; and Joe DiMaggio, the son of Italian immigrants, became one of the best-known athletes in the 1940s.

Another athlete on center stage during 1941–1945 was the "Brown Bomber," Joseph Louis Barrow, known to millions as Joe Louis, who defended his heavyweight boxing crown in January 1942. A heavyweight title fight is always a spectacular event, but when Louis and his manager, Mike Jacobs, agreed to give their earnings to the Navy Relief Fund, the stage was set for a major sporting event with a heavy overlay of patriotic fervor. The champ and big time boxing gained immense public approval by joining the sports-entertainment bandwagon to help the war. They were following the lead of professional football which had staged a highly profitable contest between the National League All Stars and the Chicago Bears a few days earlier, also for Navy Relief. Twenty thousand fans paid a gate totaling $200,000 to watch Louis deck his opponent, Buddy Baer, in two minutes fifty-six seconds of the first round. Although Baer had a forty-five-pound weight advantage and nearly ten inches more in reach, Louis floored him twice before the winning punch.

Promoted in Madison Square Garden with ample patriotic hoopla, the fight attracted a galaxy of show people and politicians. Among the famous was Wendell Willkie, unsuccessful Republican contender against FDR in 1940, who gave a "stirring address from mid-ring" before the bout. And when he went to Louis's locker room afterwards, the fighter, who could always be counted on to say the right thing, responded, "That was a fine speech, Mr. Willkie. Yes sir, that was the finest speech I ever heard that I liked."

Three days after the match, Louis, like millions of young Americans, was inducted into the army and billeted at Camp Upton near Yaphank on Long Island. And shortly after the swearing-in ceremony, attended by swarms of reporters and flashing cameras, Louis was given leave to attend an awards banquet in New York, sponsored by the Boxing Writers Association. There, on January 21, he received the prestigious Edward J. Neil Memorial Plaque—named for a writer killed while covering the Spanish Civil War—for his contributions to boxing.

Louis had come a long way from rural Chambers County, Alabama, where he was born in 1914. When his family joined the black exodus out of the cotton fields of the South in search of jobs during the Depression, he found himself a third-grade student in Detroit. Unsuccessful in the regular schools, Louis entered Detroit's Brownson Trade School as a woodworking student, and, while there, got his first taste of organized boxing. After a string of professional matches, starting in 1932 with a white fighter named Johnny Miller, who knocked him down seven times in two rounds, he finally got a shot at the title in 1937. Max Schmeling, the German strongman who later embraced Nazism and fought in Hitler's army during the war, nearly ended Louis's career in June 1936 with a knockout blow before 45,000 spectators in Yankee Stadium.

Louis avenged the Schmeling disaster in a rematch which saw the big German flattened in the first round. During his fighting career, 1935–1949, Louis won thirty-seven out of thirty-eight fights. In 1941 alone he defended his title (won from Jimmy Braddock in 1937) nine times. Yet, although he was constantly in the public eye, Louis was never free from racial slurs, particularly in the South. His time in the army was spent touring military bases with a company of athletes who put on boxing exhibitions. While visiting Camp Sibert, Alabama, during 1942 with another black fighter, Sugar Ray Robinson (who was to become the future welterweight champ), Louis was ordered from a segregated waiting area by several military policemen. An altercation in the local bus terminal ensued, which landed both men in the post stockade. Although he was released immediately, Louis thereafter made it a practice to oppose military segregation policies wherever he encountered them.

It was little wonder that millions of blacks chafed at the humiliating restrictions imposed on them by an antiquated racial code in a country fighting a war to preserve democracy. Though Louis retained an outward calm, he balked at outlandish segregation practices. Yet, revered by millions, whites as well as blacks, Louis decided to risk his title in March 1942, two months after the Baer fight, this time for the Army Relief Society. Staged in Madison Square Garden against a little-known boxer named Abe Simon, the bout brought a purse totaling $45,882, which was promptly handed over to the benefit fund. Although the six-foot champ worked out daily at Fort Dix, New Jersey, he found the training, before 3,000 soldiers difficult. He had to struggle at getting down to his proper fighting weight, 207½ pounds, and he was required to undergo an additional two hours of basic military instruction each day. And once in the ring, the 225-pound Simon presented more of a challenge than anticipated. Louis, who was happy to see several thousand of his Fort Dix messmates at ringside, knocked his stubborn opponent down in rounds two and five before finishing him off in the sixth.

Jack Dempsey, heavyweight champion in 1917, had nearly disgraced boxing during World War I by managing to stay out of uniform. In 1942, however, the forty-seven-year-old Dempsey followed Louis and other top athletes into the service, and saw extensive Coast Guard duty as a lieutenant commander in the South Pacific. But no sports figure held the public eye like Joe Louis, though he was nearly touched by scandal during the war. Shortly after the Simon fight, Mike Jacobs, his manager, approached Secretary of War Henry L. Stimson with a scheme to stage another championship match for charity. This time Louis was to fight Billy Conn, a major heavyweight contender, with match proceeds again going to the Army Relief Fund.

Since both fighters were in uniform and asked for no part of the gate except training expenses, Jacobs suggested the government help them pay overdue income tax levees from past fights. Though Louis and his promoters were no doubt sincere in the offer to help charity, the plan was scrapped after newspapermen who knew the boxing game told authorities about hidden complications. Among other things was something called "the ice," or money made on the manipulation of ticket sales beyond the regularly stated price of admission. There were other unforeseen revenues accruing to the management from a major fight promotion. The bout, scheduled for September 1942, was canceled after Stimson decided adverse publicity would offset any benefits.

If Louis told reporters who dogged him during the war, "There may be a lot wrong in America, but there's nothing Hitler can fix," black activists like labor leader A. Philip Randolph and actor-singer Paul Robeson had more forceful views about the war. American blacks supported the war because they recoiled at Nazi racism and wanted to help their country in a perilous hour, but they also objected to continued Jim Crowism, lynchings, and segregation. And the United States had its share of racial injustice in 1942. At Sikeston, Missouri, on January 25, two weeks after millions cheered the Louis-Baer fight, a riotious mob lynched a black millworker named Cleo Wright after he reportedly stabbed a white woman. Just as treacherously, blacks were systematically denied jobs in the nation's busy defense plants and "Jim Crowed" in the military, which prompted Randolph to ask in November 1942: "What have Negroes to fight for? Why has a man got to be Jim Crowed to die for democracy? If you haven't got democracy yourself, how can you carry it to somebody else?"

Randolph was a leading advocate of black rights throughout the war years and beyond. Before Pearl Harbor, when the country began preparing its war machine, he spearheaded a drive to gain jobs for blacks in the new defense industries. Asa Philip Randolph, who became the nation's most influential black leader in the 1930s, and 1940s, was born in Florida in 1889 at Crescent City on the St. Johns River. He gained national prominence after 1925 when he founded and became president of the all black Brotherhood of Sleeping Car Porters; during the 1940s his "Red Caps" union, named for the distinctive hats worn by black train attendants, had become, according to Randolph's biographer, "the most important black political institution in America."

As a major labor leader and black activist, Randolph organized the famed "March on Washington." Scheduled to take place July 1, 1941, Randolph planned to have thousands of blacks converge on the nation's capital to demand a fair share of the defense pie. President Roosevelt, not wanting to be embarrassed by a demonstration for black equality, met with Randolph and Walter White, president of the National Association for the Advancement of Colored People, two weeks before the march. Then, as the "March on Washington" continued to gain momentum, FDR issued a June 25 executive order, which created the Fair Employment Practices Commission (FEPC) and guaranteed blacks jobs in defense plants.

Labor unions and employers, however, continued to draw the color line whenever possible as a bar to black employment. As a result of continued foot-dragging, Randolph resolved to keep his protest apparatus intact; and on June 16, 1942, 20,000 people, responding to his call, jammed into Madison Square Garden to demand an end to discrimination; another 9,000 assembled during August in the city auditorium at St. Louis. Despite charges that the protest rallies were financed with Nazi funds, the "March on Washington" movement made headway. When the war ended in 1945, black membership in unions had increased sixfold over that in 1940; blacks on the government payroll had doubled during the war; and importantly, the overall income earned by blacks had risen sharply. In 1940 the wages earned by black workers were roughly forty percent of the wages earned by whites; by August 1945 black wages were sixty percent of white wages.

Another black leader who strove for the "Double V," a term used by black newspapers to call for victory over discrimination at home as well as victory over the Axis powers, was Judge William H. Hastie. Just as Randolph fought for jobs for blacks in industry, Hastie sought to end discrimination against blacks in the military. Jim Crowism was so rampant when the war started that on one occasion black GIs detailed to transport German prisoners of war through the South were denied service on railroad dining cars, while their charges were admitted and served. In 1941 there was only one black general in the army, Benjamin O. Davis, out of a total 776 general officers, and only seven black colonels out of 5,220. Hastie, born in 1904 at Knoxville, Tennessee, was a graduate of the Harvard Law School and a federal judge both before and after the war. He was appointed a civilian aide to Secretary of War Henry L. Stimson to handle black affairs for the military. But Hastie, who was also dean of the Howard University Law School, was unable to make headway against ingrained racism and resigned before the end of 1942.

Paul Robeson, the country's foremost black entertainer in the 1940s, refused to honor a singing date at Santa Fe, New Mexico, after a hotel denied him lodging. A consistent advocate of human rights for all, the massively-built Robeson, born in Princeton, New Jersey, and an all-American at Rutgers, had started his singing-acting career in the 1920s as an interpreter of Negro spirituals. A graduate of the Columbia University Law School, he made a widely-reported tour of Nazi Germany and the Soviet Union in the 1930s. Following successful stage appearances in the United States and England, Robeson visited Russia at the invitation of movie director Sergei Eisenstein, who wanted him to star in a film about the black patriot in Haiti, L'Ouverture. (The picture was never made.) Robeson's Russian experiences convinced him, according to his biographer, Virginia Hamilton, that the Communist regime had a more realistic view of minority rights than his native land did, and that he could not "identify himself with a country [the United States] that deprived its largest minority of human equality."

His politics notwithstanding, Robeson attracted wide attention during 1942 when he starred in a stage production of *Othello*, the celebrated Shakespearean play. A road company featuring his commanding performances with fellow actors Jose Ferrar and his wife, Uta Hagan, played to huge wartime audiences. "After seeing him, scholars might insist,"

Time noted in August 1942, "that Shakespeare meant Othello for a Moor and not a Negro." But his love scenes with a white Desdemona contributed to the breakdown of old taboos. Yet he maintained an unqualified stance against Nazism throughout the war as did all black Americans; when an antiFacist group put on a huge fund-raising banquet at New York's Biltmore Hotel to aid victims in Hitler's concentration camps, Robeson was on hand.

From the beginning, American women had been quick to organize for the war effort. The Washington Naval Yard eagerly advertised for women with engineering and mechanical training to work in jobs which, before the war, had all gone to men. Women with bachelor degrees in mathematics and physics were offered immediate work, though those with high school diplomas and mechanical ability also found jobs in the yard's machine shops. "Rosie the Riveter" quickly became romanticized in cartoons and song as the patriotic female doing her bit for war production. But the millions of women who flocked into defense plants as Rosie the Riveter did not get the same paycheck as the men they replaced. Equal work did not mean equal pay. A survey released early in the war by the Women's Bureau in the Department of Labor, headed by Kate Papert, showed women lagging behind in earning power in every category of manufacturing.

As the country got its first taste of nationwide savings time—called war savings time—in early February 1940, a tragedy struck the home front: the destruction of the liner *Normandie* on February 9. The majestic *Normandie*, pride of France's overseas fleet in more peaceful times, had been taken over by the U.S. Navy and renamed the *U.S.S. Lafayette*. More than 3,000 workmen, employed by Robins Dry Dock and Repair Company, a subsidiary of Todd Shipyards, and several subcontractors, worked at refitting the 83,423-ton ship for a voyage to Boston on February 14, when a disastrous fire engulfed one of the lower decks.

Subsequent investigation revealed that an acetylene torch had ignited a pile of "kapok," a cotton-like fiber used in life preservers. The fire, which killed one worker and hospitalized 125 others, was finally put out by New York City fire fighters twelve hours later, but not before choking fumes and smoke blackened parts of the city. Filled with water, the ship rolled over and settled into the New York harbor mud "with the lower rims of her funnels barely three feet above the water." Though a serious loss of life had been averted, officials were dumbfounded to learn that an American fire hose would not connect to a French valve as the fire roared out of control.

A few weeks earlier, on January 16, American movie fans suffered a blow when the enormously popular actress, Carole Lombard, was killed in a plane crash while returning to Hollywood from a war bond rally in Indianapolis. Miss Lombard, wife of movie giant Glark Gable, was killed instantly, along with twenty-two other passengers, when the plane smashed into Nevada's Table Rock Mountain within sight of Las Vegas. Buck Blaine, a construction foreman at nearby Boulder Dam who reached the crash site by horseback, told reporters: "The plane had needed another 250 to 275 feet to clear the mountain" and that bodies were strewn around the plane. The actress, whose body was identified by Gable after a hurried flight from Los Angeles, was thirty-one.

Lombard who had first achieved top billing when she starred in *Nothing Sacred*, a sophisticated comedy by Ben Hecht, had once been married to William Powell, her costar in the 1936 hit, *My Man Godfrey*. Following a 1933 divorce and a raucous courtship, she had married Gable, eleven years her senior, in 1939. Like his wife, Gable drew top billing; his dashing performance in the 1939 epic film, *Gone With the Wind*, had made him familiar to audiences worldwide. The couple's romance had attracted wide publicity because of Gable's stormy divorce from his second wife and the prying eyes of Hollywood columnists. Lombard, who demanded and got a staggering $150,000 for each picture, had forced Paramount to abandon the morals clause in her contract (which called for prompt dismissal in the event of bad publicity) in order to pursue her relationship with Gable. Two weeks after his wife's death, Gable resumed work on a movie aptly titled *Somewhere I'll Find You*.

A sharp increase in movie attendance brought on by the war had produced a heightened interest in the private lives of film stars. Literally everyone, it seemed, in those days before television and easy access to home entertainment, went to the movies. Somewhere between 55 and 60 million Americans bought movie tickets each week during 1942; Hollywood itself projected a weekly attendance of 80 million. Movie historian Charles Higham reported that theater-going during the war "was not just a habit, it was a compulsion." And *Fortune* said: "The basic explanation for the movie boom is obvious—more people with more money to spend, and fewer things to spend it on. In addition, the strains and pressures of war are goads that drive millions into movie theaters, where for a little while they can escape reality and relax in comfortable darkness."

When the war started, Hollywood was grinding out 500 films annually for 16,000 domestic movie houses plus a profitable export market. Though the threat of war had loomed on the horizon for months, American films with rare exceptions had no patriotic or propaganda overtones. But in the aftermath of Pearl Harbor, Hollywood quickly changed and began to produce a spate of war-flavored films. Concerned about their impact, Roosevelt on June 13, 1942, created the Office of War Information (OWI), headed by Elmer Davis, a former Rhodes scholar and a writer and news analyst for the Columbia Broadcasting System.

OWI's function was to foster public perception of the war by overseeing propaganda output in all parts of the media—radio, motion pictures, and the press. Yet specialists differ on how effective the Bureau of Motion Pictures, a subdivision of OWI, actually was at getting Hollywood producers to follow government guidelines in their moviemaking. One thing is certain, the prewar practice of referring to German and Japanese characters as "the enemy" was soon changed to epithets like Huns, Krauts, and Japs. "In Hollywood's battles," writes historian John Morton Blum, "the Japanese, if they prevailed, heavily outnumbered the Americans and usually tortured or mutilated their captives."

Akin to public fascination with the movies was the bobby sox phenomenon that swept the country in the 1940s. Named for the thousands of teenaged girls with turned down anklets and pleated skirts who "shrieked and swooned" around the leading male vocalists of the day, the bobby sox craze reached into every hamlet. No performer captured the youngsters like Francis Albert "Frank" Sinatra from Hoboken, New Jersey, who became the nation's number one singing idol during the summer of 1942. Sinatra, who had replaced crooner Bing Crosby in the *Metronome* and *Downbeat* polls by 1943 as the country's top male singer, was the featured vocalist on the popular *Hit Parade*, a favorite radio show sponsored by Lucky Strike cigarettes, and he has remained in the limelight through the 1980s, forty years later. Running Sinatra a close second during the war years was Dick Haymes, a nineteen-year-old singer with the Tommy Dorsey, Harry James, and Benny Goodman bands. Young girls intent on following their every move did not seem to mind that neither man entered the service—Haymes because he was an Argentine native and Sinatra because he had punctured eardrums.

The entertainment world hit the headlines in a big way March 1 when the renowned Stage Door Canteen opened its doors in the basement of Broadway's Forty-fourth Street Theater; it started operations at the same time MacArthur was struggling to keep a toehold in the Philippines and it entertained untold numbers of servicemen from every corner of the globe. The Canteen was in the news constantly because showpeople turned up nightly to entertain the crowds of soldiers and sailors. It remained open every night of the war from 9:00 p.m. to midnight, and the only price of admission was a uniform. Everything was free—there was no cover charge, no minimum, and no tipping.

On a typical evening at the Stage Door Canteen in March 1942, Hildegarde, a comely singer and one of America's best-dressed women, according to the National Fashion Academy in 1940, would be on hand in her "V for Victory" gown which featured a great plunging "V" in the front. Alfred Lunt, a stage actor who had once toured with the legendary Lilly Langtry, and his wife, Lynn Fontaine, were also there serving food and washing dishes. Lauren Bacall, a struggling young actress and later the wife of Humphrey Bogart, signed up early to be a Canteen hostess. "I was asked to dance with any soldier, sailor, or marine, who asked me—get drinks or coffee for them, listen to their stories," she wrote in her best-selling autobiography. For a brief moment, GIs lucky enough to find the Canteen's open arms were able to forget the pangs of war; it explains the popularity of Irving Berlin's hit song, "I Left My Heart at the Stage Door Canteen," written for the Broadway musical *This is the Army, Mr. Jones.*

Berlin's hit, which the New York *Times* called "the best show of a generation," became an instant wartime classic. Few relished their service in Uncle Sam's citizen army and songs like "This is the Army, Mr. Jones," "Oh, How I Hate to Get Up in the Morning," "I'm Getting So Tired I Can Sleep," and "I Left My Heart at the Stage Door Canteen" captured the GI's aversion to army routine. The show opened in New York's Broadway Theater on Independence Day 1942 with an all-military cast which included actor-singer Burl Ives. But the $45,000 raised from first performance admissions was only the beginning of the astronomical sums that the show poured into Army Relief. *This is the Army, Mr. Jones* played to sellout crowds for 112 performances before it hit the road as an equally successful touring company. And before it closed in New York, Warner Brothers paid the army charity $250,000 as a first installment for movie rights.

3 MAY-AUGUST 1942: A NATIONAL PARADOX

By the summer of 1942 war production had reached a pitch it was to maintain for the duration. It was an exciting time as the country tooled up to produce the machines of war, not only for American use but for the Allies as well. It required a complete overhaul of national economic and industrial priorities; before peace returned in 1945, every aspect of the national experience had been influenced by it. Scarcely a person was unaffected by the swirl of defense production as millions of men and women took their place on the assembly line.

America's mission as the Arsenal of Democracy was whipped into line during January 1942 when Roosevelt, after months of hesitation, finally appointed a grand overseer—a production czar—for the war effort. He had intentionally kept this country's war effort diffused among several disjointed committees, starting in May 1940 with the National Defense Advisory Commission. Robert E. Sherwood, a highly acclaimed playwright (he wrote the *Petrified Forest*, later made into a hit movie starring Humphrey Bogart) and presidential speechwriter, who had close contact with the White House during 1940–1942, wrote that FDR "steadfastly and perhaps stubbornly refused" to designate a single director. "I have never known what the real reasons were for this delay," Sherwood added.

Donald Marr Nelson, a veteran Sears, Roebuck executive, was tapped to head the new War Production Board (WPB) when it was formed on January 13, 1942. It was a demanding job from the outset, one that *Life* described succinctly: "In cold but staggering figures the president has given Nelson one-man, life and death power over the 185,000 factories, 13,000,000 industrial workers, and the $52,000,000 arms program." Nelson stayed at the helm until September 1944, when he left on a personal diplomatic assignment for Roosevelt.

The fifty-three-year-old production czar, born in Hannibal, Missouri, brought a world of industrial and government experience to his task. After getting a chemical engineering degree from the University of Missouri in 1911, Donald had gone to work for Sears. By 1930 he was vice president in charge of merchandising; and because he was in charge of the massive Sears, Roebuck catalog, he became an expert in the purchase and distribution of consumer goods. Nor was his background limited to big business. As an early member of the New Deal team, he served on a number of advisory boards of the National Recovery Administration until 1935. He returned to Washington in 1940 as coordinator of Roosevelt's National Defense Advisory Commission.

Nelson and the country had endured a difficult twenty-two months before Roosevelt decided upon a unified approach to war production. It started with NDAC, the parent defense and food production agency, which was formed in May 1940 by presidential mandate. The eight-man council that had functioned until January 1941, eleven months before Pearl Harbor, had had no administrative head. Neither had the two production boards that had followed. At a time when the Battle of Britain was raging in Europe and the Japanese threatened to plunder the far Pacific, many had thought Roosevelt should order drastic war preparations. Although pacifist factions urged restraint, the president had generally taken it on the chin for his failure to appoint one man to head defense production before the outbreak of actual fighting. Until Nelson took over as head of WPB, the Arsenal of Democracy had been run by committee.

"Of course I am war orphan number one," Mrs. Helen Nelson said as her husband took charge of the defense program. Although she remained behind in the couple's fourteen-room mansion in surburban Chicago and did not follow Nelson to Washington, she told reporters in early 1942, "the country has been given the best man for the job." She made occasional appearances at patriotic functions early in the war but despite her support of her husband's work, the Nelson marriage dissolved three years later. In 1946, when Nelson published his first-rate *Arsenal of Democracy: The Story of American War Production*, he dedicated the book to "My Wife, Marguerite Coulbourn Nelson, who rendered exceedingly valuable service to me all through my work on the War Production Board."

Earlier attempts to fashion a valid system of war production under NDAC and several later boards had proved unworkable. The entire defense program floundered in a sea of indecision until the war with Japan finally spurred the president to action. Roosevelt's resolve to abandon the committee approach in favor of a cohesive defense structure came in the face of mounting foreign and domestic pressure. From overseas Lord Beaverbrook and the British, who had a vital stake in our ability to sustain Lend Lease shipments, bombarded Washington to make sweeping changes. At home Wendell Willkie, the 1940 presidential contender, called at the White House in early January to urge implementation of a unified production system. Willkie, reported the press, "had demanded a single director for the war effort 87 times in the 1940 campaign and 37 times since." He informed FDR that he fully intended one more speech at the upcoming session of the United States Conference of Mayors in Washington. Earlier, Harry S. Truman, senator from Missouri and chairman of the Senate committee investigating the war program, informed Roosevelt that his committee was about to issue a report. It would, the Missouri Democrat related, scold the present system and reveal that "the production effort was an awesome mess."

Unquestionably, the revelations of Truman and his investigators, or perhaps the suggestion that they might go public, contributed to the production shakeup and the creation of WPB. Truman's findings were in fact released to the press, and they painted a dismal picture of official and civilian boondoggling, buck passing, confusion, graft, and plain ineptitude in war plants all over the country. Military aviation was a shambles: "The U.S. has only enough planes to furnish 'skeleton forces' and many of these are inferior; after two years there are not enough planes to give pilots adequate flying training; the standard U.S. pursuit plane is outmoded in speed, ceiling, and firepower." Widespread profiteering and mismanagement were also uncovered in shipbuilding programs for the Navy and Merchant Marine.

Truman also blasted a World War II phenomenon—the "dollar-a-year man." In order to get the Arsenal of Democracy into operation Roosevelt had encouraged top engineering and managerial executives to enter the defense program on a loan basis at little or no official salary. Although it was patriotic and good public relations for their companies it was also a sure way to avoid the draft; more times than not it was also a means to influence defense contracts in favor of their firms. Unimpressed with dollar-a-year men and their counterparts—WOC (without compensation) men—the committee recommended "that they be fired or given a regular salary." Mostly, however, the report urged appointment of a single production overseer as the best means for correcting abuses.

Roosevelt, who read the Truman report before it was released, started to act in early January when he summoned Vice President Henry Wallace and Donald Nelson directly from a production meeting to the White House. Press speculation had been rife for days that appointment of a single director was imminent, and most defense big brass hoped lightning would strike. A long line of individuals wanted the post, including William S. Knudsen, a former General Motors executive, and Sidney Hillman, spokesman for organized labor—two Roosevelt confidants in the existing production scheme. Others waited in the wings, but Nelson was given the presidential nod.

When Wallace and Nelson arrived, FDR confided immediately that a new super board would be appointed with a director to handle the production morass. Then, according to his own account, Nelson was asked what the new panel should be called. When he suggested "the War Production Administration," the president balked. "He rolled the words over his tongue meditatively, and then aroused himself and said with emphasis, 'Oh, no, that won't do. That spells WPA. We had a WPA and while I thought it was fine, some of our friends were a little cross with it. I don't think we want to confuse people with two WPAs.' "

Always the adept politician, Roosevelt, who needed a united America to confront the Axis aggressors, was in no mood to furnish his detractors with ammunition. Conservative Republicans and others who suffered through the New Deal with disdain saw the WPA of an earlier day as the epitome of Rooseveltian bumbling. That anti-New Deal, anti-Rooseveltian feeling persisted straight through the war. Therefore, while Nelson was still in his chair, FDR proclaimed that the new agency would be the War Production Board (WPB).

Nothing short of production marvels swept U.S. industry under the new defense setup. Industrial tycoons like Henry J. Kaiser, who refined shipbuilding into a delicate art, suddenly became household names and subjects of wide press coverage. Kaiser first caught the public eye when his West Coast shipyards began turning out "Liberty Ships" in unheard of numbers early in the war. The Liberty vessel, patterned after the British tramp steamer and capable of a 17,000-mile cruising range, was a general cargo hauler throughout the war and beyond. It quickly became the country's chief workhorse for transporting defense supplies across both oceans. By utilizing a streamlined section-by-section technique, Kaiser's workers were able to complete 14 vessels a month or three and a half ships every week at peak production. During 1942 alone, Kaiser, who had the green light from Nelson and the WPB, sent 600 ships down the ways.

Kaiser became a real American success story. By 1942 he was operating four shipyards: Todd-California and Richmond at Richmond, California; California Shipbuilding at Los Angeles; and Oregon Shipbuilding at Portland; and he was part owner of four other companies. Born sixty years before at Sprout Brook, New York, and educated in several colleges, including the University of Nebraska and Montana School of Mines, Kaiser's quick rise started during 1914–1930 as a highway builder in such diverse places as British Columbia, Washington, California, and Cuba. His big break came during the 1930s when he got into the cement supply business for construction of Boulder and Grand Coulee Dams.

Prior to 1939, when he bought a small yard on the Columbia River at Portland, he had never built a ship of any kind. Still, reported Newsweek in 1942, Kaiser got the lion's share of the business because of "his demonstrated ability to build ships according to specifications and to build them fast." Nor were his West Coast operations unique. All kinds of companies joined in the mass manufacture of everything from rifles for foot soldiers to flying fortresses for the Air Force. American companies not only produced the tools of war in unprecedented quantities but, with government financing, they also created jobs for millions of war workers. Chrysler Corporation, the automotive giant, turned out tanks for the army and our allies which rivaled Kaiser's production of liberty ships.

When activated in 1941, the Chrysler Tank Arsenal at Detroit was the country's largest defense plant. Its size was increased during 1942 by more than one-half to 1,248,321 square feet as a result of increased defense contracts. Chrysler needed twelve additional installations with a total of 3,200,000 square feet, employing 25,000 workers to fill its contracts with Uncle Sam. The main facility at Detroit built 25,009 tanks to twelve different designs before the war ended; Chrysler-built tanks were used by Field Marshal Montgomery for his stabbing thrusts and counterthrusts across North Africa. And they furnished the armored backbone for all U.S. forces.

Ever-increasing demands for guns meant fewer items on hardware and department store shelves as the war progressed. In January, mail-order customers of the mammoth Montgomery Ward catalog found that the section usually devoted to Riverside tires had been deleted; inserted instead was a two-page bulletin on the wartime tire situation and an advertising plug for recap business. The number of household items made from metal—refrigerators, washing machines, vacuum cleaners—was also greatly reduced. Both Sears and Ward expanded their mail order offerings of wearing apparel and soft goods to offset the shrinkage in major household goods and related merchandise.

Still, the mass infusion of defense contracts was an absolute boon to American business. Nor did it take long for the average Joe to cash in on the ready money to be found in war work, even if he had scant opportunity to spend it on consumer items and the comforts of life. Money was no object for employers with defense contracts, and jobs could be located everywhere as businesses large and small fought each other for every available worker. In Bridgeport, Connecticut, premium wages were offered by the Remington Arms Company when it got ready to turn out "more small arms ammunition than was produced by all the manufacturers throughout the four years of World War I." Five months later, in July 1942 the venerable H. J. Heinz Company of Pittsburgh, makers of the famed fifty-seven varieties, got a contract for the fabrication of plastic-plywood airplane and glider parts. Soon men by the hundreds were recruited to work on "pressure machines formerly used for canning." And so it went in every part of the country.

The sharp upturn in defense output led to an immediate decline in business failures. According to Dun and Bradstreet, the dip in bankruptcies was greatest in the second half of 1941: "For 51 weeks of last year (1941) the total number of bankruptcies was 11,924, a decline of 12.6 percent from the 13,647 registered in the like 1940 period." Moreover, the effect of government monies thrust into major defense projects unquestionably spilled over to smaller, consumer-oriented operations. Even tiny mom-and-pop stores showed an amazing prosperity because of free-spending defense workers. The widespread growth in business activity led the Justice Department to move quickly against shady companies. Thurman Arnold, an assistant attorney general in charge of prosecutions, announced that since "we are fighting a war of production," the Sherman Anti-trust Law would be aggressively enforced to "guarantee the preservation of independent business organizations as a means of making full use of our resources."

Expanded commercial activity, however, did not produce a corresponding rise in stock market volume. The New York Stock Exchange, already stagnant from the depression years, and generally fearful of New Deal planners, simply did not shoot upward with the onset of war. February 1942 was the worst month on Wall Street since the disastrous crash of October 1929, although the great Allied victories during 1943 spawned a moderate rise in stock market activity. Washington's quickness to curb speculative dividends in the aftermath of Pearl Harbor, coupled with increased taxes to finance the war effort and the drive to keep a check on inflation, kept investors out of the market.

The industrial giants may have experienced astronomical profits from defense contracts but most of the money went to retire outstanding debts and to build up reserves for postwar expansion into new product lines. Blue chip profits were not channeled into stockholder dividends. This in turn created a steady market throughout 1941–1945. Boeing Aircraft stock, for example, sold at a high of 24 ¾ in 1941 but reached a low of 17 ¼ during 1945. Other major companies experienced similiar patterns. "If stock prices remained comparatively level after 1942, while employment rose and savings increased greatly, what then did the wage earners do with their money?" asks Robert Sobel in his closely-reasoned history of the New York Stock Exchange. "Rationing and the halt to appliance, automobile, and housing production held down spending. Since there was a lot of surplus cash in the hands of the public, it might have been expected that some of it would find its way to Wall Street. This was not the case. Instead, wage earners put their money into savings banks, paid off mortgages and installments, bought insurance, and participated in Defense, War, and Victory Bond Drives." And the big investors stayed out of the market because of wartime taxes.

In spite of a depressed stock market, the suddenly expanded economy created labor-supply problems requiring government intervention. At least two agencies, Paul V. McNutt's War Manpower Commission and the War Labor Board headed by William H. Davis, were established by Roosevelt to oversee labor allocations in much the same manner Nelson's group parceled out precious resources for actual defense production.

In mid-July Nelson told reporters: "Materials are the only limiting factor on American war production." Paul McNutt, however, had an entirely different view, and the WMC, which anticipated a severe labor crunch by October, began laying plans to handle worker shortages. Although the British had had a strict labor system in operation for months, McNutt and the administration decided to wait until after the off-year elections in November before seeking congressional approval for a National Service Act—a piece of legislation to give WMC authority to meet "labor emergencies" with powers akin to those of the Churchill government in England. And since administration projections demanded another 20 million people—7,000,000 for the armed forces and 13,000,000 for industry—by the end of 1943, the War Manpower Commission obviously needed extra muscle to back up its decisions.

Meanwhile, McNutt's planners established local committees in key industrial areas "to harmonize the conflicting demands of local industry and draft boards." Fear of upsetting Democratic control of the House of

Representatives in the November elections caused McNutt to move slowly at labor regimentation. At a time when Republicans might be expected to make substantial congressional gains, WMC contented itself with issuing "toothless directives" through the summer and fall. Yet a major effort was started to have labor, business, and government bureaus establish cooperative labor agreements which would erase the need to coerce civilian workers into unwanted jobs.

A staggering variety of individuals and groups soon confronted WMC field offices and draft boards with work-related difficulties. Many, if not most, men seeking military deferment or outright avoidance of active duty cited demands of the workplace as ample justification. At Waterbury, Connecticut, a local draft board reported in May 1942 "what it believed to be the ultimate reason for deferment by the registrant." A prospective soldier, identified only as "Pete," asked for a delay in military induction because he had purchased 5,000 metal buttons with General MacArthur's picture and needed time to sell them. His plea was turned down.

A related problem cropped up early in the defense program over work hours for employees. War contractors had been prodded into a 168 hour week by government overseers and many companies used even longer work schemes to avoid "weekend blackouts." The scramble to fill production quotas and thus keep their defense contracts caused producers to offer or even demand extended overtime from their workers. Employers might appeal to patriotic fervor but the long hours begat sticky personnel problems. "There is striking evidence," concluded Princeton professor J. Douglas Brown, "that hours beyond 48 and particularly beyond 54 cause a reduction in individual output, an increase in days off, and a rise in accidents."

It was not the individual employee with a job-related beef which caused authorities the greatest headache but the nearly impossible task of placating workers and their union bosses in heavy industry. A major source of trouble arose from the eternal cat-and-mouse game between labor leaders, the union rank and file, and management. Union chiefs throughout the history of organized labor have made it an article of faith to make outrageous demands for pay hikes and work concessions, knowing full well that employers could never grant them. Their tough-man stance in labor negotiations is taken primarily to court workers who vote them into office rather than to bully management.

Labor's insatiable demands for more money and better work conditions led to formation of the National Labor Board during January 1942 as part of FDR's general reorganization of defense priorities. Headed by

William H. Davis, a New York patent lawyer, NWLB was a twelve-man board with representatives from industry, labor, and the public. And because the panel was charged to control the inflationary impact of spiraling wages, it was frequently called "a court packed against labor," by prounion spokesmen; it also had responsibility for settling labor disputes in critical industries. Davis, a Maine native and 1901 graduate of George Washington University's school of law, struggled to have NWLB hold down the so-called inflationary gap. That was a fancy economic concept to explain what happens when too much money chases too few consumer goods. Put another way, the notion prevailed in official circles that high wages paid to war workers would be spent on a constantly dwindling supply of domestic items. And the way to hold down prices was to hold down wages—lower wages, the economists said, would narrow the gap. Although labor bosses resisted that line of attack, Davis, who later headed the Office of Economic Stabilization and served on the Atomic Energy Board after the war, used NWLB's authority to influence union-company disputes.

As the War Labor Board and organized labor clashed over wages, other parts of American life seemed totally unaffected by the defense uproar. A visitor from another planet during the summer of 1942 might have wondered if the country was really at war. Official Washington might have been preoccupied with production, but for huge chunks of the population it was life as usual. Most Americans thought the easy flow of money a welcome relief from the drabness of the Depression years; they were eager to let the good times roll.

Sporting and entertainment events continually attracted large audiences throughout the war. Churchill Downs officials reported that a crowd estimated at 100,000 gathered in Louisville on May 1, 1942 for the sixty-eighth running of the Kentucky Derby. The mile-and-a-quarter Downs took on its customary carnival atmosphere as a seventeen-horse field vied for the illusive winner's circle. One wire service said the track "was flooded from turret to turf. There were people on the roofs, on the walls, and hanging from the rafters," all of them seemingly oblivious to the war.

In a paradox that would often plague the national conscience throughout the war, the cheering of the racetrack crowds at Louisville was matched by the mourning of families less than a 100 miles away at Harrodsburg, Kentucky, when word arrived that sixty-six men from that town had been swallowed up in the Japanese capture of Bataan. The men, all members of Company D, 192nd tank batallion, had been called to active duty in 1940 with the Kentucky National Guard; it was a bitter time for the families who grieved over the fate of sons and loved ones. A total 36,853 U.S. and Filipino troops had fallen into enemy hands at Bataan, and *Life* reported that the Harrodsburg families were showing "their courage in many quiet ways. They are already planning how they will dedicate a recently-completed armory when the boys of Company D come home at the end of the war. They have taken to putting snapshots of their sons in a Main Street store window for their friends to see."

War was not an abstract thing for the Harrodsburg families who read an article in the Harrodsburg *Herald* "on how to to send letters for prisoners of war in Japan or a Japanese-controlled country." Since Bataan, many of their young men fit that description. And the Kentucky families had company in their vigil for word about loved ones—"there were 35 men from Port Clinton, Ohio, in Company C of the same outfit. There were 97 men from Janesville, Wisconsin, and 89 men from Maywood, Illinois, in Companies A and B. There were similiar Companies from Carlsbad, New Mexico, and Salinas, California. . . ." Bataan had fallen on April 9. Nearby Corregidor fell a few weeks afterward. The news of these battlefield losses set a pattern that lasted until the return of peace. But except for the families directly concerned, an America preoccupied with enjoying the newfound prosperity of the war years took little notice of their fallen countrymen.

Still, the need for an increased war effort led to public acceptance or at least toleration of the first gasoline rationing plan. Although food and assorted consumer items were soon placed on the rationed list, gasoline rationing became effective in nineteen eastern states after May 15, following a stormy period in which citizens signed up for coupons at OPA field offices. Overnight every car, truck, and motorcycle in the country had an "A," "B," or "C" sticker prominently displayed on its windshield. The stickers not only indicated the vehicle's weekly fuel allotment but also the social standing of its owner. Some—doctors, congressmen, essential workers—were given higher assignments than ordinary drivers. Most got the lowly "A" badge, which was seen everywhere and which allowed its owner a mere three gallons per week. "Rationing made sweeping changes," *Newsweek* reported: "Service station operators, their already slashed stocks depleted by last-minute buying, felt they could no longer make a living. . . . Chauffeurs by the hundreds saw their jobs sputter as tanks went dry. Parking lot operators found potential playgrounds on their hands. Businessmen in suburban shopping centers feared the worst. Those in downtown locations were happy."

Although highway patrolmen grew lonesome for lack of traffic, government demands on available petroleum reserves made civilian rationing a necessity. Military aviation consumed gasoline at enormous rates, and in the Carolinas, where the 2nd Armored Division conducted 1942 maneuvers, each light tank required fifty-four gallons at a single refueling. In one night the 2nd used 92,000 gallons of gasoline. Yet the initial plan caused widespread grumbling. Rubber and sugar rationing had been accepted readily because everyone was treated alike, but the first gasoline allocations hit only part of the country.

The restrictions were not applied uniformly in the nineteen Eastern states first rationed—actually seventeen states, the District of Columbia, and the city of Bristol, Tennessee. Some counties were exempted in Maryland, New York, Pennsylvania, Virginia, and West Virginia because locally-refined gasoline was readily available; motorists by the thousands simply drove across county and state lines to fill empty tanks. The vast area west of the Mississippi was totally without rationing.

The unfairness of it all led Pennsylvania Congressman James Van Zandt, who later entered the Navy as a lieutenant commander, to introduce legislation which would have blocked funds to enforce OPA edicts. Although his bill was defeated on a voice vote, Van Zandt got off a parting jab: "The entire gasoline rationing program is a farce and a fizzle. Certain sections of the country are asked to submit to a rationing program, while their neighbors in adjoining counties are free to use the highways to their hearts' content." Car owners agreed; and in rationed zones situated throughout Appalachia and parts of the Southwest, enterprising locals found ways to beat the restrictions. Wherever natural gas wells existed around the countryside a new curiosity called "drip" burst upon the the wartime scene. It made a workable alternative to gasoline and an automobile would run on it, especially if mixed with commercially-produced fuels.

Normal production required each well to have a condensate line to "drip off" unwanted residue; in great stretches of the Southwest today the same material is burned or flared off into the atmosphere. During the war, however, when collected and "strained through an old felt hat" to remove impurities, it found its way into ration-starved gas tanks. All over Appalachia good old boys left a telltale smoke screen as their cars sputtered along on the substitute. It became a standing joke in some mountain regions that any car emitting smoke from the tail pipe was using drip.

Not everyone could find a producing gas well. The rationing scheme was no sooner announced than OPA offices were overrun by a frantic public asking for higher-bracketed rationing cards. And OPA threatened swift retaliation for anyone making false petitions for more than the minimal three gallons per week. After penalities of ten years in jail and fines ranging to $10,000 were announced, an avalanche took place as people rushed to turn in revised cards. More than 2,500 showed up in New York alone on the first day, commented *Newsweek*, "but the demand for more than three gallons per week continued. Anyone who asked for no more than a simple A card was greeted with relief at rationing boards."

If gasoline rationing did not keep sports enthusiasts at home it surely contributed to a solemn July Fourth. Unlike years past when practically everyone joined in the funmaking, the first wartime Fourth was markedly subdued. In Philadelphia, where the first Independence Day festivities originated 166 years before, "thousands stayed at home," and the customary "fanfare of city-wide parades was given up as inappropriate in wartime." At a time when Allied forces were facing repeated setbacks on worldwide fighting fronts, President Roosevelt sounded a serious note in his annual Fourth of July address: "We celebrate it this year, not in the fireworks of make believe but in death-dealing reality of tanks and guns and planes. We celebrate it also by running without interruption the assembly lines which turn out these weapons to be shipped to all the embattled points of the globe."

Around-the-clock production at war plants did in fact continue full steam ahead during the holiday interlude. Men and women engaged in the grim business of making war machines found no time for firecrackers and lemonade. Not even news that American air units had joined R.A.F. bombers for a raid on Nazi-occupied Europe was enough to shake off the national gloom. The July Fourth foray "plowed up airfields, blasted enemy planes and installations, and gunned German flying personnel in the Netherlands," said the New York *Times*. "Hangers and troop buildings at the German airdromes at Alkmaar, Haamstede, and Valkenburg," the patriotic account continued, "were bombed and set afire and Nazi airmen on the fields were shot down by low-flying attackers."

But the war did not keep baseball fans from major league ball parks on the Fourth. If the baseball adage is correct that the first place team on July Fourth will capture the league pennant, then the American and National circuit leaders in 1942 broke fifty-fifty. Joe McCarthy's New York Yankees remained four games in front of the second place Red Sox after splitting a double header in Boston. The American League leaders, spearheaded by Joe DiMaggio, one of the hottest hitters in baseball history, captured the 1942 pennant with nine games to spare. DiMaggio, whose brother "Dom," or Dominic, played for the Red Sox, remained one of the game's great heroes throughout the war years and into the

1950s; the Yankee outfielder, who closed the 1942 season with a .305 batting average, had hit safely in fifty-six consecutive games the year before to set a modern player record.

DiMaggio and manager McCarthy led the Yankees into the first wartime series forty-eight games ahead of the last place Philadelphia Athletics. In the National League, however, the Brooklyn Dodgers ended up in first place on July Fourth after sweeping a double header from the Phillies. At midseason they were nine and a half games in front of the second place St. Louis Cardinals. But it was the Cardinals and not Brooklyn who carried the National League banner into the 1942 World Series. Things had reversed themselves by season's end, with St. Louis nine games ahead of the second place Dodgers. Ironically, both Philadelphia teams brought up the tail end of the American and National circuits with the Phillies ending the season sixty-two and a half games behind the Cardinals.

The national pastime flourished during the war because Roosevelt and the administration felt baseball was good for civilian morale; the game was exempted from restrictions on wartime travel and FDR specifically allowed night games as a diversion. Though organized baseball, like other facets of home-front life had its problems during 1941–1945, the emergency did not really affect the 1942 season. But conditions changed drastically the following year: "The war had now caught up with baseball," writes Frederick G. Lieb, a World Series historian, "and riddled most of the clubs. Both the 1942 champions lost numerous key players: the Cardinals, Terry Moore, Enos Slaughter, Jimmy Brown, and Howie Pollet; and the Yankees, Joe DiMaggio, Red Ruffing, Phil Rizzuto, Buddy Hassett, and George Selkirk." As the war progressed, the military took its toll, and baseball had to resort to using aging players and rejects from the service to fill its rosters.

American and National League teams reported attendance figures in excess of four and a half million during 1942. That figure was about a million and a half lower than the last peacetime season; and the 1942 world series between New York and the Cardinals pulled in 276,717 fans and a whopping $1,105,249 gate, the highest tallies ever for a five game series. In keeping with the war spirit, the USO was given the entire $100,000 broadcast fee plus forty-nine percent of the gate for the third and fourth games—a total of $362,926.65.

In the midst of the summer's concern over baseball standings, FBI agents announced July 2 that eight Nazis arrested two weeks earlier as saboteurs would be tried as spies in a military court. According to *Time,* the eight had been "spewed upon U.S. shores like Jonas from the bellies of U-boats" at Amagansett, Long Island, and Ponte Vedra Beach, Florida.

Government agents were busy rounding up suspected spies and saboteurs throughout the summer and the arrest of the submarine-borne Nazis heightened an already charged atmosphere. Matters worsened when it was learned that all eight had previous connections in the United States and spoke English. One of them, Herbert Hans Haupt, a former ROTC cadet at an American university, had a fiancée, Mrs. Gerda Melind, in Chicago. The twenty-four-year-old widow and beauty operator told newsmen that she was "ashamed, and through with him" when questioned about Haupt's arrest. Also taken into custody were George J. Dasch, who had worked in hotels all over the country, and Werner Theil, a onetime worker in several U.S. automotive and tool plants; the five others were also discovered to have been in the United States previous to the abortive raid.

When captured, they carried maps and detailed plans for "destruction of vital war plants, key railroad centers and bridges, and water supply systems." Fear gripped the home front when their targeted destinations were learned: New York City; Alcoa, Tennessee; Newark, New Jersey; Altoona, Pennsylvania; Cincinnati, Ohio; and East St. Louis, Missouri. Speculation about their fates ended abruptly when FDR ordered a military trial; the president also issued "a proclamation denying espionage or sabotage the right of access to the civil courts." The Supreme Court even met in rare extraordinary session to rule that the would-be saboteurs were in lawful custody and that military trails could proceed. Then, "seven boot-tough generals" sat as judges while the tribunal "which stuck to due process to the point of mumbo-jumbo" meted out swift justice. After two days of testimony the military men forwarded a guilty verdict to the White House. Dasch and a coconspirator named Ernest Peter Berger got life imprisonment after they informed on their comrades, although FDR later reduced Dasch's sentence to thirty years at hard labor. The remaining six were later electrocuted in "the new south wing of the District of Columbia's ancient red-brick jail."

A crackdown on subversives during the summer included surveillance of native Americans opposed to the war and Rooseveltian policy. A chief target of Justice Department interest was the well-known "radio priest," Father Charles E. Coughlin, and his right wing journal, Social Justice. Coughlin, who originated the paper in 1936, had been a harsh critic of FDR and the New Deal since the darkest days of the Depression; and he consistently spoke out on economic and political issues from the start of his radio and publishing career.

An ordained Roman Catholic priest, Coughlin often invoked the teachings of St. Thomas Aquinas, a thirteenth-century divine, to support his conservative views. Aquinas was readily embraced to explain Coughlin's extreme theories on private property and civic responsibility. "The temporal goods which God permits to a man are his with regard to property," Coughlin proclaimed in a 1930s radio broadcast: "If the individual owner rejects his social responsibilities, it is the duty of the state to enforce them."

He gained an enormous following in the 1930s and, according to his biographer, Charles J. Tull, thought some government intervention in the economy was necessary. But he remained a staunch anti-Communist as well as anti-New Dealer. Born to an American father and a Canadian mother in 1891 at Hamilton, Ontario, and a 1911 graduate of the University of Toronto, he taught philosophy at a Catholic college in Waco, Texas, before taking holy orders in 1916. He began serving parishes in the Detroit area and in 1921 was assigned to a small congregation twelve miles north of the city at Royal Oak, Michigan. From the beginning, Coughlin had a reputation as a pulpit orator. He launched his national career over station WJR in October 1926; speaking from his church, the Shrine of the Little Flower, "his radio fame was to make him a household word within a few months."

An adjunct to Coughlin's conservative radio ministry was his magazine, *Social Justice*, edited by E. Perrin Schwarz, onetime editor of the Milwaukee *Journal*. From the first issue in March 1936, the paper grew until Coughlin claimed a circulation of six million on the eve of war. *Social Justice* not only advocated total isolation for the United States and accused Roosevelt of "warmongering," but was also blatantly anti-Semitic. Coughlin, who condemned what he called "Communist Jews," even had his paper "give praise to Hitler for solving Germany's economic problems and chide Roosevelt for failure to cure America's."

Attorney General Francis Biddle announced in April 1942 that *Social Justice* would be barred from the mails because the Justice Department said it was spreading Axis propaganda. As proof, government investigators cited a 1938 editorial which aped "a savagely anti-Semitic speech" made in 1935 by Joseph Goebbels, Hitler's propaganda chief. Shortwave broadcasts from Radio Berlin during 1942 made the most of Coughlin's troubles with Uncle Sam: "Father Coughlin, well-known in America for his undaunted struggle against Bolshevism and jewry, has once again been given a taste of the method of oppression so common in the world's freest democracy." The radio priest did not fight the edict but merely informed Postmaster General Frank A. Walker that *Social Justice* would cease publication. Pressured by the government and his church superiors, Coughlin quietly returned to his pastoral duties at his Shrine of the Little Flower.

About the time Coughlin was being run out of business for unpatriotic activities, America was treated to a new sight: women in uniform. And they attracted instant public interest. When the first 800 women reported for Army duty in July at "elm-shaded Fort Des Moines, 21 women reporters, 12 men reporters, and 22 photographers" were there to publicize their arrival. Soon, photographs and elaborate layouts began appearing almost daily in publications and newsreels glamorizing not only women soldiers—who never saw combat—but also WAVES (Women Accepted for Volunteer Emergency Service in the Navy), military nurses, women in the U.S. Marines, and lady fliers for the Army Air Force.

The 360 enlisted women and 440 officers of the Woman's Army Auxiliary Corps, shortened to WACs when the "auxiliary" was abandoned in 1943, were greeted at Fort Des Moines by Colonel Oveta Culp Hobby, newly appointed WAAC commandant. "Military tradition has given way to pressing need," Mrs. Hobby told her charges, "and you are the first women to serve as an auxiliary force in the U.S. army. Never forget it. You have taken off silk and put on khaki. All for the same reason. You have a debt and a date. A debt to democracy, and a date with destiny."

For all her grand words, another kind of date plagued WACs and the other female services, at least in the public mind. Anytime women are thrust into an all-male domain rumor and innuendo inevitably follow; tales of pregnancies and "loose women" dogged the corps through the war years and afterward. Although Mrs. Hobby gave the WACs more than able leadership, some stigmas cannot be easily overcome. Perhaps it was also a female reluctance to leave home for the rigors of camp life but the WACs never achieved more than 60,000 recruits for the duration. Original plans called for a corps strength of 150,000. Those women who did join up adjusted quickly to camp life under Mrs. Hobby's direction. And when "a nocturnal mouse invaded company No. 1's quarters," *Time*'s account of the first inductees said, "there were no screams. A WAAC cooly slew it with a well-aimed shoe." As one would expect, men in the army had more difficulty accepting WAACs than the other way round. A War Department directive in November 1942 suggested that

army officers not be embarrassed when saluted by females and that they accept "WAACs as equals in the military social scale."

Meanwhile, as the country got accustomed to the demands of war, William H. Davis and NWLB moved during the summer to bring management and labor into line over rising demands for higher wages. Although something called the "Little Steel" decision by the labor board in July set the tone for labor-management disputes, Davis's agency acted promptly against balky employers who used the emergency as an excuse to fight organized labor. When George McNear, sole proprietor of the Toledo, Peoria, and Western Railroad, with headquarters at Peoria, Illinois, "refused to recognize the operating unions on his railroad," he was summoned before a NWLB hearing in Washington. That was after the T.P. & W. had been deemed "crucial to war production"; NWLB examiners, charged with quieting upheavals in critical industries, were not impressed with McNear's attempts to thwart the union during the emergency. Get-tough orders by Davis and NWLB brought a quick end to the strike.

But it was the Little Steel decision, *Business Week* said, that "definitely marked a new era in collective bargaining in the United States." This case linked all pay raises for unionized workers to a fixed cost-of-living scale, and it evolved out of a dispute between the C.I.O. steelworkers union and several smaller companies: Bethlehem, Republic, Inland, and Youngstown Sheet & Tube—Little Steel. The decision spelled out dollar amounts any union could expect in future disputes; constant haggling over pay hikes was removed from collective bargaining negotiations for the duration. Companies were also required to maintain a dues check-off system for the union as well as a "maintenance of membership contract." The latter meant that once a labor contract became effective, each worker had "to remain a union member during the life of the contract in order to keep his job."

Ready acceptance of Little Steel by the steelworkers meant that unions, like management, were in no position to hassle with NWLB in the war atmosphere of 1942. Three weeks later, however, a confrontation occurred when 1,000 workers at a General Cable Company plant in Bayonne, New Jersey, went on strike. The walkout took place when NWLB refused a union demand for "a wage increase of 10¢ an hour and a vacation bonus of two weeks' pay." Fear that the strike would spread to a larger General Cable installation in nearby Perth Amboy was squelched when NWLB threatened to call out regular army troops.

Troops had not been used since spring 1941 when they were called to contain a strike at an American Aviation plant in California, but the threat of army intervention put labor on short notice, although future adjustments in NWLB's antiinflation policies were necessary. As summer melted into autumn and the home front braced for more rationing including a cut in home heating fuel for the winter, firm guidelines laid down in the Little Steel episode gave the country a welcome breather from unsettling labor disputes.

4 SEPTEMBER–DECEMBER 1942: IN LIKE FLYNN

A continued drive for more defense production, more rationing, news of some military successes, and the closing fanfare of state and congressional electioneering dominated the last months of 1942. Labor Day, celebrated on Tuesday, September 7, a traditional holiday for American workers, was given over to patriotic calls for guns and ships. Rear Admiral E. J. Marquart, who addressed civilian workers during a Brooklyn Naval Yard lunch break, described shipbuilding achievements since Pearl Harbor as "a staggering total almost beyond the belief of one's eyes."

The Navy Department announced that 147 ships were launched and keels for another forty-eight put down on Labor Day. But thousands seized the long holiday break for a respite from the strains of war. Although an Associated Press survey revealed a big reduction in Labor Day fatalities since 1941 because tire and gasoline shortages had kept people out of automobiles, thousands flocked to vacation spots by bus and train. New York City reported crowds at its major attractions—Coney Island, the Empire State Building, the Bronx Zoo, the Giants-Dodgers baseball game, Radio City. "So much had been published on the predicted overflow of visitors to this city for Labor Day," reported the *Times*, "that groups of pickpockets from other cities, including Pittsburgh, Boston, Philadelphia, and Newark hied themselves here in advance of a rich harvest."

The cost of supplying the mass of people pursuing the war effort at home and overseas was tremendous; and the demand for higher wages and altered work conditions was universal. In the South, "for the first time ever" shortages of servants developed: "Surprised Atlanta, Nashville, and Winston-Salem wives," commented *Time*, "find that even inexperienced Negro girls demand at least five days off a month, won't stay in, won't cope with children, won't do laundry and insist on dinner at 6 p.m. (which in wartime is practically mid-afternoon)." Union leaders everywhere denounced Little Steel with incessant calls for fatter pay envelopes. A harried WLB even made some concessions and agreed to boosts in wages for 250,000 employees of U.S. Steel and for 400 workers in thirteen St. Louis machine shops during August and September.

Alarmed at escalating wages and prices in the marketplace, FDR chose to speak out in a Labor Day address. He "laid it on the line" to Congress: either pass the necessary legislation to halt runaway inflation or he would act under his powers as commander-in-chief. Roosevelt wanted the new law by the end of September because, he said, "we cannot hold the actual cost of food and clothing down to the present level beyond October 1."

The presidential ultimatium, which demanded a $25,000 ceiling on wages, had plenty of validity. Since the outbreak of European fighting in September 1939, domestic prices had risen steadily every single month. Everything—rents, clothing, household goods—suddenly cost more. At the end of the summer of 1942, after nine months of war, the cost-of-living index had reached an uncomfortable seventeen percent above price levels at the time Hitler unleashed his Panzer divisions across the Polish frontier.

Yet Congress, faced with the November elections, was slow to act; most of September was spent in endless wrangling, not only over FDR's call for action but also over a deluge of letters from angry constituents about rising prices, shortages, and a rampant black market. Fear gripped Congress that any scheme that linked prices and wages to a common indicator would "curb purchasing power, lower living standards, and legalize inequities." And there was the troublesome problem of spot inflation areas—they were not evenly distributed. Great sweeps of the country were relatively unaffected, while areas surrounding military installations and defense plants suffered severe economic dislocations.

As usual Congress responded to public outcry; a bill to contain consumer prices—to hold the line—was sent to the White House on October 2. One day later, an old Roosevelt crony, James Francis Byrnes, associate justice of the Supreme Court and future governor of South Carolina, took over a newly formed agency, the Office of Economic Stabilization (OES), as the nation's economic chief. Byrnes, a slender, wiry sixty-three-year-old South Carolina politician, had been on the New Deal bandwagon from the beginning. Actually, OES was an eight-man board with Byrnes as director; the new agency functioned under an executive order that clamped controls and freezing restrictions on every part of the economy. Besides restrictions on farm production, hold-the-line orders were placed immediately on all salaries between $5,000 and $25,000; no person was supposed to earn more for the duration. Public utility rates and all kinds of transportation fares from streetcars and trains to transcontinental flights were frozen along with prices on food.

A plan was even set afoot to halt the unnecessary migration of labor. While the anti-inflation rules exempted all salaries below $5,000 from the freeze, it also made adjustment in handling wages beyond the Little Steel formula. There was to be "no increase beyond the highest level between January 1 and September 15." It soon became obvious that pressure from organized labor—a central cog in the Democratic coalition—would cause further changes in the Little Steel plan. A total wage freeze was not in the offing because Roosevelt's mandate gave WLB power to "correct maladjustments."

OPA chief Leon Henderson was likewise told to freeze rents everywhere as part of the attack. "Let me at 'em!" he told reporters when word came from the White House to stop the wild hikes in house and apartment rents that plagued the country. The rent order not only covered areas adjacent to military bases and war plants but also reached into rural areas.

The battle against inflation and scarcity found Henderson and the OPA in a dilemma over fixing quotas on women's hosiery later in the fall. After removal of silk and nylon from domestic use, manufacturers were forced to use rayon as a hosiery substitute. When the uproar started in November, an estimated 87 percent of all women's hose was being made from rayon. But even rayon was needed for defense purposes, including the manufacture of tires for military vehicles. Supplies of the synthetic fiber had fallen until domestic mills were only operating at 50 percent of capacity. A female chorus swelled over the unavailability of hosiery in an era more dress-conscious than the 1980s. The approaching Christmas holidays increased demand, and considerable hoarding of remaining nylon stocks took place as the outcry gained momentum. "Some leading department stores have been telling their customers they had no nylons," *Business Week* said. "Some of them haven't; others are playing their own little game of rationing by filling orders to their best charge customers, in no case allowing them more than two pairs."

In an effort to assure more equitable distribution, OPA acted to remove the profit incentive for holding back available supplies. A $1.65 price was set in early November "for most commonly full-fashioned hose." But a further flap developed when OPA said domestic manufacturers were hoarding or holding back 3,600,000 pairs of leg wear. Industry spokesman refuted the government figures by contending that their stocks were lower than OPA estimates.

While the country was reeling from FDR's hold-the-line orders and learning to live with shortages, a running battle began between WLB and Sewall Lee Avery, head of the massive Montgomery Ward conglomerate. The crusty Avery, an individualist of the old school, reportedly once fired his golf caddy because "he bothered me, forever wanting to carry the clubs." As chairman of the board at Wards, he decided that his mail order house was not an essential industry and therefore not under WLB jurisdiction.

The sixty-nine-year-old Avery, born at Saginaw, Michigan, was a graduate of the University of Michigan law school. He had never maintained a private practice, but since 1894 had been connected with several large corporations. In 1942 he was not only in charge at Wards but was also chairman of the board at U.S. Gypsum. Avery was not pleased when, during the summer of 1942, McNutt ordered Wards to enter into a "maintenance of membership agreement as well as provide for union security, voluntary checkoff, arbitration, and seniority in its agreement with the United Mail Order, Warehouse, and Retail Employees Union."

Although such pacts conformed to the Little Steel formula, John A. Barr, labor relations director for the company, told a WLB hearing panel that Wards considered such a contract illegal because it required them "to surrender principles which the company considered fundamental." WLB issued a formal directive on November 5 ordering compliance. Wayne L. Morse, a civilian member of the board, dean of the University of Oregon law school, and future U.S. senator, said "it would be a major defeat for the home front" if Avery won the day. Wards bowed to the inevitable in 1942 after Roosevelt personally wrote the company ordering it to sign the union agreement.

When the contract expired in November 1943, however, Wards informed all concerned that it would not be renewed. Though the company reopened talks, a new agreement was not reached. As a result, after April 19, 1944, the U.S. Post Office stopped delivery of first class mail addressed to Montgomery Wards, an action that devastated the company's mail-order catalog business.

When Commerce Department officials failed to seize the company, Attorney General Biddle personally arrived with Regular Army troops to take over Avery's Chicago office. That was after Avery told his stockholders he had spent more than $4,000,000 in company funds to fight WLB.

His counteroffensive, which included full-page advertisements in leading newspapers around the country, was carried out to inform the nation that he was under "duress." Sewall Avery, editoralized *The Nation* in 1944, "apparently feels it incumbent upon himself to maintain 'free enterprise' and keep the pioneer spirit alive by his own efforts." When Biddle plunged into Avery's office, the harried board chairman was fuming: "You New Dealer," he blurted, as Biddle's soldiers evicted him forcibly after he refused to recognize the legality of documents taking control of his company. A widely-circulated news photograph of Avery being carried out of the building by two helmeted soldiers was voted "picture of the year" by one of the wire services. The antics of Avery, who continued as chairman of the board at Wards until the 1950s, pointed out a serious flaw in American life during the war: how to strike an even balance between traditional free enterprise and societal demands during a national emergency.

Another bottleneck developed later in the fall when Washington acted to guarantee an adequate rubber supply. The nagging problem of domestic rubber production was resolved in September 1942 when WPB chief Donald Nelson picked William M. Jeffers to oversee U.S. rubber efforts. Jeffers's appointment climaxed months of controversy over how best to handle rubber shortages after the cutoff of natural supplies from overseas.

A stockpiling effort had started in 1940 under the direction of sixty-eight-year-old Texan Jesse Jones, another New Deal stalwart. Jones had been a lumberman, banker, and publisher of the Houston *Chronicle* before FDR made him chairman of the Reconstruction Finance Corporation in 1933. Although he became "supervisor of basic New Deal lending programs," Jones later broke with the Democrats and used his newspaper to support Republicans Dewey and Eisenhower. He also directed Roosevelt's Rubber Reserve Corporation, but after Pearl Harbor rubber supplies had become distressingly low. Jones's efforts were hampered by his ongoing feud with Harold L. Ickes, FDR's petroleum administrator. Ickes, a onetime Bull Moose Republican and, since 1933, Secretary of the Interior, had been at odds with Jones for months over the quickest way to secure a rubber stockpile.

Complicating the issue was a fight between farm bloc congressmen and the petrochemical industry. A usable rubber for tires could be manufactured from butadiene which in turn could be extracted from grain alcohol or from natural gas and petroleum products. If scientists and engineers decided to use grain alcohol as the basic ingredient for substitute rubber it would be a big boost for the nation's farmers. Farm bloc congressmen even rammed through a bill that created a "rubber czar" who would function independently of Nelson and WPB as well as dictating that "special plants be built for the manufacture of synthetic rubber out of grain alcohol." But Roosevelt reacted to petrochemical pressure and vetoed the measure.

Presidential rejection came in the face of mounting pressure to implement nationwide gasoline rationing as a means for conserving rubber reserves. Congress also authorized $650,000,000 during early 1942 to construct pilot plants for the chemical production of synthetic rubber. In May, Goodyear Rubber brought the first government-financed plant into production. It was followed, in July, by Firestone. Arthur B. Newhall, a former Goodrich executive, dollar-a-year man, and rubber coordinator for WPB, announced in July that synthetic rubber could be produced much cheaper than expected. Union Carbide Chemicals, a company that played a major role in the wartime production of rubber, supplied the raw butadiene from a combination of grain alcohol and a chemically-created product supplied by several petroleum giants. By late August it was clear that high-grade synthetic rubber could be turned out in enormous amounts and that it could be done cheaply by the petrochemical method.

Meanwhile, the need to supply the armed forces with men as well as defense hardware found many trying to avoid service, although military-aged men overwhelmingly accepted induction without complaint. As the draft net widened to gather men at the extremes of the male population fit for military duty, draft dodging surged during the fall. In some cases, the reasons made the local headlines. In Oxford, New York, for example, a forty-four-year-old inductee failed to report to Fort Dix, New Jersey, in September at the end of a two-week furlough. He did not want to leave his sixteen-year-old bride of three months. When his otherwise peaceful neighbors began picketing his home with patriotic placards, he was arrested by the country sheriff and marched off to camp. That was after his wife had spent two nights with him in the Warren County jail.

Expansion of the draft to include eighteen-to-nineteen-year-olds during 1942 caused widespread speculation that it would interfere with the college football season. Colgate president Everett Case even predicted the 1942 season would be the last for the duration. Though the draft did take its share of Saturday afternoon heroes, Case was overly pessimistic and most colleges managed to continue fielding teams.

The onset of gasoline rationing and travel restrictions caused additional problems for college football, particularly in the East. A lack of easy transportation kept people from the stands, which produced financial losses because of reduced gates. The Michigan-Michigan State game drew 70,000 fans in 1941, but in October 1942 the same contest attracted only 40,000; yet the two schools are a scant sixty miles apart. The 1942 Army-Navy tilt at Thompson Field in Annapolis was played before nearly empty stands. Admission was denied any civilian living more than ten miles from the stadium as a patriotic gesture; two battalions of midshipmen even hurrahed for Army when West Point cadets were not permitted to travel south.

A week or so after the opening collegiate football games, the country had its first wartime election since 1918 when Maine voters trooped to the polls on September 14 to select a governor, a U.S. senator, and a congressional delegation. In what became a national trend, anti-New Deal Republicans swept the state, although the Democrats retained majorities in both houses of Congress in November. The Republicans, out of power nationally for more than a decade, tended to support the administration on war-related matters, but latent hostility to a perceived socialistic thrust in New Deal programs prompted GOP hopefuls to fight FDR and the Democrats on home-front legislation.

The GOP was able to narrow the Democrat majority in the House of Representatives to an uncomfortable thirteen seats and to gain ten new senators in the off-year election. Republican candidates "surprised even their own chieftains and prophets who had predicted at the outside a gain of not more than seven seats in the senate," reported the New York *Times*. It was the largest minority party gain in any off-year election since 1918, when the GOP fought it out with Woodrow Wilson over the Versailles Treaty at the close of World War I. The Republicans won seventeen out of thirty-three governorships at stake in 1942. The GOP resurgence in November, the *Times* continued, "would jeopardize at times the control of the Roosevelt administration especially when southern and other conservative Democrats might team up to defeat the president's proposals, especially on domestic issues."

Edward J. Flynn, onetime New York secretary of state and Democratic national committeeman in 1942, started the Republican–Democratic tug-of-war by blasting the Republicans on February 2 over nationwide radio. Flynn's attack on GOP National Chairman Joseph W. Martin, Jr., a nine-term congressman from Massachusetts and speaker of the House under Truman and Eisenhower, shattered the delicate understanding between the parties that had existed since Pearl Harbor. The GOP, Flynn proclaimed, "is not as much interested in winning the war as it is in controlling the House of Representatives." And if that were not enough, he continued: "That no misfortune except a major military defeat could befall this country to the extent involved in the election of a Congress hostile to the president." Republican criticism of the administration could only help the Axis, Flynn concluded.

Martin, who stepped down as national chairman after the November elections, said Flynn was using the war to ruin the Republican party and stifle opposition politics. The GOP would continue its support of FDR's war policies, but Martin served notice that his party would "work for preservation of the two-party system and for the American right to offer any constructive appraisal or suggestion." Although most congressional candidates had already been named for the general election in November, five states—Massachusetts, New Hampshire, New Jersey, Michigan, and Wisconsin—held primaries after the Maine canvass. Nor did the war keep the usual smattering of colorful and controversial figures from seeking office. In Michigan, where Republican Harry F. Kelly was elected governor, a three-sided race for the Republican senate nomination included a right-wing extremist named Gerald L. K. Smith. A onetime associate of Huey Long in Louisiana, Smith polled over 100,000 votes while losing in the primary to Homer Ferguson for the Senate seat held by Democrat Prentiss M. Brown.

Although Ferguson, who was later named ambassador to the Philippines by President Eisenhower, was elected in November, Smith's demagogic blasts at the New Deal enlivened the Michigan primary. An ordained minister in the Church of the Disciples of Christ and a spellbinder, Gerald Lyman Kenneth Smith had been chief organizer of Huey Long's Share the Wealth Movement in the mid-thirties. Long once called him, "next to me the greatest rabble-rouser in the country"; and Smith himself told reporters it might be possible to sweep the country with his conservative ideas and "thus to duplicate the feat of Adolph Hitler in Germany." Predictably, Smith opposed the war, which he said nobody wanted "but the power-mad internationalists operating under the direction of international Jewry"; he even ran for president on the Union Party ticket, but without success.

New York and New England likewise gave the Republicans spectacular victories in the wartime election. Thomas E. Dewey, New York City prosecuting attorney with a recently acquired reputation for attacking racketeers and organized crime, became the Empire State's first Republican governor in twenty years. And his win over New Deal Democrat John J. Bennett hurled him to the forefront of national politics. Dewey's win in Roosevelt's home territory was a serious blow to administration morale. A former Brooklyn University law professor and the state's attorney general since 1931, Bennett made repeated appeals for White House help in the campaign. But, *Time* reported, the "wartime president held the politico Roosevelt in check." After opposing Bennett in the primary, Roosevelt, who wanted the popular Republican defeated, belatedly came to his aid after several polls had given Dewey a healthy lead.

Roosevelt in fact endorsed but two candidates in 1942: Bennett and "a repetition of his 1936 plea for reelection of Nebraska's famed Senator George Norris, an Independent." His decision to stay out of the 1942 fight was colored by memories of Woodrow Wilson's crushing experience in the 1918 off-year elections during World War I. Wilson, the only twentieth-century Democrat to occupy the White House before FDR, had whistle-stopped across the country for Democrats favorable to his wartime policies. The venture not only cost him a majority in the Congress but also his health (Wilson collapsed physically from the strain of campaigning). FDR had been Wilson's assistant secretary of the navy and he was a close observer of that campaign debacle.

In Massachusetts, however, where Republicans captured the state, the main issue was not the war or the New Deal, but, of all things, birth control. Yet Roosevelt's refusal to help floundering Democrats here as elsewhere made GOP victories easier. Although Republican candidates for governor and United States senator were successful in November, the party was fearful that a Democrat-sponsored referendum on the ballot that would permit doctors to disseminate birth control information might influence the state's massive Catholic vote. Because Roman Catholic clergymen actively urged defeat of the measure and 75–80 percent of all Massachusetts Catholics were Democrats, GOP politicians were concerned that a large Democratic turnout might tip the political scales.

Both Leverett Saltonstall, who was elected governor, and Henry Cabot Lodge, who was returned to the Senate, had formidable Democratic opposition in November. Francis E. Kelly, a thirty-nine-year-old Irish-Catholic ex-governor, was beaten in the Democratic primary by Roger L. Putnam, Springfield mayor and president of a large machine-packaging company. Putnam, scion of the well-known Lowell clan and a Harvard *magna cum laude*, was handily beaten by Saltonstall, another Harvard graduate, World War I veteran, and onetime speaker of the Massachusetts legislature. Saltonstall, an outspoken New Deal critic, went on to an outstanding career in the Senate two years later.

Henry Cabot Lodge, who became one of the country's most distinguished Republicans, had an Irish-Catholic opponent named Joseph E. Casey in his bid for a second Senate term. Casey was firmly in the New Deal camp and he had been backed by Roosevelt in four successful elections to the House. But a presidential blessing was not forthcoming in 1942 and the "no machine tool, square-jawed, curly-haired" Casey went down before the Republican onslaught.

In the South, where most gubernatorial terms ran for two years instead of the customary four, nearly every state named governors in the off-year canvass. The whole region, from Maryland to Texas, was under solid Democratic control, a legacy from post-Civil War days, when the party got the upper hand through suppression of the black vote and racist appeals to white supremacy. Two long years were yet to pass before the U.S. Supreme Court assisted black voting by declaring all white Democratic primaries unconstitutional in Texas. While the country was fighting Nazi oppression in Europe, racial slurs and outright baiting of blacks played a part in the defeat of Georgia Governor Eugene Talmadge by a political newcomer, Ellis Gibbs Arnall.

Talmadge, a three-term governor who returned to the executive mansion before his death in 1945, built a political dynasty through appeals to the "wool-hat boys," his name for the state's small farmers. In 1942 the elder Talmadge enlivened the contest by mailing a pamphlet, *Do You Want Your Child to Go to School with Negroes?* to Georgia voters. His racist outcry came after several University of Georgia professors had been fired for advocating integration of the state's public schools. Arnall, a member of the state legislature and an ardent Roosevelt man, managed to slip past Talmadge in the Democratic primary, which was tantamount to election. His promise to retreat from "one-man rule" in Georgia notwithstanding, Arnall was not above a little race-baiting himself. He also made several rabble-rousing speeches during the campaign.

At the other end of the South an anti-Roosevelt governor and U.S. senator won in November. A colorful, flamboyant Ohio native named Wilbert Lee O'Daniel was reelected to the Senate from Texas to join longtime New Dealer Tom Terry Connally. If Connally was a solid member of the Roosevelt team, O'Daniel, known far and wide as "Pappy," was a political maverick who went his own way. An unknown, he worked as a salesman, wrote songs, and traveled around the Southwest with a radio band called The Light Crust Dough Boys. After O'Daniel had been elected governor in 1938 and 1940, he loudly called for increased old age pensions and an end to the state's poll tax. And in the middle of his second term he won a special election for the Senate on the death of Morris Sheppard. According to noted Texas historian Wayne Gard, O'Daniel "was ineffective in the Senate, and it was reported that no proposal he ever made there received more than four votes."

Also winning in Texas was Coke R. Stevenson, who made no attempt to hide his anti-Roosevelt sentiments. He kept several pet deer on his huge ranch near Junction, and called them "New Dealers" because they were "always looking for a handout." Stevenson, "a tall, quiet, pipe-smoking, Western-type man," became an extremely popular wartime governor. After the war, Stevenson's political career was shattered by his loss, to Lyndon Johnson, in the 1948 race for the U.S. Senate by a vote of 494, 104 to 494, 191. Though he contested the election and carried his challenge to the U.S. Supreme Court, the convenient burning of ballots in Duvall County in extreme south Texas while the case was pending made an accurate recount impossible.

On the West Coast, an energetic Republican attorney general named Earl Warren moved into the California governor's mansion. Warren had already attracted national attention with his war on crime while serving as Alameda County attorney and his defeat of Governor Culbert L. Olson, a staunch New Dealer, made him a talked-about GOP presidential contender. In war-conscious California, where Japanese submarines still threatened the coast, Olson had alienated voters by squabbling with a Republican legislature over appropriations for an expanded state guard.

Warren proved an aggressive wartime governor and the national press began to report his activities immediately after the election. He shot to national prominence as a result of the 1942 campaign and speculation began that he would be the 1944 GOP presidential contender. The Californian did run for the vice presidency with Thomas E. Dewey in 1948 against Harry S. Truman, and he made a serious bid for the 1952 nomination; after that unsuccessful attempt Eisenhower named him chief justice of the U.S. Supreme Court and the rest is history. At the same time that Warren was starting his climb to national politics, an interesting sidelight in California was the election of Will Rogers, Jr., to Congress. Rogers, a Democrat and son of a famed cowboy-humorist, ran for the House from a California district while an army lieutenant. But he resigned from Congress before his term was out to reenter active duty, and unlike Warren, his political star did not rise again although he made a try for the Senate after the war.

In spite of Republican gains and a poor voter turnout nationally, it was clear that Democratic majorities in the House and in the Senate after the election would guarantee support for the administration on critical issues. Yet there can be little doubt that public disenchantment with domestic policy had produced a voter backlash. Although many Roosevelt bureaucrats would have used the emergency as justification for a planned economy, widespread New Deal opposition remained which had not been dampened by the war. In 1942 the public concluded, *Newsweek* said, "that the planners have failed to deliver. It appears safe to say, therefore, that this election marks the end of the cycle in the economic thinking of the American public. The planners will no longer have things all their own way."

Headlines about the bedroom shenanigans of movie idol Errol Flynn started to bombard the home front during the political canvass. Flynn was well-known for his swashbuckling across the screen in movies like *The Charge of the Light Brigade, The Sea Hawk, Gentleman Jim* (the movie version of heavyweight champion Jim Corbett), and *They Died with Their Boots On,* (an epic about General George Custer and the fight at the Little Big Horn); and his personal life matched his movie image before and after 1942. In 1946, Flynn's mother told reporters her son "had not only been a bad little boy, he had been a nasty little boy"; actress Ann Sheridan called him "one of the wild characters of the world." And his appetite for the opposite sex made him a Hollywood legend. David Niven, a fellow actor, related in his own autobiography that he and Flynn parked their sports car near a Los Angeles high school just to watch girls "with their golden California suntans, long catlike legs, and high, provocative breasts." As the girls filed out in the afternoon, Niven continues, "Flynn sighed and shook his head. 'Jail bait,' he said. 'San Quentin Quail. What a waste!' "

Flynn had been born thirty-three years before on Tasmania, the huge island off the south coast of Australia, the son of a noted zoologist and university professor, and he first arrived in the United States by way of England in 1935 to start making films. He rose to notoriety during October 1942 when a Los Angeles grand jury charged him with statutory rape of two teenage girls, Betty Hansen and Peggy Satterlee. The trial, which centered around two star-struck seventeen-year-olds, started January 11, 1943 and vied with news from the fighting fronts for newspaper space.

Flynn paid lawyer Gerry Giesler, the same attorney who engineered Barbara Hutton's divorce from Cary Grant, $30,000 to argue his case. Although Flynn was tried for both offenses simultaneously, the incidents had occurred at different times and places—the alleged assault on Betty Hansen in the upstairs quarters of a dinner party host in Bel Air and on Peggy Satterlee aboard Flynn's yacht *Sirocco.* A jury of nine women and three men found him not guilty after Giesler's tricky questioning confused the girls on the witness stand. Yet photographers and reporters had a field day with the proceedings as the girls answered detailed questions—all of them faithfully recorded in the press—about "putting his private parts into your private parts," "did you cross your legs," "did he remove your panties. . . ." And Flynn adroitly denied everything—even that he had nicknamed Hanson and Satterlee, "J.B." and "S.Q.Q.," short for "Jail Bait" and "San Quentin Quail."

Part of the trial centered on Flynn showing Peggy Satterlee the moon through a stateroom porthole aboard the *Sirocco* when the night's sex commenced. As a result, "In Like Flynn" became an overnight byword. In *My Wicked, Wicked Ways*, his autobiography (ghostwritten by Earl Conrad), Flynn says: ". . . a new legend was born, and new terms went into the national idiom. . . A GI or marine or sailor went out at night "sparking" and the next day he reported to his cronies, who asked him how he made out, and the fellow said with a sly grin, 'I'm in like Flynn.' "

Shortly before Errol Flynn made his questionable contribution to the language, a more remarkable and lasting literary event took place in October 1942 when Scribner's brought out the first volume of Douglas Southall Freeman's *Lee's Lieutenants*. Within two years Freeman had completed the two remaining volumes of his classic study of Robert E. Lee and the Army of Northern Virginia during another American conflict, the Civil War. His three-volume study of the men under Lee is nothing short of monumental; it was an immediate hit in 1942 and has remained a favorite with scholars and general readers. Because the work had been in preparation for some time, it was a bit ironic that a detailed account of one terrible conflict should appear in the midst of a second. And it is Freeman's minute, highly readable descriptions of nineteenth-century battles, as well as his brilliant word pictures of the lieutenants who served under Robert E. Lee that give the books their marvelous appeal.

Meanwhile, the country pressed on day and night with the war. As the public watched the spicy doings of Hollywood or read about Confederate glories during the fall of 1942, things like construction of the Alaska Highway and the Big Inch Pipeline reminded people of the deadly business afoot. Since its purchase from the Russians by Secretary of State William H. Seward for $7,200,000 shortly after the Civil War, Alaska had been known to legions of schoolboys as Seward's Folly, and had remained isolated from the continental United States. A connecting road across the trackless wastes of British Columbia and the Alaskan wilderness simply did not exist; ship transport from Seattle, San Francisco, and other

West Coast ports was the only means of supply for the vast northern territory. Pearl Harbor, however, and the Japanese stab at Dutch Harbor and the Aleutians drove home the urgency of an overland link between Alaska and the "lower states."

An Alaska highway had been discussed for years, as was a proposal to connect it with the Pan American Highway from Texas to Argentina. American-Canadian joint financing of the project languished for decades because Congress did not want to fund what many viewed as a Canadian road, while politicians north of the border saw it as an expediency to benefit American interests. But the outbreak of fighting in 1941 changed things. On February 11, 1942, Roosevelt agreed to follow a 1930 international commission report which recommended building the Alcan Highway. Construction commenced immediately after Roosevelt's decision to go ahead, with Canadian assistance. It was an immense job, with staggering obstacles; by May more than 30,000 men were working on the high-priority project. Alaska historian Ben Adams put it this way: "The army moved in seven engineering battalions, four white, three Negro. There were 30,000 civilian workers under 54 different contractors. The men worked ten-hour shifts, seven days a week. . . . An almost bottomless morass of muskeg, decayed vegetation, and water had to be attacked in northern British Columbia. The weather was often too hot or too cold. Layers of ice would block the road in winter. . . ."

Finally, the last stones were in place and the highway, from Edmonton, Alberta—the "jumping off place"—to Fairbanks, Alaska, was opened to vehicular traffic in the spring of 1944. It was not a perfect road, but it was better than poorly defined wagon tracks or no road at all. Before the highway opened, "a newspaper publisher in Ketchican had had printer's ink brought up in a purser's cabin—just like a basket of fruit," a wire service dispatch said. "Gasoline stocks were extremely low. Worry was expressed over canned goods. Freight piled high on the Seattle docks owing to government priorities." Although connecting roads had to be built to Anchorage, Seward, and other wilderness cities, the highway ended Alaska's separation from the rest of the country. During the war it meant that matériel from defense plants could be moved northward without interruption for the final thrust at Japan. And it meant that the territory created by Congress in 1884 was on its way to statehood.

A related construction project for the defense effort was the Big Inch Pipeline. A twenty-four-inch steel pipe, which Donald Nelson had had constructed from materials salvaged from other valuable needs, it reached from Longview, in the heart of the east Texas oil fields, to Illinois; an eastern leg extended through Indiana and Ohio to Phoenixville, Pennsylvania, with several branch trunks to the East Coast and New England. Like the Alcan Highway, both segments were crash programs to deliver 300,000 barrels of crude oil daily from Gulf Coast fields to refineries in Philadelphia and New York City. Like the Alcan Highway, the pipeline was completed by thousands of men working at premium salaries.

The Big Inch, built under the close supervision of petroleum administrator Harold L. Ickes, was intended to relieve pressure on overladen rail facilities and on coastal tankers plying through U-boat infested waters in the Gulf of Mexico and the Atlantic. When completed in the summer of 1943, it transported the daily equivalent of seventy seagoing tankers. A futile hope—especially in Congress, where antirationing sentiment was rising—swept the country during the fall that the $60,000,000 pipeline would be completed in time to halt additional gasoline curtailments.

Public disenchantment with partial rationing, and repeated warnings that rubber be conserved forced Roosevelt to implement gasoline rationing for everybody. Identical letters were sent from the White House on November 26 to rubber chief William J. Jeffers and OPA boss Leon Henderson ordering nationwide rationing to start six days later. It was necessary because "our military requirements for rubber have been greater, not smaller."

Good old boys throughout Appalachia and the southwest still cruised around on "drip," but others now came forward with cockamamy ideas for fuel substitutes. A 1942 article in *Chemical Industries* by Brooklyn Polytechnic Institute's Robert S. Aries wanted to follow the European example and use wood instead of gasoline in automobiles. In pre-1939 Germany, France, and Italy it had been common practice to burn wood in large vehicles such as buses and tractors; nearly twenty-five pounds of wood did the work of a single gallon of gas. The idea called for "a stove-like generator to convert the wood into combustible gasses for the engine." Aries thought a sawdust-chopped or "hogged" wood mixture would produce sufficient carbon monoxide to fuel most American cars, although filters were necessary "to remove tar, water, and dust."

Like efforts to find substitutes for rubber tires, the fuel alternative ideas were meaningless to the average car owner. For disgruntled motorists a better approach was pressuring Washington into abandoning rationing altogether. Actually, car owners throughout the country were told to sign up for ration coupons before the November 26 edict, which precipitated a massive letter-writing campaign. So many form letters and cards from the Midwest asking for a delay in rationing started arriving at congressional offices and OPA headquarters that "Bull" Jeffers asked the FBI to investigate their origin. Todd Stoops, director of the Hoosier Motor Club in Indianapolis, "with no more equipment than a typewriter and a stack of stationery," raised enough money to send out 5,000,000 pieces of mail. While Stoops told government agents that his people were merely exercising their right to protest, Indiana Senator Raymond E. Wills received 17,000 signed cards in a short period. Congressmen from every state were inundated with protest mail, and Leon Henderson told reporters that he had ceased trying to keep count of the letters reaching his office.

The protest notwithstanding, Henderson and Jeffers went on nationwide radio to "lay down the law": universal rationing would "become effective Tuesday, December 1, on schedule." And both blasted the petition gatherers and letter writers. Henderson lashed out at those who argued that gasoline cutbacks would have no impact on rubber conservation, and he pulled no punches: "People are being told that the 35-mile speed limit will save all the rubber that is necessary. That isn't true. The wheels can be driven off an automobile at 35 just as well as at 60. It merely takes longer." The OPA chief, who was soon hounded from office, said the petition takers were "men who would gamble America's future, not for a mess of pottage, but for a gallon of gasoline."

Gasoline rationing was never popular during the war; and otherwise patriotic people who wholeheartedly supported the war grumbled at fuel cutbacks for the family car as unnecessary and looked for ways to beat the OPA regulators. In Newark, New Jersey, eleven men, indicted by a federal grand jury, pleaded guilty to charges of dealing in illicit ration coupons. They were arraigned on December 1—the very day that rationing became effective in the West and Midwest—for stealing ration books from several OPA offices in northern New Jersey. It was by no means an isolated incident; throughout the war, clandestine markets traded in gasoline and other ration coupons. And in some areas outright counterfeiting was rampant.

Trading outside OPA regulations was not confined to gasoline coupons. Ready cash in the pockets of defense workers and others led to widespread buying and selling of all kinds of products. Geoffrey Perrett, a careful observer of the war years, notes that "somewhere between 25 and 50 percent of all American business was estimated to be in the black market, and the higher figure is probably more accurate than the lower; in 1944 OPA investigations of several thousand businesses revealed that not less than 57 percent were violating price controls. In some areas the figures soared to 70 percent." Labor bosses anxious to twit government planners complained that Bureau of Labor Statistics data did not take into account black market prices when calculating fair wages under Little Steel guidelines. Although price controls and rationing held down the cost of living, they also contributed to a black market in consumer goods.

Black market buying and selling rapidly became identified in the public mind with bootlegging and racketeering; but unlike the case of Capone-era gangsterism, there was almost no evidence of large-scale dealing in proscribed goods during the war. Mostly it was individuals making private deals for needed items and food on the rationed list. Even the term "black market" meant different things to different people. "Consider, for example, the case of meat, so often the subject of black market operations," a national journal proposed in June 1943: "Strictly speaking, any meat is 'black market' if any government price or supply control has been violated at any stage in its course from the purchase of cattle to the retail butcher's counter. But this very spread of opportunity for illicit procedure suggests that the offense may vary all the way from pure black to pale gray." At least one exception to the small-man theory was a ring of cattle buyers in the West who channeled their slaughtered animals directly to chain stores in several eastern cities.

Like the crackdown on New Jersey counterfeiters, OPA kept a tight watch on those seeking to short-circuit rationing regulations. Officials enlisted junior and senior high school students in several cities "to stop illegal practices in handling gasoline coupons." At Denver, commented school superintendent Dr. Charles E. Green: "In general assemblies at schools, administrators from the War Price and Rationing Board have addressed student bodies. The black-market problem has been given careful attention in social science classes. . . . In all senior high schools, the student councils have given consideration to the matter."

Chester Bowles, who took over OPA following the departure of Leon Henderson, proclaimed the black market a serious obstacle to the war effort. "I do not say every time someone connives to get a pair of shoes illegally, or pays higher than the ceiling price for a wrist watch or a turkey, we will lose a battle. But in the aggregate, the entire black market is so vast, touching the vital necessities of our fighting way, and so widespread, measuring its its damage in billions of dollars, that it does serve to slow up certain parts of our military."

Every conceivable item from straight pins to radio tubes found an outlet on the black market. Tubes and parts for radio repair were often traded on the underground market—again, those involved were small dealers and individuals functioning outside government restrictions—in this case, to keep their antiquated sets playing. Wrist watches particularly were in heavy demand throughout the war, selling for $50 or more above ceiling prices. "The scarcity of household articles made of metal has given rise to black market sales of such items as garbage cans, electric irons, cooking utensils, and used vacuum cleaners," Bowles continued. And though it seems petty by later standards, "steel wool used for scouring pots and pans" sold in some parts of the country at fourteen cents above the approved price.

The very restrictions that drove thousands onto the black market indicated wide dissatisfaction with wartime rationing, although the public was outwardly supportive. But gasoline remained the nation's number one headache, and officials worried about the public outcry tried various schemes to alleviate the mounting irritation. A "carless Tuesday" was attempted and then abandoned in Peoria, Illinois. That bit of bureaucracy began with octogenarian mayor E. N. Woodruff tossing a silver dollar in the air, and, when it came down heads, ordering all cars with odd-numbered license plates off the streets for one day. OPA had thought up the plan and its officials descended on central Illinois to plug its 1942 version of car pooling; it was called "share-a-ride."

Unimpressed by the Peoria experiment and OPA's efforts to use community ration boards, as well as by the failure to shape rationing to local conditions, congressional opposition mounted until Henderson was forced to quit. GOP Senator Arthur H. Vandenberg of Michigan said gasoline rationing was "premature and inadvisable in view of the fact that alternative methods of conserving rubber had not been thoroughly explored." Hatton W. Summers, anti-New Deal Democrat from Texas and chairman of the House judiciary committee, backed off from a move to block gas rationing by congressional action after OPA promised changes to compensate for local conditions. More than others, congressmen from the West were outspoken because their constituents were faced with long driving distances and almost no alternative transportation. Jed Joseph Johnson, Democratic senator from Oklahoma, and leader of the anti-ration bloc, even threatened to cut off Henderson's 1943 appropriations unless OPA made changes.

Finally, Henderson resigned from OPA in late December, unable to withstand the sustained sniping. His troubles were compounded by Republicans who had been swept into office during the off-year elections and who viewed OPA as just another of Roosevelt's regulatory agencies. They lost no time in joining the chorus. John Kenneth Galbraith, Harvard economist, New Deal planner, and Henderson's assistant in 1942 (and later John F. Kennedy's ambassador to India), thinks coffee—which was also put on the rationed list in early December—was the chief cause for his return to private life. Coffee rationing had an enormous impact on the November elections in the Midwest, according to Galbraith: "Scandinavian and German voters, among whom coffee use reaches addiction, were thought to have voted their indignation." He also notes in his own memoirs, A Life in Our Times, that "Leon Henderson was, I believe never completely happy again. Divorced from public concerns, he did not wholly exist."

Although grumbling about coffee, gasoline, and shortages remained a part of wartime America, most people were willing to accept rationing in the face of mounting battle sacrifices. GIs had been dying and getting captured in places like the Coral Sea, Midway, and North Africa throughout 1942. Mingled with news of increased rationing in the daily press were battle dispatches by an army of war correspondents. "I attached myself to a group who were wounded in a dreadful way. They had no open wounds; they shed no blood; they seemed merely to have been attacked by some mysterious germ of war that made them groan, hold their sides, limp, and stagger. They were shock and blast victims," wrote John Hersey (later the author of A Bell for Adano and other war novels), describing one firefight near the Mataniku River on Guadalcanal.

And, Hersey's piece in Life continued: "There were not enough corpsmen to assist more than the unconscious and leg-wounded men, so we set these men to helping each other. . . . The rain and trampling had made the trail so bad now that a sound man walking alone would occasionally fall, and in some steep places would have to crawl on hands and knees, pulling himself by exposed roots and leaning bamboo trunks. We slid, crept, walked, wallowed, waded and staggered, like drunken men. One man kept striking the sides of his befuddled skull with his fists. Another kept his hands over his ears. Several had badly shattered legs, and behaved like football players with excruciating Charley horses. . . ." Before it ended in February 1943, the United States had lost twenty-four fighting ships and several thousand men in the battle for Guadalcanal. It was a toll that reduced home-front carping about gasoline for Sunday pleasure drives to the merest pettiness. Yet a goodly number of people resisted all rationing until the end of the war.

As the United States and the Allies increased pressure upon Germany and Japan the country got its first glimpse of enemy POWs during late 1942. Though the big influx of German and Italian prisoners from the North African fighting did not start coming until 1943, some of the nearly half million POWs in the United States before the war ended had already arrived. Pearl Harbor caught the country unprepared to handle captured enemy soldiers. In April 1942 the War Department moved to deal with POWs by putting out a booklet, *Regulations Governing Civilian Enemy Aliens and Prisoners of War,* but the first captured troops were sent here to ease pressure on overcrowded British camps. After several months of badgering from London, the State Department reluctantly consented to take 50,000 POWs from camps in England.

The provost marshal's office opened several military posts on September 15 to house and care for the incoming aliens. Arnold Krammer, historian of the prisoner of war camps in America, notes that "any family out for a Sunday drive along U.S. Highway 6 near Atlanta, Nebraska, could watch POWs enthusiastically kicking a soccer ball across the field, while hundreds of wildly cheering fellow POWs supported their favorite team." Americans living near detention camps could easily see enemy prisoners on the other side of barbed wire fences. This writer has vivid memories of gazing as a twelve-year old at German prisoners of war from a Seattle city bus. POWs were located in practically every state; only Nevada, Montana, North Dakota, and Vermont had no camps. And Washington quickly put down regulations governing the security and location of detention areas. "All POW camps should be as isolated and as heavily guarded as possible. . . . [They] could not be located in a blackout area extending about 170 miles inland from both coasts, a 150-mile-wide 'zone sanitaire' along the Canadian and Mexican borders, or near shipyards, munitions, or vital industries." As a result, Krammer continues: "Two-thirds of the base camps (containing approximately three-fourths of the prisoners) would be located in the south and southwestern regions of the country."

A few POWs managed to escape from prison camps and survive in the larger society; one fellow owned and operated a successful bookstore in Chicago for several months before his recapture. At least one POW remained at large as late as 1970. But the overwhelming bulk of the prisoners sat out the war in American camps until 1946 when the POWs were funneled into East Coast debarkation ports for transportation home. Nearly four years after the first Axis prisoners came to American in late 1942, the remaining 1,388 German officers and men sailed from New York, July 23, 1946. "The last to leave American soil," Krammer writes, "—a 22-year-old former electrician from Heidelberg—ultimately made seven 'last trips' up the ramp at the request of insistent newsmen: three in continuous motion for the newsreel cameras and four with stops at fixed points to satisfy the still photographers."

Jarring tragedy hit the home front as 1942 drew to a close when the Coconut Grove, a popular Boston night spot, burned on November 28 with enormous loss of life. The catastrophe resulted in more than 500 deaths and became the second greatest disaster of its kind in American history. The worst remained the 1903 fire at the Iroquois Theater in Chicago which took 575 lives.

The Coconut Grove was filled with more than 800 revelers—many of them servicemen from surrounding naval bases and local boys winding up Thanksgiving furloughs, as well as merrymakers from the Holy Cross-Boston game that afternoon—when the conflagration started. Every table was occupied and the dance floor packed when bandleader Mickey Alpert raised his baton to start the Star Spangled Banner as a prelude to a patriotic floor show. Then, with deathly quickness, the whole upper level of the night spot was engulfed in flames. Within twenty seconds the interior, which was festooned with paper palm trees and brightly colored streamers, literally exploded into flame. A blind scramble for exits caused more deaths than the fire and smoke did. "The chief loss of life," reported the wire services, "resulted from the screaming, clawing crowds that were wedged in the entrances of the club."

Flames shot through the roof illuminating the night sky and attracting curious onlookers which complicated rescue efforts. Priests from nearby Catholic churches administered last rites as corpes were hauled to hastily erected morgues in adjacent buildings and stores. Buck Jones, a well-known cowboy star in B Westerns, was among the victims. The governor imposed martial law on the scene as sailors and shore patrolmen dug at charred bodies piled six feet deep at one entrance. It was a calamity of the first order. National media concentration on the fire temporarily diverted public consciousness from the battles raging in North Africa and on a little-known island in the far Pacific named Guadalcanal.

People at home and in the armed forces were learning to cope with the privations of war after a full year of fighting. Rationing, price controls, consumer shortages, and the drafting of loved ones were now taken in stride. Thousands of servicemen traveled by bus and train to be with wives and families over Christmas and New Year's and the masses of uniformed men seen in every American hamlet drove home the immediacy of war. Holiday shoppers struggled to find gifts on depleted department store shelves and *Esquire*, then as now a popular men's magazine, ran ads for new subscribers that carried a two-part bonus: "The 1943 Varga Girl Calender and A Hurrell Girl Jigsaw Puzzle." Christmas 1942 was a time of introspection—a time to reflect on the war in which the national temper had become focused in its resolve for a massive push at the enemy.

5 JANUARY-MAY 1943: OFF-COLOR SHENANIGANS

N ew Year's Day 1943, which opened the fourteenth month of fighting, found Americans listening to bowl games over nationwide radio hookups and getting braced for stricter food rationing. It also brought a refreshing eighty-three year-old artist popularly known as Grandma Moses to public notice. Although her meticulous landscapes had been "discovered" in the late 1930s, it was a December 1942 showing of her work in New York's British-American Gallery that shot her to wartime recognition. Within a short time her folksy paintings were made into Christmas cards that made her known all across the country. (After the war, she was to make appearances on the popular television show "See It Now," hosted by Edward R. Murrow, and highly publicized visits to the Truman White House.)

Anna Mary Robertson had been born in 1860 on a farm in upstate New York, where she spent an idyllic childhood until 1870, when, according to her autobiography, "came the hard years." She received little schooling because "little girls did not go to school much in the winter, owing to the cold, and not warm enough clothing. . . . When twelve years of age I left home to earn my own living as then was called a hired girl." After her 1887 marriage to Thomas Soloman Moses, a local farmer, she lived on a Shenandoah Valley horse farm in Staunton, Virginia. She mothered ten children, although several died in infancy, before she returned to an Eagle Bridge, New York, homestead in 1905. After her husband's death in 1927, Mrs. Moses continued to work the family farm—located near the Vermont border—with the help of a son and his wife.

Grandma Moses's paintings were like a breath of fresh air during the war. In marked contrast to the dry monumentalism of official Nazi art, Mrs. Moses offered minutely-crafted landscapes depicting nineteenth-century American farm life. With paints and brushes from a mail-order catalog, she had, indeed, patterned some of her early works after the ever-popular Currier and Ives prints. Although her father had encouraged childhood drawing, Grandma Moses did not begin serious painting until 1938, when she was nearly eighty years old.

Her overnight notoriety caused the unassuming artist some anxious moments. When she appeared at a December 1940 showing of her pictures at Gimbel's Department Store, instead of talking about her craft, she lectured her audience "on the popular topics of canning and preserving." Grandma Moses had not been in the city since 1918 and she was dumbfounded by the changes. "She had always been a conscientious and thrifty housekeeper and she could not understand why she should get so much money for her work," explains Otto Kallir, her mentor and biographer. "She never had the idea of selling her paintings for high prices," and when several went for prices beyond what she had been paid at the farm, Kallir continues: "No sooner had the check been mailed than it was returned by Mrs. Moses with the remark that everything had been paid for, she was not owed anything, and she did not want the money."

Kallir, owner of New York's St. Etienne Gallery that sponsored her early work, described her painting as "white, or winter pictures; light green, or spring pictures; deep saturated green, or summer pictures; and brown, or autumn pictures." And novelist Louis Bromfield, who teamed up with Kallir to produce a 1946 biography, *Grandma Moses, American Primitive*, found her appeal in "her understanding of the eternal importance of small things." Tiny, frolicking figures surrounded by detailed farm animals accentuate nearly all of her paintings. Perhaps a country that wanted to recoil from the trials of combat was eager to embrace the "American primitive" and her art of yesteryear.

Although Grandma Moses and her landscapes brought a respite from worries over rationing and growing casualty lists, several opinion surveys by pollster George H. Gallup around January 1, 1943, found people concerned with the war and its impact upon their lives. An Iowa State Ph.D. and one time journalism professor at Drake University in Des Moines, the forty-one-year-old Gallup first appeared on the national scene in 1935 with his American Institute of Public Opinion. From the outset, his findings had revealed much about the American character, and a poll released January 13, 1943, showed undue optimism about the length of the war. Thirty-one months, or two and a half years, lay ahead before the return of peace in August 1945; yet 14 percent of the country told Gallup's polltakers it would be over in six months; 35 percent said one year; 19 percent, two years, and only 5 percent predicted a duration lasting three additional years.

In the patriotic fervor of early 1943, few people thought the country should withdraw from the conflict. But 60 percent said some aspects of war policy should be handled differently, and without listing percentages Gallup found numerous gripes: Washington should have shown more vision and acted quicker to ration scarce items; there should be greater efficiency in government and less "red tape" in domestic programs; labor unions and strikes needed a firmer hand; and there should be "less sugar coating" of bad news.

Gallup's findings unmistakably demonstrated that the war was affecting the way Americans lived. Yet food rationing—other than sugar and coffee—had not really taken hold by January 1, 1943. Thanksgiving and Christmas dinner in most homes had been the customary family feast with all the trimmings because food curtailments were not implemented until the new year. If the family larder was full on New Year's Day, the average family was nonetheless feeling the stress of war. The basic fiber of American life was changing, and the mobility of millions during the war induced a permanent alteration in the national lifestyle—in the fundamental way family members relate to each other.

"More of the story is told by what happened to the members of the family themselves," Newsweek said: "The son in the armed forces, the father in civilian defense, the mother in a war job, the daughter in one of the volunteer services. The vast tasks and migrations of the war have affected millions beyond the power of statistics to reveal. As in Europe the impact is falling on every family. But the full impact of it has hardly been guessed." The cliché, "How can you keep 'em down on the farm once they've seen Paree?" took on new meaning as the war continued. Easy money in war plants, quick mobility, and a release from old societal bonds because of the emergency meant that life would never be the same.

Strict food rationing was announced during the first week in January. Secretary of Agriculture Claude R. Wickard and Elmer Davis, director of the Office of War Information (OWI), explained how the scheme would work over nationwide radio. According to Wickard, rationing would become effective March 1 and he warned the country to expect restrictions on meat consumption later in the year.

His new order covered the gamut of processed food—all canned or bottled soups and juices, practically all canned, dried, or frozen fruits and vegetables. Housewives were advised that food on the restricted list would require coupons from War Ration Book Two, which was slated for issue in late February at neighborhood schools and similar meeting places. Although he promised "an adequate and healthy diet" for every citizen, Wickard painted a dismal picture for 1943: "Our armed forces and our fighting allies need 25 percent of the food we produce, including half of our canned fruit and vegetables."

Davis, on the other hand, explained Washington's rationale for the announcement several weeks ahead of implementation. Advance preparation was needed by wholesale houses, "hundreds of thousands" retail stores, and more than 1,500,000 local OPA volunteer workers to become acquainted with the point system. The OWI chief was a well-known radio newscaster, newspaperman, and novelist before taking over the government's top propanganda agency the previous summer. Several agencies were fused to form Davis' OWI but his was neither a well-received nor effective group, though he remained personally popular. Throughout the war, whether attempting to influence the content of Hollywood productions or seeking to explain government war aims, the bureaucrats under Davis did not enjoy public approval.

When Davis left active broadcasting to assume control of OWI, he had an estimated 1,500,000 daily listeners and earned a staggering $53,000 annual salary. His own network claimed that "half of all U.S. families heard him at least once a week." He had risen to national prominence from a small Indiana town along the Ohio River where his father was the town banker. A graduate of Franklin College in Indiana and a Rhodes Scholar at Oxford, Davis had worked ten years for the New York *Times* covering major news stories before he got his big break when CBS asked him to fill in temporarily for their top commentator, Hans V. Kaltenborn. In January 1943 Davis told American housewives to expect even stricter food rationing; and in an effort to make rationing more palatable he said that the British and Australians were shipping almost as much food into the U.S. as we were sending overseas.

Coupon rationing was necessary, the Agriculture Department said, because farmers "cannot produce all the food the American people want and all the feed their livestock need." Supplying the armies of the Allies remained the hitch; otherwise, the country could continue to gorge itself on every conceivable food item. Shortages were anticipated in spite of record farm outputs during 1942, when weather conditions were ideal throughout the farm belt. Favorable growing conditions since 1935 across the nation's breadbasket had produced healthy crop surpluses. But many experts predicted that seven years was a long time for good farming weather to prevail. Though serious droughts did not come until the late 1940s, Wickard and the Agriculture Department proceeded with contingency plans in the event of difficulties. In January 1943 quotas were set for meat products as well as "milk, vegetables, poultry, and eggs, a little more corn, less wheat, oats and barley."

Wickard added that each person would be allotted thirty-three pounds of canned food in 1943—roughly thirteen pounds (or 28.3 percent) below normal consumption. OPA spokesmen placed 300 processed foods in early January on the rationed list and said their point values would vary with military demands. Housewives were told to present War Ration Book One—already in use for sugar and coffee—at local OPA boards in order to get a new coupon book. And nearly 146,000,000 copies of the new book, containing twenty-eight billion food stamps, began rolling off ninety-six printing presses in various parts of the country; the books were parceled out to 5,500 ration boards before the March 1 deadline.

The new books were handed out by volunteer workers at local boards scattered around the country. OPA relied on community volunteers to handle distribution in an effort to court popular acceptance of the point system. A typical seven-member board at Bristol, Connecticut, was composed of two women and five men. Joseph M. Donovan, "a cigar chewing lawyer whom everyone called Judge," was the chairman. He said that he was trying to run the Bristol program honestly but that many of the directives from Washington made him "mad as hell." He was assisted in the thankless job by a housewife and by another woman who was superintendent of a local hospital, an assistant plant manager, a metal worker, a factory director, and an ordnance inspector in a defense plant. Similar panels throughout the country wrestled with every conceivable obstacle, including a "dowager in Evanston, Illinois, who demanded 17 ration books for her 17 cats."

Upwards of thirty-five million housewives trudged to thousands of schoolhouses in late February to get the books. Nationwide registration proceeded smoothly because most people simply ignored an OPA rule requiring declaration of five or more packages of any rationed item. Yet every grocer knew that hoarding was commonplace preceding the sign-up date. A fellow in Milwaukee was discovered with a stockpile of 158 pounds of coffee—a ten-year supply under OPA regulations—and a well-to-do family in Philadelphia said they had 4,500 cans of food "which would cost them 108 eight point stamps for 41 years." Small grocers by the thousands went out of business anticipating a sharp decline in sales;

the ready availability of war work for former grocers and the start of coupon rationing undoubtedly paved the way for the supermarket boom in postwar America.

Little wonder that the Victory Garden craze already underway accelerated during the new year. Government agencies, 4-H groups, and public schools all promoted cultivation of home gardens from the moment of Pearl Harbor. It became almost unpatriotic for people living in middle America not to have a victory plot beside the family home. Almost everyone was doing it during the war years—even big-city apartment dwellers were urged to plant vegetables in window boxes. Newspapers and magazines printed how-to-do-it pieces and occasionally ran photos of buxom young ladies in the proper getups for victory gardening. Gallup produced a two-part survey in January 1943 saying that 54 percent of its respondents intended to plant a victory garden in the spring, while 44 percent had no plans to be a wartime gardener. Overall, the figures represented a 6 percent increase over the number of people who had had gardens in 1942.

Victory Garden festivals were commonplace during the fall to praise patriotic contributions of home gardeners. Agriculture secretary Claude Wickard spoke before a giant rally in Chicago's Soldier Field during September to endorse Washington's support of the program. Whether it was patriotism or a means to supplement the family larder, Victory Gardens produced 8,000,000 tons of food from 20,000,000 individual plots during 1943, enough production to make a difference in national food supplies.

Other troublesome shortages developed in the first months of 1943 as stocks of consumer goods on store shelves and in warehouse bins since Pearl Harbor were used up. The shunting of precious raw materials into defense production meant that supplies were not replenished. An example was the lowly safety pin. The Office of Civilian Supply (OCS) in Nelson's WPB had cut domestic output to 50 percent of prewar levels in early 1942. And those manufactured were soon useless from rust because they were made from steel instead of from the customary copper and brass. When a Duquesne, Pennsylvania, hospital was forced to use scotch tape as diaper fasteners in its nursery for lack of pins, a local Lions Club launched a collection drive that brought in 6,000 safety pins.

The Duquesne episode was symptomatic of widespread supply problems facing the nation. By April, OCS was considering a report on "hard goods" for civilian use which included a variety of items from "axes, hammers, and files to churns, mopsticks, and garbage pails." In Seattle, where defense workers carried fat paychecks from teeming aircraft plants, naval bases, and shipyards, the big downtown Bon Marché department store reported substantial changes in civilian buying patterns. And the store resorted to all kinds of merchandising substitutes to fill its depleted shelves. Forty-one buyers instead of the usual eighteen were sent to New York in January to stock up on spring and summer wares. Although powerful efforts were expended to woo potential suppliers, attempts to get coveted items were a vain exercise. When Bon Marché buyers went after fast-selling goods—alarm clocks, zippers, hairpins, safety pins, bed springs, needles, fountain pens, lamps, woolen blankets, garden tools, electric blankets, small radios—they found them unavailable.

As Nelson's WPB—which included OCS—began to fill its war production and lend lease quotas, more and more restricted materials were gradually released for civilian use. But the large items—cars, trucks, washing machines, major household appliances—were not available until 1946 or later. In February 1943, however, Bon Marché announced that it had an "ample" supply of women's undies when alternative fashions were put on store counters. A bra-and-corset outfit with a "drop seat" was merchandised at the Seattle emporium which one magazine said was "a great time-saver for overhauled women" in defense plants. And Bon Marché had plenty of bras and corsets because "all new merchandise uses limited amounts of elastic."

Perhaps the reduced elastic in undergarments contributed to a new freedom of the soul and changes in personal behavior. But whatever the cause, and in spite of the deprivations of war, the country continued to have a merry time. The good times of the war years, like a hound chasing its tail, fed a widespread disregard for social conventions. "There was a peculiar spirit around New York in those days," Shelly Winters notes in her best-selling autobiography: "It was almost as if people who weren't actually fighting the war were in some way enjoying it. Under the guise of patriotism there seemed to be a general loosening of morals and manners, with everyone living for that day or night and to hell with tomorrow."

The twenty-one-year-old Winters, born Shirley Schrift in St. Louis but reared in Brooklyn, was a struggling young actress in New York and later Hollywood during the 1940s. After arriving in the movie capital in 1943 to start a motion picture career that eventually catapulted her to stardom and an Academy Award, she found time to join other starlets at California's Hollywood Canteen and on the entertainment circuit at "military hospitals in driving distance of Hollywood." Like other Americans, young and old, the bright-eyed girl from New York City was caught up in the good-time swirl of the war. And her observation about the what-the-hell atmosphere in wartime New York had a wider application; it described a new morality that reached into every corner of the nation. The anxieties of the times produced an upsurge in vice and deliquency as well as sexual abandon. After all, nothing could equal an amorous interlude to relieve worries over the uncertainties of war and separation from loved ones. The prevailing ethic was fast becoming: "If you can't be near the one you love, then love the one you're near."

Wartime newspapers were filled with unpleasant aspects of the new morality and off-color shenanigans of the young. A Jacksonville, Florida, high school reported that 25 percent of the unmarried girls in its 1942 graduating class were pregnant. New York City police said the crime rate among eleven-to-thirteen-year-old girls shot up an alarming 30 percent during 1942. In San Francisco a crackdown on teenage activities began when authorities found two girls, ages twelve and thirteen, in a downtown hotel room with two musicians. Juvenile misconduct in the California metropolis led to police patrols at bus depots and thoroughfares which turned back unescorted girls flooding into the city. And at Victoria, in south Texas, civic leaders and parents searched for ways to dissuade junior and senior high school girls from flocking around airmen at nearby Aloe and Foster air bases.

A whole new category of young female appeared on the scene. Variously labeled "Victory Girls" or "Cuddle Bunnies," they could be seen everywhere, but especially around army and navy installations, seeking the attentions of servicemen. They might be anywhere from twelve years up, though generally in the fourteen-to-seventeen age bracket. Wearing snug-fitting sweaters, bobby sox, the latest hairdos, and up-tilting bras, the girls more times than not gathered around the "juke joints" of the period.

Although teenage Cuddle Bunnies caused soul-searching among social workers, parents, and lawmen, authorities were more concerned with the outright prostitution that flourished wherever servicemen congregated. Attempts to deal with organized vice usually produced different forms of the illicit rendezvous. Something called "taxicab troubles" developed in many cities, causing sharp police crackdowns; it was simply sex in the backseat. "Trailer girls" also set up shop at trailer parks and sleazy tourist courts on the outskirts of army and navy towns where civilian and military police could not reach them.

Professional prostitutes, call girls, and their procurers in big cities and around military installations not only thrived during the war, but became a chief source of vice. Joining in the search for illicit sex was the "sometimes" prostitute or semi-professional; *Newsweek* said that such women were "camp followers hanging around bars and night clubs near military camps and indulging sometimes for profit, sometimes not." Things got so difficult in Florida that base commanders asked Governor Spessard L. Holland to summon a special legislative session to strengthen the state's liquor and curfew statutes. In Chicago, authorities responded to the problem by prohibiting hostesses from working in bars and searching for excuses to close liquor joints; a favorite police tactic was to arrest owners for serving drinks to minors. New Orleans systematically closed brothels, yet call girls openly plied their trade in early 1943. And San Francisco, which had its share of vice, dealt with the problem by raising bail for arrested prostitutes from the customary $25 to $2,500.

Widespread prostitution and the general moral laxness brought on by war produced rapid increases in the reported cases of veneral disease. Although police efforts to halt indiscriminate lovemaking were doomed to failure, medical discoveries in the 1930s made the large-scale treatment of VD a practical goal. Doctors at induction centers across the country noted an incidence rate of sixty cases per 1000 for syphilis and gonorrhea in the general population as they examined draftees. Military commanders, determined to stop the spread of VD among servicemen, started a program in late 1942 to set up treatment centers or prophylaxis stations in key areas.

Soldiers and sailors were forced to check into the centers or suffer reprimand if detected with infections, but getting civilians to seek help was another matter. Some came into stations which were located at "fire houses, police stations, and health centers" in large cities and near military posts. Civilian registrants were never numerous and the treatment of service personnel was a much more common practice throughout the war. A treatment center doctor in New York told reporters: "Imagine the meeting of two persons at a prophylaxis station after an affectionate parting an hour before."

The enormous influx of women into the job market led to a new dilemma: sex in the factory. Over two million women had gone to work in defense plants and shipyards by the end of 1942 and another three million were to enter previously all-male work bastions before 1945. Most were either unattached or had husbands and boyfriends in uniform which created potential consequences for overworked plant managers.

Sex-related goings-on in the workplace were part of wartime living, and strong measures were taken by company superintendents to cope with philandering and outright lovemaking on the job. The "Dorothy Dixes" hired by some plants kept an eye on employees and served as counselors for their personal and work-related behavior. These plant matrons' job was to police workers in an effort to minimize liaisons during working hours. Flirting on production lines led to production pileups which became so rampant at a Douglas Aircraft facility in Santa Monica that a plant bomb shelter was closed after "swing shift couples" found it convenient for intimate trysts during lunch breaks. Although women in defense plants began wearing slacks—a further breakdown in old conventions—according to *Newsweek*, thousands balked at wearing safety suits and goggles; and most women in the plants "flatly refused" to wear coverings over their hair.

An undisputed connection developed between the new morality and the draft, which had moved into high gear by early 1943. Draft age men were called up daily and many women left behind, who were unable or unwilling to be content, began to seek companionship elsewhere. It order to allay apprehensions, the Office of War Information issued a statement at the beginning of January indicating that 350,000 men per month would be conscripted in the immediate future. By the end of 1943, the bulletin said, "the grand fighting force would be 9,700,000 and 4,200,000 men will be inducted to meet that figure."

High monthly quotas continued throughout 1943 and Selective Service warned able-bodied men in April to prepare for active duty. Only three categories could hope to escape: key workers in defense plants and other essential industries, farmers and farm workers, and those with "undue family hardships." Men with minor children were told not to expect deferments; otherwise, only those with "invalid wives" would be deferred. The Selective Service raid on the nation's pool of family men had far-reaching social and economic consequences. One spinoff was economic hard times for nearly 3,000,000 million families, roughly one-tenth the total population. Fathers going into uniform simply did not earn their former salaries. Although service allotments and allowances to wives and children picked up some of the slack, women with small children either had to enter the workplace or scrape by on limited incomes while their husbands were away at war.

Not every young family was confronted with economic disaster, because 40 percent of those called up were rejected on the basis of job deferments or physical deficiencies. Ever since the introduction of machines in the eighteenth century, following the Industrial Revolution, armies in Europe and America had undergone a decline in physical fitness. Modern living in advanced countries and a shift away from subsistence agriculture had led to a decrease in brute muscle power once men were freed from the need for backbreaking labor. Military doctors and post commanders noted deficiencies in overall fitness of draftees from the beginnings of Selective Service. It was not serious at first because the reservoir of unmarried men under twenty was tapped first for induction. In March 1943 Major General Louis B. Hershey, longtime director of the draft, bluntly told Congress "that the pool of unmarried men for the army and navy was practically exhausted." Authorities reported a steady decline in the fitness of males from eighteen to forty-five even though the draft only reached to age thirty-eight; the older the man the greater likelihood of health defects that precluded military service. And the decline became more pronounced in the thirty-five to forty-five age bracket; more were rejected than accepted in this group. Hershey also said "the weight of the draft must fall on the man under 30, married or not" because of fitness difficulties with older men. Eighteen- and nineteen-year-olds, bypassed in earlier callups, had been ordered to register in December. The initial drafting of men under twenty started in January 1943 and continued at the rate of 100,000 per month to offset health drawbacks with older draftees.

Families by the hundreds of thousands were disrupted by their menfolk going into uniform, but particularly disheartening was the "lonely wife" or young married woman without children who was left behind. Frequently living beyond the reach of their own families with little money or meaningful job prospects life was tedious for such women. And they were often the target of "wolves," the 1940s term for philandering males. Ethel Gorham, a staff writer for the New York *Times*, turned out a book for the woman alone, entitled, *So Your Husband's Gone to War*. Among other things, the 1943 Doubleday publication advised: "On the whole, it is wiser to try and stay on in the same fashion you did before the war. Perhaps in a less spacious, cheaper house, but with intrinsically the same setup, the same furniture, you as the mistress of the house—instead of another female or assorted females—your husband as the master when he returns on furlough."

Women at home were admonished to stay busy—doing war work, additional schooling, volunteerism, any useful activity to help them pass the time. Letter writing to soldier husbands, *Life* observed, "eased the ache of loneliness" for most women. When their husbands did come home on leave, according to Gorham, "he will want to do what he has always done. If he liked gay parties, he won't want a romantic twosome. If he was the pipe-and-slippers type, he won't want to go out on the town." No two women faced the same obstacles, although the lonely wife remained a wartime dilemma for untold thousands. Gorham also told her readers to write their husbands regularly but to leave "details of your personal upheavals" out of the letters.

The rapid military buildup was necessary to meet urgent demands on American manpower. By early 1943 the United States was fighting in North Africa and the Pacific and engaged in heavy convoy duty to England and the Soviet Union. While no American troops were committed to the Russian front, shipments of war matériel along the torturous sea route around the top of Scandinavia to Murmansk demanded strenuous sea duty by British and American personnel. In all, forty-one convoys, totaling 811 ships, of which fifty-eight were lost and thirty-three turned back, made the "Murmansk Run" after 1941, carrying lend lease supplies to the Soviets. More than 5,000 tanks and 7,000 planes were delivered from American factories, a decisive factor in the final Russian victory over Hitler's panzers.

"Uncle Joe Stalin" was our ally in the crusade against Hitler, and OWI was anxious to present a favorable image of the Communist dictatorship. The country was inundated with newsreel and press coverage during January 1943 of the savage fighting at Stalingrad. A press account for January 11 had "the Germans burrowed into cellars and turned into 'bearded beasts' who subsisted on short rations of horse meat." Stalingrad—later changed to Volgograd after some unfathomable shift in Soviet policy—was the high tide of German penetration toward the rich oil fields of the Caucasus. Located on the Volga, 1,300 miles from Berlin, Stalingrad was the focal point of German-Russian combat throughout the winter of 1942–1943.

German tanks first penetrated the city of 450,000 in September 1942, following a headlong drive across southern Russia. But Stalingrad never surrendered. Brutal house-to-house fighting continued until January 31 when General Friedrich Paulus—made a field marshal by Hitler and told to make a last-ditch stand—surrendered the Nazi garrison. Further surrenders on February 2 brought the number of German prisoners to more than 90,000 in the final Soviet assault. Paulus's capitulation on the Volga not only shifted the eastern campaign in favor of the Allies, but was also a major turning point in the entire war. After January–February 1943 the Nazi warmacht was put on the defensive, a stance that persisted until the final great collapse of April 1945.

It was a different story in June 1942 when Hitler unleashed Operation Barbarossa—named for a crusading Teutonic knight of the thirteenth century—against Russia. The Axis onslaught ended the Russo-German

Pact of August 1939 which had kept the Russians at bay while Germany blitzkrieged its way through Poland and France. Although the German offensive was delayed because of stubborn resistance to Axis thrusts into Greece and the Balkans, Stalin failed to put his armies on full operational alert; even the British secret service knew Hitler was ready to make war. Three great armies, Army Group North under Field Marshal Wilhelm von Leeb, Army Group Center under Field Marshal Fedor von Bock, and Army Group South under Field Marshal Gerd von Rundstedt marched with startling quickness across the Russian flatlands in the summer and fall of 1942.

The Red Army, which was never completely foiled by the German attack, not only regrouped to throw back Group South at Stalingrad, but also halted Hitler's other spearheading columns. After a brief pause to rekindle his armor von Leeb's vanguard arrived at Leningrad during the first days of September. Though completely ringed by German panzers and Field Marshal Carl von Mannerheim's Finns, the city of three million—nearly one million of whom died from starvation during the siege—held out until January 1944. Leningrad was blockaded for seventeen grueling months; yet the city never capitulated, one of the great triumphs of the war and one forever commemorated in the seventh symphony of Dimitri Shostakovich. Russian defiance at Moscow was equally devastating when von Bock's armored divisions got close enough to see a city water tower but no closer. Hitler, unlike Napoleon a century earlier, failed even to enter the Russian capital.

Six months after Stalingrad the world's greatest tank battle took place at Kharkov in the Kursk Salient during July 1943. It marked the beginning of the final rout of Hitler's panzers from Russian territory. Harsh winters and "General Mud" hastened the German defeat, and by January 1945 Soviet units had crossed the frontier into East Prussia. The Russian counteroffensive, helped by American military supplies via the Murmansk Run, carried unbelievable cruelities in its wake. Nazi barbarities inflicted on Russian civilians notwithstanding, no German was safe from Russian molestation; Marshal Zhukov's troops celebrated their arrival on German soil on January 20, 1945, with a "lurid and violent sack" of Hahesalza, a small town in East Prussia, which continued for three days.

If raging battles on the Russian front seemed remote and slightly unreal in January 1943, the heroics of Mess Sergeant Floyd Archiquette did not. An American Indian with our troops in New Guinea, Archiquette shot an enemy sniper outside his mess tent while American and Australian units fought for control of that remote island. "He was making a nuisance of himself," he told war correspondents, "and somebody had to get him—so I got him." The public readily identified with soldiers like Archiquette and his GI buddies who were locked in a death struggle for mastery of the southwest Pacific. After all, the United States lost 2,800 men and the Australians another 5,700 in the six-month campaign to drive Japanese forces out of New Guinea.

Although Japan lost four carriers at Midway in June, and therefore lost the advantage in their fight with the United States, the warlords in Tokyo forged ahead in the South Pacific by launching a two-pronged move in the direction of Australia. First, Japanese troops landed on the north coast of New Guinea in the old German colony of Kaiser Wilhelmsland to prepare for a thrust across the Owen Stanley mountains into Papua, formerly a British colony but now under Australian control. Next, with their bases on Bougainville and Guadalcanal, the Japanese hoped to capture the British Solomons.

After initial landings on July 21, Japanese forces encountered heavy opposition from American and Australian contingents when they started to push southward along nearly impregnable jungle paths over the Owen Stanley range. Port Moresby on the southern coast, only 320 miles from Australia across the Coral Sea, which they hoped to use as a debarkation port, was never captured. The Japanese, who lost 12,000 men in their abortive campaign to get a foothold at Port Moresby, were soon put on the defensive. Though Japanese units had been cleared from eastern New Guinea by January 21, 1943, two weeks before their withdrawal from Guadalcanal, enemy forces remained on other parts of the island. After MacArthur started his "leapfrogging" strategy of bypassing Japanese pockets, Allied forces under General Sir Thomas Blamey fought westward along the northern New Guinea coast until 1945. Some enemy troops in fact stayed in the interior jungle until the final surrender was signed in Tokyo Bay.

Meanwhile, American reconnaissance planes spotted an airfield under construction on Guadalcanal, an island ninety-miles long and twenty-five-miles wide, 650 miles east of New Guinea in the Solomons group. The airfield posed the deadly threat of land-based enemy bombers and stirred Nimitz and the United States Navy to feverish activity, although no United States forces were put ashore until August 7. When 19,000 marines, commanded by Major General Alexander A. Vandergrift, landed on Guadalcanal, they found the beaches undefended and none but construction workers on the island. But the Japanese, anxious to keep their toehold in the Solomons, started the famed "Tokyo Express" or the running of fast-moving destroyers down "The Slot" from their huge base at Rabaul. By using a narrow channel down the length of the islands at night, Yamamoto and the imperial navy strengthened and supplied their land units on Guadalcanal for another six months.

Harvard historian Samuel Eliot Morison called Guadalcanal "the most bitterly contested campaign in American history since the Campaign of North Virginia in the Civil War." And a major factor in the ultimate victory was the first-day capture of the island's airfield. Renamed Henderson Field in honor of a U.S. Marine flyer killed at Midway, the field was used effectively against the enemy after it was completed and lengthened by American engineers. A climax in the Guadalcanal fighting took place September 13–14 over a small "grass-covered hump" known as Edison's, or Bloody Ridge. Here, Samuel B. Griffith, a marine officer turned chronicler, writes: "Edison's Raiders sustained 135 casualities, the Parachutists 128." The Japanese, however, lost more than 1,000 men in the two-day slaughter.

Although American losses were high on Guadalcanal, enemy fatalities were nothing short of staggering. The Japanese army left behind 21,000 fallen soldiers when their withdrawal took place during the first week in February. Other islands in the Solomons chain and the Bismarck Archipelago remained in Japanese hands as the "island hopping" toward the Philippines and Tokyo got underway. And the enemy continued to use The Slot to resupply their forces on Bougainville, Munda, and New Georgia after the American victory on Guadalcanal. American use of fast PT-boats to jab at the enemy in the Solomons campaign and throughout the Pacific was vitally important to a future president of the United States.

PT-109, commanded by a young Navy lieutenant named John Fitzgerald Kennedy, was "run down and knifed" by the destroyer *Amagiri* on the night of August 1–2 while steaming through The Slot south of Kolombangara. Unwilling to give up in a life-threatening situation, Kennedy and a wounded comrade swam the Blacket Straight to a small island in the dead of night. Friendly natives found the exhausted lieutenant, paddled him to safety in a well-camouflaged canoe, and the rest is history.

At the start of 1943, home-front America also watched great events unfold in North Africa, where U.S. forces were stabbing at Rommel's panzers in Tunisia near the Moslem holy city of Kairouan. American and Allied forces from the United States and Europe made simultaneous landings in French Morocco and Algeria in early November as part of Operation Torch. Carefully planned by another future president, Dwight

D. Eisenhower, Torch was designed to open an attack on the Axis in western North Africa at the same time that Field Marshal Montgomery's Eighth Army was driving westward after the great British victory at El Alamein. The Americans, also using tank columns commanded by General George S. Patton, met little resistance at first in their headlong rush for Tunis and the jumping-off point to Italy. In spite of 60,000 German casualties at El Alamein, Rommel and the Axis high command mounted a terrible delaying action during January–February 1943 as the American–British vise tightened around the Tunisian coast.

The area was secure enough for Roosevelt to meet British Prime Minister Churchill in late January 1943 "in the enclosure of a Casablanca hotel surrounded by barbed wire and bristling guards." The Morocco meeting took place to plan the next moves against Hitler. Roosevelt, always the consummate politician with an eye on the next election, shattered precedent when he journeyed to wartime North Africa.

In January 1943 the public was told a great deal about FDR's first airplane ride since 1932 when he "rushed to Chicago to accept the Democratic presidential nomination," but very little about the Casablanca meeting. Yet momentous decisions came out of the Roosevelt–Churchill deliberations, which continued for ten days. Russian dictator Joseph Stalin, who had been clamoring for a "second front" to relieve pressure on the Red Army, found it convenient not to attend, "even for a day, as it is just now that important operations of our military campaign are developing." Stalin's communiqué answering an invitation to the conclave reminded Roosevelt and Churchill of their "promise to establish a second front in Western Europe in the spring of 1943." But the legions of civilian and military advisors from the United States and Britain at Casablanca concurred on one thing: any attempt at a cross-channel operation into France was out of the question for another year. A decision was made for a landing in Italy or what Churchill called the "soft underbelly of Europe" when the remaining Nazi forces were cleared from North Africa.

Increased military operations overseas touched the country in ways both tragic and whimsical. For one thing, it became almost commonplace for boys too young for military service to be found in uniform. Fifteen-year-old Johnny Maras had already earned three stripes as a U.S. Army sergeant and been shipped to an East Coast debarkation center for transport to North Africa before his real age was discovered. The Milwaukee lad had undergone basic training at Camp Roberts, California, and received advanced schooling at Fort Meade, Maryland, unnoticed by army brass. That was after he had hitchhiked to California following the death of a Marine chum in the attack on Pearl Harbor.

Maras had tried both the U.S. Navy and Marine Corps before he convinced Army recruiters that he was over the legal age for induction. But a suspicious colonel checked with Wisconsin officials to learn that he had been born in June 1927, which made him fifteen years of age in January 1943. When confronted by his commanding officer, the young sergeant stoutly maintained he was eighteen. "I figure," he told reporters who covered his January discharge, "that when I was home at Christmas somebody found out how good I was doing in the Army and turned me in . . . So now I have to wait a year and a half before I can get in there and pitch. I can't get into the Marines or the Navy until I'm 17 and the Army won't take me back until I'm 18." Undaunted, Maras was afraid the war would be over before he could reenlist.

A more serious outgrowth of the war was a rash of violent plane crashes that plagued the country during the early months of 1943. Scarcely a day passed from January through April without news of another military crash. Four widely separated mishaps—at Boise, Idaho; Camp Lee, Virginia; Shreveport, Louisiana; and Mitchell Field, Long Island—resulted in the death of eighteen fliers over a two day period, January 15–16. Ten perished in the Boise crash of an army bomber; a fighter pilot waited until he was fifty feet from the ground before jumping to his death over Camp Lee as thousands of drilling recruits watched his plane from nearby Richmond Air Base barely miss the camp's "crowded barracks, class-rooms, and drill grounds." Two young pilots, Richard O. Simmons of Alexandria, Louisiana, and Richard W. Nellis of Watertown, New York, both twenty-two-year-old lieutenants, were killed in separate accidents the same day near Mitchell Field, New York. Simmons died, a wire service report said, "when his fighter plane dropped out of formation and crashed this morning on the Camp Upton Reservation"; his plane erupted in flames when it hit the ground. Nellis bailed out over Jones Beach but drowned when he landed "a few hundred feet offshore."

At Barksdale Field near Shreveport five men were killed and two escaped unhurt when a medium-size bomber upended on takeoff. The uninjured men, both sergeants—a radioman and a gunner, were riding in the tail section; the other five were trapped in the burning wreck after the plane, according to army spokesmen, "lifted only a few feet off the runway when it dipped to the ground and burst into flames at the south end of the field." Another army plane crashed into the farm of Francis Schleppi on January 25 near New Albany, Ohio. Schleppi and his neighbors found eleven bodies in the wreckage, which was scattered over 600 feet of his farm.

And eleven more men died the same day when "a heavy bomber" from Topeka Army Base went down in rough mountain country eighty miles north of Alamogorda, New Mexico. Sgt. John J. Mikolich, "believed to be the first American-born professional hockey player in the armed forces to die during the war," was among those lost. The twenty-four-year-old Mikolich had played two seasons for the Kansas City farm team of the Chicago Black Hawks before entering the air force. Nor was that all. Three other military craft were reported down on January 25–26 at Rapid City, South Dakota (ten officers and men lost), at Dalhart, Texas, where a glider crashed with five fatalities, and at Flomaton, Alabama, when nine men, seven of them officers, perished on a flight from Drew Field near Tampa.

The sharp rise in the number of training flights and military activity in the United States produced almost daily fatalities for several months. Further military crashes were reported during February at Newberry, South Carolina, when two planes in formation collided, killing fourteen crewmen, and in California where a bomber ditched in the Pacific one mile offshore with a loss of eighteen men. A sensational crackup occurred in Seattle on February 18 after "a four-motored Boeing bomber crashed and exploded atop a packing plant." Fourteen people died in the mishap, and "4 officers and a technical sergeant" perished on February 28 near Austin, Texas, when a transport crashed from nearby Valle Field.

Despite such constant reminders of the war as these frequent air crashes by inexperienced young pilots and the country's continuing rationing difficulties, some Americans found no difficulty in going their own individual way. One of these was Margaret Wilson, a daughter of President Woodrow Wilson who had moved to Pondicherry, a French enclave on the east coast of India. Fifty-six-year-old Miss Wilson, described by one journalist as "the spit and image of her father," was staying in a Hindu ashram.

After she had spurned the strict Presbyterianism of her family—she did so by stalking out of a church communion service—Miss Wilson made her way to India "to acquire a state of serenity." That was after she had read a book in the New York Public Library, *Essays on the Gita*, written by a Hindu mystic named Sri Aurobindo. She subsequently joined the seventy-year-old guru, who had been educated at Cambridge and who appeared but four times a year to his followers. Miss Wilson had taken a new name, Dishtra, which means "the discovery of the divine self" in Sanskrit. She had to abandon a strict vegetarian regimen because of health difficulties, and she was "allowed to wear American clothes, read magazines and newspapers, and puff on an after-dinner cigarette." Nonetheless, she told journalists her new life "was extremely hard."

While Margaret Wilson sat out the war in Asia, Josephus Daniels, a prominent member of her father's wartime cabinet, remained as crusty as ever in his North Carolina newspaper office. Daniels, editor-owner of the Raleigh *News and Observer* since 1894, made the news by celebrating his eighty-first birthday. His good health, Daniels said, resulted from "an avoidance of exercise and a refusal to retire from social and political hurly-burly." Except for his intervals at government service, Daniels remained an uncompromising crusader for social justice and a staunch Democrat. In May 1943 he was writing editorials urging North Carolina to adopt its first nine-month school term with full state funding. "I believe the Bible from cover to cover except where it says that a man's life is three score and ten. That Sir, is a lie," he told newsmen.

Others catching the public eye were Stephen Vincent Benét and J. Pierpont Morgan, who both died in the spring of 1943, taking a part of Americana with them. Benét's famous refrain, "John Brown's Body Goes A Marching On," from his epic *John Brown's Body*—written in 1926–1927 while he was a Guggenheim Fellow—was known to every schoolboy. The Pulitzer Prize-winning poet died March 16 in Manhattan after suffering a heart attack at age forty-four. He had also penned the well-received novel, *The Devil and Daniel Webster*, that was made into a highly successful movie during the war years. Nor had the duration dampened his literary output. Benét wrote several scripts for patriotic radio shows, one of which, *Dear Adolph*, attracted wide notice, and his "Prayer for the United Nations" was read over the air by FDR as part of his 1942 Flag Day address to the nation. "A tall, loose-limbered, slyly humorous, friendly man with a boyish look despite his mustache and thick-lensed glasses," Benet had published his first volume of poetry in 1916 while still a teenager.

J. Pierpont Morgan, a dominant figure in American finance for decades, suffered a heart attack on a New York-to-Florida train and died on March 13 at Bocagrande in the Florida Keys. Known the world over as Jack, he was the son of J. Pierpont Morgan (Maximus), financial titan and founder of the House of Morgan on Wall Street. Morgan had used his private funds to float loans for the British and French governments on the eve of WWI. He conducted what amounted to a private lend lease program for the allies until the United States entered the war in

1917. And when the stock market crash of October 1929 sent shock waves around the world, Morgan led other Wall Street tycoons in an abortive scheme to save the plunging market. Though he managed to raise 240 million dollars to avert the crash and subsequent Depression, his more realistic partner at the House of Morgan, Thomas W. Lamont, retorted: "There is no man nor group of men that can buy all the stocks that the American public can sell."

When summoned before the Pecora Investigating Committee after the crash, Morgan steadily maintained that "if a banker had power, it was because of his reputation for integrity." A highpoint of the 1934 investigations came when a circus agent for P.T. Barnum placed a female midget on his lap and barked to waiting photographers: "The smallest lady in the world wants to meet the richest man in the world." At the time of his death in March 1943 if he was not the richest man in the world he was certainly one of the near richest. *Time* estimated his personal estate at $50,000,000, a good part of it his holdings in J. P. Morgan and Company.

In the spring of 1943, the public's imagination was captured by another kind of court action, this one taking place in Boston and very different from Morgan's troubles with a liberal Congress. Prosecuting Attorney Robert T. Bushnell, swept into office with Governor Leverett Saltonstall in November 1942, gained several indictments stemming from the disastrous Coconut Grove fire. The final body count had reached 491 in the fire, and the forty-six-year-old Bushnell, a maverick Republican, was anxious to make political hay from the tragedy. Capitalizing on the public's continuing fascination with the catastrophe, not only locally but nationally, Bushnell began to act, bypassing the Boston police department. But because city police commissioners had been gubernatorial appointees since 1906, he encountered difficulties with Saltonstall and the Republican establishment. Bushnell promptly blasted them for foot-dragging because "there are too many politicians who are interested primarily in the tenure of their office."

The indictments came from a Suffolk County grand jury after Bushnell presented evidence gathered by state police. In a widely-publicized trial in Boston, Barnett Welansky, Coconut Grove owner and club president, was sentenced April 15 to prison for manslaughter; two others connected with the popular night spot were acquitted of any wrongdoing. Also indicted by the same grand jury were the city building commissioner and the night commander of the police district surrounding the club (which explained why Bushnell had bypassed Boston officials in his initial investigations). And as if that were not enough, "the big and popular Police Commissioner Joseph F. Timulty" was forced to take a leave of absence along with six subordinates after gambling charges were lodged against them as a result of the Coconut Grove probe.

The war did not deter other enterprising politicos like Bushnell from making a name for themselves. Even before the return of peace, many bright boys in uniform were planning to use their military service as a stepping stone to a postwar political career. In fact, practically every politician who was to rise to prominence over the next forty years had seen active duty in the war. With the sole exception of Harry S. Truman (who had been an artillery captain in World War I), every single American president after 1945 had served in the military during World War II: Dwight D. Eisenhower, John F. Kennedy, Lyndon B. Johnson, Richard M. Nixon, Gerald R. Ford, Jimmy Carter (an Annapolis midshipman), Ronald Reagan, and George Bush.

6 JUNE 1943: DAYS OF PROTEST

S ummer 1943 found America convulsed by an ugly wave of protest
that tested the national patience. Although news from the fighting
fronts continued to be favorable, with American and Allied armies
advancing steadily against the bastions of Nazism and the Japanese
warlords, the pent up frustrations arising from nineteen months of continuous warfare erupted in a storm of racial violence and labor unrest at
home. Much of the racial discord had its roots in the war-caused population shifts that had moved groups of people from differing ethnic and
cultural backgrounds into close contact for the first time. Cross-cultural
conflict and street confrontations in cities like Los Angeles, Detroit, and
New York were agitated by economic inequalities. Meanwhile, during a
seven-month period, from May through November 1943, John Llewellyn
Lewis and the soft-coal miners shut down all bituminous production on
four different occasions because they could not abide Roosevelt's Little
Steel freeze on wages. Even the Jehovah's Witness religious sect precipitated a minor constitutional crisis when its schoolchildren balked at
saluting the flag.

The United Mine Workers work stoppage had its origins in the 1940
presidential campaign, when Lewis supported Wendell Willkie. He had
convinced himself that an "unholy alliance" existed between his newly-
created CIO and the New Deal president. Although organized labor
remained a mainstay in the Democratic coalition, Lewis insisted that the
party had lost its zeal for protecting rank and file union men. His anti-
Roosevelt stance became a public quarrel after January 1940, when Lewis
addressed the twenty-fifth annual UMWA convention at Columbus,
Ohio: "Labor today has no point of contact with the Democratic administration in power, except for casual and occasional interviews which are
granted its individual leaders. In Congress, the unrestrained baiting and

defaming of labor by the Democratic majority has become a pastime, never subject to rebuke by the titular or actual leaders of the party."

John L. Lewis, whom 550,000 soft-coal miners followed with near-religious fanaticism with their battlecry, "No contract, No work," was a formidable opponent in any league. A natural orator and spellbinder, the fiery Lewis was born February 12, 1880, into a family of Welsh descent in the coal producing region of south central Iowa. A precocious lad, whose father was blacklisted for union organizing activity in the Iowa fields, he was raised in a milieu of hatred for coal barons as well as in the uncertainty and poverty of life underground. At age fifteen he joined his father and brothers in the pits. Union activity came naturally to Lewis, and after a move to Panama, Illinois, in 1909, he caught the eye of American Federation of Labor organizer and president Samuel Gompers. But Gompers's dedication to the skilled trades did not suit the young Lewis, who soon abandoned the AFL and its commitment to trade unionism. He became president of the UMWA in 1920 after a meteoric rise through the ranks; and his enthusiasm for all-inclusive industrial unionism, as opposed to the more elitist AFL approach, led him to form the CIO during 1936.

The secret to Lewis's hold over the miners was his tough-minded attention to their needs. After more than twenty years on the ramparts, the crafty, bushy-browed "John L.," one of the most powerful men in America, was unimpressed with Roosevelt's plea for support in the crusade for democracy. When most union chiefs rushed to join in the no-strike pledge following Pearl Harbor, Lewis held back; and throughout the war he fought the Little Steel formula with its brake on wage increases. What was more threatening to labor peace, Lewis never recognized the NWLB, which he viewed as another Rooseveltian device to limit the aspirations of working men.

The second coal strike, which began June 1, grew out of Lewis's earlier calls for portal-to-portal pay and a two-dollar-a-day pay hike. Portal-to-portal pay was an issue close to every coal man's heart and it remained a sticking point throughout the troubles of 1943. Miners often spent up to an hour in travel once they went underground simply to reach the diggings, which caused Lewis to demand extra pay for transit time at the mine site. Though coal operators agreed to his demands, portal-to-portal pay was in effect a wage increase that the NWLB could not allow because of its commitment to "holding the line" on wages.

Lewis, always the realist, knew the national mood would never tolerate an extended strike and ordered his miners back to the pits on June 7.

That was after Roosevelt and Interior Secretary Harold Ickes, who had charge of the nation's coal mines, upheld an NWLB back-to-work order; throughout the four strikes, Roosevelt threatened to use his powers as commander-in-chief to force the union into compliance. Undeterred, Lewis served notice that his miners would renew the walkout on June 20 "unless a new agreement is reached with the Appalachian bituminous and anthracite operators."

A prolonged coal strike in the middle of wartime was not only unthinkable, it was also potentially devastating to defense production quotas. During the June 1–6 stoppage no less than eleven blast furnaces were forced to close, hampering steel output. The six-day shutdown prompted a hue-and-cry against Lewis and his union that jarred the home front. Production boss Donald Nelson warned that a halt in the flow of coal to defense plants would threaten "the making of steel, synthetic rubber, aviation gasoline, and the like." Another labor boss, James C. Petrillo, head of the American Federation of Musicians, joined the anti-Lewis chorus: "With hand gestures," the New York *Times* said, "he pooh poohed John L. Lewis as a 'guy' calling strikes 'every two weeks' and not having anything to show for it." Roosevelt repeatedly blasted the UMWA organization as well as Lewis, but avoided damning individual miners; without calling names, FDR on June 24 said their actions had "rightly stirred up the anger and disapproval of the overwhelming mass of the American people."

Perhaps Lewis's harshest detractor was the armed forces journal, *Stars and Stripes*. An issue printed in Cairo for Eisenhower's North African troops carried a cartoon that showed Lewis in miner's garb; he was using a coal shovel to throw dirt on a fresh grave of a GI killed in the desert war. A hastily drafted poll by the paper reported that 90 percent of American troops favored "drastic action against the miners"; several GI respondents offered to change places with the strikers and, in an oft-quoted editorial, *Stars and Stripes* accused Lewis of treason: "He had betrayed the spirit of democracy. . . . He had betrayed the belief of the American soldier that his would be a war in which individuals' interest would be sublimated to the common purpose.

"Speaking for the American soldier: John L. Lewis, damn your coal-black soul."

Congressional wrath resulted in passage of the Smith-Connally Anti-Strike Act, named for Texas senator Tom Connally, a New Deal stalwart, and Virginia congressman Howard W. Smith; it was designed to deal with this and future work shutdowns. Smith and Connally, both veteran

Democrats on Capitol Hill, had been foes of big labor since the early 1930s. Lewis told Saul Alinsky, his biographer, "Every time Smith introduced a union-busting bill we fought him with all our strength." Howard Smith of Virginia, Lewis continued, "is a labor-baiting, crackpot fool, a menace to the nation."

Be that as it may, Lewis and the miners had prompted a shift in the national temper, and when finally passed, the act required thirty days advance notice for any strike. Moreover, penalties were established for anyone who "directed, instigated, or aided strikes in mines or plants operated by the United States government." Though FDR, anxious to keep organized labor loyal to the New Deal coalition, vetoed Smith-Connally, presidential objections were hurriedly brushed aside by a Congress intent on bringing Lewis to heel; within days it was repassed over presidential objection.

Even the Communists, a faction normally expected to support labor's fight with industry, joined the anti-Lewis groundswell. The party's national committee issued a statement on June 20—the first day of the second shutdown—assailing Lewis and urging miners to return to work immediately. Signed by William Z. Foster, committee chairman, and Earl Browder, general secretary, it scored Lewis for "setting himself up above the labor movement and the country." The Communist brass not only smacked him for abandoning the no-strike pledge, but also reminded miners that Roosevelt and Ickes had given assurances they would be treated fairly. "Lewis is trying to assume a veto power over United States participation in the war," they said. "He sets himself above the labor movement and above the government." Moreover, the Communists declared miners would have to choose between the country and their union boss.

Condemnation of any labor group was bitter medicine for the Communists and typified a paradox faced by the party. Prior to June 1941, when Hitler unleashed Operation Barbarossa, American Communists not only opposed war in Europe but also cautioned against any United States participation. The isolationist clamor commenced after Hitler and Stalin signed their nonaggression pact of May 1939. When Germany invaded Poland the following September, labor was asked to ignore the conflict: "This war cannot be supported by the workers. It is not a war against facism, not a war to protect small nations from aggression, not a war with any of the character of a just war, not a war that workers can or should support. It is a war between rival imperialisms for world domination."

Since Lenin, the master Communist theorist of all time, had branded imperialism as enemy number one, the leftist battlecry became: "Keep America Out of Imperialist War!" But the moment Hitler crossed the frontier into Russia, it was a new ball game. An instantaneous flip-flop occurred for American Reds. Foster, Browder, and their followers now unashamedly demanded United States involvement and ordered Communists to support America's Arsenal of Democracy. "The Communist Party," Foster wrote in his remarkable *History of the Communist Party in the United States*, "with its characteristic vigor activated all its members in the unions, in its press, and elsewhere to speed the wheels of industry. None served with better results in winning the war than did the Communists."

Although Lewis had courted Communist help in his earlier battles to establish the CIO, he soon, along with most Americans, became bored with left-wing sloganeering. Still, Foster was a man well suited to speak for the Communist cause. Born in 1881 and a onetime railroad worker, he remained in the forefront of worker causes until his death in 1961. Before joining the Communists in 1921, he had been in the Socialist party until 1909, when he left because of ideological disputes with Eugene V. Debs, head of the party. He stayed in the radical labor movement by becoming national secretary of the newly-created Syndicalist League of North America in 1920 at Chicago. Once in the Communist party he rose rapidly through the ranks until 1924, when he carried its presidential banner against Calvin Coolidge. Foster was also Communist candidate for president in 1928 and 1932.

James W. Ford, a black steelworker from Alabama whose father had been killed by klansmen, ran with Foster and later with Earl Browder for the vice presidency. The party under Foster and Browder had in fact made ongoing efforts to enlist blacks throughout the 1930s, especially in the South. A newspaper, *The Southern Worker*, was set up by James S. Allen at Chattanooga in 1924 to spread the message among southern blacks. Communist-paid lawyers regularly intervened in legal cases involving blacks during the 1930s, the most famous being the Scottsboro Boys. Party funds were used to defend nine youths accused of raping two white girls on a freight train in Depression-ravaged Alabama. Although they were given horrendous prison terms, a nationwide publicity campaign by the Communists probably saved the Scottsboro nine from hanging. (The last of the nine was finally pardoned by Governor George Wallace in the 1970s.) Yet Communist efforts to take up the "Negro standard" in a Jim Crow-dominated South were not applauded by all black leaders. Black newspapers like the Birmingham *Recorder* and the Richmond *Planet* cautioned their readers to eschew "radical remedies" for the plight of blacks.

After Foster suffered a crippling heart attack in the late 1930s, Browder took over the party leadership, which was extended through the war years. For most people in the 1940s not associated with left-wing activism, Browder typified American communism. Ten years younger than Foster, he had been born in 1891 at Wichita, Kansas; an early advocate of radical causes, he was jailed in 1917 for opposing United States participation in World War I. He had joined the Communists by 1920 and, following a much-heralded trip to Russia, became general secretary of the party ten years later. In 1936 and 1940 Browder and James W. Ford headed the party presidential ticket against Roosevelt. Because of wartime exigencies, the Communists not only declined, under his urging, to put up a presidential slate in 1944, but threw their support behind FDR during his precedent-shattering fourth bid for the White House. Browder's change of heart came after Eisenhower and the Allies opened a second front in Western Europe during June, thus relieving pressure on Russia.

Meanwhile, Harry Bridges, Australian-born head of the International Longshoremen's and Warehousemen's Union, though not officially in the Communist party, also blasted Lewis in 1943. During the coal strikes Bridges said Lewis was a "black disgrace to the laboring men and women of America. . . . in his personal vindictiveness against our government and its Commander-in-Chief." And as if that were not enough, Bridges stated that "[Lewis] had become the single most effective agent of the fascist powers within the ranks of labor." Lewis, on the other hand, busy with his ongoing fight with NWLB and the mine owners, had no time for international strategies. From the start of the first strike on May 1 until November 4, when the fourth strike ended, Lewis gave every ounce of his energy to the struggle. Wags said he planned to worry Roosevelt and the government into submission.

As criticism mounted, Lewis found he had some well-wishers in his fight with Uncle Sam. *Newsweek* published a letter from PFC George Kalinchock in Kingman, Arizona, which gave a different view of miner determination to get more money—war or no war. His father, a coal miner in eastern Pennsylvania, the army private said, worked for "6.07 per day, daily risking his life or being buried alive down deep underground." He was disturbed, he said, that a buddy who was also a relative had "received $12 a day for sweeping the four corners of a single floor of a defense plant till the day he was inducted into the service." Though

Kalinchock opposed the strike, he thought the miners should get their "measley" two-dollar raise. Similar letters poured into Lewis's Washington office as he got ready to renew the fight.

While everybody watched Lewis slug it out with Roosevelt's inflation fighters, and kept an eye on Mark Clark's Fifth Army inching its way up the Italian boot, several racial outbreaks rocked the country. In early June the notorious "zoot suit" riots started in Los Angeles, when hundreds of GIs roamed Mexican-American sections of the city yelling, "Kill the Pachuco Bastards!" Nor was anti-Hispanic rioting confined to the West Coast, although Los Angeles experienced the worst disorders. Similiar troubles erupted in cities along the Texas-Mexican border, Toronto, Detroit, Philadelphia, and Baltimore. The riots even led to a momentary diplomatic flap with Mexico, a situation that threatened relations with a valuable wartime ally.

In the 1940s, the zoot suit was worn by Hispanic and black youths as a badge of defiance against the mores of Anglo-America. Faced with unrelenting ostracism and forced into menial jobs, Spanish youths in Los Angeles and along the Mexican border to Texas banded together for sociability and support. Unfortunately, gangs who wore the zoot suit frequently engaged in vicious pranks and outright hooliganism; police in Los Angeles, for instance, soon noted a correlation between the zoot-suited youths hanging out at street corners and an increase in crime. They were often accompanied by "cholitas," or girlfriends, who wore a distinctive garb of black blouses and slacks or short skirts with fishnet stockings. The girls not only carried weapons for the pachucos but sometimes also served as lures to attract unwary servicemen into their boyfriends' clutches.

Although wartime restrictions on amounts of material used in clothing manufacture all but outlawed the flashy zoot suit, renegade tailors readily supplied them for a price. Worn by pachucos, who took their name from the area around Pachuca in central Mexico known for its flamboyant native dress, the suit stood out on American streets like a beacon. Nor was its use confined to Spanish youths. Nonconformist black and white youths were also attracted to it. "The suit is distinctively something bottom drawer," Newsweek said: "Its origin is obscure, although its main features—pegged trousers and long coat—resemble those suits of the early 1900s. Its creation had been attributed variously to a Negro busboy in Georgia and to costumes worn by Clark Gable in Gone With the Wind. No one actually knows or can prove where the suit actually started.

Harlem is its acknowledged gate to popularity, however, and there had flourished in all of its glory the neat pleat, drape shape, and stuffed coat."

For middle America the suit was an object of ridicule and outright scorn; in Los Angeles the stage was set for an explosion when young draftees from the hinterlands began flooding into surrounding military installations. Trouble started when word spread through service barracks that zooters and their cholitas had roughed up servicemen in downtown Los Angeles. In May two sailors were manhandled outside a nearby Venice dance hall after making passes at several Hispanic girls. Then, on the night of June 4, bands of club-wielding sailors and white youths invaded the Mexican section of east Los Angeles, smashing heads and roughing up every zooter in sight.

The following night found the pachucos grouped and ready for action. They had gathered tire irons, steel chains, knives, broken bottles, metal bars, and monkey wrenches for the renewed melée. Soldiers and sailors poured into the city on successive nights to join the rampage; in downtown Los Angeles, one news account read, "A Pachuco of 17 tried to sneak through a crowd of civilians following a band of soldiers. Men pushed him back; fists smashed into the frightened brown face. The boy went down, hands ripped off his coat and pants and tossed him into a garbage truck while the crowd roared approval. . . . The police could or would do little but make belated arrests."

After proclaiming that "no group has the right to take the law into its own hands," Governor Earl Warren did what all politicians do when faced with hard choices—he appointed a commission to investigate the disturbances. The Los Angeles city council passed an ordinance that made the wearing of zoot suits a misdemeanor. And German shortwave broadcasts had a field day with the American upheaval as outbreaks spread to other cities. In Toronto, Canadian sailors and zooters clashed for several nights on a Lake Ontario beachfront; zoot-suit-wearing blacks in Detroit, a city that had its share of racial violence in 1943, attacked a group of high school boys and stabbed one of them, leaving him in critical condition. Two members of Gene Krupa's dance band, on their way to work in Philadelphia, were punched out by several sailors. The costumed bandsmen had been mistaken for zooters, the red-faced sailors later told authorities.

A week or so after the Los Angeles flare-ups, another kind of racial trouble broke out on the Texas Gulf Coast. In mid-June, fighting between blacks and whites at Beaumont caused the governor to declare martial law; more than 100 state troopers and 1,600 national guardsmen were needed to restore order. The trouble commenced after rumors swept a Neches River shipyard that a black had raped the wife of a worker. Instantly, mobs of white workers fanned throughout the town's black section looking for the attacker. A news dispatch said the whites were "armed with shotguns, pistols, axes, hammers, and other tools as they stormed the jail and the Negro district." Calm did not return until a well-known Beaumont physician could find no evidence of violent attack after examining the mother of three. But that was after a number of blacks had been thumped around, their shops looted, their automobiles demolished, and their homes ransacked.

At about the same time near Greenville, Pennsylvania, racial fighting erupted at the Shenango Personnel Replacement Center. In the fray white and black inductees nearly wrecked the camp. In fact, the Shenango difficulties reflected the frustration and discontent of blacks throughout the armed services. Angered by discriminatory practices in the army as well as in civilian life, a group of black soldiers stole into the supply depot following an altercation with whites at the segregated base. According to Shenango public relations officers, blacks began firing into an area reserved for white inductees after arming themselves with rifles and ammunition. One black was killed in the melée and six more hospitalized with gunshot wounds.

Blacks' disenchantment with the American dream reached far beyond the army in 1943. Back in the South the massive Alabama Dry Dock and Shipbuilding Company at Mobile, which employed 30,000 defense workers, was the scene of a vicious black–white outbreak on May 25. Managers at the giant shipyard, who did not agree with Washington-imposed work regulations, were accused of making assignments that produced the riot. Company failure to explain work duties not only fueled a racial confrontation that injured eighty workers, but also halted vital defense production.

A tacit understanding at the yard mandated that "crews of Negro riggers, welders, and their helpers" would work exclusively on specific shipways; other sections were reserved for white crews. But on the May 24 night shift, the company made work changes that assigned an all-black crew to a white area. No whites were at work in the section, yet fearful of losing jobs and resentful of the black presence, they were ready for a fight the next morning. A later investigating board came down hard on the company for not explaining its work policy to its white and black workers. The policy had not been stated, critics said, because management wanted a confrontation to force government overseers into changing labor rules in the sprawling facility.

Previously the company had objected to an agreement that set aside four ways for blacks' use only; the company wanted worker segregation ended and permission to make its own inplant assignments. And the company was upset because the Maritime Commission did not want the Washington-dictated policy made public. The work rules and their implementation had led to a senseless upheaval. As usual nearly all of the eighty men injured in the "bloody rioting" were black. Still, one of the worst hurt was a white "who attempted to rescue a Negro worker from two of the company's guards who were beating up on black workers." Several military units arrived at the shipyard almost immediately, which indicated that authorities had had advanced warning of an impending clash.

A June 4 statement released in Washington scored the company for not making its work policy public. "The simple text," it said, "which provides four ways for Negro workers and disturbs no traditions shows that the issue was met in a straightforward fashion." In the war climate of 1943 authorities outside the company were more interested in having the agreement implemented than in stifling segregation.

The black drive for economic fairplay produced racial outbreaks in Indianapolis some weeks before the tortuous Detroit disturbances. Though the city's black population had not increased much during the war, a serious housing shortage developed around the inner-city—a problem common to cities throughout the Ohio Valley and the Midwest. Indianapolis experienced an influx of Appalachian whites from the hill country of Kentucky and Tennessee, many of them young women who came to work in the city's hosiery mills. Racial mistrust and tensions invariably arose when the hill folk—many of them as poor as the city's blacks—began to vie with them for cheap housing. Assimilation of the white newcomers, particularly where white–black relations were concerned, proved an impossible task.

Blacks, both men and women, had readily found work in the city's defense facilities and foundries. Crowding and the racial mix around the midtown area had already precipitated minor street disturbances and clashes with police. Indianapolis had roughly 50,000 Negroes in a total population of 400,000, mostly concentrated near the center of town and in three other areas. The real difficulties arose when blacks with defense money in their pockets wanted to move into better housing—the same housing coveted by newcomers from the southern Appalachians.

Although the great mass of black workers who sought a slice of the American pie during 1941–1945 ran into a wall of indifference or outright venom, other blacks, mostly performers and athletes like Joe Louis and Paul Robeson, were given a cordial, even enthusiastic welcome. Throughout the early months of 1943 a young singer with a sultry voice began to enthrall her audiences with songs like "Honeysuckle Rose." "Each year in New York's after-dark world of supper clubs," *Life* reported, "there appears a girl who becomes an overnight sensation—this year that girl is Lena Horne, a young Negro who has been appearing at the Savoy-Plaza Lounge. . . . Singing without a microphone, she makes old song favorites sound new and exciting." And what a sensation she was! Even in the star-studded galaxy of the early 1940s, Lena Horne was able to take the limelight and hold it for the next forty years.

Born in 1917 into an upper-class Brooklyn family, a family which included teachers, government workers and ministers, Lena Horne had sung in Ethel Waters's shows and at Hollywood's Little Troc Cafe before she sang at the Savoy-Plaza. When she joined other starlets entertaining troops during the war, she adopted an ironclad rule: She would never sing where black soldiers were not admitted. "It frightens me a little," she told reporters in 1943, "but I haven't got any voice. I don't know anything about music. I am like the fellow who was dreaming, all he could say was 'don't wake me up.' " Another wartime dispatch said she "seethed her songs with an air of a bashful volcano." That singing style and starring roles in several movies—*Stormy Weather, Death of a Gunfighter, Two Girls and a Sailor,* coupled with television appearances after the war have made her a leading American entertainer.

Even before Miss Horne was on her way to becoming a household name, Josephine Baker, a black singer with an entirely different stage presence, had reached the pinnacle of success in Europe. Josephine Baker Lion Bouillon, known to millions the world over simply as "Josephine," was an international phenomenon who first captured the limelight in the Paris of the 1920s and remained in the public eye until her death in April 1975. Her every move in the cafes of Paris and the continent was reported on this side of the Atlantic.

In the 1920s, Josephine Baker had became the toast of Paris "as a gay darling who lived in a turreted chateau, surrounded herself with monkeys and birds, kept a perfumed pig, walked abroad with two swans on a leash, and fed on rooster combs and champagne." For millions at home watching the world conflagration, counting their ration coupons, and reading about her work for the Free French, she was the exciting "Negro girl" from St. Louis who showed the Europeans how to live. After the Germans occupied Paris in June 1940, Josephine made her way to French North Africa where she lived and worked for the remainder of the war.

In North Africa, Josephine Baker rendered valuable service to Charles de Gaulle and the Free French resistance movement as spy and entertainer. She traveled the length of North Africa and the Middle East entertaining Allied troops until her return to France. With the American landings in Morocco she began singing for GIs almost as soon as they came ashore. Her wartime performances invariably ended with the unfurling of a gargantuan French Tricolor as the band roared out the Marseillaise; and she remained a lifelong friend and confidant of Charles de Gaulle because of her services. By October 1944 she was again back in Paris recording and performing at night spots.

Unlike Lena Horne and Josephine Baker, both of whom gained world renown as performing artists, many top black athletes in the war years were almost unknown to the larger public. A case in point was Joshua "Josh" Gibson, a first-rate black catcher who would have been a valuable asset to any major league club but who was relegated to a career in the relative obscurity of "Negro baseball." Before Jackie Robinson broke the color barrier in organized sports by joining Branch Rickey's Brooklyn Dodgers in 1947, black players were forced to play in the two Negro leagues. Gibson dominated black baseball in 1943, and the immortal Walter Johnson once claimed that the player was worth $200,000 to any white club in the country. And that was before the big-bucks contracts of the postwar era became commonplace.

Gibson, a regular for the Hometown, Pennsylvania, Grays (a team which played a good portion of its games in Washington's Griffith Stadium) earned a reported $750 per month; in addition, he received "an occasional bonus." Sportswriters said the 215-pounder resembled "a very dark Babe Ruth." Moreover, Gibson was well known for his distinctive stance at the plate—with his tongue curled into a circle and sandwiched between his lips, he could literally hit the ball a country mile. He was a consistent long-ball hitter who dazzled the stands with his flashy performances. Against the Memphis Red Sox in 1938, he swatted four home runs in a single game. In 1930 Gibson hit a ball officially measured at 563 feet from home plate at Monessa, Pennsylvania; Babe Ruth had only managed a record 550 feet.

By early July 1943, Gibson was the leading hitter in "Negro baseball." When he reached the .541 mark to lead both leagues, one wire service said "it was a little less than super because he had been at bat only 39 times." His batting average was almost always higher than contemporary white hitters. And the four-baggers continued to pour from his bat. Earlier in 1943 he had hit three homers in Griffith Stadium, one of which sailed 485 feet.

Teams in the two "Negro leagues"—the American and the National —played a fifty-game regular season in 1943 besides 100 or so exhibition games with white semipro and amateur clubs. Although money problems abounded, black teams regularly rented white ball parks in major league cities where they often outdrew their white counterparts. Gibson's team played in Griffith Stadium every Saturday when the Washington Senators were on the road—in one 1943 game, 32,000 fans watched Gibson and the Grays trounce the Cuban Stars. And crowds of whites regularly packed the stands. Satchel Paige was another black player who was a great favorite among white spectators during the 1940s.

The success enjoyed by a handful of black performers and athletes did not typify the lot of blacks in the segregated world of wartime America. Still, the old patterns of discrimination and injustice that had plagued the race since slavery times acted as a catalyst for action because an affront against one was an affront against all. A lengthy court battle involving Odell Waller, a twenty-five-year-old sharecropper, provoked a massive, although unsuccessful, campaign during 1943 to save him from the Virginia electric chair. Black activists, including future Supreme Court justice Thurgood Marshall, who helped file legal briefs in his behalf, and singer Paul Robeson, who gave benefit concerts to raise money for lawyer fees, joined in the effort to save his life. And the Communist-financed Workers' Defense League conducted his losing fight through the Virginia and federal courts. The Defense League later made a last minute appeal to the White House for a stay of execution, although Roosevelt refused to act.

Waller's legal difficulties started in the summer of 1940 when he shot and killed Oscar Davis, his white employer, in rural Pittsylvania County, near Gretna, Virginia. The two had disagreed over division of a wheat crop that Waller farmed on land owned by Davis. Following a row in which Davis refused to give up Waller's share, Waller had whipped out a gun and fired four shots, two of which struck and killed Davis. Prosecution witnesses insisted Davis had promised to give Waller his share of the crop at a later time.

The case attracted national attention after the Defense League and others sympathetic to black and civil rights causes found a constitutional issue. Waller's lawyers contended that the jury, which found him guilty of murder, had all paid a poll tax, and that Waller "belonged to that class which did not pay such taxes." Convinced that their man had been denied equal protection under the law, his defenders launched a countrywide petition-signing and fundraising campaign in his defense. People from every walk of life, including Eleanor Roosevelt, telegraphed and made repeated appeals to save him. But Governor Colgate W. Darden, a later president of the University of Virginia, who "did not believe payment of a tax of $1.50 a year had the effect of dividing the people of the Commonwealth into economic classes," remained unresponsive. He called the drive to rescue Waller a propaganda campaign without regard to legal facts: It had the effect of "sowing racial discord at a critical time when every loyal citizen should strive to promote unity."

After failure to secure his release on the questionable grounds of unfair treatment because he did not pay his poll tax, Waller died, July 2, 1943, in the electric chair at Richmond. When he was executed, this poorly educated man left a poignant statement for reporters; after asking for divine forgiveness, he said that he had "worked hard from sun up to sun down trying to make a living for my family and it ended in death for me. . . . I accident (ly) fell and some good people tried to help me. Others did everything they could against me so the Governor and the coats (courts) don't no (know) the facts." Black churches in Virginia and New York's Harlem joined in a special day of prayer imploring the courts to be "divinely guided and establish democracy for poor folks."

The traumatic Detroit riots in the summer of 1943 were rooted in the very issues raised by Waller's execution: more opportunity and fair play for economically depressed blacks. The violent convulsions that started on June 21—one day after John L. Lewis began his third coal strike—and lasted for nearly a week were the nation's worst wartime disorders. While other riots originated in a distaste for the zoot suit or in work disagreements at isolated defense plants, they were symptomatic of a more basic flaw in American life. Newsweek said Detroit was a "stark explosion of racial hatred burgeoning across the land as war and population shifts threw the races into mounting contact and frictions."

The trouble began on a hot Sunday afternoon at a giant municipal park located on Belle Isle in the Detroit River between Lake St. Clair and Lake Erie. A predominately black crowd, estimated at 5,000, was milling around the lagoons and groves in the huge facility when a "group of whites objected to their monopoly of the park." Officials in Michigan who tried to cope with the explosion were powerless to stem the first brawls on Belle Island that spilled across a bridge into Detroit proper.

Gangs and mobs on both sides gathered reinforcements as full-scale riot-ing broke out after dark.

Before federal troops reinforced military police from Ft. Custer and River Rouge Park with orders "to clear the streets," a rampage convulsed the black east side along Hastings and Woodward Avenues. As evening approached blacks in isolated groups roamed the streets wrecking auto-mobiles, stoning taxicabs, breaking windows, and looting storefronts. Around 8:00 p.m. a policeman trying to stop a fight was shot six times with his own sidearm, and there was widespread sniping at prowl cars from adjacent apartment houses. A shoot-out erupted later as several blacks were spotted entering a building with shotguns and revolvers. Police used tear gas and fired nearly a thousand rounds of ammunition into one apartment before the fight ended two hours later; two blacks and a city officer were killed in the exchange. By 10:30 p.m. twenty blacks and three whites were reported dead. Finally, an uneasy calm was restored around midnight when army troops began patroling the streets with guns at the ready.

Soon 3,500 troops arrived at the request of Governor Harry F. Kelly, who flew into the city from a National Governors Convention at Co-lumbus, Ohio. Kelly immediately declared martial law in the wake of stabbings, shoot-outs, lootings, and brawls over wide parts of the city. His edict covered three surrounding countries—Wayne, Oakland, and Macomb—besides metropolitan Detroit. All firearms were banned, movie houses and places of entertainment closed, and the sale of spirits forbidden. The edict did not, however, close the civil courts nor suspend normal police operations. Roosevelt responded from Washington with an order for all rioters "to disperse and retire peacefully to their respective homes"; and he instructed General Henry S. Aurand and the Sixth Service Command to use whatever force necessary to stop the disturbances.

The episode that had originated with a fight between one black man and one white man on the bridge connecting Belle Isle with the mainland soon had the entire city paralyzed. Rumors of more troubles and Kelly's marital law edicts contributed to a near panic. Nor was the rioting carried out by Negroes alone. The following morning blacks trying to reach jobs in the city were dragged from streetcars along Woodward Avenue, a major thoroughfare, and beaten by angry whites. Private automobiles driven by unsuspecting blacks were set upon and their occupants roughed up. El-ementary schools were forced to close when frightened parents kept their children at home. Because of the riots numerous defense assembly lines ceased production. C. M. Boldson, a local War Production Board official, announced that "very few Negro workers reported for work on the afternoon shift." Officials at a Ford plant said hundreds of black workers left work after getting telephone calls from worried families.

Martial law restrictions were eased on Wednesday, June 23, following a conference between Kelly and military commanders. A postponed game at Briggs Stadium was played between the hometown Tigers and Cleveland Indians under tight military scrutiny. Some 350 "rifle-bearing soldiers" from the Michigan National Guard were on hand to take care of troublemakers. Tiger's managers said the presence of armed troops was a first in the history of major league baseball. An uneventful double header, which took five hours to complete, saw the Tigers take the opener, 3-to-1, and Cleveland the nightcap, 9-to-6, on a game winning homer by Jeff Heath. There was so little to do that most guardsmen spent the evening clustered around the Cleveland dugout "chatting with players and collecting autographs."

If Detroit blacks had reached the breaking point in June 1943, thousands more were actively engaged in winning the war. On the same day that Texas congressman Martin Dies threatened to probe un-Americanism among Detroit blacks, Secretary of War Henry L. Stimson announced, that "the air force's first squadron of black pilots, the Ninety-ninth Fighter Squadron, had weathered its first aerial combat very creditably." Primarily a support and escort fighter group, the Ninety-ninth went on to greater glories in the European war. Commanded by Lieutenant Colonel B. O. Davis, Jr., son of the army's first black general, the outfit shot down several German fighters over Pantelleria, a tiny island between North Africa and Sicily. In a lively engagement, part of Mark Clark and the Fifth Army's drive to land in Italy, the all-black Ninety-ninth had fought the Luftwaffe head on.

Then, right in the midst of the Detroit upheavals, the country faced a new threat when John L. Lewis and the coal miners went on strike for the third time in seven weeks. The June 21–22 walkout certainly slowed heavy production. In Pittsburgh the Carnegie-Illinois Steel Corporation was forced to bank six of its blast furnaces. The company was preparing for deeper cuts because insatiable demands for high defense outputs made the stockpiling of coal impossible. Wartime America simply could not tolerate a major production shutdown, and just as quickly as the strike had started Lewis reacted to public pressure and ordered his men back to the pits.

Amid the incessant outcries by Lewis, the National Headliners Club took time to recognize war correspondent Ernie Pyle for the year's "best foreign feature reporting." Newspaperman Pyle had become the best-known, best-liked reporter of the war years; literally millions read his descriptions of everyday GIs as they fought their way across North Africa and up the Italian peninsula. "Ernest Taylor Pyle," *Time* reported, "is an inconspicuous, frail 110-lb man of 42, homely and quiet-mannered. He looks exactly as if he came smack off an Indiana farm—which he did two decades ago." Like John Hersey and other overseas correspondents, Pyle's accounts in daily newspapers about suffering and dying by regular American Joes contributed to the country's unwillingness to countenance production stoppages by Lewis and other labor chiefs. "It must be hard for you folks at home to conceive how our troops at the front actually live," he had written about the Tunisian fighting: "Some have not slept in a bed for weeks. . . . They never take off their clothes at night, except their shoes. They don't get a bath oftener than once a month. . . . Nobody keeps track of the days or weeks. . . . You find men sleeping anywhere, any time."

Pyle, also described as "pixey-like," had begun his newspaper career on the La Porte, Indiana, *Herald*. In 1923, he had joined the Washington *Daily News* as a reporter. "By 1932, after a brief fling at Manhattan newsrooms, he became the *Daily News's* managing editor. Unhappy, in 1935, he asked for a roving assignment. Pyle has been a roving reporter ever since prowling around the United States, Alaska, South and Central America, by train, ship, plane, horseback but mostly by auto, and writing chatty, personalized copy, always digging out the ignored, and ignoring the obvious." Although numerous trophies befell the unassuming Pyle, including an honorary doctorate from Indiana University, he did not survive the war. Ernie Pyle was killed by "Japanese machine-gun fire" on the island of Ie, west of Okinawa, at age forty-four during 1945 at the height of his wartime popularity.

As the country read Pyle's folksy accounts of GIs in battle throughout the summer, the Supreme Court handed down a landmark decision on June 14 upholding a longstanding complaint by the Jehovah's Witness sect. A basic tenet of the fundamentalist group was refusal to salute the Stars and Stripes, which they viewed as being sacrilegious and contrary to Holy Writ. For them, the flag symbolized the earthly power and dominion of the state, which they considered evil. All kingdoms and states, according to their interpretation of Scripture, would be swept away after the final battle of Armageddon; to salute the flag therefore was to take part in a ritual opposed to the divine plan. They rejected military service for the same reasons.

The salute controversy had been around since 1898, when New York enacted a statute requiring a pledge of allegiance by all schoolchildren during the Spanish American War. Occasional difficulties had arisen during the years when other states passed similiar laws; but the patriotic fervor associated with World War I spurred an avalanche of statutes that required daily flag exercises on pain of expulsion from the public schools. Though the Supreme Court had ruled against the Jehovah's Witnesses three years earlier in a case involving Pennsylvania children, the high tribunal reversed itself in June 1943. The wartime case that prompted the ruling that all salute laws were unconstitutional started in Kanawha County, West Virginia, where children from two Jehovah's Witness families were barred from school for refusing to participate in flag ceremonies.

In January 1942 the West Virginia State Board of Education had ordered "that during the formative period in citizenship, schoolchildren should exercise patriotism by saluting the emblem of freedom." When opposition to the edict began to mount, the state panel ruled that "mere possession of convictions which contradict the relevant concerns of political society does not relieve the citizen from the discharge of political responsibility."

This set the stage for a near explosion in the hollow communities around the capital city at Charleston where the Witness movement was strong; there were three congregations in Charleston alone and the sect was active throughout the state. Among those expelled from Kanawha County schools were two small daughters of Walter Barnette, who worked in a local petrochemicals plant. Barnette and his family had long associations with the church and adhered rigidly to its teachings.

Witness lawyers filed a class action suit in behalf of the Barnette children as well as all those removed from the schools, several of them children of Barnette's relatives. Moreover, extensive litigation resulted from a countersuit by the state attorney general who sought compliance with the salute order by the recalcitrant families. The U.S. Supreme Court, which chose to hand down its decision in *West Virginia State Board of Education vs. Barnette* on Flag Day 1943, "upheld the right of Jehovah's Witnesses to refuse to salute the American flag at public schools contrary to their sect's beliefs," by a 6-to-3 vote. Justices William O. Douglas and Hugo Black, both of whom had voted against the church in the earlier case, reversed themselves when the West Virginia appeal reached the high court. "Long reflection," they declared in separate opinions, had convinced them "that neither our domestic tranquillity in peace nor our national effort in war depend on compelling little children to participate in a ceremony which ends in nothing for them but a fear of spiritual condemnation."

June 1943 was by far the worst period for domestic protest, although more racial and labor unrest was to plague the country before the year was out. Still, the American Civil Liberties Union reported in July that the country was experiencing less hysteria and fewer infringements on the civil rights of individuals than it had during World War I. The organization, however, did take Washington to task for internment of Japanese-Americans in what it termed "virtual concentration camps." Others contended that, at one such camp anyway—Tule Lake in the farmlands of northern California—18,000 Japanese internees reportedly had everything they needed for a comfortable life except personal liberty. Nonetheless, although most residents at the Japanese-American "relocation centers" lived quiet lives waiting for the war to end, several hundred internees considered "fanatically disloyal" by authorities had either been jailed or placed under surveillance.

Overall, despite protests from interned Japanese, disgruntled labor unionists, and economically depressed blacks, the ACLU concluded there was "no organized, powerful radical and pacifist opposition to the war." The country was plainly in favor of Washington's war policies at home and overseas. The riots and disturbances during the summer were nothing but temporary aberrations in the drive for total victory. The overwhelming majority of Americans continued to see the struggle against Germany and Japan as righteous vindication of the national honor.

*FDR, 1944, by B. Movin-Hermes,
photographer to the King of Sweden.*

*Lord Beaverbrook meets with OPM
representatives, August 1941. (l to r)
Sidney Hillman, John Lord O'Brian,
Edward Stettinius jr., Lord Beaverbrook,
William Knudsen.*

*Supply Priorities and Allocations Board,
September, 1941. (Seated, l to r) Harry
Hopkins, William S. Knudsen, Henry
A. Wallace, Donald M. Nelson.
(Standing, l to r) James Forrestal,
Robert Patterson, Leon Henderson,
Sidney Hillman.*

Program for 1942 Rose Bowl.

*Production conversion in auto plants,
January, 1942. (l to r) R. J. Thomas
(UAW-CIO President), Sidney Hillman,
Leon Henderson, Paul Hoffman
(President, Studebaker), William S.
Knudsen, C. E. Wilson.*

Cocoanut Grove, Boston,
November 1942.

Salvage begins
on the Liner Normandie,
February 10, 1942.

Col. Oveta Culp Hobby,
April 1943.

Women war workers—
westcoast aircraft factory,
May 1942.

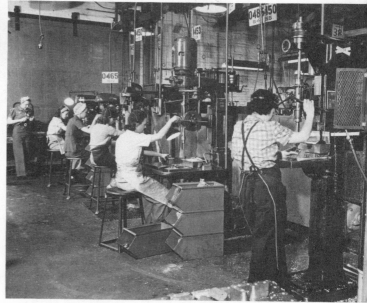

"Old Mr. Kondo" in
Tanforan Assembly
Center, San Bruno,
California, June 1942.

America's arsenal of democracy:
P-38's roll off the assembly line,
July 1942.

W. Lee O'Daniel's hillbilly band, 1942.

*Comedian Eddie Cantor sells war
bonds.*

*Actress Joan Blondell on USO
Tour, April 1943.*

USO "Flying Boat" Tours—Laurel and Hardy in the Caribbean, April 1943.

*Comedienne
Judy Canova tells
country to save
scrap rubber,
September 1942.*

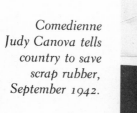

They've got more important
places to go than you!...

Save Rubber
CHECK YOUR TIRES NOW

"A Streetcar Named Desire," New Orleans.

Pete Gray, Memphis Chicks, 1943.

Wartime disasters—Philadelphia, September 1943.

*Launching of the S.S. Carol Lombard, Wilmington ship yard,
January 1944. Irene Dunne breaks bottle; Clark Gable and Louis
B. Mayer lend a hand.*

*Ashford Hospital,
located at fashionable
Greenbrier resort in
West Virginia,
March 21, 1944.*

Mrs. Roosevelt in South Pacific, 1943?

Wartime travel: Union Station, St. Louis, July 4th, 1944.

*Barbershop at Parker, Arizona, c. 1944, near Colorado River Center
for Japanese Americans.*

*New President Harry
S. Truman confers
with Texas Senator
Tom Connally and
Under Secretary of
War Robert P. Patter-
son, April 13, 1945.*

Richard Wright, author of Black Boy, *in his Paris apartment after the war, 1948.*

Joe Louis chats with General Benjamin O. Davis at an American base in the European theater of operations, August 1945.

Rosie The Riveter: Women war workers. Exact date unknown.

*St. Louis Browns clinch 1944
Pennant before record 37,815
fans, October 2, 1944.*

THE GREENBRIER

*Convalescent GI's playing golf during stay at
Greenbrier Resort. Date unknown.*

Roosevelt funeral train, Greenville, South Carolina, April 1945.

Roosevelt burial at Hyde Park, April 1945.

General Leslie Groves and
Robert J. Oppenheimer
at Los Alamos, July 16,
1945.

*Alamogordo, July 16, 1945. (l to r) Ernest Lawrence,
Enrico Fermi, I. I. Rabi.*

Nagasaki, August 1945.

7 JULY-DECEMBER 1943:
A SUBVERSIVE AUTUMN

After the raucous events of June, the country settled into quiet acceptance of the war for the remainder of 1943. *Life*, the pictorial magazine of Henry R. Luce which found its way into millions of homes, ran an article in November depicting life in Hamilton, Ohio, as scarcely ruffled by the war. It focused on the 300 block of Progress Avenue between Rhea and Gray Streets: "Its two-story frame houses, some white clapboard and some brown shingle, all are set back from the sidewalk by pieces of lawn. Maple and sycamore trees, their branches into each other over the roadway, grow in straight rows down the block." Barely 230 miles south of battle-torn Detroit on the Miami River, Hamilton in wartime was described as "an American Anyplace—plain, satisfied, friendly." War, the photographic essay said, "has not yet scarred or even marked this block."

There was not even noise until the morning hours when children clamored off to school. While husbands worked—a junior high school mathematics teacher, a physician, an industrial foreman, a monument company owner, a draftsman, wives kept house and "rolled bandages two days a week at the Elks club"; other families were pictured preparing boxes of "goodies" for sons in service or writing daily letters to them as neighborhood children whizzed down leaf-covered streets on roller skates: "This is a very lucky block in a world so full of misfortune; it accepts its luck without questioning it. But in the even current of life, the block has a tremendous reserve of power, a great strength built up by its peaceful ways."

Not everyone could remain in safe havens like Hamilton. The wholesale movement of people around the country continued at a fast clip. The nation's antiquated rail network—most of it built in the decades following the Civil War with little subsequent upgrading—transported most of the migrants and was vastly overworked. And it was plagued by a rash of spectacular train wrecks in 1943 when hardly a month passed without additional disasters. Fourteen people died on May 23 at Delair, New Jersey, aboard a fifteen-car passenger train bound from Atlantic City to New York. The train had left the tracks two miles north of Camden. A baby was born during the derailment, but the mother perished.

Miraculously, 150 passengers escaped death and serious injury aboard a Worchester-to-Boston run which derailed near Smithville, Massachusetts, on June 24. The engine and five coaches—two of which burst into flames—wrecked after two army fighter planes collided "at a high altitude and plummeted" onto the tracks. Two young boys "ran around a bend in the railroad tracks to halt the train which was due soon after the crash. One of them pulled off his red shirt and waved it as a signal, but the engineer was unable to stop," said one press account. The engineer, who was injured slightly, told authorities that heat from the burning planes caused the rails to spread apart. One of the pilots was killed while the other parachuted to safety.

One of the worst rail disasters happened September 6 at Frankfort Junction inside the city of Philadelphia. Like many other rail mishaps it resulted from equipment failure on grossly overworked trains. The wreck, which occurred four miles east of North Philly Station from a burned-out "journal" (the housing at the end of an axle), claimed eighty victims. The Congressional Limited, the "famous Washington-to-New York express of the Pennsylvania Railroad," was rounding a curve at nearly seventy miles an hour when the bearing gave way between Glenwood and Frankfort Avenues. Immediately the seventh car—the passenger coach with the defective journal—shot vertically into the air. "As it came down it dragged with it from the tracks a second coach, two diners, and four Pullman chair cars, but the last two cars of the train remained on the tracks. So did the first six cars, although the rear truck of the sixth car was derailed."

More than eighty people were found in a single coach, and said a news dispatch, "all eight of the derailed cars were sprawled like match sticks across the four tracks of the Pennsylvania's main line." Although FBI agents rushed to the scene to search for evidence of sabotage, an earlier scrutiny by government inspectors found the tracks in good shape. Servicemen among the 541 passengers performed heroic rescue efforts among crash survivors. One sailor smacked a frenzied woman inside an overturned coach telling her "to close your damn mouth before everyone in here becomes hysterical." The New York *Times* account said that "quieted her down."

American railroads had done yeomen service during World War I but had fallen into disrepair like other parts of the transportation–industrial system during the Depression years. The advent of war found the country with 25 percent fewer freight cars, 30 percent fewer passenger coaches, and 32 percent fewer engines than had been operational during World War I. In World War II operation of rail lines was further complicated because the 1917 war required shipment to Atlantic coast ports only; empty freight and troop trains could be returned to points of origin without difficulty. War with Japan and Germany, however, necessitated rail traffic to both coasts and played havoc with the nation's rail handling capability. "Between Pearl Harbor and V-J Day," writes railroad authority John F. Stover, "American railroads furnished 97 percent of all domestic troop movements and about 90 percent of all domestic movements of Army and Navy equipment supplies. In the forty-five months of war, 113,891 special troop trains moved 43,700,000 members of the armed forces, or an average of nearly a million men a month." That was in addition to the heavy flow of civilians.

A Senate investigating committee chaired by Missouri Senator Harry S. Truman released a December 1943 report which said changes were necessary to keep the trains running. Heavy use of equipment and trackage caused the panel to warn it was "folly to assume that there is no limit to the strain the transportation system will stand." Earlier the German propaganda machine had speculated that the nation's rail network could become America's Achilles' heel; Truman's committee apparently agreed and called for increased production of "freight cars, passenger cars, rails, trucks, buses, and tires." Otherwise, it said, wartime transportation would collapse. Some weeks earlier WPB and the Office of Defense Transportation (ODT) had authorized several lines to begin manufacture and use of diesel-powered locomotives, an order that changed the fundamental nature of American railroading for all time. It spelled an end to the romance of steam locomotives with raw displays of power on the rails. Within a few years they were replaced by impersonal diesel-driven electric engines that moved down the tracks of America like innocuous boxes of green cheese.

Despite home-front acceptance of the war in late 1943, constant reminders of the conflict remained near at hand. Housewives still had to count their ration coupons; and the availability of meat for the family table became a political issue during the fall when an actual beef–pork glut developed from a meat shortage. An over-supply of meat resulted from an OPA policy of price supports on a per pound basis for cattle and hogs which caused midwestern farmers to hold livestock from the slaughterhouse and to feed them corn for maximum weight. Farm groups and no less a politico than New York Mayor Fiorello LaGuardia repeatedly lambasted OPA for subsidizing farmers to withhold animals from the marketplace. Because the practice led to short-term shortages, LaGuardia suggested that Canada, which had plenty of meat but little liquor, work out a swap with New York City, which had plenty of liquor but no meat. His criticism of OPA heated up in early September; changes had to come, he roared, or OPA would "bust wide open."

Unmoved by pleas from around the country, Chester Bowles, acting OPA administrator after the resignation of Leon Henderson, ordered nationwide registration for War Ration Book No. 4 on September 15. The new coupon book had the same approach to meat and other food items, although OPA spokesmen were hopeful it would be the last ration book needed for the duration. Housewives were required to sign up for the new book at schoolhouses during the last ten days of October; a notorious, somewhat flimsy plastic token was distributed in January for use with the coupons.

Vacation time in 1943 also produced difficulties because of travel restrictions and the absence of gasoline and tires for family automobiles. Defense work had stuffed plenty of wallets, but there was scant opportunity to spend money on travel or the good life. On the East Coast the use of private cars was illegal even to visit an army camp, and travel by rail or air was out of the question without special permission. From Washington the Office of Defense Transportation put out a blurb urging people not to travel far and to do so only on "slack days." One-day vacations were recommended. "If you can't go fishing, go to the aquarium and look at the fish," suggested the Chicago Chamber of Commerce: "Interested in faraway places? Visit the new foreign exhibits at the Field Museum." Newly constructed miniature golf courses popped up in Atlanta for the stay-at-home crowd; and in New York "bicycle renters" reported a hot demand throughout the summer while the Bronx Zoo registered record attendances.

For people in Boise City, Oklahoma (population 1,144), there was more than enough excitement in 1943 without leaving home. Although no one was injured, six bombs—each with four pounds of explosives and ninety-six pounds of sand and shell—landed in the middle of town at one o'clock in the morning. The panhandle town twenty miles from the Texas border was bombed on a clear July night by a "fledgling pilot" from a training squadron at Dalhart, Texas, forty-five miles to the south. "We ran as fast as we could," Coleen Jones said. The "daytime soda dispenser" had just left a local movie theater for a stroll through the courthouse square with four other girls and their soldier dates from Dalhart when the bombs rained down. Frank Garrett, a power company worker, saved the town serious trouble by running out of the Southwestern Public Service building and pulling the city's main power switch.

The plane unleashed its payload from 30,000 feet on a Baptist church and Forrest Bourke's garage in the center of town. A door was blown ajar and a stained glass window broken at the church which prompted a quip from Pastor R. D. Dobbs: "If one fourth of the people who came to see the hole made by the bomb would only come to church." In the flat, open spaces of the Southwest the lights of Boise City had been mistaken for a practice bombing range near Colin, Texas, used regularly by fliers from Dalhart and located thirty miles to the southeast. The Boise City *News* was induced to demand more searchlights and antiaircraft guns after the excitement.

While mainstream America wrestled with the pinpricks of war and braced for the draft net to reach the fathers of small children in late 1943, unresolved social flaws remained to torment the country. Racial disturbances during July and August again rocked several urban centers, including St. Louis and New York's Harlem. In St. Louis racial disharmony was primarily confined to talk interspersed with random incidents—racial slurs, innuendoes, and fisticuffs between whites and blacks. Great numbers of blacks from the upper South had crowded into St. Louis looking for jobs during the Depression years, increasing the area's minority population appreciably. And an already difficult situation of fitting the newcomers into an essentially Southern milieu was agitated by the migrations of low-income—in the 1970s and 1980s they would be called "deprived"—whites looking for defense jobs after 1940. The whites came mostly from the Ozarks of Arkansas and the Flat River country of southern Missouri, where blacks were rare and racial feeling acute. The southern whites found work in the defense plants, often as foremen or skilled workers, while black job-seekers were pushed aside.

A further strain was created by nearby Jefferson Barracks, which housed a high concentration of "Negro troops." With black soldiers readily visible on St. Louis streets and seething resentment among black civilians over jobs, rumors of potential racial conflict swept the city in the weeks following the Detroit riots. The heresay reports took the form of anonymous phone calls, postcards, and letters to the mayor's office, police, newspapers, civic organizations, religious leaders, and to prominent community leaders. Finally a "rumor clinic" was set up to search out trouble spots, a move that diffused an explosive situation.

The lid blew off, however, in New York's Harlem during August when a racial explosion resulted in the death of six blacks, injury to 550 rioters and police, and a dusk-to-dawn curfew for the whole borough. Mayor LaGuardia was on the radio from the outset appealing for calm, and proclaiming that "shame" had come to New York: "This was not a race riot. This was the thoughtless, criminal acts of hoodlums, reckless, irresponsible people."

Newsweek said Harlem in 1943 was New York's "inner city of Negroes, a vast stretch of squalid tenements, unabating noise, and crowded streets extending from Central Park and east of 8th Avenue." A majority of the 300,000 people jammed into the area were good citizens, but, the magazine continued, "as a jungle of jive, of cheap poisonous liquor, marijuana, and frequent muggings, it has been the city's major sociological problem. Since Detroit, police had dreaded the spark that would set off the dynamite." The fuse was ignited on a sweltering Sunday night when police were summoned to quiet "a disorderly Negro woman" at a Harlem hotel. An off-duty black M.P., who happened to be nearby and who objected to the ensuing arrest, clubbed a white policeman. Then, in a fast-developing scenario, the city policeman pulled his revolver and fired a single shot that slightly wounded the M.P.

Although no one was seriously injured, news of the encounter swept the city. Within half an hour thousands of angry blacks poured from tenement houses and bars, and began to loot liquor stores, grocery stores, and pawn shops, and smash windows and burn automobiles. More M.P.s, many of them black, were rushed in to clear the streets of black soldiers on leave who had joined the rioters. The disorders lasted a full twenty-four hours before police and army troops restored calm. Long afterwards, LaGuardia and other authorities held to the line that the riots were the work of hooligans. Yet undeniably, the pent-up frustrations of blacks who were crowded into "cramped, rabbit-warren housing" and deprived of economic advantages fueled the outbreak. In addition to the six blacks killed, more than 500 people of both races were injured, nearly 400 people were arrested, and property losses exceeded $1,000,000.

National tranquillity was shattered once more during the first days of November when John L. Lewis and the soft-coal miners went on strike for the fourth time. Lewis, who continued his war of nerves with Roosevelt and the WLB, ordered the new walkout to begin at midnight, October 30. It ended the truce between Ickes and the United Mine Workers that had been in effect since the third work stoppage in June. Although it was another short strike that terminated on November 3, every union miner in the country obeyed the "no contract, no work" dictum. And it was the usual story. The nation lost more than 2,000,000 tons in coal production as Lewis pressed for his vaunted two dollar-a-day pay hike.

Roosevelt acted quickly, again ordering government seizure of the mines as WLB struggled to preserve Little Steel and "to hold the line" on salary increases. This time, however, the crafty union boss got what he wanted. When finally hammered out by government negotiators, his new agreement granted the miners increased wages for overtime and travel, although the additional money was less than Lewis had demanded, and the UMWA was forced into one small concession—lunch hour in the pits was reduced by fifteen minutes. An elated Lewis, suffering from influenza throughout the hassle, told newsmen it was "a satisfactory wage agreement."

Peace had no sooner returned to the coal fields than other union chiefs began eyeing the coal pact and calculating their own chances for pay hikes. It made no difference that OPA had recommended in late November a 60¢ per ton increase in the price of coal to offset production costs. Others wanted in on the action. And mounting pressure for higher wages influenced Washington planners to relax their hard-line stance. *Time* reported in November that "since enactment of the Smith-Connally Act, NLRB had had 404 notices for strike votes. Out of 69 strike elections, 64 resulted in strike calls, almost all to put pressure on WLB. This was the real meaning, and the big news behind the country's 4th coal strike."

Although Little Steel was dead by late 1943 and individual workers could expect higher pay envelopes for the remainder of the war, other economic-business confrontations gripped Washington. A long-boiling dispute within FDR's inner circle came to a head during mid-July that materially affected Washington's handling of overseas business transactions. The disagreement, which developed between Vice President Henry A. Wallace, who doubled as overseer of the Board of Economic Warfare, and the wealthy Texan, Jesse Holman Jones, secretary of commerce and head of the Reconstruction Finance Corporation (RFC), was part personal, part ideological. Since the heady days of March–June 1933, when Roosevelt put his New Deal into operation, a threatening conservative–liberal split had lain below the surface of all Democratic party deliberations. But following Pearl Harbor, FDR had worked to hold party liberals in check and to placate the conservative faction concentrated primarily in the South in order to prosecute the war.

Wallace, who had impeccable credentials to lead the liberals, had been a New Dealer from the start, as well as Roosevelt's secretary of agriculture, 1933–1941. He sprang from a long tradition of midwestern agricultural liberalism, though like all the Wallaces, he had started as a Republican stalwart. His father, Henry C. Wallace, had served as secretary of agriculture under Harding and Coolidge, and his grandfather, the first Henry Wallace, had turned down the same post in McKinley's administration. Following graduation from Iowa State in 1910, young Wallace went to work as an agricultural experimenter and writer for the widely-distributed *Wallace's Farmer*, founded by his grandfather at Des Moines. The family, including Henry Agard Wallace, shifted away from the Republicans in 1928 after Al Smith and the Democrats embraced the McNary-Haugen Farm Bill, which called for liberalization of national farm policy. During his editorial years at Des Moines and also as vice president, Wallace spoke out forcibly for a wide spectrum of economic, political, and social reforms. When Roosevelt asked him to head BEW upon its creation in December 1941, Wallace seized the opportunity to put his philosophy of government and international relations into operation. BEW, which replaced the earlier Economic Defense Board, was designed "to negotiate directly with foreign governments in matters pertaining to the shipping and procurement of all strategic materials." Wallace and Milo Perkins, his chief lieutenant at BEW, according to Wallace's biographers, "considered speed, sure acquisition of scarce materials, and international goodwill more important than mere price tags."

Jesse Jones, on the other hand, epitomized the conservative wing of the party and remained fixed in the conviction that New Dealers and Wallace in particular were a bunch of liberal visionaries. The Texan had generaled RFC since its formation under Herbert Hoover in 1932 and he remained in Washington under FDR as director of the agency and also as secretary of commerce, 1940–1945. RFC had been used to finance most New Deal programs for national recovery from the Depression, and the 1941 War Powers Act extended its functions "to create subsidiary corporations, first for advancing national defense and then for furthering the war effort." Jones therefore not only held the purse strings over Wallace but also ran RFC according to strict banking practices. He frequently balked at handing over money for BEW activities, and later wrote in his memoirs that Wallace ran operations at BEW that were "practically eleemosynary in nature."

In addition, personal animosities separated the two men, animosities that Roosevelt tried to ignore. Jones had wanted the vice-presidential nomination after FDR decided to replace his fellow Texan John Nance Garner on the national ticket. And following the 1940 election each man grabbed the newspaper headlines with sensational charges that the other had muffed the pre-Pearl Harbor rubber-stockpiling program. Things came to a head in July 1943 when the president was forced to intervene in the dispute between his vice president and his secretary of commerce. The interagency wrangling was further complicated by injudicious statements made by Milo Perkins. Perkins had just lost a young son fighting with the Marines, and he looked upon Jones as a conservative obstructionist to the war effort.

While reporters enjoyed a field day with the counter accusations and innuendoes, Roosevelt called upon James F. Byrnes, director of the Office of War Mobilization, to settle the dispute. An earlier White House mandate had warned administration functionaries not to criticize other agencies in public or through press leaks. "I ask you," Roosevelt had written to department heads, "that when you release a statement for publication, you send me a letter of resignation." With Wallace and Jones in clear violation of that order, the impasse was resolved by abolishing BEW and creating a new agency under Byrnes's control, the Office of Economic Warfare headed by Leo T. Crowley. *Newsweek* said Crowley was a "New Deal administrator from way back, and a relatively conservative one."

The foreign purchasing bottleneck was no sooner resolved than the administration moved on a wide front to insure a better flow of manufactured goods for domestic use. And it was clear from directives out of Washington that the war was perceived to be winding down. In December 1943, six months before the Normandy invasion and another twenty months before the Japanese surrender, Fred M. Vinson, who had taken over as director of economic stabilization in May, told manufacturers the "War Production Board would formulate plans and programs to secure the production, in needed volume, of essential consumer goods." The Kentucky congressman turned federal judge who became chief justice of the Supreme Court after the war, ordered Donald Nelson at WPB and Chester Bowles at OPA to implement the new policy immediately. Businessmen objected to Vinson's directive that manufacturers produce items for domestic consumption at cost if need be, or face the prospect of having profit-making raw materials withheld from them. But it also meant civilian life would improve in the months ahead.

A further indication of a widening gulf between home front and war front was increased lobbying by special interest groups for advantage while wartime regulations remained. Everybody wanted the country to win on the battlefield, but no one wanted to be left out in the scramble for defense dollars or peacetime upsmanship. An undoubted overoptimism about how soon peace would return pervaded the country during the autumn; congressmen and bureaucrats at every level were swamped with demands for relaxed restrictions from every conceivable sector. Everybody from organized labor to midwestern farmers clamored for adjustment in governmental mandates to fit their notions of the good life. But politicians soon learned it was disaster to court the special interest lobbyists.

Although a lessening of war-induced strictures on the economy continued and Washington worked to increase the supply of household goods, domestic shortages in many areas remained. Cigarettes for instance—at least the desired brands—were often difficult to purchase in many communities. And smoking was at universally high levels throughout the war years among civilians and servicemen alike; the rush for cigarettes was so great in some communities that even children were hurried off to corner drugstores or the neighborhood grocery to stand in line for "a couple of packs" after word of a new shipment. It became almost a badge of manhood for young men to walk about with a cigarette package tucked tightly in the shirt sleeve. The wide usage of tobacco to relieve tension during World War II—in the days before tranquilizers—may well explain the upsurge of cancer-related deaths during the 1970s and 1980s.

After two years of war, civilians had not only learned to cope with shortages and make-do substitutes, they had also became adept at circumventing Washington-imposed regulations. By the end of 1943 an under-the-counter black market was operating all over the country to furnish whatever people wanted. It was not an organized, illicit operation, simply average folks getting around restrictions on wartime living to secure cigarettes, gasoline, scarce food items, or rationed clothing. Mark Miller, an enterprising Texas newspaper reporter, found a way to make an issue of what everyone knew—that gasoline could be purchased with or without official coupons. Miller set out from Brownsville on the Rio Grande in his private automobile without a single gasoline coupon and ended up in International Falls, Minnesota, on the Canadian border. He not only used 123 gallons of bootlegged gas but he also got enough coupons along the way for an additional 190 gallons. After selling his story to *Collier's* magazine, OPA revoked his 1944 ration book with a slap-on-the-wrist, warning that "the war effort would be promoted better by emphasizing individual responsibility. . . . rather than pointing how easy it is to break the law."

Nose-thumbing at food rationing became nearly as rampant as the use of black market gasoline. The War Food Administration in December put out a report which claimed that "American pantries are bulging with the largest stocks of canned goods in history." Housewives continued to can food raised in victory gardens or bought from local farmers in massive quantities; but extra food did not keep them from using every available coupon, which in turn led to widespread hoarding. "Most housewives," *Newsweek* continued, "use up their points regardless of home canned supplies, storing up their purchases."

But 1943 Christmas shoppers found fewer gift items than the year before, and the widespread hoarding of food was undoubtedly influenced by an absence of consumer merchandise on local store shelves. It was as if a general get-what-you-can psychology gripped the country. About the only items not in short supply at year's end were, of all things, comic books. Even in the face of 15 percent reductions in paper allotments, roughly two dozen publishers turned out 125 titles a year which were purchased as quickly as they hit the newsstand, primarily by well-heeled schoolchildren and servicemen. About twenty-five million copies of "escapist" comic fare were sold monthly during 1943 with a price tag set at $30 million. Although youngsters read most of the 10¢ "funny books," men in uniform were a close second; a 35,000-copy special edition of *Superman* was dispatched monthly to our overseas forces.

The serious-minded Christmas shopper, however, was hard-pressed to find suitable gifts because of lingering shortages. Whiskey, for instance, became nearly impossible to buy for holiday cheer because of an edict that distillers hold 100 million gallons of a 303 million gallon supply in reserve for postwar use. Rum quickly became the country's number one selling liquor, and when a Washington store advertised it "had 8,000 bottles of real rye, bourbon, and scotch for sale," *Time* reported: "A mob that made a football crowd seem tame waited outside through ten freezing hours for a chance to carry a bottle away." With patience, gifts other than the second-rate neckties which were reportedly in good supply might be found on store counters. Good, dependable toys, children's clothes, and metal household items were nonexistent, and parents had to content themselves with flimsy cardboard and wood substitutes. And worst of all, the desirable but scarce items were expensive because money was no object for many shoppers. A large downtown store in San Francisco discovered that its customers had given up on finding the "right" Christmas present and had fallen back to a reliable standby: the gift certificate.

"OPA did it!" or "It's OPA's fault!" was the popular cry whenever items were difficult to find on the open market or were restricted because of rationing. The Office of Price Administration, the famous or infamous OPA of World War II, touched literally every household and, rightly or wrongly, remained public enemy number one in the eyes of most Americans. By the close of 1943 the agency was regulating eight million prices and thus the availability of goods in three million business places. Through its coupon rationing operations it had direct contact with thirty million housewives and thirty-nine million automobile owners.

Despite never-ending hassles with wartime rationing, not only comic books but amusements of every kind, including the movies, stayed in demand as popular diversions. Hollywood's latest outpourings made local theaters a hub of activity in the days before television. Everyone from junior to grandpop flocked to feature films—many of them with war related themes—the minute they hit town. It was the golden age of filmmaking with actors catching the public imagination in a way that is almost difficult to understand in the 1980s. More times than not, the films were accompanied by "selected short subjects" that included cartoons and adventure serials like *Commander Don Winslow and the U.S. Navy*. Such entertainment not only drove home the immediacy of war but also bred an intense patriotism and allegiance to national policy. During October alone, estimates of total movie admissions reached $145 million—a $16 million increase over October 1942.

An offshoot of the nearly universal movie going was a widespread interest in the personal lives of movie stars which were reported on in numerous magazines and daily newspaper columns. *The Motion Picture Herald*, a trade publication, released a survey in November listing Hollywood's ten most glamorous stars in terms of box office draw. Many of those listed remained household names long after the war: 1) Betty Grable, 2) Bob Hope, 3) Abbott and Costello, 4) Bing Crosby, 5) Gary Cooper, 6) Greer Carson, 7) Humphrey Bogart, 8) Jimmy Cagney, 9) Mickey Rooney, 10) Clark Gable. Betty Grable, who was married to Harry James, the popular dance-band leader and trumpeter, was not only a widely-photographed glamor girl but also the number one pinup girl for fighting men at home and overseas. Humphrey Bogart, a stage actor turned movie performer, shot into the top ten for the first time after his stunning appearances in *The Petrified Forest, The Maltese Falcon, The High Sierra,* and the greatest World War II film classic of all, *Casablanca*, with Ingrid Bergman. (He had been twenty-fifth on the list the previous year.) Even more spectacular was the audience appeal of Clark Gable, whose memorable performance as the dashing Rhett Butler in *Gone With the Wind* fixed his place in movie history for all time. Gable had been in the top ten since 1932 when the *Herald* survey first appeared. Rated tenth in the 1943 poll, he had made only one movie in 1943 because he was serving as an air force captain in Europe, where he really flew combat missions.

An actor not on the top ten list but nonetheless one of the best-loved movie stars of all time was Charles Spencer Chaplin, Jr.—the immortal Charlie Chaplin—known the world over for his portrayals of a lovable but rascally screen tramp. Chaplin found himself embroiled in a sensational scandal during 1943–1944. Not since the romantic escapades of Errol Flynn had the press latched on to a story so intensely, primarily because of Chaplin's worldwide visibility. Television host and author Alistair Cooke wrote in 1977 that "throughout the 1920s and into the 1930s Chaplin was the most famous man on earth. . . . He was mobbed by ordinary people of all types, of all ages, was known to every country, and was the sought-after guest of kings, statesmen, authors, artists, celebrities of every sort." His fame rested on his movie roles as a tramp with baggy pants and small derby, a figure who in his own words, "was a gentleman, a poet, a dreamer, a lonely fellow, always hopeful of romance and adventure. He would have you believe he was a scientist, a musician, a duke, a polo player. However, he is not above picking up a cigarette butt or robbing a baby of its candy. And of course, if the occasion warrants it, he will kick a lady in the rear—but only in extreme anger."

Chaplin's troubles started in June 1943 when Joan Barry, a twenty-three-year-old actress and onetime friend of oil tycoon J. Paul Getty, accused him of fathering her unborn child. Miss Barry was "well-built," Chaplin wrote in his autobiography about their first meeting at a California restaurant, "with upper regional domes immensely expansive and made alluring by an extremely low decolleté summer dress, which on the drive home, evoked my libidinous curiosity." Cooke, who knew Chaplin personally, also writes: "From his earliest slapstick days, when director, cast, actors, and crew were vagabonds, there was always some mischief brewing with one or other of the Mack Sennett bathing beauties. . . . He was also remarkably handsome, extremely attractive to women and instantly susceptible to them." And the actor himself summarized his often uproarious affairs with characteristic accuracy: "Procreation is nature's principal occupation and every man, whether he be young or old, when meeting any woman, measures the potentiality of sex between them. Thus it has always been with me."

When the Joan Barry scandal hit every front page in the country, Chaplin stoutly proclaimed his innocence of paternity charges. Unabashed, Barry filed suit to have Chaplin pay a $10,000 lump sum for "medical expenses" plus child support in the amount of $2,500 per month. The court, however, ruled on June 17 that settlement of the case must await birth of the child in September. At that time three physicians—Chaplin's, Barry's and a third mutually agreed upon—would determine if Chaplin was indeed the the father. If the medicos said maybe—a positive yes was medically impossible—Miss Barry could press her claims for support.

Chaplin, who never relinquished his British passport, and who was knighted by Queen Elizabeth in 1975, was working on a film, *Monsieur Verdoux*, when the scandal became public. Ironically, he had met a daughter of playwright Eugene O'Neill, whom he subsequently married in June 1943 while fighting the Barry suit; seventeen-year-old Oona O'Neill became his fourth wife.

When Barry's daughter was born in October, three months after the O'Neill marriage, a panel of doctors declared Chaplin was not the father because of blood differences. But Joan Barry engaged a lawyer of the old school, Joseph Scott, who attacked Chaplin in an April 1944 trial on personal and emotional grounds; he simply ignored the blood tests. Scott not only wondered aloud why Chaplin had never bothered to become a citizen, but also engaged in damaging courtroom theatrics. After accusing the actor of past indiscretions, sexual and otherwise, he had Joan Barry hold her infant daughter so the jury could compare her looks with Chaplin. That did it. After a three-hour deliberation, the jury found for Barry, whereupon the presiding judge ordered Chaplin to make monthly support payments until the child reached twenty-one. The imbroglio made spicy reading for the home front and when it ended, Chaplin faithfully complied with the court judgment.

A genuine tragedy struck wartime Hollywood in November—while the Barry-Chaplin scandal was in full swing—when Lou Costello's young son drowned in the family swimming pool. In the amusement-crazed atmosphere of the 1940s "capering, cornfed" comedian Costello and his straightman partner Bud Abbott, were the nation's best known funnymen. Their silly, slapstick routines were watched by millions at theaters around the country, and their skits are considered by many to be classic adaptations of the comic art form to American life.

Abbott and Costello made their first film in 1939 for Universal Pictures after years of vaudeville and burlesque work. When the war came along they made a string of comedy pictures built around war-related topics. In films like *Keep 'em Flying, Buck Privates,* and *In the Navy,* they made a specialty of high-jinx stunts in uniform which made audiences laugh about an otherwise serious war. Over the airwaves they were just as zany, performing their slapstick routines that they had perfected during years on the vaudeville circuit. "The famous baseball spoof, 'Who's on First?,' " writes broadcast historian Jack Dunning, "was developed for a live audience, but it was especially adaptable to radio. Their skits developed their images: Abbott became the stern taskmaster, while Costello fumbled his way through life and shrugged off his bumbling with 'I'm a baaaad boy!"

Born Louis Francis Cristillo, March 6, 1908, in Patterson, New Jersey, Costello became known as "Hard Luck Lou." Educated in the public schools, he first met William "Bud" Abbott in 1929 while performing at a Brooklyn theater; but one year later he was working at the Culver City studios of Metro-Goldwyn-Mayer as a laborer and part-time movie extra. Abbott, the stony-faced straightman, born 1889 at Asbury Park, New Jersey, to circus-performing parents, began his show career in 1918 as a movie cashier. He first met Costello in fact when the pudgy funnyman was booked at a theater where he was collecting tickets.

Costello earned his "Hard Luck" handle in March 1943 when he was forced to abandon his work because of rheumatic fever. Although other comics were suggested to take his place, Abbott refused to work without his partner. In November, Costello returned to their famed Abbott and Costello Show over network radio and was in dress rehearsal for his first broadcast when word arrived that Lou, Jr., had drowned. The toddler, one day short of his first birthday, had opened a playpen slat to reach the family pool. Other actors including Mickey Rooney, Jimmy Durante, Bob Hope, and Red Skelton offered to take his place on the live broadcast, but Costello said "No." He went ahead with the show as the two wisecracked their way through a thirty-minute spot "with jokes about topics such as life insurance."

The need to be entertained that drove people into movie houses to laugh at the silliness of Abbott and Costello or to become maudlin over the combat melodramas of John Wayne and Humphrey Bogart also lured thousands to Broadway and the New York stage. Wartime conditions reduced the overall number of Broadway productions—the last year of war in 1945 saw only thirty New York plays—but those that were running packed the theaters up and down the Great White Way. "On Broadway there was something for everyone," observed Brooks Atkinson, writer and longtime New York *Times* reporter: "It was choked every night with servicemen looking for a good time. But it was supported by many unworldly people who for the first time in their lives had more money than they knew what to do with. There were hundreds of enterprising merchants to help them. At the head of Times Square, at 47th Street, Broadway, and Seventh Avenue, the bank of three signs put everything in proper proportion: Four Roses, at the top, Kinsey's Blend, in the middle, Pepsi-Cola at the bottom."

Broadway sponsored a wholehearted commitment to the entertainment of servicemen through the USO and its own Stage Door Canteen. Virtually every stage actor of any standing—including such luminaries as Katharine Cornell, Raymond Massey, Al Jolson (who made a specialty of singing "Sister Susie's Sewin Shirts for Soldiers") Ethel Waters, Alfred Lunt, Lynn Fontain, Gracie Fields, Helen Hayes, and Fredric March —joined the effort. General George C. Marshall himself traveled to New York City in June 1942 to give a boost to the USO and to unveil a new USO sign on Broadway. The huge neon board, which displayed a picture of FDR, dominated the Broadway-Times Square area: "The USO Deserves the Support of Every Individual Citizen," it told theatergoers and passersby. Before the war ended USO had fifty-nine companies of Broadway and Hollywood stars on the road in this country and another 228 overseas, employing more than 2,000 actors. Their comings and goings were reported in the daily press far beyond the pale of Broadway.

While plays like *This is the Army, Mr. Jones, The Barretts of Wimpole Street, GI Hamlet, Oklahoma,* and *Carmen Jones,* attracted nightly crowds, the fundamental nature of wartime Broadway was altered by the war. The civilians and servicemen who invaded Times Square were basically moviegoers from small-town America accustomed to theaters in which shirt-sleeves, casual dress, and popcorn were the norm. Yet the same people—their wallets stuffed with defense factory money—thought nothing of purchasing front-row seats for a night on the town.

And sports fans in the larger cities flocked into pro football stadiums as if they had never heard of the war. Although the National Football League was forced to accept a forty-game season and to make some manpower concessions, its turnstiles in 1943 jingled with cash and customers at Sunday afternoon games. League officials reported in November that Sunday attendance figures averaged 25,383. This was a 4,500-per-game increase over the previous year. With total league attendance in excess of 1,100,000 for 1943, the NFL had its best financial season ever (except for 1941 when each club played a longer season).

Nearly 43,000 fans jammed into Manhattan's Polo Grounds on December 19 to watch "slingin" Sammy Baugh and the Washington Redskins trounce the New York Giants, 28-0, for the NFL Eastern Division title. Reared in west Texas, at Sweetwater, Baugh had played college ball at Texas Christian University in Fort Worth under coach Dutch Meyer before joining the Redskins in 1937. He is thought by many to be the greatest thrower in football history with a lifetime pass completion average of 70.3 percent after sixteen seasons in pro ball. Samuel Adrian Baugh, who once starred in a Hollywood-produced serial, *King of the Texas Rangers*, threw sixteen sucessful passes to give his team the upper hand in the Polo Grounds playoff. The twenty-nine-year-old Texan was mobbed by exuberant fans at the fifty-yard line before he was rescued by police. Baugh earned a cool $15,000 yearly for throwing baseball-style passes that hit their mark with brutal accuracy.

Baugh and the Redskins reached the Eastern Division playoffs by winning six, losing three, and tying one during the regular season. But the championship game, played before 34,320 fans on December 26 in Chicago's Wrigley Field, was a fiasco for the Washington eleven. What should have been a passing duel between Baugh and ace Chicago quarterback Sid Luckman turned into a 41-21 rout for the Redskins. Luckman, who connected fourteen times—five of them touchdown passes for a total 276 yards—was nearly as well known as Baugh to wartime football crowds. One of the first modern T-formation quarterbacks, Luckman had broken into the NFL three years after Baugh. The former standout at Columbia played twelve seasons for the Bears.

Luckman left for active duty with the Merchant Marine shortly after the Chicago-Washington game. But, like big league baseball, the NFL took plenty of criticism earlier in the year when several players left defense jobs to don football uniforms. As part of Washington's policy to encourage entertainment and diversion during the war, the War Manpower Commission in early 1943 had ruled that "football was their major occupation and permitted the switch." Still, the sight of grown men busting heads for pleasure every Sunday afternoon while millions remained in uniform did not appeal to large sections of the home front.

The NFL, organized in 1921 although pro teams in Ohio and Pennsylvania had been playing each other for money since the 1890s, was forced to make operational changes. After raising nearly $700,000 in 1942 through benefit games for War Relief Charities, the league found it necessary to adopt a free substitution rule in 1943 because of manpower shortages. Though many players managed to avoid military duty, others soon joined Luckman in uniform. A case in point was Byron "Whizzer" White who left the Detroit Lions in April 1942 for the army. White, a Rhodes scholar, graduate of the Yale Law School, and onetime Pittsburgh Steeler, became the first pro-football player to sit on the U. S. Supreme Court. Athletes like Luckman and White were not unique; when the war ended in 1945 at least twenty-one former NFL griders had lost their lives in combat.

The NFL was headed during the 1940s by Elmer Layden, who was appointed commissioner after club owners decided a baseball-style overseer was needed—a decision that came about following the 1940 championship game in which Chicago thumped the Redskins 71-0. Layden, former head coach and athletic director at Notre Dame, struggled under heavy odds to keep pro-football going during 1941–1945. Among other things, he reduced the NFL to a streamlined eight teams—Chicago, Green Bay, Detroit, St. Louis in the western division; Washington, New York, Philadelphia-Pittsburgh, Brooklyn in the eastern division. The Cleveland Rams quit after the 1942 season and the Pittsburgh Steelers combined with the Eagles of Philadelphia to form a new team officially dubbed the "Pittsadelphia Steagles." The NFL did not return to full strength until the 1950 season, when the league reorganized itself.

The number of people flocking to resorts and night spots along Florida's Gold Coast reached near scandalous record proportions in the winter of 1943–1944. At Miami's Hialeah race track, where para-mutuel betting hit $1 million for the first time ever, cars with C and B ration stickers could be seen on the parking lot from a dozen states or more. And once inside, the horse players were so busy placing bets that a war bond booth manned by local matrons was totally ignored. At nearby West Flagler Kennel Club the dog races took in $100,000 nightly, a gigantic sum in the 1940s. While other parts of the country were struggling with Christmas shortages and ration books or were keeping anxious track of the awesome military confrontations going on overseas, south Florida took on an indulgent, carnival-like atmosphere. Prayers for peace and the return of loved ones at special Christmas services in countless small town churches held little interest for the high rollers.

As 1943 came to a close, most Miami hotels were booked solid through March; though several large resorts and hotels had been taken over by the army in 1942, most had been promptly returned to civilian use. "It was as if someone had called off the war," one correspondent said: "Upon these hotels, upon every boardinghouse and cottage in the city, hordes of hedonists, defying the Government's request not to travel for fun, descended from the north by train, by bus and in private cars propelled by black market gasoline." The second year of war ended with a single Miami night spot, the Latin Quarter, seating an average 800 nightly and more than 1,000 on weekends. The funseekers ate dinners from $3.50 upwards while scantily-clad chorus girls gyrated across a brightly lit stage for their entertainment.

8 JANUARY-APRIL 1944: WAR IS HELL

In the first months of 1944 the country braced for a final assault on Hitler's Fortress Europe and for additional island battles in the Pacific as U.S. forces pushed toward the Japanese homeland. The year 1944 was the first presidential election year in wartime since George B. McCellan ran against Abraham Lincoln in 1864, which meant that the country was embroiled in politicking for most of the twelve months. Continued agitation by labor bosses to get rid of Little Steel caused more industrial unrest, although wages remained high. And the man-in-the-street went on grappling with gasoline and food rationing.

Gallup's pollsters found in mid-January that less than half the country thought the war would end before the year was out; according to 46 percent, or slightly under half of those interviewed, Nazi Germany would be beaten in the second half of 1944, but 31 percent said it would take another full year, and 5 percent even thought victory in Europe would not come until 1946. Only 6 percent thought Japan would collapse during 1944. A January 11 poll was evenly divided on the Pacific fighting: 33 percent said war would end there in 1945: 33 percent opted for 1946. A majority obviously thought Hitler was nearer defeat than Tojo a full six months before the Normandy invasion.

The population appeared to be in good health; another Gallup survey on January 22 found only 13 percent of all American households reporting some member with the flu. And either because they supported Washington's pleas to conserve food or, more likely, because they were trying to get ahead of the rationing game, 75 percent of housewives said "yes" when asked if "you or your family put up (home canned) any cans or jars of food this year." It is difficult to believe, but the respondents claimed an average 165 jars for the year. If Gallup's ubiquitous polls said nothing else about wartime America, they found the nation united in its determination to win the war. Moreover, Americans overwhelmingly supported Washington's bipartisan approach to the fighting but were widely divided when asked who would be the best Republican candidate to oppose Roosevelt in the November election. There was no rush to outlaw liquor; when asked, "If the question of national prohibition should come up again, would you vote wet or dry?" 66 percent said, "wet."

World leaders in America and Europe told their people to expect hard days ahead. A New Year's message from Hitler said self-denial was the only way to shake off the noose around Nazi Germany. Domei, the official Japanese news agency, released an equally pessimistic statement attributed to Premier Tojo to the effect that Japan was facing "a crucial test and that it was the sublime duty of everyone to sacrifice body and soul without a single atom of interest." Roosevelt, incapacitated with the "flu and grippe," found time to put the social goals of his administration in an international context: "It is fitting," he said, "that we direct our thoughts to the concept of a United Nations." Unwilling to repeat past mistakes when America rejected League of Nations membership at the close of World War I, he urged a "need to continue when peace comes the mutually beneficial cooperation we have achieved in war."

Heroic declarations aside, New Year's Day 1944 dawned on an America not only scarred by conflict but also still conducive to stout-hearted individualism. Helen Dortch Longstreet, the eighty-year-old widow of Confederate General James Longstreet of Civil War fame, was working at an aircraft plant in Atlanta. She had attracted national attention during 1943 when she appeared on a network radio show, "We the People," to talk about her life. Mrs. Longstreet, a classmate of the general's daughter, Sarah, at Brenau College in Georgia, had married in 1897 when Longstreet was seventy-six years of age and she, thirty-three. The plucky war worker, who had once campaigned for Roosevelt in California, told reporters: "I am going to assist in building a plane to bomb Hitler and the Son of Heaven [the Japanese emperor] to the Judgment Seat of God."

Other American women, too, caught the public eye during January. Former First Lady Mrs. Herbert Hoover, past president of the Girl Scouts and a gracious White House hostess during her husband's presidency, died in New York on January 7. Born Lou Henry at Waterloo, Iowa, in 1876, she had met and married the future president while both were students at Stanford. A day earlier, eighty-six-year-old Ida Mae Tarbell also passed away at Bridgeport, Connecticut. Known to millions as a writer and muckraker of the early twentieth century, she gained great notoriety in 1904 with her *History of the Standard Oil Company*—a book which made her the "Terror of the Trusts" and led to the breakup of John Davison Rockefeller's Standard Oil conglomerate.

Fanny Hurst, another popular writer, brought out her twelfth novel, *Hallelujah*, in mid-month. Hurst's book, her second in wartime, "which the public bought like crazy," according to one reviewer, was "a long, carefully worked-on story of Lily Browne, a 'normal' girl in a small midwestern town, whose mother murdered a man with a butcher knife, spent six years in the penitentiary, and came home bringing a good-hearted, darkly-skinned prostitute named Oleander to look after Lily." The novel dealt with all sorts of questions such as the war, the bad effect of inherited money on children, and the light burning in people which made Lily cry out: "Hallelujah!"

In the midst of nagging gasoline problems and changes in the draft, Frank Hayden, a rancher near Pueblo, Colorado, diverted attention from the war by displaying his two-headed calf to eager newsmen. Soon magazines and newspapers carried accounts of the abnormal creature to every American home. "Though most double-headed animals do not survive," the *Newsweek* account said, "this one is thriving. It has one brain, two heads, four eyes, two noses, two mouths, two tongues, two sets of teeth, and the two throats join in the digestive tract." Then, suddenly, similiar animals cropped up in circus sideshows and in traveling menageries around the country; it seemed that the public had developed an instant fascination with the bizarre and unusual in order to forget the war.

There was nothing bizarre, however, about the gasoline shortages that struck the West Coast after January 1. Even Ralph K. Davies, Deputy Petroleum Administrator in Washington, experienced difficulty while driving from San Francisco to Sacramento. Although the former president of Standard Stations had sufficient ration coupons, he was stranded in Vallejo because he could not locate a station with gasoline. For two days in Sacramento during late December, only five taxicabs had had enough fuel to answer emergency runs before government officials released enough gasoline to restore partial service. Meanwhile, in Portland, Oregon, buses were packed with riders after 12 percent of the city's filling stations closed. And in Salt Lake City a very expectant mother who needed gasoline for a hospital visit won a battle with local rationing czars by threatening to stay in their offices until she got the gas.

If gasoline scarcities were not enough to nettle the home front in the early months of 1944, the Selective Service Board announced on January 15 that it planned to double the draft by digging deeper into the pool of fathers with young children. Stronger measures were needed after the draft quotas for October, November, and December failed to reach projections. Most of the new inductees had children born before Pearl Harbor; until January 1944 only 90,000 men in this category had been drafted. The total number of men in uniform stood at 10,709,000 on December 31, nearly 30,000 below what the war planners considered adequate. Even more families were touched as fathers were called up during January–June, boosting the number of men in the service to 11,130,000 by July 1.

Then, as the military build-up mounted for a crosschannel attack a railroad strike that had menaced defense output since November was settled. Many unions, including the railroad workers who observed Washington's reaction to Lewis, lost no time in asking for greater concessions from WLB. Actually, the railroads had been controlled by Secretary of War Stimson since December, when Roosevelt had seized them to prevent a work stoppage. Although the president agreed to a settlement on the 14th which granted a 9¢ hourly raise in addition to vacation and overtime concessions for 1,450,000 railway workers, the railroads were not returned to private ownership until January 18.

Although concessions to organized labor were designed to court the union vote in November, this renewed abandonment of Little Steel brought about an industrial peace that was needed for both the anticipated French invasion and the air war against Hitler. Strategic needs in Europe and the Pacific demanded an unbroken flow of military hardware from the nation's factories. One month after settlement of the rail dispute, the so-called "Big Week" in the bombing war took a heavy toll in men and machines; during February 11–26, 1944, the RAF and American Eighth Air Force commanded by General Carl Spaatz pounded German cities and military bases incessantly. Despite heavy Allied losses, a badly-mangled Luftwaffe managed a few raids over London and southern England.

In an American–British attack on February 22 against aircraft plants in Bernburg, Achersleben, Halbertstadt, and Regensberg, the Eighth Air Force lost fifty-two planes and shot down fifty-eight. Three nights later the Allies lost another thirty-five aircraft over Schweinfurt. London was attacked the same night, February 25, and a bomb that hit the Marie Curie Hospital provoked a frantic search for a half gram of radium lost in the raid. More than 1,800 tons of explosives were dropped on submarine works at Ausburg on February 26 by British, Canadian, and Australian groups with a loss of twenty-four planes. During the "Big Week," writes historian C. L. Sulzberger: "The R.A.F. put 2,300 bombers over Germany at night, and the American Air Force 3,800 during daytime. Desperately trying to fend off this particular series of assaults, the Luftwaffe lost 450 planes, a rate it could not long sustain."

Although Hitler's air chief, Reichmarshal Goring, uttered his famous boast, "If bombs ever drop on Germany, my name is Meyer," the Luftwaffe, which was never intended for extended combat, was gradually beaten down by unceasing American-British pressure. American bombers first hit Nazi targets in August 1942 and they carried the fight until the very end. But the RAF, which had seen the Luftwaffe defeated during the Battle of Britain, refused to undertake daylight raids because of heavy losses they incurred. A September 1942 agreement between Spaatz and Sir Arthur "Bomber" Harris of the RAF produced a strategy in which the Americans bombed in daytime and the British at night. A maneuver called "windowing"—the dropping of tinfoil strips to confuse German radar—often proved effective. And in several notorious cases—Dresden, Hamburg and Nuremberg—the Allies dropped incendiary bombs to create firestorms that devastated the cities and caused horrible suffering to civilian and military personnel.

The backbone of American air power over Europe and the Pacific was first the B-17 "Flying Fortress" and later the B-29 "Super Fortress." Produced in staggering numbers at Boeing plants in Seattle by Douglas Aircraft in Tulsa, and by Lockheed at Burbank, California, "the big ass birds" made a difference in the air war because of their long-range and high-altitude capabilities. Yet a flying altitude of 25,000 feet did not make the B-17 immune from Luftwaffe attacks. In one raid over Germany in October 1942, the Eighth Air Force lost sixty planes and had another 138 damaged out of 219 Fortresses, leaving England with a heavy escort of American-built Thunderbolt fighters. But the short-range Thunderbolt, which could not fly beyond Aachen on the German-Belgium border, was shortly replaced with another marvel of American production, the P-51B Mustang. With a powerful Packard-built Rolls Royce Merlin engine and a cruising range of 1,000 miles at 5–600 m.p.h., the new plane exceeded anything in the Nazi arsenal. It permitted the Fortresses to bomb most of occupied Europe at will.

A long-term debate that grew out of the war was the contribution of American air power to the collapse of Hitler. While bombs alone did not do the job, they were a major factor in the Nazi defeat: in three raids on Dresden alone during February 1945 American and British planes killed 35,000 Germans. And constant hammering at the Luftwaffe, as well as at German cities, hampered Axis ability to resist Russian and American-British ground attacks. In that sense the air war quickened the return of peace. By 1945 the Luftwaffe was helpless to defend the Reich because the American home front had built the planes and bombs to bring down Goring's eagles.

American air power was also part of the thrust against the "soft underbelly of Europe" that grew out of a January 1943 meeting between Roosevelt and Churchill at Casablanca. Though Rome did not fall until June 1944, the drive into Fortress Europe started on July 10, 1943, when the first Allied forces to reenter the continent hit the beaches of southern Sicily under General George S. Patton and Field Marshal Montgomery. After the first amphibious landings of Patton's Seventh Army at Licata, Gela, and Scoglitti on July 10, the relentless Patton drove straight across the island and captured Palermo on the northern coast by July 22. Montgomery's Eighth Army, meanwhile, which fought its way up the eastern coast from Cape Passero, met heavy resistance around Mt. Etna, the famed volcano that dominates the Sicilian landscape.

Frederick Blesse, Eisenhower's chief medical officer, said Patton's frantic effort to reach Messina before Montgomery caused his GIs "to march the skin right off their feet." The campaign across northern Sicily caused an uproar when Americans learned of the now-famous incident in which an over-enthusiastic Patton struck an army private in a field evacuation hospital. Actually, Patton gave way to two such outbursts; in the second episode, which occurred August 10 in another field hospital, he threatened to shoot an enlisted man suffering from "anxiety neurosis." Eyewitnesses said he hit the fellow and grabbed one of his pearl-handled pistols. As the man cried out, Patton added: "I should shoot you myself, you goddam whimpering coward."

Eisenhower, who made his headquarters on Malta during the Sicilian operation, had to struggle in order to save his friend Patton from a serious reprimand. Meanwhile, both armies reached Messina simultaneously and by August 17 "the last German soldier had been flung out of Sicily," an official report said. But the enemy had pulled off one of the war's great coups; over a seven-day interval, before the British-American arrival on August 17, nearly 40,000 German troops and over 60,000 Italians had been withdrawn to the mainland. "Although the Italians left behind all except 200 of their vehicles," Liddell Hart added, "the Germans brought away nearly 10,000 vehicles, as well as forty-seven tanks, ninety-four guns, and 17,000 tons of supplies and equipment." But the Germans and Italians together left behind 135,000 prisoners, as well as 32,000 dead and wounded. Allied losses totaled 31,000 in the fight for Sicily.

Following a three-week lull, Allied forces made the move to the Italian boot. Montgomery's Eighth Army had a comparatively easy advance northward after landings at Reggio on September 3, but six days later Mark Clark's Fifth Army ran into pure hell on the beaches of Salerno. The German commander, Field Marshal Albert Kesselring, was able to pin down Clark's GIs for almost a week at the waterline with his reorganized units. Secretary of War Stimson told a Washington news conference that American losses in the four-week Salerno campaign were "511 killed, 5,428 wounded, and 2,368 missing, or a total of 8,307." He warned the country to prepare for "very heavy fighting because the Germans now have in Italy 20 to 25 divisions, or from 300,000 to 375,000 men."

Among the wounded at Salerno was the American novelist John Steinbeck, who reported on the campaign for the New York *Herald Tribune*; he had previously covered some of the North African fighting where Ernie Pyle had told him, "If ever I hear another G.I. use 'fuck' as an adjective, I will cut my fucking throat." At Salerno with the Fifth Army, relates Steinbeck's biographer, Jackson Benson, he found himself under attack by a German bombardment: "At one point a round had come in nearby, blowing a stack of fifty-gallon oil drums every which way, one of which was thrown up in the air, hit the ground, and then rolling slammed against his head, neck, and back. He had already badly twisted an ankle while jumping out of the landing craft unto the beach, and both eardrums had been burst so that he could barely hear." Steinbeck suffered blackouts and episodes of memory loss after the incident.

After the prize-winning novels of the 1930s, *Of Mice and Men*, *The Red Pony*, *Tortilla Flat*, and *The Grapes of Wrath*, the California-born Steinbeck had already used his pen for the war effort. While playwright Arthur Miller wrote about army boot camps, he toured army air bases at the suggestion of General Hap Arnold "and wrote a straightforward account of their life and training." His book, *Bombs Away*, which appeared in late 1942, earned him a $250,000 honorarium from Hollywood which he turned over to the Air Force Aid Society; it was followed a few months later by a war novel, *The Moon is Down*, about Nazi occupation of "a vaguely Scandinavian country." It was made into a lackadaisical movie and appeared as a Broadway production. Although the Norwegian king decorated Steinbeck for the "contribution the work made to the liberation movement," others did not think it equaled his previous books. Clifton Fadiman called the novel "unsatisfactory" in a review for the *New Yorker*, and another journal labeled the Broadway version "ineffectual."

After the Salerno affair Steinbeck returned to New York in November 1943. He had spent five months with the Fifth Army, and his wartime dispatches, like those of Ernie Pyle and John Hersey, were sharp reminders that Americans were dying in a lot of unfamiliar places. Within six weeks, however, he had recovered enough to commence work on *Cannery Row*. It was published in 1945 and became one of his best-known books. Steinbeck had already received the 1939 Pulitzer Prize for *The Grapes of Wrath*, which was made into a successful movie starring Henry Fonda. Additional works by Steinbeck—*The Wayward Bus, East of Eden, The Winter of Our Discontent*, and a host of others—followed after the war. Before his death in 1968 at age sixty-six the writer achieved worldwide literary fame and was awarded the 1962 Nobel Prize. In 1958, thirteen years after the war, he published an account of his adventures in North Africa and Italy, *Once There Was A War*. He served briefly as a correspondent once again during the Vietnamese struggle.

The march on Rome continued. But the advance was hampered by Kesselring's hastily-constructed Gustav Line thrown across the Italian boot from Gaeta on the Mediterranean to Pescara on the Adriatic. From October 1 when Naples fell until the first GIs entered the Eternal City on June 4, the campaign involved some of the war's meanest fighting, including an ill-conceived attack on Monte Cassino. Perched on a hill overlooking the road to Rome, Monte Cassino, a monastery founded by St. Benedict in the sixth century, became a natural German fortification to block the Allies. Though Eisenhower had cautioned against destruction of "historic buildings," the abbey was bombed after hard combat at Anzio but with little impact on its Nazi defenders. Worst of all, the abby was destroyed in the face of worldwide condemnation and German propaganda.

Even a spectacular eruption of Mount Vesuvius, which spewed vast clouds of volcanic ash over both armies in March, did not blunt the American-British momentum. And the invading troops found a cheerful reception when Rome was finally reached. Zeke Clark, a war correspondent with the spearheading tanks, noted the enthusiasum: "As the GIs drove through the moonlit streets, hundreds of the populace leaned out of windows, shouted 'vivas!' clapped hands, and rushed out offering vino despite the lateness of the hour." Although wild merrymaking followed capture of Mussolini's capital on June 4, more hard fighting awaited the Allies in northern Italy; Kesselring erected another defensive barrier across the boot—this one called the Gothic Line—again slowing the drive toward Germany. After hard fighting around the so-called Argenta Gap near Bologna, American units finally reached Milan and Turin in early 1945. The last Nazis withdrew through the Brenner Pass on May 6 to close the war's most controversial campaign.

Four days after Clark's dispatch from Rome, American neighborhoods were awakened on the morning of June 6 by newsboys hawking "extras" that proclaimed the long-awaited French invasion. Operation Overlord —as the massive landings on the Normandy coast were called—had been on the planning boards for months, and Roosevelt appointed Dwight Eisenhower on December 5, 1943, to command the invasion. Eisenhower, who immediately took charge in England, assembled a formidable array of subordinates, including Walter "Beetle" Smith, Omar Bradley, and George S. Patton. Though Patton's appointment after his slapping incidents evoked a hue-and-cry at home, Eisenhower—now supreme Allied commander—stood by his old-comrade-in-arms: "I have no intention of throwing valuable men to the wolves because of one mistake," he told General Marshall in response to an anti-Patton campaign abetted by radio commentator-columnist Drew Pearson.

After six months of constant planning, Ike gave the go signal for 4:45 a.m., June 6, 1944, from his invasion headquarters at Southwick House a mile or so north of Portsmouth. A huge funnel of men and ships from the south of England, from Falmouth to Newhaven on the Kentish coast, converged on the Contentin Peninsula east of Cherbourg. Immediately radio stations and wire services blared out the news to an enthralled America. A second front had been established on five beaches extending from LaMadelleine to Ouistreham: Utah and Omaha Beaches were occupied by American units under Omar Bradley, while the British, commanded by General Miles Dempsey, went ashore at Gold, Juno (Canadian), and Sword. By nightfall on D-day eight miles of Hitler's Fortress Europe was firmly in Allied hands.

By mid-August the liberation of Paris had taken place, as German field commanders struggled to retreat through something called the Falaise-Argentan Gap near the Orne River. To the disgust of many Americans, Patton and the Third Army were held in check to avoid embarrassing Montgomery. The unquenchable Patton, who nursed a monumental dislike for Montgomery and his Tommies, later told Omar Bradley: "To hell with Monty. We'll win your goddamn war if you'll keep the Third Army going." Once unfettered by Eisenhower, his tanks were poised on the banks of the Seine by August 17 within sight of the French capital. But as a concession to de Gualle, who remained as quarrelsome as ever,

French units fighting alongside the Allies were allowed to enter Paris alone.

American units had occupied Aachen near the Belgium-Dutch border by October; it was the first city on German territory to fall but still forty miles from the Rhine, Hitler's final defensive barrier in the west. A temporary halt in the Allied advance occurred in December when the Wehrmacht mounted its last counter-offensive of the war. The Battle of the Bulge—named for a huge backward "bulge" in the American-British front—commenced December 16 and lasted until Christmas Eve 1944. An entire Nazi army group under Von Rundstedt attacked the Allies under heavy fog cover, which precluded use of air power in the snow-clad Ardennes region of eastern France. The fighting peaked at Bastogne, where U.S. General Anthony McAuliffe sent his famed one-word reply, "Nuts!" to a German surrender ultimatum. After the Bulge, Nazi units were constantly on the defensive until the final collapse of April–May 1945.

June 1944 was also a watershed in the fight with Japan. "The Great Marianas Turkey Shoot" on June 19—part of the Battle of the Philippine Sea—was not only a stunning victory for the United States, but gave American movie audiences a realistic look at the Pacific war. Millions saw newsreels shot from fighting decks that showed azure skies ablaze with flak and spiraling planes. There was something spectacular about the reports made by war correspondents standing aboard ship that could never be matched by those who followed the land war in Europe. The Battle of the Philippine Sea, which followed the American landings on Siapan four days earlier, was American fighting at its best: a great air–naval battle in which the enemy lost two carriers and 346 aircraft—literally knocked from the skies like sitting ducks—while our losses were thirty planes shot down and one partially damaged battleship.

The Siapan-Marianas operation, led by Admirals Chester A. Nimitz and Raymond A. Spruance, was the northernmost of a two-pronged counterattack across the Pacific. The Nimitz-Spruance Central Pacific Task Force had previously made several successful amphibious assaults: Tarawa and Makin in the Gilberts on November 20; Kwajalein on January 31; and Eniwetok on February 17. (The last two were in the Marshall Islands.) The extraordinarily difficult maneuver at Tarawa—across a low-lying atoll where the enemy was braced behind a coconut log barrier—although it cost 1,500 Marine casualties was a long-run asset: it set the tone for future attacks in the Pacific after American commanders saw the need to "soften up" enemy positions with air and naval bombardment before landing troops on jungle-covered islands. The Central Pacific Fleet recaptured Guam—which had been under United States control for forty-five years before Japan's rampage across the Pacific—on July 21, and Tinian three days later.

"Strategically located 1,300 miles from the Philippine Islands and an equal distance from Japan," Newsweek told the home front, "the Marianas will provide territory from which B-29s can range freely over both. Likewise, they will provide land bases to stage large troop forces for the westward drive to the Philippines and China, and an advanced naval base from which American task forces can intercept Japanese convoys to and from the home islands—a longtime navy ambition."

Meanwhile, the South Pacific Task Force, headed by MacArthur and Admiral William F. "Bull" Halsey, converged on the Philippines from the south. After fighting his way along northern New Guinea with a charged-up Australian–U.S. force, MacArthur leapfrogged to tiny Morotai in September. Situated 300 miles from New Guinea in present Indonesia, the island was still 600 miles short of the first landings in the Philippines. Following the humiliations of Bataan and Corregidor, recapture of the islands—a United States possession since the Spanish American War in the 1890s—remained this country's chief strategic goal in the Pacific short of Japan itself. Although initial landings were made October 20, 1944, at Leyte Gulf, it was another two months before American forces stormed the beaches at Lingayen on the large island of Luzon which held the key to the entire archipelago.

History's greatest sea engagement—the Battle of Leyte Gulf—took place after the Leyte beachhead. Forced into a do-or-die situation, Japan's imperial navy had assembled a fleet of seventy ships from its dwindling resources, in a futile effort to check the advancing Americans. Stripped of virtually all carrier planes after the Marianas shoot-out, the Japanese resorted to Kamikaze attacks for the first time to save themselves from total annihilation. And to their chagrin, several ships "dredged from the mud of Pearl Harbor" were thrown into the fray. The brilliant American victory over Admiral Toyoda Soemu who directed his fleet from Tokyo enabled MacArthur to reoccupy the Philippines with the knowledge that Japan could not resupply her garrisons. MacArthur himself landed on Leyte in late October and by January 9, 1945, his forces had a foothold on Luzon. Notwithstanding the later fighting on Okinawa, Manila fell in March, following a stubborn resistance. MacArthur announced on July 5 that the Philippines operation was complete.

Some months earlier, presidential politicking at home had started with a ban during January–April 1944. In fact it was Republican infighting that intensified among three of four front-runners for the nomination; Roosevelt's fourth term intentions were a foregone conclusion, although he did not formally announce his candidacy until July. With the Democratic nomination already decided, political attention focused on the GOP. A few days before the "Big Week" in the European air war, and while the fight for Eniwetok and Marshall Islands was taking place, 2,000 Lincoln Day galas over the February 12 weekend gave Republican hopefuls an opportunity to seize the limelight.

The Republican dinners and fund-raisers were accompanied by the inevitable preelection polls which appeared in newspapers during the first weeks of active campaigning. In the Midwest, where "isolationist" sentiment was strongest within the party, a survey on January 6 gave New York Governor Thomas E. Dewey a thirteen-point edge over Wendell Willkie, the party's 1940 standard-bearer and a man well known for his "internationalist" stance. General MacArthur—then engaged in directing the life-and-death struggle to regain the Philippines—Ohio Governor John Bricker, Ohio Senator Robert A. Taft, and several favorite sons brought up the field. Another poll in mid-January that was limited to Maine, Vermont, and New Hampshire, put Willkie on top (with 55%) by a healthy margin while Dewey (with 26 percent) and the others trailed badly. Willkie was ahead in the East where his liberal and "one world" views were received more favorably in the Grand Old Party.

The isolationist-internationalist hassle dominated early Willkie-Dewey infighting for the 1944 nomination. The issue had plagued the GOP throughout the war years. Since the 1930s, the Republican old guard—centered mostly in the Midwest and united in disliking Willkie—had thought the country should go slow with foreign entanglements; likewise, GOP senators and congressmen with isolationist leaning had made it an article of faith to oppose early Rooseveltian support of the Allies.

The fact that Roosevelt and the Democrats exploited every isolationist vote in Congress and tried to brand the entire party as obstructionist in regard to the war did not keep Harrison Spangler from blurting out: "My job is to build up an army of voters in the United States to defeat the New Deal, and I don't think there are any votes in China, or Mongolia, or Russia that I can get for the Republicans." Spangler, GOP national committeeman, Iowa lawyer, and ally of Robert A. Taft, was lambasting the "dreamy internationalism" of Vice President Wallace at a Washington news conference when he let fly at reporters. But his remark, however ill-chosen, drove home the great Republican dilemma: how to oppose administration policy and at the same time not oppose the war effort.

With Spangler's blessing, the party high command called a meeting in late 1943 to repair the mischief. Though Willkie, the party's chief exponent of international agreements, was excluded, the Republicans committed themselves "to responsible participation by the U.S. in a postwar cooperative organization among sovereign nations."

Willkie made his appearance at a Lincoln Day dinner in Tacoma, Washington, while on a campaign swing through the West. Speaking before a crowd of 4,000 at the Masonic Temple and two "wired-in" auditoriums, he warned "the Republican party not to permit the forces of discontent and discord to write its platform and dictate its nominee." Earlier, at Twin Falls, Idaho, he "flayed the myth" that Roosevelt and the Democrats had a monopoly on foreign affairs. At Salt Lake City, when challenged on his position that taxes "must go up" and on his foreign policy views, Willkie replied: "All I'm trying to do with reference to the Republican party is to make it worthy of the high traditions Lincoln gave it." Many politicians continued to think he had led the GOP to defeat with his internationalist views in a time of opposition to involvement in the European war. Then FDR sent him around the world after the election as unofficial goodwill ambassador. His best-selling book, *One World*, which described the journey as well as his liberal foreign policy positions, damned him forever in the eyes of GOP stalwarts.

While Willkie was calling for a redirected Republican party committed to liberal principles, Bricker, darling of the conservatives because of his attacks on Rooseveltian bureaucracy and mismanagement, spoke to a Lincoln Day gathering of 1,500 "well-groomed and notable Republicans" in Washington's Mayflower Hotel. Bricker concentrated his fire on administration stands on taxation and domestic issues, but the lid came off with a standing ovation when he briefly mentioned foreign affairs: "Time and again I have said the U.S. should take her place in a cooperative organization among sovereign nations after this war. We want no supergovernment, no central world authority over us." The isolationist old guard, already disenchanted with Willkie and the "One Worlders," made sure that Bricker was handed the vice presidential nomination four months later.

Another governor, Thomas E. Dewey of New York, was likewise courting the conservatives and isolationists in early 1944. Dewey, a native of Owosso in central Michigan and a 1923 graduate of the University of Michigan, had reached national prominence by way of the Columbia Law School and prestigious New York law firms. In 1933 he was appointed U.S. district attorney for the southern district of New York. But it was his role and his flamboyant style as special prosecutor in the much-publicized crackdowns on organized crime that thrust him into the political limelight. After putting several underworld figures behind bars, Dewey, the gangbuster, got himself elected district attorney for New York County. From that platform he made an abortive stab at the governorship one year later. In November 1942—when the first wartime election ushered in modest Republican gains—he carried New York Republicans to victory by capturing the executive mansion in Albany, a house once occupied by Franklin Delano Roosevelt.

Dewey, who had not spoken publicly since the gubernatorial campaign, like Willkie, seized the opportunity to counter any supposed monopoly on foreign affairs by the Democrats. He told a Lincoln Day crowd in New York's Waldorf-Astoria Hotel that people were turning to the Republican Party "at an accelerated pace since we entered the war because they are so desperately anxious that we shall build well and strongly in international cooperation after this war. . . . They know that with a self-willed executive who wars with Congress they will have a repetition of the same catastrophe which happened in 1919. . . . The people realize that the only hope of America for world peace is that it be won by an administration which is not seeking power for the sake of power."

Although Willkie, Bricker, and Dewey continued their search for convention delegates after the Lincoln Day fêtes, the important Wisconsin primary on April 4 left Dewey in unchallenged control of the field. Moreover, on the very eve of the primary Willkie reiterated his stand on foreign affairs—that he had supported lend-lease and selective service long before any other Republican got on the bandwagon—while addressing an audience of 3,000 in the civic auditorium at Norfolk, Nebraska; yet he did not win a single Wisconsin delegate to the national confab. Dewey was the big winner in the primary balloting for the state's twenty-four-man delegation. He won fifteen delegates with two others who were uninstructed leaning in his direction; General MacArthur got three, and Harold Stassen, four.

Roosevelt's supporters tried to label the entire GOP irretrievably isolationist. But the Milwaukee *Journal* said, "We are not isolationist," after the Wisconsin primary. And *Time* editorialized: "Wisconsin clearly voted no confidence on global goodwill and a foreign policy of generalities. They voted against the 'crusade' kind of internationalism—a crusade against which was hopelessly confused with New Dealism." By rejecting the One Worldism of Willkie the Republicans had turned, *Time* reasoned, to Dewey and a "realistic" approach to international cooperation after the war.

Although Willkie withdrew from the race after Wisconsin, an event with far-reaching socio-political consequences took place on April 3—one day before the Wisconsin primary, when the U.S. Supreme Court ruled 8-to-1 that all-white primaries in the South were unconstitutional. Southern Democratic organizations had long used the whites-only primary to keep blacks from the polling booth, except in general elections where their rights were protected by the Fifteenth Amendment. Rulings by the Supreme Court in 1935 and 1941 that "a political party was a private organization and hence arbiter of who might participate in its primaries" had aided the southern diehards. Reversal of these mandates was heralded by the black community and by liberal-leftist groups who equated discrimination in this country with Jewish oppression in Europe.

Things came to a head in wartime Texas when Dr. Lonnie E. Smith, a Houston dentist, brought suit against local election officials. He charged that Texas Democratic election judges S. E. Allwright and James E. Liuzza had kept him from voting in a party primary "because of his race and color." The new decision came down on appeal from the lower courts: "When primaries become part of the machinery for choosing officials, state and national, the same tests should be applied to the primary as to the general election. The right to vote in such a primary, like the right to vote in the general election, is a right secured by the Constitution." Although Texas attorney general Grover Sellers reargued the case in Washington, saying "the Democratic party in Texas is a voluntary association and is therefore not an instrument of the state or any governmental agency," the court on May 8 reaffirmed its earlier decision.

Immediately, the National Association for the Advancement of Colored People, which had used its legal fund to fight against discrimination for years, began to badger the Justice Department for implementation of the decision. But white politicians fought back with often-devious shenanigans to thwart the courts. When a black Baptist minister announced for the Dallas County school board, his frightened opponent took out several blazing newspaper ads: "Vote the Straight Ticket." And Florida Senator Claude Pepper, later a liberal stalwart, cried out: "The South will allow nothing to impair white supremacy."

A different political phenomenon in the wartime South was a bid for elective office by several country and western singers. In Louisiana James Houston "Jimmy" Davis was elected governor in April 1944 and Roy

Acuff made a strong bid for the Tennessee state house during 1944 and 1948. Two years earlier, Texas had sent W. Lee "Pappy" O'Daniel to the U.S. Senate. O'Daniel's successful politicking came in the wake of travels across the Lone Star State with his Light Crust Doughboys, a band that included the immortal Bob Wills, known later as the "king of Western swing" and a widely imitiated musician through the 1980s. Davis, Acuff, and O'Daniel were among the host of singers and performers who skyrocketed to fame, primarily in the South but also in other parts of the country, when country or "hillbilly" music reached unheard-of popularity during the war years.

Davis, a Shreveport native who campaigned with a band "recruited partly from the Shreveport police department," was a widely-known singer-composer. Sworn into office on May 9, he had been elected by a 33,000-vote plurality over a slate of candidates backed by the late Huey Long's political machine; his gubernatorial opponent, Lewis L. Moran, had been Long's personal attorney. But in 1944, Louisiana voters turned to the forty-two-year-old Davis, composer of the classic, "You Are My Sunshine," after a campaign that featured a heavy diet of country and western music including a song or two from Davis himself at each appearance. Born in poverty, he rose to prominence as college professor, cowboy movie actor, and composer of popular hits: "It Makes No Difference Now," "Nobody's Darling But Mine," "Sweethearts or Strangers," "When It's Roundup Time in Heaven." Earl Long, brother of the deceased Huey, was defeated for lieutenant governor by Davis' running mate, Emile Verrett, a political unknown. "Don't elect him," the irascible Long told reporters about Davis, "We'll never know whether he is here or in Hollywood."

While Democrats O'Daniel and Davis successfully pursued political careers, Republican Roy Acuff was unable to launch a winning combination in Tennessee. Following graduation from Knoxville's Central High in 1924, Acuff, a natural performer who learned to fiddle from his father, Neil Acuff, an east Tennessee lawyer and judge, began a singing career that has continued unabated through the 1980s. With a band he dubbed the "Crazy Tennesseans" he began fiddling and singing his way across Tennessee and adjacent states in the early 1930s, and in 1936 he recorded "The Great Speckled Bird," a religious ballad based on an Old Testament passage from the Book of Jeremiah. That song, his biggest all-time hit, was followed by "The Precious Jewell" (1940), "Wreck on the Highway" (1942), and "The Wabash Cannonball" (1947) among a host of others. All quickly became staples of the country music repertoire.

Acuff first appeared on the premier country music show during February 1938, the famed Grand Ole Opry. Already well-known throughout the white South, he shot to national prominence in October 1943 when the National Broadcasting Company began carrying his Saturday night portion of the Opry over a network of more than 125 stations. According to country music historian Bill C. Malone, Acuff "dominated and symbolized" country and western music during the war; in 1944 when he first dabbled in politics he was earning $200,000 a year from recordings and personal appearances. Nor was Acuff's popularity limited to audiences in the South. During a bonzai attack in the desperate struggle for Okinawa, Japanese soldiers were heard to yell: "To hell with Roosevelt; to hell with Babe Ruth; to hell with Roy Acuff."

His entry into politics started in 1943 when Prentice Cooper, three-time governor and tool of Boss Ed Crump of Memphis, could not run for reelection under Tennessee law. Shortly after his first coast-to-coast broadcasts over NBC, a group of reporters at the Nashville *Tennessean* with nothing better to do got up a petition and entered Acuff's name for the Democratic gubernatorial nomination. Upon hearing that he might be a candidate, Crump, who had dominated Tennessee politics for more than a generation, said he could not "believe that the people of Tennessee want a man who knows nothing what-so-ever about governmental affairs." Although Acuff allowed himself to be courted by anti-Crump Democrats, he announced in late October: "I know I'm a good fiddler—but I don't know that I'd make a good governor." And since his family were Republicans in the mountains of east Tennessee, he faced a dilemma. Just two years before he had campaigned with his band—then styled the Smoky Mountain Boys—for his father's reelection as Republican judge in Knox County. Acuff, who had also appeared in several Hollywood movies, ended speculation about his political ambitions on February 7, 1944, by officially withdrawing from the Democratic primary.

Unabashed by his disavowal, GOP groups in various Tennessee counties began to sponsor him for the Republican nomination. But Acuff issued a formal disclaimer on June 23 asking "his friends over the state not to consider me as a candidate for this, the highest office in their gift." Although he decided not to seek office during the war, it was a different story four years later. After winning the Tennessee GOP nomination in 1948, he joined longtime Republican Congressman B. Carroll Reece, a candidate for the U.S. Senate, in a wide-ranging contest for governor. But his postwar campaigning proved a disaster, although he told one 1948 campaign crowd that he was running "like the 'Wabash Cannonball' and the 'Night Train to Memphis' rolled into one." The 1948 gubernatorial campaign ended Acuff's political ambitions.

The astounding popularity of country music during the war among southerners surely fueled the political aspirations of Davis, O'Daniel, and Acuff, and nonmusical politicos regularly used hillbilly bands to enhance their image with white southerners. The wartime migrations of people to and from every part of the country spread the music's influence. Good old boys from Virginia to Texas not only carried their love for hillbilly harmony to military bases in the North and overseas but also clamored to hear the down-home tunes over the radio and in bars wherever they went. Defense workers from the South who went to other parts of the country in search of war jobs also sought out country and western music over local radio stations and on juke boxes in jive joints and eateries. Because many southern and Appalachian whites never returned home, their music stayed with them in the North and on the West Coast.

Radio, more than any other vehicle, spread the art to other sections of the country. Listening audiences reached an all-time peak during the war when literally everybody kept an ear tuned for the latest fighting news and for the newest in popular entertainment. Thirty million homes had at least one radio in 1944, and while no country music show was listed among the top ten programs in the national ratings, country and western performers were featured on hundreds of local broadcasts. Bill Malone, acknowledged dean of country and western historians, estimates that in 1944 more than 600 hillbilly programs were beamed over the airwaves. Practically all major country and western artists of the war and postwar eras got their show business start by performing on local broadcasts. Greater radio exposure for both popular and hillbilly musi-cians in turn led to recording contracts and increased public acceptance of their work.

Universal radio listening during the war years encouraged a broad-casting style that has survived into the 1980s—the barn dance, or Grand Ole Opry-type country and western format. The Opry, oldest and best known of the shows, first went on the air in 1925 over WSM at Nashville. Originating from historic Ryman Auditorium, the program was heard weekly in more than thirty states and occasionally as far away as Alaska. Though most of its artists "could not read a note of music," the lively show with its catchy mountain tunes had a tremendous audience through-out the 1940s. Featuring such performers as Acuff, Bill Monroe,

"Cousin" Minnie Pearl, Rod Brassfield, Eddie Arnold, Cowboy Copas, and the Texas Troubadour, Ernest Tubb, the Opry was heard over millions of radios tuned to the powerful 50,000 watt transmitter at WSM.

The average citizen, who waited for the return of sons and husbands from war fronts and who listened faithfully to down-home music from Nashville, created an eager audience for other country and western broadcasts, some national in scope, others purely local. Station WCHS in Charleston, West Virginia, made its "Old Farmer's Hour" a Saturday night staple in the 1940s. Like other regional programming it not only highlighted local mountain talent, but it also launched several performers on careers at the Grand Ole Opry and opened the way to contracts with major recording companies. The regional productions, however, were overshadowed by shows like the National Barn Dance, "a kissin cousin" to the Opry, that started in 1924 over WLS in Chicago, another 50,000 watt clear-channel station. Gene Autry, reputedly the highest paid wartime country and western singer before his 1942 induction into the army, was a onetime performer on the show. Other "hillbilly" broadcasts included the WLW Barn Dance from Cincinnati and the famed Renfro Valley Show; the latter originated from rural south-central Kentucky near Mt. Vernon, a small hamlet that was miles from the nearest population center. Yet it had Saturday night crowds during the war that averaged 5,000 foot-stomping fans.

Though the "Camel Caravan," named for a popular wartime cigarette manufactured by the Reynolds Tobacco Company and staffed by Grand Ole Opry singers, became the best known, the larger barn dances also put together touring companies. Even before 1941 organized troupes were on the road spreading country and western music to countless small towns and hamlets; these shows, which entertained civilians and servicemen alike, were encouraged throughout the war as a way to foster home-front morale. Mostly they further popularized the Nashville sound during 1942–1945 by giving locals a chance to see and hear top hillbilly showmen perform at movie houses and high school auditoriums.

Many artists specialized in songs with patriotic and war-related themes—"Praise the Lord and Pass the Ammunition," "There's a Star Spangled Banner Waving Somewhere," "Cowards Over Pearl Harbor," "Smoke on the Water"—which made country and western music an integral part of wartime America. That tradition, which included songs like *Filipino Baby* and *My Fraulein,* was carried unbroken into the 1950s and 1960s. And forty years after the conflict, down-home singers are still belting out mournful tunes about the war. A widely heard song in 1982, "*War is Hell*," told how a sixteen-year-old Georgia boy got his first taste of love in 1942; his partner was an older woman whose husband had entered the service. "War is Hell," a refrain blared out, "for the woman left behind."

9 MAY-JULY 1944: A MOUSEY-LOOKING LITTLE MAN FROM MISSOURI

ummer 1944 found 140 million civilians preoccupied with every conceivable activity, much of it far removed from the war. While national attention was fixed on the massive troop build-ups in England for the Normandy invasion, a survey of dress and dating habits among teenage girls in several states revealed little interest among them in anything as abstruse as the Allied crusade for democracy. Although "slick chicks at west coast schools insisted on white shirts and dungarees, most girls seemed to favor the time honored sloppy joe outfit," or, according to *Life*, "a loosely-fitting sweater, string of pearls, pleated skirt, and shoes." Tight-fitting sweaters and blouses were considered bad taste. At Atherton High School in Louisville the in-dress for girls included plaid sport coats which had been left behind by boys in uniform. It was called the "Sinatra look," after crooner Frank Sinatra who was still a popular singing idol. The *Life* survey in May concluded that among high school girls: "1) the craze for wearing men's clothing—shirts, bow ties, sweaters, and jackets—is spreading; 2) white bobby sox have replaced colored anklets; 3) moccasin-type shoes [loafers] are being worn in place of the no-longer-available Oxford." About the only rebellious or radical fad among pre-military age boys was "their deliberately sloppy way of wearing short shirts outside their pants."

Another survey in mid-1944, this one by the J. B. Pierce Foundation of New York—an outfit interested in postwar housing construction—examined middle-class bedroom-bath practices. A sample of 131 "typical families" earning between $3,000 and $4,000 per year found, among other things, that 87 percent of the couples interviewed slept in double beds; but nearly half the wives said twin beds would make a better sleeping arrangement. The twin bed mania, made popular by countless movie scenes with couples always sleeping apart during an era in which Hollywood did not dare film a man and woman in the same bed, was only part of the Pierce findings. "In summer," the survey learned, "70 percent of the wives sleep in nightgowns, 24 percent in pajamas (10 percent more switch to pajamas in winter), 1 percent in shorts, 5 percent nude." Furthermore, 63 percent of the women claimed they usually dressed and 72 percent undressed in front of their husbands, while 20 percent said they never did; 6 percent were too embarrassed to do either.

Two groups that materially affected the country in the post-war era continued to arrive in this land of quaint sleeping habits through the summer: war brides and refugees from wartorn Europe. GIs by the thousands stationed in England and Australia not only found the local lasses attractive but also desirable as wives; boatloads of the new Americans began to reach the home front, and more times than not they arrived without their husbands to live with in-laws. An army transport ship which docked at San Francisco in April 1944 carried ninety women as well as 2,000 veterans of Guadalcanal, New Guinea, and the Pacific naval war. The women had frequently married following whirlwind courtships, and one Australian bride who was on her way to the home of in-laws in Humboldt, Nebraska, said she had met her husband, a naval chief petty officer, eighteen months before at a Sidney dance hall: "He just asked me to dance and I kept dancing with him all night." Another, described as blue-eyed and self-assured, had first encountered her husband at a Sydney zoo two years earlier. Then, in a seemingly typical response, she told reporters that she was "forgetting how he looks and how he talks." Fourteen of the ninety brides were accompanied by young babies.

Other ships during the summer brought the war to these shores in a different way. Although the boats carried a mere trickle of refugees from the European Holocaust, these latecomers were seldom greeted with the same enthusiasm as the brides from Down Under. The refugees who managed to slip by rigidly-enforced alien-exclusion laws usually came with little or no wealth and no relatives to welcome them at dockside. When 983 refugees from internment camps in Italy landed in New York on August 3, they were hustled off immediately to an "army barracks" at Fort Ontario in Oswego, New York. All were considered temporary visitors because they had entered the country outside existing immigration quotas.

Once here, "the visitors" were placed under the jurisdiction of the War Relocation Authority, the same agency in charge of detention camps for Japanese-Americans. Most of the 983 refugees were Jews from various parts of Europe who somehow made their way to Italy after word spread across the continent that Eisenhower had landed in France. Mrs. Eva Bass, a nightclub singer in Paris before the war, traveled sixty kilometers through several combat zones with two small children to reach the Allied lines and safety. Trapped in Milan at the outbreak of war, she had been given "free confinement" at a camp in southern Italy because of her status as a Swiss Jew. Like the other refugees she made an overnight train ride from New York to Oswego without a stop-over upon leaving the boat. The army used "gas chambers" to disinfect their clothing before handing each "two towels and a cake of soap." Then, as curious townspeople peered from outside the post fence, Mrs. Bass and her fellow refugees were assigned their quarters.

It is doubtful if the reception accorded war brides and refugees once crossed the minds of an estimated 60,000 to 70,000 fans who crowded into Churchill Downs at Louisville to watch the seventieth running of the Kentucky Derby. Like others with money in their pockets and bent upon the good time, they whooped it up as Pensive, "the son of the 1936 English Derby winner, Hyperion, bounded home four and one-half lengths ahead of Mrs. George Poulson's Broadcloth of Los Angeles." The three-year-old Pensive, from Kentucky's Calument Farm, earned $65,200, the richest purse in Kentucky Derby history, with a first-place time of two minutes and four seconds. Although $655,372 was bet on the Louisville classic, the highest ever one-day take at a racetrack crossed the boards one week before at Jamaica, Long Island. The old record for a seven-race program on a single day was $2,852,414, bet at the same track during 1943. The new record was $3,176,553.

Yes, segments of the home front seemed to ignore the conflict, but others continued to do their part until the very end. Nowhere was the curious mix of pleasure-seeking and patriotic concern more evident than in a peculiarly wartime phenomenon called the paper drive. Like the effort to roll bandages for the troops at Red Cross headquarters or the collection of food for the overseas needy, the paper drive was a means of socializing with neighbors in the name of patriotism. The unprecedented demand for paper and paper products in defense production—a single P-51 Mustang fighter required 1,069 square feet of paper packing for overseas shipment—prompted calls for the public to save leftover paper. Agencies of the army and navy reportedly needed a billion paper containers in 1944 alone for the shipment of foodstuffs.

Every community of any size had its paper salvage committee in place for the duration to oversee collections. Just about everyone in small-town America, from Brownie troops to senior citizens to housewives joined in the periodic drives. Although OPA set a $14 per-ton ceiling price for waste paper, organizations of every kind joined in paper drives as fund-raising techniques. In Teaneck, New Jersey, a VFW post was able to payoff its lodge hall mortgage with money raised through paper collections. The War Production Board, which supervised paper gathering operations, issued patriotic pennants to communities and civic groups meeting prescribed quotas. Average paper per capita consumption at home in 1944 was twenty-four pounds per month; each citizen therefore was asked to hand in seven pounds monthly to make up a serious shortfall.

Professional junk dealers before the war supplied 250 wastepaper mills with five million tons annually; by 1944 demand had risen to eight million tons to supply 600 paper processing plants. With the patriotic impulse to turn in paper high at first, collections sagged as the emergency progressed, though many communities kept up their quotas straight through the war. Conscientious individuals like Henry Leuders of Teaneck, described as "an indefatigable picker-up of stray paper," gathered 2,500 pounds in a single collection drive. And people like Leuders cropped up all over America.

But others were not so anxious to help the Allied cause. Driving home the ever-present problem of disloyalty was the trial of twenty-eight men and two women accused of sedition, which opened April 17 in Washington's Federal District Court Building and lasted throughout the summer and winter. Although the court proceedings bordered on the farcical at times, they dramatized the dilemma of a freely-elected government trying to defend itself against a citizen's constitutional guarantee of free expression. And clearly, loose talk was all that the thirty defendants could be charged with, because FBI director J. Edgar Hoover had released a report before start of the trial that out of 147 convictions for sedition, sabotage, and failure to register as an enemy alien in the preceding year "there was no evidence of foreign-directed acts of destruction." In nearly all cases prosecuted, his report concluded: "The sabotage was committed by individuals because of maliciousness, spite, or as a prank."

Those placed on trial represented a who's who of American Bund leaders, Ku Klux Klan spokesmen, and Nazi apologists. Nine of the thirty were already in jail on various charges. Among the others were Edward Smythe, who spoke regularly at German Bund and KKK rallies, and James True, inventor of the "kike-killer," a short rounded club made in two sizes, one for use by women (he even held a valid U.S. patent for the thing). George Deatherage, a leader in the Knights of the White Camellia, was also on trial, along with William Pelley, chief of another pro-Nazi outfit called the Silver Shirts, and George Sylvester Viereck, reputed to have been an intimate of ex-Kaiser Wilhelm. Since the case was styled, *United States vs. Joseph E. MacWilliams, et. al*, Joe MacWilliams, another Bund activist, was also among the accused. *Time* said MacWilliams was "a handsome soapbox führer who used to berate Jews and laud Hitler on Manhattan street corners."

When the trial opened, its two women defendants—Mrs. Elizabeth Dilling and Mrs. Lois de Lafayette Washburn—got sensational media coverage for their often hilarious antics. Washburn, a direct descendant of Revolutionary War hero Marquis de Lafayette and the leader of something called the "Yankee Minutemen," was outspoken in her defense of Hitlerism. According to John Roy Carlson, author of *Under Cover*, which appeared in 1943 and detailed his experiences as an undercover agent in the antiwar movement, "more serious than her leaving the shade up while undressing was her insistence that Pearl Harbor was arranged by the New Deal." Always signing her letters "T.N.T. Washburn," she was the object of a widely-circulated photo thumbing her nose at the federal courthouse and calling out: "I am a Facist." Elizabeth Dilling, described as "Führine" of a group called the Mothers Crusade, was also well known, because of her writings and her picketing in front of the senate office building in Washington. Author of a book called *A Red Network*, and defended by her lawyer ex-husband, she appeared in court wearing "a big rose-trimmed hat and a becoming dignity."

Although the Chicago *Tribune* called all thirty "crackpots"—a view shared by most everyone, the government proceeded against them with deadly seriousness. But the public lost interest as the thing dragged through November and December. And press coverage slackened after the first blast of publicity; though twenty-eight newsmen were initially assigned to the proceedings, their number had dwindled to three "regulars" by November: United Press, International News Service, Washington *Star*, and "an occasional visit from the *Daily Worker*." By early November, when the trial entered its thirtieth week, *Newsweek* reported: "The record has already run to more than 15,000 pages of bickering, objections, argument, testimony and rulings. . . . Thirty-six government witnesses have been heard: another 75 still to testify. . . . With bland resignation the jury of 10 men and women have surrendered their private lives indefinitely . . . and no one can tell when it will all end."

Then, with a classic twist of irony, the curtain rang down on the spectacle a few weeks later without a decisive outcome. One defendant, Elmer J. Garner of Wichita, Kansas, publisher of *Publicity*, a pro-Nazi paper, had died and three others had been granted severances of trial because of illness. (They included James C. True, inventor of the "kike-killer.") Others had quit attending. Lois de Lafayette Washburn, who gestured suggestively at the start and who wore "a pale blue nightdress" to open court, had stayed away since August teaching a night course for secretaries. After all the uproar and hours of painstaking testimony, the trial ended suddenly on the 102nd day when the presiding judge, Edward C. Eichler, a onetime New Deal congressman from Iowa, died of heart failure.

Ironically, as proceedings against the thirty dissidents swung into high gear, the country entered into serious mainstream politics on June 26 when the Republican National Convention opened in Chicago. A total of 1,057 delegates from forty-eight continental states and the territories gathered in a staggering heat wave to choose a presidential nominee from three candidates still in the running: Bricker of Ohio, who kept plodding for every possible convention vote and who was the only active candidate to make the trek to Chicago; Harold E. Stassen, onetime Minnesota governor and then attached to Admiral Halsey's staff in the South Pacific; and "youthful" Thomas E. Dewey, who made sure newsmen learned that he was inspecting operations at his Pawling, New York, farm when the spectacle opened. The conventioneers met with the foreboding knowledge that Roosevelt had upstaged them by unleasing Eisenhower and the Normandy invasion two weeks earlier. Although organizers timed convention sessions for peak radio listening hours, it was difficult to be enthusiastic for the Republican banner with Roosevelt riding a good turn in the war.

Ohio Senator Robert A. Taft, chairman of the platform committee, held hearings for one week before the opening gavel in a much-publicized effort to write a vote-getting document. Working on the premise that everyone should be heard, Taft and his platform drafters listened to a parade of speakers—many of them grasping at a national podium for their harebrained schemes. Speakers included Gerald L. K. Smith, head of the America First Committee, Clark M. Eichelberger, an "internationalist" who spoke for the United Nations Association, and aging General Jacob S. Coxey, organizer of the famed Coxey's army in the 1890s. The final draft, rejected by a sulking Willkie because it was "ambiguous," like most party instruments, had something for everyone. For the black vote it recommended "establishment of a Fair Employment Commission, passing of anti-lynching legislation, adoption of an anti-poll tax amendment to the Constitution and investigation of racial discrimination in the armed forces." Social Security for all workers was advocated, as well as "elimination of excessive business regulations." On the all-important foreign policy issue the platform called for "a postwar cooperative organization among nations," but it declared against creation of a "world state."

With the country glued to convention broadcasts, Wednesday, June 28, was reserved for nominating speeches and the selection of candidates. Nebraska Governor Dwight Parker Griswold, who had served with Black-jack Pershing in Mexico during his chase after Pancho Villa, was picked to nominate Dewey. Griswold, a future U.S. senator, stepped before a conclave stripped of ostentatious display because of the war to proclaim Dewey "the spokesman of the future." "For his efforts," notes Dewey's biographer, "Griswold was rewarded with a short, sweaty display of applause that included nearly every state standard, and a brass band pounding out 'Anchors Away' and 'What do we do on a Dew, Dew, Dewy Day?' Alf Landon could be seen in the crowd doing a little dance of joy. Dewey's supporters waved professionaly lettered placards which had been brought from New York. 'Dewey Will Win,' they promised. 'Dewey, the People's Choice.' "

After that outburst (which lasted only seven minutes because of the heat), other Republican hopefuls withdrew from the contest. With Dewey clearly the man of the hour, they came forward to proclaim their loyalty. First, Bricker withdrew his name as the band played "Beautiful Ohio" and his followers shouted "No!" "No!" Senator Joseph Ball of Minnesota followed him to the podium to say Stassen was no longer in the running; and last, Illinois Congressman Everett McKinley Dirksen, who had conducted a low-keyed campaign, bowed out. Since Willkie and MacArthur had already withdrawn from the race, the only remaining business was to call the roll for Dewey. After a single ballot the tally stood: Dewey, 1056, MacArthur, 1; a lone holdout in the Wisconsin delegation, fifty-four-year-old Grant A. Ritter, a Beloit diary farmer, was the only recalcitrant. "I'm a man, not a jellyfish," he told his delegation chairman, when implored to change his vote.

Although his mother, Mrs. George H. Dewey, had journeyed from the ancestral home in Owosso to watch the convention, Dewey and his wife followed radio accounts of his selection in the executive mansion at Albany. He was nominated at 2:25 p.m., and six hours later he was in Chicago to give his acceptance speech, which had been prepared in advance. When Dewey arrived by special plane, newspaper accounts of the flight played on the irony that FDR had done the same thing twelve years before when he too traveled from the New York executive mansion to Chicago by air to accept his party's nomination. After shaving and donning a new suit—crafted by the Duke of Windsor's New York tailor—Dewey stepped with his wife before the roaring conclave at 9:08 p.m. John Bricker of Ohio who had been handed the vice presidential nomination as a sop to midwestern conservatism, was also on the podium. Dewey stood before 25,000 people, sweating and jammed into an auditorium designed to hold 21,000, as he hurled down the political gauntlet: "I come to this great task a free man. I have made no pledges, promises, or commitments, expressed or implied, to any man or woman. I shall make none except to the American people. . . ."

As Dewey left Chicago on Friday, June 30, to take up the campaign trail, the home front was wild with the ouija or swami board craze then sweeping the country and with preparations for the upcoming July Fourth holiday. The so-called ouija board—a come-on for the gullible if ever there was one—was made from plastic materials instead of the wood that had been utilized in earlier versions. Designed for use on a table or lap with one or two players, it consisted of printed letters on a rectangular surface. A "pointer" with small legs was supplied to glide across the contraption; it operated by placing the fingers lightly on the pointer and letting it mysteriously "spell out" future events and omens.

Young girls particularly were attracted to the device to learn if or when Prince Charming might arrive. Seemingly unaffected by wartime restrictions on construction materials, the hot-selling item could be found in shops and stores everywhere. The board had been popular during World War I and the fad was resurrected in 1941–1945 by enterprising merchants. "They're mysterious," read an advertisement offering the boards for $1.69 each: "They're uncanny. They're like golf and solitaire—once you get started you're a fiend. These boards are sweeping the country— you've got to have one to be in the swim. Talking boards are taking the place of ping pong and a dozen other things. What else can tell you when you'll have a letter from him?"

But the hardships of war were evident when the country celebrated its 169th birthday; travel restrictions once again dampened vacation plans for millions over the Independence Day weekend, although more than a few found ways to enjoy the work break close to home. Police in New York said train travel was far below expected levels during the Saturday through Tuesday holiday; and the Associated Press reported record low "accidental and violent deaths for the period." Several deaths amid the July Fourth oratory and lemonade-guzzling resulted from various mishaps. These included a spectacular train wreck twenty miles west of

Flagstaff, Arizona. The Santa Fe Chief, with 158 passengers aboard heading for the West Coast, derailed after it "eased over a mountain hump, rounded a slight curve, and headed into a long straightaway." Indians from a nearby reservation tended bonfires through the night as crewmen worked to free the vital east-west track for military traffic.

At the other end of the country a fire of undetermined cause destroyed the wooden grandstand used by the Baltimore Orioles. The old ball park, which had come near to being a national landmark, had been home to baseball greats such as Lefty Grove, Joe Bailey, Thomas Thomas, and Babe Ruth. The team not only lost its stadium but also its uniforms and equipment along with those of the visiting Syracuse Chiefs. While no one died in the Baltimore inferno, another fire a few days afterward claimed 167 lives, eighty of them children, when a Barnum and Bailey circus big top burned on July 6 at Hartford, Connecticut. The worst disaster in Barnum and Bailey history took place while the famed Wallenda family was performing on the high wire before a packed house of 7,000. "More than 1,000 animals, including 40 lions, 16 tigers, 30 leopards, 20 bears, 40 elephants, and lesser beasts, were in the corral just south of the circus tent when it flamed, but they were kept under control. None broke out." Most of the victims suffocated when the burning tent collapsed around the main pole.

Another kind of tragedy—one involving family relationships—came to light on July 3 when a twenty-three-year-old draft resister was hauled into federal court at Miami. Thousands of conscientious objectors, religious fanatics, and an occasional backswoodsman who did not understand the law had plagued selective service officials since implementation of the draft, but in this case a man simply did not want to serve. He had remained "hidden" in his parent's home for three years without leaving the house. His saga started in 1941 when he failed to register, he told the court, because of illness. The father, who worked at a Miami shipyard, his wife and the son were released on $500 bond each after federal prosecutors indicated that the youth, described as "emaciated and pale," was unfit for military duty. Prosecutors recommended physical and psychiatric treatment before continuing the case. But game to the last, he told the judge: "I am the guilty one. I got mother and dad into this trouble. I knew what I was doing. I just waited too long to register." He objected strenuously, however, when the court set bail and bound him over for future action because he "did not want to go home and face the neighbors."

Meanwhile, Admiral Ernest J. King joined a parade of patriotic speakers on July Fourth at the giant Philadelphia Naval Yard, where he addressed 50,000 military and civilian workers. Besides urging greater industrial output to end the war, King, Fleet Commander and Chief of Naval Operations, thought, like nearly everyone else, that the conflict was approaching a climax: "The current offensives against Japan and Germany," he said, "have so restricted the enemy's areas of occupation as to bring close at hand when the Axis forces must stand and fight." Secretary of the Treasury Henry F. Morgenthau and James V. Forrestal, Navy Secretary, were also there to present citations for bond purchases by naval personnel because King's address was part of the well-orchestrated Fifth War Bond Drive.

Seventy-five miles away, at the Federal Shipbuilding and Dry Dock yards near the Newark suburb of Kearney, New Jersey, July Fourth was observed by launching "a heavyweight destroyer and two destroyer escorts." Although public perception of the war's end matched that of King, the American Arsenal of Democracy could still supply the military hardware that "counted." A 2,200-ton destroyer launched on the Passaic River at Kearney was the *Boire*, named for Edward Adolphe Boire, Secretary of the Navy under Ulysses S. Grant. It was sent down the ways by Mrs. Albert Nalle of White March, Pennsylvania, a great grandneice of Boire. She had christened an earlier version of the *Boire* during World War I, but the ship had been torpedoed in November 1942 while fighting a German U-boat.

Since the start of the defense build-up, the federal installation at Kearney had built eighty destroyers, giving wartime jobs to thousands. But the company furloughed 800 workers one week after launching the *Boire* and announced plans to lay off 700 more before the end of July. Federal was not the only defense manufacturer to initiate massive terminations within weeks of the Normandy invasion. Navy spokesmen called for immediate cuts in landing-craft construction and an equally sharp reduction in the building of Hellcat and Wildcat fighters produced by Grumman Aircraft plants on Long Island and the West Coast. At Baton Rouge, Louisiana, a recently-built aluminum plant closed its production lines for lack of defense contracts. And a Budd Manufacturing installation in Philadelphia was forced to layoff 2,000 workers during the summer, when orders for stainless steel cargo planes were canceled.

A debate raged for the remainder of the war about whether the demand for defense production had peaked, and if so, what to do about it. Conversion to a peacetime economy got entwined with election-year politics, as labor leaders, businessmen, and politicians warned that plans for returning servicemen and furloughed defense workers required immediate attention. Millions of workers who perceived the end was coming wanted to leave their jobs in defense plants and get a jump on good peacetime spots. And as desertions from the assembly line mounted, the War Manpower Commission—still charged with worker allocations—was faced with hard choices: whether to impose restrictions on the work jumpers or turn a blind eye as they looked for other work.

The reconversion argument reached fever pitch during June when War Production Board chairman Donald Nelson released his own plan for ending defense production. He issued a four-step reconversion program in the middle of the presidential campaign at a time when everyone wanted consumer items after thirty-one months of doing without. It resulted in his fall from grace in wartime Washington. The first three proposals aroused little notice since they primarily freed aluminum and magnesium for the manufacture of consumer items, and they allowed companies to begin purchasing tools and machinery for non-military production. But his fourth step raised a storm from military planners and a faction inside WPB that was opposed to Nelson's enthusiastic approach to the manufacture of civilian goods. The order permitted companies whose defense contracts had expired to start turning out any of seventy-nine household products: "vacuum cleaners, electric irons, pots and pans, bedsprings, juice extractors, bicycles, and most of the other wonderful useful items that one used to be able to find in department stores." Those items, the military men said, would divert precious raw materials from the war effort.

Meanwhile, army brass raised an outcry at Nelson's Order No. 4, which he scheduled for release on July 1, less than a month after the first landings on the French coast. Under Secretary of the Navy Robert Patterson went over his head to have the directive delayed; and Roosevelt's chief defense coordinator, James F. Byrnes, ruled that when it did take effect on August 15, "no plant could actually start making any of the 79 items without permission of the War Manpower Commission." When labor leaders fearing mass unemployment and layoffs because of Order No. 4, joined in the crescendo FDR hurriedly relieved Nelson at WPB. But FDR did not turn Nelson away entirely. He dispatched him to China on a high-level diplomatic mission. Wags and Republicans said Roosevelt wanted Nelson out of the country during the presidential canvass because he feared that he might speak out for more civilian production, a popular notion among voters.

As early as November 1943, cutbacks in defense contracts had started a downward spiral in domestic employment. By June 1944, more than a million workers had been thrown out of work since the New Year; and blacks—especially black women—were hardest hit by the fall in jobs. In all too many cases they had been the last hired and the first to be let go. A 1982 study by University of Arizona Professor Karen Anderson noted that during the war "the percentage of the black female labor force in farm work was cut in half, as many from the rural South migrated to urban areas in response to the demand for war workers. The shift of large numbers of black women from work in farms and homes to work in factories resulted in the proportion of black females employed in industrial occupations rising from 6.5 percent to 18 percent during the war." Minority women, and indeed all women, who had managed to get a toehold in wartime plants were bumped from decent paying jobs without mercy, but their male counterparts also received short shrift from an economy hell-bent on peacetime reconversion. Although some companies relented under Fair Employment Practices pressure and gave employment to black women for the duration, they seized the opportunity to fire them when defense contracts began to disappear. Other outfits, like the Carter Carburetor Company in St. Louis "managed a minimal compliance with FEPC orders to cease discriminating when it came to black men, but refused in April 1944 to hire any black women on the grounds that it had no intention of hiring any more women."

Black workers—men and women alike—had been an integral part of the migrations and population shifts during the war. And if some discriminatory barriers were broken in the process, old patterns of race relations were quickly reestablished by the reconversion process. "Both during and after the war," Anderson concludes, "black women entered the urban labor force in large numbers only to occupy the lowest rungs. Largely excluded from clerical and sales work, black women found work primarily in service jobs outside the household and in unskilled blue-collar categories. . . . For black women, especially, what is significant about the war experience is the extent to which barriers remained intact."

Around the country during the war, many low-income whites had joined the higher-paying work force. Taking their place were black workers from the rural South who moved to the industrial centers of the North in search of defense jobs or domestic service work. The great exodus of blacks had a marked impact on some parts of the country. In the South, Mississippi had more whites than blacks for the first time in a century because of the many blacks who had either moved to the North or joined the armed services (12,000 Mississippi blacks had done the latter). The

Jackson *Advocate,* a black newspaper, noted that 50,000 had left the state and that more were going every day because they were "frustrated and confused by the South's racial bigotry." Racial discord in fact worsened in the war period, particularly around Mississippi's military camps, where black soldiers like Joe Louis ran afoul of white supremacist customs. As local politicans thrashed away at administration efforts to improve the lot of blacks, the *Granada County Weekly* editorialized in 1944: "The good darkies of the South should remember that, at best, Eleanor [Roosevelt] will be boss of the U.S. a limited time, while the good white people of the South will be here forever."

Hostility toward blacks in a shrinking workplace was not confined to the South. In Philadelphia an August 1 strike against the city's transit system nearly shut down the nation's number two defense production center. The trouble started when eight blacks were given jobs as apprentice motormen on city streetcars. Although the strike ended within a week, the man-hour loss in war production was enormous. *Time* called it the worse transportation stoppage of the war: "Philadelphia's 900,000 war workers (who make everything from hub caps to vital radar equipment) hitchhiked, trudged miles on sweltering sidewalks—or stayed home."

The transit company, which employed 600 blacks, had experienced no race-related labor difficulty until the decision to elevate the eight motormen after a training period on the city's lines. Then 6,000 workers walked off the job. White workers used the call-in-sick ploy and stayed home. When word got out that blacks would run some streetcars on their own, the entire transit system collapsed: "Hardly a streetcar or a subway train left the barn. Flying squads in automobiles chased after the few that were already in operation. By noon every one of the city's 1,900 street cars, 632 buses and 541 subway and elevated cars were idle."

Philadelphia's racial woes and strike ended when FDR ordered 8,000 army troops into the city with guns at the ready. Major General Philip Hayes, in charge of the force, immediately evoked the Smith-Connally Act, which resulted in indictments against thirty-five strike leaders by a hastily-summoned grand jury. And Hayes not only hoisted an American flag over the city car barns but also came down hard on white trouble-makers; go to work or loose your draft-exempt status for the remainder of the war was his message. When union men objected to the continued presence of the black motormen, Hayes was equally blunt—they would stay on their jobs. Although the Philadelphia episode was spawned by racial discontent, the strike itself was not unique. It made little difference that the country was locked in the third year of war, as labor all but abandoned its earlier no-strike pledge and official Washington gave its tacit approval. After all, the administration could hardly deploy 8,000 regulars everytime workmen walked off the job. And walk off the job they did throughout 1944. Most wartime strikes and work stoppages were purposely held to short intervals by union bosses. Like a quick kick on the football field, the fast strike before public opinion and officialdom could mobilize against the strikers proved very effective in labor's fight against Washington's effort to maintain a stable workforce.

The Bureau of Labor Statistics—charged with keeping records on such matters—apparently had difficulty in recording the man-hours lost in vital defense production as a result of the near-constant strikes. Bureau statisticians in 1943, for instance, withheld production figures for three months on the flimsy pretext that "a reduced budget at the Office of War Information kept BLS from receiving reliable data." Republican newspapers called that explanation "silly" and even hinted that it was part of an administration cover-up of labor's poor showing in wartime. The best available information revealed that some 2,565 work stoppages had occurred during the first six months of 1944.

Fighting men, like people at home, were not impressed by labor's record. A minor controversy arose during July after officers and men aboard the *U.S.S. Coos Bay*, a seaplane tender in the Pacific, got up a $412 contribution "to buy off" 12,000 strikers at a Wright Aircraft plant in Lockland, Ohio. That work stoppage, which started on June 5, lasted four days, halting defense production after seven black workers were transferred to an all-white section of the plant. The shutdown ended as quickly as it began when union and company leaders came down hard on the recalcitrants, although 240 diehards were fired for refusing to work. But reasons for the strike made little difference to the *Coos Bay* crew. They saw only that 12,000 men at home had halted defense production while they stood toe-to-toe with the Japanese war machine.

A letter and $412 in pennies was sent to an Associated Press manager in San Francisco, asking him to become their "go-between in buying off the strikers." The navy men made no bones about their anger: "Our enemies at home we cannot reach, therefore, in desperation, we can think of nothing but to offer our money 'to buy' them back to work. . . . Ask them not to strike in the future but, instead, to let the men in war zones know of their displeasure and we will gladly chip in each month to save them from starvation so that they can continue to produce arms for us to defeat their enemies as well as ours." Then, after asking if the strikers wanted to see them after the war, the sailors added a postscript: "If the

Wright strike is over, choose another. There are always plenty around."

Washington bureaucrats were not happy with the *Coos Bay* gesture. Although Navy Secretary James V. Forrestal received the pennies from the AP with a snappy "no comment," the administration could hardly reprimand the sailors for speaking out. Navy brass chose to return the money in late June with a terse statement for a bemused public. "The navy holds no brief with strikes in wartime. . . . Neither does the navy condone expressions by its personnel of resentment, however sincere, which are in disregard of official regulations. . . ." If Washington was upset, the labor bosses were more so because the boys on the *Coos Bay* had touched a raw nerve. Automobile Workers president R. J. Thomas, whose union represented the aircraft strikers, immediately claimed the navy men had been "propagandized." But, Thomas warned, the UAW would have to change its ways: "Our union cannot survive if the nation and our soldiers believe that we are obstructing the war effort."

Wartime strikes in Philadelphia and Ohio were nothing compared to the avalanche of overseas events and quickening political pulse that seized the nation during late summer. As the last Nazi strongholds crumbled in Europe and Democrats prepared to nominate Franklin D. Roosevelt for a fourth term at their Chicago national convention, July 19–21, a catchy little tune called "Mairsey Doats" was heard everywhere. Although the thing was on the radio constantly—a movie even featured it—a survey found 75 percent of the population did not know what it meant. That "Mairsey doats and dosey doats and lillamsey divey . . . ," translated into "Mares eat oates and does eat oats and little lambs eat ivy." If Americans found time to whistle silly songs in the midst of war, the German nation facing certain defeat in July 1944 was forced to make hard decisions. Berlin Radio announced on July 20—one day after the Democrats began their twenty-ninth presidential caucus—that Adolph Hitler had been nearly killed by a group of disgruntled officers. The conspirators, headed by Colonel Claus Von Stauffenburg, had tried to destroy him with a bomb planted in his military command post at Rastenburg in East Prussia. By some design of the gods Hitler, though hurt, escaped death. The bloodbath of executions that followed, when hundreds of officers were brutally put to death for their alleged part in the conspiracy, sent shivers through the civilized world.

Then, as America learned about the death by poisoning of Field Marshal Erwin Rommel, the legendary Desert Fox, for his role in the Rastenburg conspiracy, the Democrats assembled in Chicago for their convention. Speculation was rife that the president's health would keep him from serving another full term. Forced to wear bothersome braces wherever he went as a result of a bout with poliomyelities in the 1920s, Roosevelt was obviously a very sick man in 1944; Lord Moran, Winston Churchill's personal physician and confidant, who observed the president during this period, noted that he was a dying man. At age sixty-three he was soon to be the oldest standard-bearer of either major party since 1856, when James Buchanan was nominated by the Democrats at the age of sixty-five. "He had entered Bethesda Naval Hospital in March 1944," observes party historian Otis L. Graham, "after six months of extreme bronchical troubles, and the doctors found his heart enlarged, his blood pressure high, and that he suffered from arteriosclerosis and hypertension. He lost weight at doctor's orders, further accentuating the gaunt outlines of age."

After Bethesda Roosevelt traveled to Bernard Baruch's plantation retreat near Georgetown, South Carolina, to recuperate. By May 7 he was back at the White House telling reporters he "was feeling a great deal better." In spite of a press understanding never to photograph him in the act of standing up or sitting down because of his lameness, the public could see a plainly weakened chief executive in other photos. Like all politicians, Roosevelt enjoyed playing a coquettish game over his fourth-term ambitions, although no serious observer doubted he would run. Finally, on July 11, FDR did what everyone knew he would do—he sent a letter to Democratic national chairman Robert Hannegan saying he would run "If the convention should nominate me for the Presidency": "Reluctantly, but as a good soldier," he told party chiefs and public alike, "I repeat that I will accept and serve in this office, if I am so ordered by the Commander-in-Chief of us all—the sovereign people of the United States." That noble rhetoric came two weeks after he had "laughed off" questions about the campaign.

On June 23—the same day Thomas E. Dewey was nominated by the Republicans and FDR scoffed at fourth term speculations—a killer storm sliced through western Pennsylvania and north-central West Virginia. In a part of the country seldom bothered by twisters, the death toll ran into the hundreds. The tornado, which originated around Indiana, Pennsylvania, hometown of movie actor Jimmy Stewart, tore through surburban Pittsburgh leaving scores dead. It leveled radio transmitting towers and injured factory workers when roof sections were ripped from three steel mills around McKeesport. In Green County, where the Mason and Dixon strikes the Endicott Line northward to Lake Erie, the havoc was awesome. At Chartiers, a tiny mining community near the county seat at Waynesburg, upward of fifty homes—nearly the whole town—were destroyed and more than fifteen people killed. The storm continued its deadly path southward to three West Virginia counties. Steep mountain hollows hampered rescue efforts throughout the region; and at Shinnston, where the death count soared, ambulance drivers said they counted dead bodies along the roadway as they fought their way up tree-strewn Shinns Run.

A political storm also raged through the summer as conservative Democrats waged a war of their own to dump Henry A. Wallace as FDR's 1944 running mate. It started when Jim Farley, former postmaster general, Coca-Cola bigwig, and New York Democratic boss, resigned as national committee chairman following the 1940 campaign, and Roosevelt replaced him with Ed Flynn, another New York politico. Edward Joseph Flynn, Roman Catholic, lawyer, and one-time sheriff of Bronx County, though he was replaced as national committeeman by Hannegan in 1942, spearheaded the get-Wallace fight. First, he "forced" liberals from party positions whenever possible, and, secondly, he orchestrated a conservative drive to impress the president with Wallace's unacceptability among party rank-and-file. Although Wallace kept up a brave front by speaking for a Democratic party committed to liberal principles as he traveled and lectured, he could not meet the mounting onslaught. Roosevelt, a weary, as well as sick man, who wanted a harmonious national gathering as the war wound down, finally capitulated to the forces led by Flynn and Hannegan. He announced on July 17 that he would stay out of the vice presidential tug-of-war and leave the choice of a running mate to the convention.

The move to return the party to its traditional moorings was influenced by Republican and conservative Democratic gains in the 1942 off-year elections. Roosevelt's own popularity showed signs of slipping because of his failing health, the fourth-term issue, and public apathy toward "liberal New Dealism." A poll after the Republican convention by Elmo Roper indicated that 27.6 percent of the population—less than one third— "were out-and-out for Roosevelt for a fourth term." That compared to 29.6 percent who said they intended to vote for Dewey and the Republicans. Yet it was certain that Roosevelt would be reelected even before his nomination. When Roper asked, "Regardless of what you hope for the future, who do you think will win?" the response was clear: 66.4 percent said, "Roosevelt," 21.9 percent said "Dewey," and 11.7 percent were undecided.

With the liberals determined to renominate Wallace in an open convention, the Democrats were badly divided on the eve of their national conclave. Not only the liberal-conservative fight for control, but also the longstanding North-South division in the party complicated matters. Josephus Daniels, old-time North Carolina newspaperman and Woodrow Wilson's Secretary of the Navy, summed it up this way: "There is the South, where the party is strongest, yet no Southerner has been elected President since the Civil War. One of the biggest Democratic groups is the Catholics, and Al Smith was defeated on that ground. Another group is the Jews, and no Jew can sit in the White House. Finally, there are the Negroes, and they are excluded."

Life said party divisions were the result of history: "This state of affairs began, of course, when the Democratic party was split wide open by the Civil War. When the Civil War was over, the party consisted of the Solid South and whoever in the North had reasons to go along. The most important people to go along were the biggest of the big city bosses. But, in grandpa's day, the South plus the big-city machines couldn't make a national majority—and so the Democrats had to welcome a third element which may be roughly called reformers—reformers of every sort." It was the New Deal reformers who found themselves fighting for the upper hand as they marshaled forces to preserve their notion of what the Democratic party should be.

Forty thousand delegates, newsmen, and hangers-on, who found a way to Chicago in spite of wartime travel restrictions, jammed into Chicago Stadium for the Democratic convention. National chairman Hannegan tried to bar the sale of spirits in the convention hall but later had to rescind the order—there were no drinking fountains in the Stadium. Hannegan's change of heart and a July heat wave caused beer concessionaires at the Democratic confab to do a barnyard business; the conventioneers devoured 125,000 bottles of soft drinks and more than 100,000 hot dogs as they deliberated the party's future. Beer sales averaged 40,000 bottles a day.

Oklahoma governor Bob Kerr opened the gathering with a rousing defense of Roosevelt and party policy. The next day, June 20, Kentucky senator Alben Barkley—disappointed at not getting FDR's blessing for the vice presidential nomination—took forty minutes to put the president in formal nomination. Then followed the customary seconding speeches by party functionaries, one of them by Wallace who seized the occasion to say, "the Democratic party cannot survive as a conservative party." The soon-to-be-deposed vice president demonstrated his appeal by receiving a prolonged ovation upon entering the hall. Roosevelt of course got the nomination on the first roll call, although a band of disgruntled southerners cast a few votes for Virginia senator Harry F. Byrd. The final tally: Roosevelt 1086, Byrd 89.

Frantic dealings through the night over second place on the ticket made it clear that Harry S. Truman, U.S. Senator from Missouri since 1934 and protegé of the infamous Pendergast machine, was the choice of Roosevelt and party caciques to replace Wallace. Roosevelt in fact considered several men for the vice presidency, including Supreme Court justice William O. Douglas and West Virginia senator Harley M. Kilgore. In spite of his disavowal of any preference for a candidate, the president was involved in the final choice. Besides liberals and New Deal bureaucrats in the convention, Wallace's chief support came from organized labor. Sidney Hillman, still Roosevelt's right arm among labor men, had created something new on the American political scene—a Political Action Committee, designed to further labor causes in the coming campaign. PAC, which was bankrolled by the CIO organization, had its own well-oiled staff and headquarters in Chicago, and controlled fifty delegates and seventy-five alternates from twenty-eight states. And PAC stood four square behind the renomination of Henry Agar Wallace. "Wallace . . . Wallace . . . Wallace. That's it. Just keep pounding," CIO president Philip Murray told a clandestine meeting of PAC-labor delegates before the vice presidential roll call. But 1944 was not a good year for liberal causes as conservative-southern forces tightened the screws: on the first roll call it was Wallace 429½, Truman 319½, with 393 votes scattered among thirteen favorite sons. Although the Democrats had been in session for six and a half hours with a PAC-manipulated gallery clamoring for Wallace, convention chairman Sam Jackson, fearing a Wallace groundswell, ordered an immediate roll call. Halfway through the second ballot, when it was Truman 342 and Wallace 286, the favorite son delegates began a mad scramble to get on the winning bandwagon. The bosses had carried the day. The Democratic ticket would be Roosevelt and Truman.

Although PAC and its liberal allies did not win for Wallace, they were able to influence the nomination of Truman in their backstage maneuverings. Several liberal planks were put in the platform at their urging, and Truman's selection was soon dubbed the "Missouri Compromise." PAC and the conservatives had agreed on Truman because he had an unblemished voting record on New Deal issues and he could always be counted upon to follow the party line. And he "voted right" on "Negro-related measures" which enhanced his acceptability to the liberals. Because he was a "plodder" and a faithful party stalwart, Kansas City political boss Tom Pendergast had made him a road supervisor and, after 1933, a county judge. Then followed two terms in the U.S. Senate with Pendergast support, but Pearl Harbor plunged him into the limelight as chairman of a Senate investigating committee to oversee war expenditures. The sixty-year-old Truman, a decorated artillery captain with the A.E.F. in France during World War I, soon found himself shouldering a large part of the campaign for an ailing Roosevelt. Thirty-two months into the war Truman traveled the nation pounding Dewey and "the do nothing Republicans." Finally, on doctor's orders, he was forced to cancel a campaign address at St. Joseph, Missouri, in early August. The reason: he had shaken 10,000 hands within one week of the nomination. A smiling, irrepressible Truman was unbothered when *Time* called him "the mousey-looking little man from Missouri."

10 AUGUST-DECEMBER 1944: BALLOTS AND BASEBALL

In the fall and winter of 1944, as the country watched a presidential canvass in which one of the candidates was running for an unprecedented fourth term, a dairy cow named Elsie stole the public imagination. Actually the "Elsie Phenomena" was part of an ongoing advertising gimmick by the Borden Company to promote the company's line of milk products; through ads in magazines and commercial appearances, Elsie-the-Cow became a familiar sight throughout the 1940s. It all started in 1939 when Borden publicity men used a Jersey cow named "You'll Do Lobelia" from a Massachusetts dairy farm for their display booth at the New York's World Fair.

Elsie/Lobelia, who had appeared in earlier company cartoons, became such a hit, said the New York *Times,* that 60 percent of all questions asked attendants at the Borden fair display concerned her. After all, her measurements were impressive: "hoof circumference at bottom, 16 inches; length from horn to tail, 84 inches; throat, 32 inches; and neck at shoulders, 46 inches." Other questions were divided almost evenly between operations at Borden plants and location of toilet facilities at the fair.

One Borden spokesman explained that "in the late 1930s buying milk at the store was still a recent phenomenon. Because the Jersey is a small, friendly breed that gives milk rich in butterfat, it was the breed that was most often chosen as a family cow. So many adults recognized Elsie as just like the cow we used to have." As her popularity spread, Elsie was awarded the keys to more than eighty-five cities and when she went to Hollywood for a movie appearance in *Little Men,* Elsie-mania ruled supreme. According to writer Martha Thomas, "Borden followed close behind, selling the rights for such novelty items as Elsie mugs, cigar bands, jigsaw puzzles, soap, and neckties. In Hollywood Elsie was greeted by Kay Francis, Spencer Tracy, Frank Sinatra, and John Wayne. She planted her footprints on Hollywood Boulevard, and was given a baby shower two days before the birth of her daughter Beulah." Early in 1945 a survey by the Psychological Corporation found "48 percent of those surveyed knew of Albert Einstein, 43 percent knew who movie idol Van Johnson was, 57 percent recognized Secretary of State Edward Stentinius, and 58 percent knew Elsie the cow."

Amid the country's fascination with lovable dairy cows, Hollywood again made sensational headlines at the end of 1944 with word that Lupe Velez, "the Mexican Spitfire," had overdosed on sleeping pills. Known more for her string of lovers than for serious acting, the thirty-four-year-old Mexican-born actress, appeared in several comedies for Hal Roach Studios at the same time that Jean Harlow and Carole Lombard were getting their start in films. In Hollywood she struck up a tempestuous romance with another young actor, Montana-born Gary (James Frank) Cooper.

Cooper broke into films during 1925 as a cowboy extra. Besides starring in some of Hollywood's best-known productions over the next thirty-five years, including the immortal *High Noon* with Grace Kelly, Cooper wooed some the world's most alluring women. Unlike his buddies Clark Gable and Jimmy Stewart, he did not enter the service, but stayed at home making films like *Sergeant York*, *Pride of the Yankees*, and *For Whom the Bell Tolls*. Although Cooper himself afterwards wrote in the *Saturday Evening Post*, "I guess I was in love with Miss Velez or as much in love as one could get with a creature as elusive as quicksilver. . . ." Their sizzling romance ended in near disaster.

Cooper, who encountered opposition from his mother and his Hollywood press agents over Velez, decided to break off the relationship in 1929, at the same time he planned on taking an extended leave from moviemaking. As he boarded an east-bound train from Los Angeles to New York to board ship for a trip to Italy to visit with American-born countess Dorothy di Frasso, the fiery Velez suddenly appeared on the train platform. After shouting a suitable profanity, the five-foot, 109-pound spitfire whipped out a pistol and blasted away at Cooper. Fortunately she missed, but the episode attracted much press attention for both actors.

After Gary Cooper, according to *Newsweek*, the curvacious Velez had affairs with "John Gilbert, Ronald Coleman, Ricardo Cotez, Johnny Weissmuller, and Arturo de Cordova." Her cavalier approach to men caused her to brush off a young French actor just a week or so before her death, in December 1944, with a flip, "I told him to get out. I like my dogs better." A few days later, she returned from a premier of her latest film, *Zaza*, to her "lavish Hollywood bedroom" and, the *Newsweek* account continued: "She put on her pale blue silk pajamas and wrote two notes. Then she swallowed an overdose of sleeping tablets. Several hours later her secretary and companion, Mrs. Beulah Kinder, found her dead between the silken sheets of her oversize bed."

The graphic portrayal, not only of Lupe Velez's romantic life, but also of the details of her death was not unique to wartime journalism. Popular magazines as well as mass circulation newspapers and tabloids smothered their readers in sensationalism and cheesecake, especially in their Hollywood reporting. Collectively, the press contributed mightily to "a new morality" in a time of personal laxness brought on by the war. *Life* magazine, for instance, ran a story in July 1944 about movie actress Deanna Durbin, featuring a full-page photograph that left little to the imagination about her breast structure. And the photograph did its work. Two issues later the magazine ran another photo of Miss Durbin with a letter from a flying officer at a Pueblo, Colorado, training base: "After one look at Deanna Durbin we have unanimously decided to christen our Liberator 'The Demi-Durbin.' Fully armed, the B-24 in which we are training for combat packs only half the wallop of Deanna." The actress, who received 16,000 fan letters each month, had plenty of admirers on both sides of the Atlantic. William Manchester, in his massive biography of Winston Churchill, says the British prime minister's favorite actress during the war was Deanna Durbin.

In spite of home-front fascination with the bosoms of Hollywood starlets—the death notice of Lupe Velez in one national magazine carried a torrid photograph from a better time in her life—rationing and consumer shortages remained its number one headache. Various shortages of meats, canned foods, tobacco products, and household goods nettled the public in late 1944. Cigarettes especially were in short supply. Everybody seemed to want a cigarette during the war and the race to get them even produced a new joke: "Give me a pack of stoopies." It was a jab at the practice of store owners who "stooped" under the counter to retrieve a pack for favored customers.

Partly as a result of Republican nominee Thomas E. Dewey's slashes at administration reconversion plans, James F. Byrnes, still FDR's home front boss, formulated new strategies to get additional liquor and food to the country as the election neared. One result was a new phrase, V-E Day, to signify the defeat of Hitler or victory in Europe. Byrnes and his Washington bureaucrats handed out edicts that would release everything from whiskey to refrigerators for immediate consumption once Germany collapsed. By late August, *Time* reported: "The administration began to unwind the rationing program. Gin was already flowing out of distilleries in place of war alcohol; whiskey was back on dealers' shelves in plain view of voters. And then September 17, 1944, was set as the day when all processed foods except canned fruits and a few other items would be unrationed."

A moratorium on the manufacture of whiskey, however, was reimposed later in the year. Alcohol distillers were simply given a thirty-one day holiday from government restrictions under Byrnes's August mandate. But that had been long enough to grind out 13,500,000 gallons of whiskey, 21,000 of rum, 897,000 of gin, and 460,000 of brandy. And that was not enough. Thirsty civilians had consumed Byrnes's windfall by the middle of November, which brought demands for more spirits before the Christmas rush. Retailers joined the clamor for replenished liquor stocks, but once the election was over, War Production Board chief Julius A. Krug said, "No." "At the present time," continued Krug, who had replaced Donald Nelson, "in view of the critical nature of military requirements throughout the world, we are not in a position to declare a holiday." Drinkers were told that excess alcohol was needed for the manufacture of synthetic rubber. Bourbon stocks were especially hard hit because corn supplies had to be diverted from the liquor distilleries to the nation's chicken farmers.

Clothing scarcities likewise plagued the country for most of the year; cutbacks in textile and wool production led to a 40 percent reduction in the availabilty of civilian underwear below peacetime levels. First priorities by military procurers made it almost impossible for housewives to buy new towels and other linens. An accompanying dilemma was the lack of moderately-priced linens and clothing of all kinds. Not only clothing and textile manufacturers, but other domestic suppliers as well growled that OPA regulations prevented them from turning a profit on lower-priced goods, which all but disappeared from retail shelves. The result was a flood of costly merchandise beyond the reach of low-income families.

Paper shortages also led to a reduction in the number of new books for the reading public. When a panel of ten literary critics including Norman Cousins of the *Saturday Review* met in December to award prizes for the year's best books, they discovered 6,819 new titles for 1944. The 5,513 general books and 1,306 novels represented a 1,602 drop from the preceding year. John Hersey's war classic, *A Bell for Adano*, was judged the best novel; another novel about the war by Harry Brown, *A Walk in the Sun*, received high praise as well from the critics. Brown's book "was a straightforward, quiet story of a small band of American soldiers on an Italian beachhead."

Sumner Welles's elegant plea for postwar cooperation among nations, like other general works about the war, was turned aside by the literary men. Although *A Time for Decision* by the career diplomat and onetime undersecretary of state had been on the New York *Times* best-seller list for weeks, they went to an earlier time in American life for the best general work. It was a giant biography of Washington Irving by Van Wyck Brooks. Before his death in 1963 at age seventy-seven, Brooks had established himself as the country's chief writer about writers, a fact that no doubt accounts for his acclaim in 1944 by other literati. *The World of Washington Irving* published by Dutton was one of a series of Brooks's biographies about American men of letters: Emerson, Twain, Melville, Whitman, and Henry James. With proceeds from his monumental study of Ralph Waldo Emerson, *The Flowering of New England*, published in 1936, Brooks purchased a home "on the top of an isolated hill four miles from Westport, Connecticut." There the Harvard Phi Beta Kappa turned out his literary masterpieces during the 1930s, 1940s, and 1950s. Brooks told reporters that he had difficulty obtaining the quart of black ink he used each year because of the war.

More train wrecks struck an America already troubled by food and paper shortages and by Thomas E. Dewey's run against a three-term president who said he was too busy to campaign. At Stockman, Georgia, an Atlantic Coast passenger train from nearby Waycross, bound for Montgomery, Alabama, sliced through a section gang; forty-five black workers were killed and nearly 300 others injured in the August 2 disaster. Another rail accident was averted at Annapolis, Missouri, in September by an alert station agent who warned unsuspecting trains to go slow after spotting an open block signal. FBI agents said a fifteen-year-old boy opened a Missouri Pacific switch by busting a padlock and forcing a rail spike between the rails. "I never saw a train wreck, and I always wanted to see one," the youth told St. Louis *Globe-Democrat* reporters. Even though the switch remained partly open, several trains, including two loaded with troops, kept using the rails at reduced speeds near the small hamlet 100 miles southwest of St. Louis.

Even Dewey was not immune from wrecks as his campaign special crossed the country. His train struck a parked troop and passenger hookup at Castle Rock, Washington, sixty miles north of Portland, Oregon, where the Republican candidate was headed for a major campaign appearance. The September 19 accident occurred after a troop train halted because of a previous wreck on the mainline to California. But serious trouble was averted when E. A. Welles, a Seattle engineer operating Dewey's train, saw the engine ahead. "He reported that he was rounding a curve at 55 miles an hour and managed to get the speed down to about 30 when the train hit." It was enough to send reporters and typewriters sprawling through the aisles, and Mrs. Dewey reportedly had a banging headache after striking her head on a door to her Pullman compartment. Her husband was unhurt, although he had a close encounter with a flying waterbottle. "After several hours of delay," reported a New York *Times* writer traveling with the Dewey campaign, "it was decided to abandon the wrecked train for the time and proceed to Portland by automobile. Hastily gathered state police took the immediate Dewey party into their cars and, stopping passing motorists, rounded up enough transportation for the rest of Dewey's people."

Dewey had left the governor's mansion at Albany on September 6 for a whistle-stop tour to the West Coast and back. While heading westward, the Chicago *Daily News*, formerly published by Roosevelt's secretary of the navy, Frank Knox, came out for the New Yorker. Knox, a onetime supporter of FDR's Republican cousin Theodore, had died April 28. The paper's anti-fourth-term stance—because "the American people do not want a perpetual president"—was a boost to Dewey's campaign. Roosevelt may have been a popular wartime leader who capitalized on a "don't change horses in midstream" campaign, but a fourth term did not sit well with many people.

As Roosevelt remained ensconced in the White House with his war advisers and tried to stay aloof from the campaign, Dewey stumped the country in an all-out fight to unseat him. At San Francisco on September 21, he lashed out at administration plans for peacetime reconversion before a cheering 15,000. The country needed "a green light," Dewey proclaimed, "so it could produce peacetime miracles." His jabs at the administration were laced with an anti-New Deal clamor as he demanded a reduction in taxes. "Washington social dreamers" who would spend their money on do-good schemes had no shortcut to the good life, he told his applauding audience. Dewey called for "American ingenuity" to solve peacetime problems—"A new viewpoint in the relationship between government and the planning of our economic security."

Although the campaign sponsored radio spots announcing that "Dewey would clear everything only with Congress and the American people," it was John Bricker, his running mate, who blasted the Democrats for their purported connection with Communists and fellow travelers. He did it in a September 21 speech at Baltimore while urging a breakup of the Democratic hold on the solid South. Bricker developed a two-pronged argument: 1) that the way Democrats could regain control of their party was to cast a Republican tally in 1944; and, 2) that rank-and-file Democrats had lost out to Sidney Hillman and his CIO-sponsored Political Action Committee.

Bricker and the Republicans seized on an apparently off-the-cuff remark by Roosevelt while the Democratic national convention was in progress: "Clear Everything with Sidney!" According to a widely-circulated version of the incident by insiders, FDR, en route to the West Coast, had his private coach switched to a siding near the convention hall. As the fight to keep Wallace off the Democratic ticket bubbled, the party's national chairman, Robert Hannegan, was summoned to the presidential train: "Go down there and nominate Truman before there's any more trouble. And clear everything with Sidney." Gleeful Republicans were soon spending $1 million through various state committees to get the message to every American voter.

Hillman's PAC had an army of volunteers knocking on doors and spending money by the barrelful to defeat not only Dewey but Republican candidates everywhere, which further enflamed GOP passions. His Lithuanian birth coupled with his identification with leftist and labor causes was used by the GOP to maximum effect: and, notes Dewey's biographer, Robert N. Smith, "getting as much publicity as Hillman was Earl Browder, the Kansas-born chairman of the Communist Political Association, a successor to the party dissolved as a measure of wartime unity. Four years earlier, Browder, echoing the party line at the time, stood on a stage in Madison Square Garden and denounced Roosevelt for scheming to lead the nation into imperialist war. Now Browder did an about face, hailing FDR, along with Stalin and Churchill, as 'one of the great architects of the new world a-coming' . . . and warned against the election of Dewey as sending unfriendly signals to the Soviet Union." Dewey, Bricker, and countless GOP candidates in congressional and state house races lost no opportunity to drive home the Hillman-Browder-Roosevelt connection.

Meanwhile, Dewey—press reporters said it was a nervous Dewey—appeared at a West Coast gala on September 21 which featured some of the grandest names in Hollywood. Lavishly staged by movie moguls Cecil B. DeMille and David O. Selznick in the Los Angeles Memorial Coliseum, the get-together attracted 90,000 people. Although veteran actor Lionel Barrymore, who headed a Dewey Committee in Hollywood, was not there, plenty of personalities were on hand: Adolphe Menjou, Eddie Bracken, Ginger Rogers, Hedda Hopper, Edward Arnold, Walt Disney, Gene Tierney, and Joel McCrae. Still critical of Rooseveltian policy, Dewey called for a new program "to pick up and carry forward a system of social progress to fight the difficulties of old age, unemployment, and ill-health."

Roosevelt finally broke his aloofness on September 23 with a speech before an AFL-Teamsters convention in Washington. His first major campaign appearance before a friendly audience was aimed at what the president called "the most obvious or common garden variety of fraud." Or fraud that resulted from unnamed GOP candidates who sought to claim credit for the New Deal. "The whole purpose of Republican oratory these days," he told the truck drivers, "is to persuade the American people that the Democratic party was responsible for the 1929 crash and Depression." Roosevelt said he was too old to be taken in by the Republican ruse.

Dewey, whistle-stopping across the southwest on his return to Albany, answered Roosevelt the next day at Berlin, New Mexico. FDR, he crowed, had resorted to charges of "fraud and falsehood" because he had no constructive program to offer the country. At Oklahoma City, where 10,000 crammed the Municipal Auditorium, including a company of anti-fourth term Democrats from Texas, Dewey spoke "with fury in his voice." He concentrated on Roosevelt's fourth-term aspirations as well as on his supposed indispensibility to the war effort. After quoting General Hap Arnold, Senator Alben Barkley, and even FDR's own running mate, Harry Truman, Dewey said flat out that Roosevelt had not prepared the country for Pearl Harbor. Then, as the crowd stomped approval, he continued: "Sure he's indispensible to Harry Hopkins, Madame Perkins, Harold Ickes. . . . the mayor of Jersey City. . . . to Sidney Hillman. . . . to Earl Browder. Shall we perpetuate one man in office to accommodate this motley crew?" Actor Gary Cooper, who later had reason to regret his outspokenness, said during the campaign that Roosevelt deserved condemnation "for the company he keeps." Cooper, like other conservatives, thought "the country should be saved from foreigners."

Roosevelt, on the other hand, had his own supporters among Hollywood's elite. A star-studded shindig in Madison Square Garden on September 28 drew 20,000 cheering Democrats. Not quite as big as Dewey's affair in Los Angeles, the meeting featured Roosevelt's lame duck vice president, Henry A. Wallace. After urging the reelection of his chief because "he is a great Liberal," a string of actors—Betty Davis, Orson Welles, and Frederick Marsh—came forward to applaud the Democrats. Blind activist Helen Keller and novelist Sinclair Lewis were also there to lend support. The 20,000 partisans paid from 60¢ to $2.40 for seats at the fundraiser. Out in California, a Hollywood committee of New Dealers, which included Rita Hayworth, Olivia de Havilland, Katherine Hepburn, Harpo Marx, Lana Turner, Walter Huston, and Fanny Brice, also worked for Roosevelt.

While Dewey rested in Albany and at his Pawling, New York, farm, he received a visit from Colonel Carter C. Clarke, chief of the War Department's cryptographic intelligence branch. He came at the request of General George C. Marshall, who had become alarmed at Dewey's remarks in Oklahoma about Roosevelt's lack of preparations for Pearl Harbor. Dewey in fact later spoke with Marshall personally but he went to his grave convinced FDR had had a hand in the matter to quieten him during the campaign. After Marshall and his lieutenants told the Republican nominee that the nation's security was at stake—that to pursue the issue of Pearl Harbor on the hustings would tip the enemy about ongoing U.S. code-breaking activities—Dewey decided to let the matter drop.

In a renewed assault on the New Deal, he proposed "a reduction of individual taxes and corporate income levees as part of a complete restructuring of the federal tax system" during another nationwide address from Albany. Tax reform was mandatory, Dewey proclaimed, "to remove a roadblock in the way of progress." And Bricker kept up the anti-Roosevelt rhetoric. First, at Nashville on October 2, the Ohio conservative called for a "complete housecleaning in Washington" because of financial irresponsibility. "The federal payroll has expanded under the present administration, from 560,000 employees to a staggering 3½ million." Then, two days later in St. Louis, he directed his guns at Hillman and Browder for "seeking to tie the noose of communism around the whole American people." Further, he took up the now familiar theme: "The New Deal destroyed the Democratic party and now the radicals and communists of the Hillman–Browder stripe have taken over the New Deal."

An angered Roosevelt responded to the Republican charges in early October. In what was termed his "second avowed political speech of the campaign," the president invited a small group of intimates, including Fala, his pet Scotty, to the White House, to watch him address the nation over radio. Following the usual nonpartisan appeal for every American to vote regardless of party, he got down to business. FDR did not mention

Dewey's name as he charged political propagandists with bringing "the red herring of Communism" into the campaign. "Labor baiters and bigots and some politicians use the term 'Communism' loosely and apply it to every progressive and social measure and to the views of every foreign-born citizen with whom they disagree. They forget that we in the United States are all descended from immigrants. . . ." With that apparent reference to Sidney Hillman, Roosevelt concluded: "I have never sought and I do not welcome the support of any person or group committed to Communism, or Fascism, or any other foreign ideology."

As the polls pointed to an easy Roosevelt win, the charges and countercharges of presidential contenders as well as the Allied advance toward Berlin were pushed aside as the country awaited the 1944 world series. The St. Louis Cardinals won the flag from baseball's hard luck team and their hometown rivals, the American League Browns, on October 8, during the Roosevelt-Dewey tug-of-war. Prospects of an all-St. Louis series had stirred sports fans for weeks—all the more because the "Brownies," usually in the league cellar, had not won a pennant since formation of the club in 1902.

Although the Cardinals had clinched the National League title by September 21, the Browns were forced to battle the Detroit Tigers for the American crown until October 1—a mere three days before start of the series. The winning game before 37,815 fans in Sportsman Park set an all-time attendance record for a Brown's home game, and the team set a league record by trimming the New York Yankees four straight to win the pennant. St. Louis, the hometown *Globe-Democrat* said, "is in the limelight all over the world and the United States as the Browns climaxed their sensational dash to their first American League championship . . . thereby making the 1944 world series an all-St. Louis affair." After all, besides the novelty of a Brown victory, only two cities had ever kept the series at home. Chicago had hosted the classic once in 1906 when the White Sox thumped the Cubs, and New York had been the scene of five world series titles between the Yankees and Giants: the Giants won in 1921 and 1922, the Yankees in 1923, 1936, and 1937.

By September 26 the Browns had moved into a tie with Detroit by trouncing the Boston Red Sox 3-1 in Sportsman Park; both St. Louis teams in fact used the same stadium by scheduling their home games to alternate with the other's road games. Present at the September 26 game was Leo A. Fohl—then a security guard at a Cleveland, Ohio, aluminum plant—who had managed the Browns until 1929. Fohl told reporters after the Browns's triumph that he hoped his old team would win the pennant because "this had been a very strange year in baseball." When he piloted the club during 1922, the Browns had come within a single game of beating out the Yankees for the league championship.

Two days after the tie for first place the Browns were back in second place after a 4-1 loss to Boston. Detroit romped over the Philadelphia Athletics, 4-0, before 7,293 fans and the Tigers split a doubleheader with the Washington Senators the same day. In spite of some sensational pitching which carried the team to victory, the Browns were afraid the season might end in a dead heat with Detroit. Because of an American League rule that dictated a single game to decide the title in case of a first-place tie, a coin was actually tossed to determine the locale for a playoff match. The single contest that would be played on October 2 was decided in favor of Detroit.

The coin toss by Associated Press writer Charles Dunkley was not necessary. The Browns won the pennant with an October 1 triumph over the Yankees. Following the win, reported a wire service, "Browns fans sat dazed for a couple of minutes after Oscar Grimes fouled out to George McQuinn at 3:40 yesterday afternoon in Sportsman Park. They sat there, automatically yelling and looking out at the field, and the mass of Brownie players roaring out of the dugout to pummel their teammates. . . . Confetti, seat cushions, hats, scorecards, and assorted items of paper filled the air." And it was a good time in St. Louis following the win in spite of wartime conditions; even some Cardinal fans joined in the fun: "The celebration that had been 42 years in the making," continued the press wire, "spread out over the city. Oblivious to the Sabbath and gas rationing, the reaction was not as hilarious as it might have been—a score or more of Browns fans tied tin cans and washtubs to the backs of their cars, bore down on horns, and toured the city in raucous parades."

Although 34,000 fans crowded Sportsman Park to watch the Browns capture the American League pennant, the subdued celebrations following the win were symptomatic of baseball's problems. Manpower shortages because of the draft, as well as wartime restrictions on travel, still plagued every major league team. Several sportswriters maintained that during 1944 only the St. Louis Cardinals played prewar quality ball. The Browns, in the attempt to field good men during their headlong race for the pennant, signed a one-armed player, Wyshner Gray, for the 1945 season on September 29.

Wyshner Gray, known to baseball fans as "Pete," joined the 1945 Browns from the Memphis Chicks of the Southern Association. The highly popular Gray, who collected enthusiastic press notice and roaring crowd approval, had lost his left arm in an automobile accident as a child. Although he played only one season in the majors, he went to the Browns with an enviable minor league record. At Memphis during the 1943 season the gregarious Gray hit .333, including five homers, and stole sixty-eight bases to set a Southern Association record. The year before, Gray played for the Three Rivers club in the Canadian-American League where he also captured the league batting title with a respectable .381. In a shortened forty-two game season he rapped sixty-one hits in 160 times at bat.

When he joined St. Louis Gray was twenty-eight-years-old, unmarried, weighed 170 pounds, and stood six feet one inch. Born in 1917 at Nanticoke, Pennsylvania, of Lithuanian-American ancestry, Gray, who became a symbol for wounded servicemen, broke into professional ball during 1940 with the semi-pro Bay Parkways of Brooklyn. "Although Pete can catch a ball and throw it back to the infield in many ways," *Collier's* reported, "he always uses the same method in a game. As he catches the ball, he brings the glove up to his right armpit, letting the ball roll down his wrist against his chest. Then he holds the glove between the arm stump and his body, pulls his hand out, lowers it, and the ball rolls back into his palm, all ready to be tossed. It's all done so fast that it looks like a comic-strip performance of Super Man." In the majors, however, his batting fell to .210 after sixty-one games and, according to *Newsweek*, he "had difficulty handling sizzling grounders and balls hit to his right."

Meanwhile, the 1944 world series, which ran six games before daily crowds of 35,000, opened October 4 in Sportsman Park. Although the Browns won the first and third games by 2-1, 6-2 margins, their hometown rivals were odd-on favorites from the start. The Cardinals had netted eight pennants since 1925 and National League championships in 1942 and 1943; try as they might, the Browns could not overcome the superior play of the Red Birds. The all-St. Louis series, which saw the Cardinals win their fifth world crown, did not attract the crowds of yesteryear; a mere 31,630 paying fans turned out for the sixth and final game. Yet the country had a sentimental attachment for the underdog Brownies and Harry Truman even took time from the campaign to watch them win the third game.

Wartime spectators, seemingly oblivious to the hard fighting by U.S. troops in Europe and the Pacific, flocked to football games and other sporting events in swelling numbers; nothing, not even the upheavals of World War II, could dampen public enthusiasm for sports. Horse racing absolutely boomed throughout the war and "hushed audiences" crowded New York's Hotel Capital to watch Welker Cochran snatch the world billiards title from the legendary Willie Hoppe. Both men had dominated three-cushion billiards for decades; Cochran, who won a $2,500 first prize in the November tournament, had been world champion in 1933, 1935, and 1936. And football as well, drew huge crowds in spite of the duration and, like professional baseball, college football teams used freshman and draft rejects to complete their rosters. Ohio State captured its conference crown and a 1945 Rose Bowl berth by thumping Michigan 18-14 with a team of "17 year olds and 4Fs." But football's lack of beefy manpower did not keep fans at home. The annual Army-Navy game, played in Baltimore's Municipal Stadium, drew 66,000 spectators who purchased $58 million worth of war bonds for seats. Army's eleven, generaled by Felix "Doc" Blanchard, not only downed Navy but also won every game during 1944—their first perfect season since 1916.

Even though nonessential industries and big-time sports limped along with make-do workers and players until the end, a manpower thaw commenced in late 1944 as numbers of servicemen started coming home. The army announced on September 6 that 1,000,000 men would be returned to civilian life as soon as Germany was defeated. A week earlier the Pentagon said that it had a 150,000-man cushion beyond its planned strength of 7,700,000. But demands in the Pacific forced the navy to ask for 195,000 recruits to bring its total contingent to 3,200,000.

Returning servicemen and their hometown receptions were in the news constantly during the fall and winter. And the men returned to a home front not only locked in debate over how to find them jobs after reconversion to peacetime conditions but also a home front enjoying good mental health. If lowered suicide rates indicate an improvement in morale, then America was in good shape. The Metropolitan Life Insurance Company concluded in August that the nation was too preoccupied with the war to worry about suicide. From a peacetime average of 19,000 suicides per year the national total in 1943 dropped to 13,000; actuarial experts at Metropolitian said the decline came from general economic prosperity and high civilian morale; the largest decline was among twenty-to-twenty-five-year-old women.

If marriageable women were in demand with millions of bachelors in uniform, their lot improved still more when those same millions started coming home; finding a girl, getting married, landing a good job and raising children was on every serviceman's mind. And the hometown girls were anxious to find the right husband. When a troop train carrying furloughed marines stopped briefly in Moberly, Missouri, in August, local girls "in their pretty summer dresses" descended on the train to give the returning warriors rides around town in their automobiles. "Your wife know you're coming?" a reporter asked a few days later when the train reached Baltimore. "Damn right, its been 27 months. . . ." As he neared the East Coast that sergeant spoke for married GIs everywhere.

Regardless of their marital situation, most returning veterans had little time for the several thousand conscientious objectors who had managed to evade military service. After thirty-three months of war isolated instances still surfaced of men who either refused to register or who missed the draft altogether. A single issue of Newsweek in August 1944 reported widely-separated draft evasion cases in California and Alabama. In Los Angeles, a nineteen-year-old Mexican-American youth was found residing in a Nisei relocation center at Manzanar, California. He had registered as a Japanese-American during 1942 with several Oriental school friends; "Like a lot of fellows here I'd prefer being in the war," he told inquiring reporters—also that he planned to enlist as soon as possible. The Alabama case involved a twenty-four-year-old man who had been hiding in a cave near his farm since 1942; "equipped with animal traps, blankets, and one razor blade, the fellow did not know the country was at war."

Most conscientious objectors sought to avoid military duty on religious grounds. Upwards of 2,500 men landed in federal prisons and specially-created civilian work camps after selective service bureaucrats refused them 4-E classifications; "COs" made up roughly one-third of all federal prison inmates during the war. Christian Century speculated that the men went to jail because selective service chief General Lewis B. Hershey purposely distorted the law: "He insists on applying a definition of 'religious training and belief' not intended by Congress. Congress implied by its discussion of the point, and the courts have affirmed, that conscience is by its nature religious. Nevertheless General Hersey in a letter dated March 5, 1942, insisted that a registrant who is a conscientious objector must believe not only in a diety but also in a creator diety. This definition cuts down the incidence of conscientious objection."

A man was thus obligated to prove genuine religious commitment to gain a draft deferment. Hershey, apparently with presidential approval, ignored provisions in the Selective Service Act that permitted alternative public service. Instead, public service camps were created to house COs who refused military induction; but more times than not, the COs were shipped directly to federal penal institutions. One camp near Baltimore housed ninety-eight conscientious objectors; and when New York *Times* reporter Robert Van Gelder visited the facility in September 1942 he found that Mennonites, Brethern, and Quakers composed most of its population. Men from these sects, along with Jehovah's Witnesses and a handful of intellectuals, accounted for nearly all COs. Van Gelder talked with a Mennonite objector named "Walt," who was described as an "unspoiled individual": "It ain't fittin for me to speak for my church," he said. "I mightn't know enough to tell you right, but we can't fight, not in my church. The Brethern, they feel much the same."

Although perfectly sincere in their convictions, Walt and his fellows found little sympathy. Public disgust with Jehovah's Witnesses, Mennonites, Brethern, and similiar fundamentalist believers was likewise heaped upon others including movie actor Lew Ayres and Robert Lowell, a socially prominent poet, who sought objector status. Average citizens had enough trouble understanding religious obstacles to military service, let alone those who passed up the draft on intellectual grounds. And the difficulty arose in part from a misconception of individual guarantees under the Bill of Rights. A survey by the National Opinion Research Center in Washington during 1944 found that 23 percent of the country "did not believe in true free speech, nor that newspapers should be allowed to criticize our form of government, even in peacetime." Not one American in three, the researchers discovered, could explain what the Bill of Rights guaranteed.

Unlimited freedom of dissent did not include the CO, as men like Lew Ayres soon found out. Widely-known for his Dr. Kildare movies— the same 1930s films familiar to millions of educational television viewers in the 1980s—and his starring role in the anti-war classic, *All Quiet on the Western Front,* Ayres ran afoul of religious interpretation of the selective service laws. After refusing to enter the army in 1942 because of "deep philosophical thought arising from a religion of his own," he was ordered to a public service camp near Wyeth, Oregon. Although his films were canceled by movie houses in Hackensack, New Jersey, and other cities, MGM bigwigs thought he could ride out the storm of public abuse. As he worked on firebreaks and felled trees in the Oregon wilderness, other actors were assigned to make his already contracted-for pictures. Ayers later sought a noncombatant classification, but the New York *Times* said he had destroyed his career "by registering as a conscientious objector." After the war, however, he was able to create a new film-television career that reached into the 1970s.

"In 1941 we undertook a patriotic war to preserve our lives, our fortunes, and our sacred honor against the lawless aggressions of a totalitarian league: in 1943 we are collaborating with the most unscrupulous dictators to destroy law, freedom, democracy, and our continued national sovereignty." Thus, Robert Lowell, Harvard graduate, scion of a wealthy Boston family, and poet who would later win two Pulitzer Prizes for his work, wrote to Roosevelt in answer to a ubiquitous presidential "greeting" from his local draft board. "Lowell Scion Refuses to Fight," trumpeted the Providence *Journal* as his refusal of induction was referred to the federal courts. His biographer, Ian Hamilton, tells what happened next: "Lowell . . . was sentenced to a year and a day in the Federal Correctional Center at Danbury, Connecticut. While waiting to be shifted there, he spent a few days in New York's tough West Street Jail. Lowell's famous poem on the subject is augmented by the recollections of a fellow inmate: 'Lowell was in a cell next to Lepke, you know, Murder Incorporated, and Lepke says to him: I'm in for killing. What are you in for?' 'Oh, I'm in for refusing to kill.' And Lepke burst out laughing. It was kind of ironic."

Conscientious objection was an agonizing ordeal for the liberal community and the men involved, although most, like Lowell, received surprisingly light sentences. But the plight of COs was totally overshadowed by the Roosevelt-Dewey campaign during October-November 1944. "The campaign, in all, was not enlightening," observed historian Otis L. Graham: "Dewey spoke once or twice of alternative approaches to the broad goals of the New Deal, but talked mostly of Roosevelt's dictatorial tendencies, his association with labor bosses, machine politicians, women cabinet members, and CIO communists. Roosevelt toured military installations to emphasize his role as commander-in-chief, defended the New Deal when he spoke, and reminded listeners that the Depression was a Republican invention."

Try as he might, the diminutive—wags called him the little man on the wedding cake—Dewey could not capture the national pulse. At Minneapolis in late October he attacked Roosevelt's failure to consult Congress on foreign policy and claimed he had not prepared the country for war; it was an old saw by this time as he scrapped a prepared speech on farm policy to say that FDR had dropped the ball in 1941. The next night, before 500,000 in Chicago Stadium (Chicago mayor Ed Kelly, a Democrat, said the crowd was closer to 120,000) Dewey told applauding zealots that Roosevelt had continued to sell the Japanese American oil until four months before Pearl Harbor. Then, as the vice presidential contenders, Truman and Bricker, toured the country aping their bosses,

Roosevelt undertook an 1,800 mile-campaign circuit in the company of his personal physician, Vice Admiral Ross T. McIntyre. And when his thirteen-car special reached Fort Wayne, he answered his Republican accusers: "I am in the middle of a war and so are you. . . . It's quite a job, but I am perfectly able to take care of it and so are you."

Another candidate with his eye on the November 7 returns was the Socialist spellbinder, Norman Thomas. The Ohio-born Thomas had carried his party's banner in every election since 1928 and would do so again in 1948; an absolute master of the spoken word, Thomas and his oratory were known to millions of Americans. In June, the Socialist National Convention at Reading, Pennsylvania, not only tapped Darlington Hoopes, a three-term member of the Pennsylvania legislature, as Thomas's running mate but also drafted a platform written by Thomas himself. His appeal to wartime America, summarized by Thomas biographer Harry Fleischman, demanded "a political peace offensive pledging equal rights for all peoples and self-determination plus organized political and economic cooperation to remove the causes of war, settle disputes, conquer poverty and guarantee security." And he wanted the United Nations to "free the European colonies overrun by Japan or under white rule. Domestically, his platform stressed the traditional Socialist proposals for socialization of the commanding heights of the economy plus a variety of civil rights and civil liberties planks." With the "red herring" of Communism a big issue in the campaign, Thomas generated little enthusiasum for his left-leaning appeal.

Although the cry by Thomas and the Socialists for greater egalitarianism in American life was ignored by Roosevelt and Dewey as well as by the established media, the old campaigner did what he could to deliver his message. For all his efforts in 1944—including several broadcasts to overseas servicemen after Congress made provisions for soldier voting—Thomas polled his lowest vote in six campaigns for the presidency. His 80,518 votes was a far cry from the 25,000,000 and 22,000,000 polled by Roosevelt and by Dewey respectively. The year 1944 was not a good time for minority parties; Thomas finished a poor third in the presidential canvass, a meager 6,000 votes ahead of the Prohibition candidate. His Socialist vote varied from 13,295 in Wisconsin to a scant forty-six in New Hampshire and he did not even get on the ballot in twenty states.

In the Roosevelt-Dewey contest thirty-six states landed in the Democrat column and twelve in the Republican; more than 48,000,000 Americans trekked to the polls in the first wartime ballot for president since the Civil War. Immediately afterward there was a fear that a tally of the "soldier vote" might alter the result in two or three states, but a final count changed nothing. At the same time that Congress enacted legislation to permit absentee voting by GIs, strict penalties were imposed against politicking among servicemen. Senator Robert A. Taft, a fierce Republican stalwart, fearful lest Roosevelt and his subordinates manipulate the soldier vote, inserted a provision that disallowed polling servicemen about political preferences. War correspondents in Europe were warned during August by army public relations officers to leave GIs out of their reporting about the campaign at the risk of a $1,000 fine and a two-year imprisonment. Zealous commanders went to the extreme of ordering removal of certain "political books" from post libraries and rec rooms.

Although Carl S. Schoeinger, national commander of the Veterans of Foreign Wars, said "American troops show an utter lack of interest in the upcoming national elections," over 3,000,000 service votes were cast. A post-election analysis by the New York *Times* in seven states—California, Colorado, Maryland, New Jersey, New York, Pennsylvania, and Rhode Island—that reported separate returns for the soldier vote found that Roosevelt got 59.3 percent of the ballot, as opposed to 51.5 percent of the civilian tally.

Dewey received the largest electoral count—ninety-nine to Roosevelt's 431—of any losing presidential candidate since 1924, and the popular vote was the narrowest since the 1916 contest between Woodrow Wilson and Charles Evans Hughes. The governorships stood at twenty-two Republican and twenty-six Democrat after the election. Moreover, Democrats picked up twenty-nine seats in the House of Representatives to retain control of both branches of Congress. Three women, all Democrats—Helen Gahagan Douglas, movie actress and onetime opera singer; Mrs. Emily Taft Douglas, wife of an Illinois college professor; and Mrs. Chase G. Woodhouse, former secretary of state in Connecticut, were also elected to the house. Their first-term elections raised the number of women in Congress to nine.

Two weeks after the election, novelist-playwright Arthur Miller came to public attention when his first Broadway production, *The Man Who Had All the Luck*, ran for four days at New York's Forest Theater. Although the play closed on short notice, it set Miller on the path toward his later recognition as a major American playwright. Miller himself thought "it merely a preparation, and possibly a necessary one for the plays that followed." And follow they did through the postwar era: *All My Sons* (1947), *Death of a Salesman* (1949—Pulitzer Prize), *The Crucible* (1953), *The Misfits* (1960—a screenplay), *After the Fall* and *Incident at Vichy* (1964). *The Man Who Had All the Luck,* which lasted "long enough for the performers to get into their make-up before it perished of fiscal anemia," according to one source, was "didactic and inexpert." Others, including Burton Rascoe, onetime collaborator with H. L. Mencken and wartime reviewer for the New York *World-Telegram,* thought it one of the best plays to appear in the past twenty-five years.

The twenty-nine-year-old writer had already churned out more than thirty scripts for college and amateur productions as well as radio scripts, which, says his biographer Leonard Moss, "all ask a general question and demand an answer." Miller was born on Manhattan's Upper East Side in 1915. After graduation from Brooklyn's Lincoln High School in 1932, he was unable to attend college because of family losses during the Depression. "He therefore found a job as a stock clerk in an automobile warehouse." Hard work and frugal living enabled him to enter the University of Michigan two years later; with assistance from a New Deal agency and his earnings as night editor of the *Michigan Daily,* he received a bachelor's degree in 1938. There at Ann Arbor, Miller served his apprenticeship by publishing several prize-winning college plays.

Miller returned to New York upon graduation to write scripts for both CBS and NBC radio networks; then, in 1944, he was hired by a Hollywood producer who sent him around the country visiting army boot camps to gather material for a movie based on Ernie Pyle's *The Story of GI Joe.* The result was a book, also published in 1944, entitled, *Situation Normal,* which presented his own impressions of World War II army life. "Mr. Miller saw a great deal and has recorded it racily and informatively, considering that he seems to have been pretty much in a hurry all during his tour. . . . I have never seen the excitements and bewilderments of basic training better recorded, and the good Lord knows practically every reporter in the country has had a try at doing it," commented the New York *Times;* and *Bookweek* called it "a fine book that sneaks up on you." At a time when things military dominated the national psyche, Miller's precise descriptions of camp life added to his growing stature.

That stature, however, suffered—at least in conservative circles—when he ran afoul of congressional investigators during the postwar hysteria over Communist penetration of American life. Miller's subsequent smashes on Broadway as well as his well-received novel about anti-Semitism, *Focus,* which appeared in November 1945, made him a highly visible personality by the mid-1950s. When summoned before the House Committee on UnAmerican Activities in 1956, he "freely admitted past associations with ultraliberal, left, or Communist groups," but refused to implicate others he had encountered at leftist meetings. Although found guilty and handed a light jail sentence the following year, he was later exonerated by a federal appeals court.

In November-December 1944, however, Miller's legal difficulties lay in the future as the country turned to the upcoming Christmas season. Shortages still plagued shoppers who looked for gift bargains. OPA bureacrats faced a "nightmare" during November when toymakers who grossed more than seventy-five dollars a year were forced to submit their wares for price fixing and approval of raw materials. Yet Christmas toys for 1944 were judged the best to appear since 1941; although several playthings turned up made from metal, most toys were again wood and paper concoctions. Jeeps had been the 1943 favorites for boys, but now manufacturers pushed tractors for boys and dolls for girls. "In spite of material shortages," *Life* reported, "OPA had kept prices as low as those of 1942. A wooden steam shovel costs $3.95. A large woolen Sandy Andy sells for about $2. A toy helicopter that maneuvers like a yo-yo costs only $1.29."

An unabashed buying spree fueled by the easy flow of defense dollars commenced after Thanksgiving and continued until Christmas eve. Consumers not only bought every gift in sight, they also purchased war bonds in record numbers. Along with Christmas buying that surpassed anything known previously, the Sixth War Bond Drive during mid-December was over-subscribed. Although the sale of small denomination E-bonds had fallen somewhat, overall volume passed expectations; treasury officials announced that the drive had exceeded their national goal of $14 billion by more than $1.5 billion.

As the search for Christmas presents intensified, it was the same old story: OPA pricing policies made it difficult for manufacturers to compete in a nonprofitable market. Moderately-priced items all but vanished from department store counters by the first week in December, leaving shoppers with more expensive goods. "In every big U. S. city," *Time* reported, "black (and very transparent) nighties revealed the intimate mechanics of window dummies." Although negligees for the ladies were costly, numerous newspaper ads assured them 1944 was "a return to femininity." Other hot-selling items were handbags in the $100 range and a variety of perfumes, some of which, like *Dans la Nuit*, were going for $1,000 per seventy-two ounce bottle. Flashy merchandise might have been beyond the reach of most, but it caught the imagination of wartime shoppers. Yet, the *Time* account of last-minute Christmas buying continued: "Customers reached for absurdly-priced costume jewelry as eagerly as pygmy tribesmen bartering for trade beads. . . . The old standbys of yester-Yule, things like the 15¢ handkerchief and the $1 necktie, were extinct as the dodo. Christmas, 1944, might be merry; it would certainly be costly."

As the hard, brutal fighting to check Von Rundstedt's "bulge" around Bastogne taxed American fighting reserves abroad, the War Department announced that "persons of Japanese ancestry whose records have stood the test of army scrutiny during the last two years will be permitted to return to their West Coast homes." By and large, Americans of all walks of life could be thankful for a Merry Christmas. The war after all had hardly touched these shores. Thousands attended ball games all over the place, bought $150 cigarette lighters for dad, and with the exception of gasoline and a handful of rationed items, continued to enjoy the good life. But when several thousand people were asked what they wanted for Christmas there was one resounding reply: "To have the boys back home."

11 JANUARY-MARCH 1945: HOW TO GET MARRIED

Besides the usual ballyhoo and hangovers, the New Year opened with news from Washington that the home front could expect to tighten its belt because of setbacks in the European war. Although it was the last year of the war, one last push—really a dying gasp—by the Nazis to hold Eisenhower and Montgomery at bay in the west created shock waves on this side of the Atlantic. Once the 1944 elections became history, James F. Byrnes and the administration had no qualms about grinding out mandates following the German counterattack around Bastogne.

The War Production Board started with bad news for the drivers who were trying to prod a few more miles from their aging automobiles; all tire-rationing schemes were scrapped and the number of tires for passenger cars cut by 1,600,000. And as if that were not enough, "A" card drivers—those with the least rationing priority—were told to either find recapped tires or park the family sedan. All production of goods for civilian markets was frozen until the military crunch lessened.

Byrnes, no doubt upset by the size of the crowds attending New Year's Day bowl games and by the rampant gambling at race tracks, came out with a double-barreled blast: he suspended horse racing for the duration and ordered the reexamination of all 4-F athletes, including collegiate players, by their draft boards. Colonel J. Morgan Johnson, director of Defense Transportation, joined the fray with a warning that race track closures would be followed by more drastic steps unless unnecessary civilian travel was eliminated. It was not only the big daily crowds at the tracks that attracted his attention. "Railroad equipment has been taxed to the limit," he told reporters: "Needless passenger movement is getting to the point where it is embarrassing the war effort." The ODT chief speculated that "rationing train travel" would lead to an administrative nightmare and he predicted that new travel regulations would make it difficult for civilians to "gad about."

Byrnes held a press conference in early January to elaborate his views as the wire services buzzed with news from Bastogne and the Ardennes fighting; Hitler did not break off the western offensive until mid-month, when his panzers were forced to counter a new Russian advance along the Eastern Front. Although Byrnes personally favored some form of "universal service," he said key congressmen had warned him privately that such a law was out of the question. He had given "no thought" to a complete reform of sports under his wartime powers, but he was "clearly upset" with current practices. "And he plainly said," continued press accounts, "that when he saw football players who had been physically disqualified, he wondered if their ear drums might be good enough to hear a sergeant as well as a quarterback's signals, and he went on, co-lorblindness did not interfere with the players seeing the tinge on sweaters." Almost all 4-Fs, Byrnes thought, were capable of some military or defense plant service. But his ban stopped short of shutting down nightclubs or interfering with boxing and baseball.

Byrnes did have a point. On New Year's Day more than 230,000 fans packed the four major bowl games. An observer could be excused for wondering if the country even remembered it was fighting a war. At Pasadena, California, 91,000 showed up for the Rose Bowl to watch the Trojans of Southern California trim a University of Tennessee team that had had to travel 2,000 miles for the January classic. Although not quite as well attended, the remaining bowl games drew roaring crowds to watch "17-year-olds, 4-Fs, and other draft escapees" carry the pigskin. The Cotton Bowl at Dallas attracted 37,000 for Oklahoma A&M's 34-0 trouncing of Texas Christian University; in New Orleans it was Duke 29, Alabama 26 before a crowd of 72,000 in the Sugar Bowl. And in Miami's Orange Bowl 30,000 "sun-drenched" spectators watched Tulsa plough Georgia Tech under, 26-12. It was Tennessee State 13, Tuskegee Institute 0 in the all-black Vulcan Bowl at Montgomery, Alabama; 6,000 partisans turned out to see William Bass, a 1944 black all-American, spear-head the State victory with a series of "brilliant passes late in the game."

But Byrnes was fighting a losing battle in his struggle to dampen public enthusiasm for football and wartime sports. And it was more than col-legiate bowl games. Every crossroads college, army–navy installation, and high school in the nation was playing football, war or no war. While Byrnes was decrying the crowds at sporting events in this country, "25,000 GI Joes and GI Janes" gathered in Florence for the first "annual" Spaghetti

Bowl. Nazi units still lingered in northern Italy when the New Year's Day game was played before boisterous American servicemen. It featured two bands, "a barelegged drum majorette who shivered and strutted," plenty of hot dogs, and a P-38 squadron overhead to ward off prying German planes. But the Luftwaffe failed to show as corporal "Big Train" Moody, onetime black all-American at Georgia's Morris Brown College, carried the Fifth Army "Krautclouters" to victory. Moody and his compatriots won an easy 20-0 victory over a Twelfth Air Force team.

A racing crowd at Miami's Tropical Park on New Year's Day bet a record $777,674 on a nine-race morning program. If Byrnes's horse racing ban was designed to cut down on wartime travel, 14,745 patrons at Tropical Park were undeterred as they set a 1944–1945 attendance record. Also unaffected by Byrnes's action was the tiny Vermont hamlet of Londonville. Two weeks after the racing edict, city fathers went ahead with their annual sulky race down main street; although drivers were forced to manipulate through two-feet snowdrifts as townsmen cheered in ten-below-zero weather, observers close to the action said there was no betting among spectators—at least "no overt gambling."

An increased demand for war workers and draftees led to cut-backs in the production of consumer goods after January 1, and the earlier release of men and raw materials to produce items for home front consumption was reversed. Byrnes's orders, designed to relieve the manpower crunch, were echoed by Roosevelt himself. In his January State of the Union message the president minced no words: "There is an old and true saying that the Lord hates a quitter, and this nation must pay for all those who leave their essential jobs for nonessential reasons. And . . . that payment must be made with the life's blood of our sons." Roosevelt asked for a national service law as well as congressional authorization "to require the 4,000,000 men now classified 4-F—the physically and mentally unfit— to do war work." It was his second call for a service law, although Washington observers did not think that presidental support would persuade Congress to act.

But 4-F deferments were another matter. Byrnes told reporters after Roosevelt's address that "We must use the means at hand—if we can't ride a horse, then ride a mule." General Hershey immediately increased draft .quotas from 60,000 to 80,000 for January and February. WPB ordered a freeze on the manufacture of all civilian goods until further notice. And the War Manpower Commission began a roundup of men working at nonessential jobs. Defense workers leaving the assembly line in cities like Detroit became such a headache to production officials that thousands were told "to stay put or else." During the first week in January WMC agents "swooped down" on an exclusive country club in Denver and, following interrogation of every employee, "ordered five—a cook, a watchman, and three attendants—to report to jobs in man-hungry factories." No section of the country escaped the clamp-down.

While the country braced for additional regulations, news arrived from Europe that popular band leader Glenn Miller had died in a plane crash. Miller, according to George T. Simon, historian of the big band era, was the premier bandsman of the 1940s. "Of all the outstanding popular dance bands, the one that evokes the most memories of how wonderfully romantic it all was, the one whose music people most want to hear over and over again, is the band of the late Glenn Miller." He typified the large swing bands that had their heyday during the war. Miller's death in late December, while flying from England to Paris to join his Army Air Force Dance Band, stunned a home front accustomed to the "Miller sound." Although big band music on a grand scale was first introduced by the Dorsey brothers, Tommy and Jimmy, in the early 1930s, Miller had invented a style of his own—a style that seized the country.

Following his induction into the United States Army Air Force during October 1942, Miller, commissioned a captain, was authorized to organize what became known as "the Great AAF Band." Until June 1944, when he was sent overseas to entertain American GIs and British Tommies, Miller's group, which contained many holdovers from his civilian band, toured army–navy installations throughout the United States, appeared on patriotic radio broadcasts, and performed at war bond rallies. Miller, in fact, proved as popular on the war bond circuit as he had been on the dance podium. "His grosses were exceedingly impressive," Simon comments: "At one rally in Garden City, New York, he raised $2.3 million in pledges. A few weeks later, at two rallies in Chicago and St. Louis, he helped to bring in more than $4 million per night."

Miller and his band stayed in England until personal orders arrived from Eisenhower to take the outfit to Paris. Before it left in mid-December, the band was as popular as ever, not only with GIs, but also with British listeners. Miller had been in Europe less than a week when the renamed group—"Captain Glenn Miller and His American Band of the Supreme Allied Command"—began regular broadcasts over armed forces networks as well as on the BBC. After receiving instructions to proceed with his band to France, Miller made hurried arrangements to fly the channel in an unscheduled single-engine plane assigned to Colonel Norman F. Baesell and piloted by a seasoned British flying officer named F.

O. Morgan. Lieutenant Don Haynes, Miller's civilian business manager who followed him into uniform, kept a diary of the ill-fated last days and his parture from England in threatening weather: "Glen and the Colonel climbed aboard. The Colonel seated himself in the co-pilot's seat and Glenn sat in a bucket seat directly back of the Colonel facing the side of the ship. Morgan climbed into the pilot's seat, and, as they all fastened their seat belts, I waved goodbye. 'Happy Landings and Good Luck. I'll see you in Paris tomorrow,' I said, as Glenn replied, 'thanks Haynsie. We may need it.' "

Born Alton Glenn Miller, March 1, 1904, at Clarinda, Iowa, he was a true son of middle-America; before Miller graduated from high school in Fort Morgan, Colorado, in 1921, his father, a railroad man, had moved the family to towns in Iowa, Nebraska, and Missouri. Always an apt musician, he started to make his way on the band circuit in 1923, following a year or so of unsuccessful studies at the University of Colorado in Boulder. Not only fame but fortune as well accompanied his climb; no less a personality than crooner Bing Crosby wrote a letter of recommendation for Miller when he applied for officers candidate school during 1942. When required to list his assets upon entering the service, Miller penciled in $344,000—a tidy sum for the 1940s.

Although public acceptance of big band music reached record heights during 1941–1945, most of the big bandsmen remained jazz musicians at heart. All of them had started in jazz bands, but only aficionados appreciated jazz in the 1920s and 1930s, while everyone listened to swing. From the mid-1930s onward it was swing and big bands for the in-crowd. But the war also changed the bands. "The armed forces," writes band historian Herb Sanford, "pulled both band personnel and customers. The Stage Door Canteen in New York and USO centers everywhere entertained customers who were now servicemen stationed at nearby bases before shipping out. Fewer spots were available to the large number of bands that had been built up. Maintaining a big band with top personnel and steady bookings was not easy. The bands played on, played the swing music of the thirties on through the forties, on the home scene and in the theaters of war."

A survey of music tastes by *Life* concluded: "No soldier who likes swing hears as much of it as he would like. Hot music is a native American institution and love of it is a national trait. Here at home there has been no dearth of swing." And the top swing musicians in the closing days of World War II were the same artists who had led the pack in 1941. When Pearl Harbor was bombed the favorite swing tunes were "Deep in the

Heart of Texas," "Don't Sit Under the Apple Tree," "Blues in the Night," and "Tonight We Love." In the first months of 1945 the country still wanted its music "tuneful and sentimental": "I'll Walk Alone," "Swinging on a Star," "Time Waits For No One," "Is You or Is You Ain't," "Amour," "I'll Be Seeing You," "It Could Happen To You," "I'll Get By," "and It Had to be You."

Miller's death in December took place as the Bulge-Ardennes fighting raged to a climax 175 miles east of Paris. By late January 1945 the European war was clearly coming to a close after Eisenhower unleashed his broad-front attack on the German homeland. The drive to clear the Rhineland—that part of Germany west of the Rhine—was temporarily slowed in January by Nazi defenses along the Roer. A tributary of the Maas, or Meuse, which reaches the Atlantic at Dordrecht in the Netherlands, the Roer drains much of the Rhineland along the French frontier. The Allied momentum headed by Montgomery's British and Canadian troops, as well as by the American Ninth Army under General William Simpson, slowed when the Germans emptied a series of dams along the river. Dispatches reaching the home front in March said the offensive across the Roer that had been scheduled for February 10 had been delayed due to flood waters. "At Duren it was 50 to 60 yards wide, and the current was running at six to seven miles an hour."

Simpson's battalions made straight for Dusseldorf, twenty-two miles to the east and situated on the Rhine, after forcing the Roer on February 23 at Julich. The American First Army crossed a day later at Duren and made for Cologne, also on the Rhine. By the first week in March Nazi resistance began to falter across the entire Western Front; the British advance eastward through the Low Countries bridged the river at Wesel north of Dusseldorf on March 22: "After Montgomery completed his elaborate preparations for the grand assault," writes his countryman Liddell Hart, "he had concentrated twenty-five divisions, after a quarter million tons of ammunition and other supplies had been amassed in dumps on the west bank. The thirty-mile stretch of river where he planned to attack was held by only five weak and exhausted German divisions."

Earlier, the U.S. Fifth Army commanded by General Courtney Hodges—the same outfit that had crossed the Roer three weeks before—captured the famed bridge at Remagen. Two tank battalions of Hodges's advance units unexpectedly found the Ludendorff Railroad Bridge over the Rhine intact following a German retreat. On March 7, with good old Yankee daring, the Americans seized the span before it could be destroyed, and by nightfall a bridgehead east of the Rhine had been firmly planted. This unforeseen setback goaded Hitler to replace Von Rundstedt on the Western Front with Field Marshal Kesselring, fresh from the Nazi collapse in Italy.

Although Remagen abruptly altered Eisenhower's war plans, the Rhine crossings produced some uneasy moments for the Anglo-American alliance. Montgomery wanted to spearhead the cross-Rhine thrust with his massive effort at Wesel; and General George Patton for one was not slow at telling the home front through sympathetic war correspondents about GI disgust at being held back while "Monty" pressed forward. Even so, the Americans quietly reinforced Hodges and the Ninth Army bridgehead at Remagen. And it was no mean task. General Omar Bradley later wrote in his memoirs, A General's Life: "The Germans rushed elements of some twelve divisions (including four panzers) onto the bridgehead, but most of these units were undermanned and undergunned or green to combat. The Germans brought up heavy artillery, aircraft, floating mines, frogmen. They even fired eleven V-2s at the bridge—the first and only tactical use of either V-weapon in the war." The bridge soon collapsed, but not before Hodges had his units beyond the Rhine.

Once across the Rhine, Allied forces advanced on a wide front from Montgomery on the north flank to Patton on the south. By April American units had reached the Elbe and the fateful link-up with the Russians took place on April 25 at Torgau, sixty-five miles south and slightly west of Berlin. In the days of the U.S.–Russian cooperative effort to smash Hitlerism, newspapers and magazines played up the historic juncture. At 4:40 p.m., Newsweek's account ran, "on a ruined bridge at Torgau, Second Lt. William Robertson of Los Angeles shook hands with Pvt. Nicolai Ivanovitch Andreyeff of the Russian 58th Guards Division in the meeting that the United States, Great Britain, and Russia decided to make official." Actually, first contact between the two armies had taken place a few hours earlier, when a twenty-eight-man patrol from the 69th Division, led by Lieutenant Albert K. Kotzebue of Houston, Texas, bumped into a group of Russians at Riesa, a small village near Torgau. Life used its Picture of the Week to feature a soldierly clasp between Robertson and medal-bedecked Lieutenant Alexander Sylvashko of the First Ukrainian Army. "To symbolize the momentous occasion," the Robertson-Sylvashko picture was splashed across front pages around the world.

American, British, and Canadian forces with a few French units remained frozen on the Elbe-Mulde-Ergebirge line—from the North Sea to the Czech border—following the April 25 meeting with the Russians.

Several units under Patton advanced down the Danube to Linz, while its left flank crossed the Czech frontier and occupied Pilsen; although Patton could have moved into Prague in another day or so, he was halted short of the Czech capital. Other GI units moved into Hitler's mountain retreat at Berchtesgaden and Innsbruck before joining up with advance columns of Mark Clark's Fifth Army coming north through the Brenner Pass from Italy. And while Simpson's Ninth Army sat on the Elbe a mere sixty miles from Berlin, waiting for the war to end, the Soviets moved into the city on April 22 after their drive eastward after victories at Leningrad, Moscow, and Stalingrad. Allied failure to reach Hitler's last bastion before the Russians meant a divided Berlin would dominate east-west relations for the next forty years. In April–May, 1945, however, the American home front was preoccupied with ending the war and "bringing the boys home." Concerns about a future cold war would have to wait.

Nazi forces were powerless to hold the Russians at bay once they entered Germany itself during January. Zhukov's First Army reached the Oder near Kurstin, now in Poland, on January 31, and sat poised, like a tiger ready to spring, within fifty miles of Berlin. Marshal Konev's Ukrainian group was at the Oder-Neisse line—the present German–Polish border—three weeks later. The Russians had marched against Hitler from the Baltic to the Carpathians with unbelievable might; that the Soviets had the upper hand in men and supplies by 1943–1944 was no longer in doubt. Hitler's panzer chief Heinz Guderian told him that the Russians had an "11-1 superiority in infantry, 7-1 in tanks, and 20-1 in artillery and planes." Military historians Ernst and Trevor Dupuy set German losses on the Russian front at "1 million killed; 800,000 men, 6,000 aircraft, 12,000 tanks, and 23,000 guns captured" in the last three months of war.

While people in this country fussed over rationing piques and restrictions on sporting events, Germans by the millions were desperately seeking ways to avoid the Soviet onslaught. High-born ladies who were ready to sell themselves and their jewels were often no better off than common folk in the race for transport to the West; soldiers in the rapidly crumbling panzer divisions joined the dash toward the Allied armies. "An estimated million and a half fugitives and four army divisions," writes Dupuy and Dupuy, "were evacuated from Kurland, including 157,000 wounded. In turn, Danzig, the present day Gdansk, and Gdynia (March), Konigsburg and Pillau (April 25), and Kolberg (mid-April) were successfully evacuated by the German navy. In these operations Allied air power nibbled away

German naval strength. By April only the cruisers *Prinz Eugen* and *Nurnberg* were still afloat. But the task had been accomplished."

Joining the exodus was Wernher Von Braun and his team of rocket experts at Peenemunde on the Pomeranian coast. Unlike many of their countrymen, the engineers and scientists who masterminded Hitler's V-weapons were successful in reaching the Allies. Once in this country with their rocketry know-how, they changed the course of history at Huntsville, Alabama, by developing the NASA hardware that put Americans on the moon two decades later. James Michener, in his best selling novel, *Space*, tells the story of their achievements in this country as well as the gripping tale of their frantic race across the dying Third Reich, one step ahead of the Reds. Everyone in Germany but Der Fürher himself, notes Barbarossa historian Albert Seaton, knew the war was over by 1945. When the Soviet generals unleashed the final thrust at Berlin on April 16, they did it with one Russian soldier "for every 13 feet in front of the attackers." The Russians marched on, right onto the avenues of Berlin while the Western Allies watched; by May 2 they had secured the city with British and American forces still sixty miles away on the Elbe.

The quickness of victory in Europe caused this country to overlook the high casuality lists among GIs and the Allies. With our forces poised on Saipan for the last plunge at the Japanese home islands, Byrnes issued further edicts to focus attention on the Pacific war. In late February, as the struggle raged for Iwo Jima, a curfew was placed on "all nightclubs, sports arenas, theaters, dance halls, road houses, saloons, bars, and similiar enterprises, whether public or private, excluding restaurants, engaged exclusively in serving food." Every kind of night spot, from roadside beer joints in the rural South to swanky New York and San Francisco supper clubs was ordered to close at midnight. Byrnes, *Newsweek* reported, felt the move was necessary "to save coal consumed in heating and providing electricity." When night spot operators, including New York's Billy Rose whined that difficulties in keeping contracts with caterers and musicians would threaten certain bankruptcy, WMC bureaucrats refused to budge: "They could be stripped of all but maintenance employees; power and fuel could be withdrawn; they could face a ban on deliveries of food and other commodities."

The closing edict was hardly noticed for the simple reason that it interfered with the pleasures of few people. Between 85 and 90 percent of the population was already in bed by midnight. And if those with money could not enjoy the fast life, there were other places to drop a few bucks.

Practically everything not covered by OPA price restrictions increased in cost during the war, and nothing more than real estate values; construction of new homes ceased after Pearl Harbor and few household units had been erected in the Depression years. In 1945 war workers with money to spare and returning servicemen with accumulated savings—and access to favorable GI loans—wanted a home of their own. The resultant upsurge in house prices was enough to make the head spin. In Miami and Miami Beach, for instance, houses had more than doubled in cost since 1941. A small cottage in Surfside, north of Miami Beach, which had sold for $6,500 in 1940, was being offered in 1945 for an astounding $16,500.

Meanwhile, the Pacific war, which remained an exclusively American undertaking, entered its final phases following the capture of Saipan, Guam, and Tinian in the summer of 1944. While MacArthur destroyed isolated Japanese garrisons in the Philippines, Nimitz, Spruance, and the Central Pacific Task Force, which now became the Fifth Fleet, prepared for an assault on Iwo Jima, 600 miles from Tokyo itself. After the capture of Luzon, which cost the United States 7,933 dead and 32,732 wounded, to say nothing of 192,000 Japanese casualties, MacArthur was through with the war. Although he directed the American occupation of Japan, the remaining fight in the Pacific was left to other commanders. And Iwo Jima in the Bonin group was the next target on the island-hopping express to the Rising Sun.

The first American wave "hit the sands of Iwo Jima" on February 19, following a concentrated air and naval bombardment. Samuel Eliot Morison says the ensuing battle was the "most prolonged and also disappointing of any Pacific island." Although our war captains wanted the place for only one reason—an air field—it cost the country dearly. Every inch of the island was fought over before the Japanese capitulated on March 16. It was mean, trench-to-trench warfare from start to finish; American losses reached a mind-boggling 26,000 dead marines, while the navy reported nearly 900 killed or missing and 2,000 wounded. Enemy losses climbed to more than 20,000 in the three-week fight. Luckily, Japanese air power was not a major factor because of Iwo Jima's isolation, although a lone Kamikaze slammed into the *Saratoga* on February 21, destroying forty-two planes, killing 123 men, and wounding nearly 200.

The struggle for Iwo Jima was chiefly complicated by its peculiar geography. According to Morison, it was an awesome locale for combat: "Shaped like a bloated pear, Iwo is only 4½ miles long and 2½ miles wide. The inactive volcanic crater of Mount Suribachi rises 500 feet above sea level. The northern part of the island is a plateau with rocky, inaccessible shores, but beaches extend from the base of Mount Suribachi for more than two miles north and east. These beaches, the land between them, and a good part of the terrain are covered with brown volcanic ash and black cinders which look like sand, but are so much lighter than sand that walking is difficult and running almost impossible."

General Tadamichi Kuribaysashi's 22,000-man garrison had made the unoccupied island into a fortress with underground passages and caves, concrete pillboxes, concealed gun emplacements, and fortified positions. Although enemy pockets remained on the island until March 16, the murderous combat subsided following capture of Mount Suribachi on February 23. The flag-raising ceremony on February 24, when four battle-hardened marines hoisted the Stars and Stripes over the volcanic mountain, soon electrified the home front. No other battle, not even Normandy, "was watched with more intensity than Iwo Jima," *Time* commented: "Henceforth, Iwo will be a place in U.S. history to rank with Valley Forge, Gettysburg, Tarawa. Few in this generation will ever forget Iwo's shifting black sands, or the mind's images of charging marines, or the sculptured picture of Old Glory rising atop Mount Suribachi."

On May 16, one day after the capitulation of the last Japanese troops, B-29 Superforts returning to Saipan from bombing runs over the home islands used captured airfields on the island. Actually, air and naval attacks on Japan had been underway for several months, although the big planes lacked fighter escorts until Iwo Jima. Nimitz had launched his carrier forces against Tokyo as early as July 10, and in the following weeks scarcely a Japanese city, harbor, or military compound escaped poundings from the air. As dwindling fuel and naval hardware hampered the enemy's ability to strike back, the American armada crept ever closer to the Rising Sun. Even British warships led by H.M.S. *King George* V joined the U.S. Third Fleet in shelling coastal towns before the war ended.

Regular bombing raids on Tokyo and other cities from Saipan were underway by November 24. In January, General Curtis LeMay, who later became Alabama governor George C. Wallace's vice presidential running mate, was placed in charge of the airwar from Saipan and the Marianas; planes and bombers were transferred from as far away as Burma and China for the assault. With P-47 Thunderbolts and P-51 Mustangs from Iwo Jima as escorts for the heavy bombers on Saipan, an incessant rain of conventional bombs continued until August 1945 when the decision was made to use atomic weapons. Even before Iwo Jima, a home front already reeling from one victory after another read daily press reports about the bombings. Lieutenant John T. Gavin, who piloted a Super-fortress during a February 16 raid on Tokyo and the Kasumigaura naval base fifty miles away, guessed he had seen 1,200 U.S. planes in the attack, which lasted nine hours. In another giant bombing raid by 334 Superforts during the night of March 9–10 "a total 1,667 tons of incendiary bombs" poured down on the Japanese capital in a wave of destruction that paralleled the fire storms that had destroyed Nuremberg, Hamburg, and Darmstadt.

Meanwhile, the Nimitz-Spruance-Halsey task force inched closer to Tokyo with the assault on Okinawa. Planning for Okinawa, called Operation Iceberg, was well underway before the capture of Iwo Jima. The huge island, largest of the Ryukyu chain, was needed as a staging platform for the final thrust. Its size and location—sixty miles long by eight wide, 340 miles from Formosa and equally distant from Kyushu, southernmost of the Japanese islands—made it a formidable military target. The Japanese imperial high command had massed upwards of 100,000 troops under Lieutenant General M. Ushijimi as well as ships and aircraft which had been held in reserve for the final defense of the home islands.

On Easter Sunday, April 1, 1945, 116,000 marines and army personnel attacked several miles of Okinawa beaches. The massive landings, which were unopposed on orders from Tokyo, followed a two-week "softening up" period. Although enemy strategy permitted our forces to gain an easy foothold, it took three months of brutal fighting to secure the island. Besides determined resistance behind something called the Machinato Line, the Japanese sent coordinated naval and air suicidal waves at the Americans, starting April 7, when more than 800 Kamikaze planes struck the fleet. That assault alone cost two U.S. destroyers and destruction of twenty-eight other vessels. The *Yamato* the world's largest battlewagon, was dispatched on a one-way mission to wreak havoc on the encircling armada, although Mitscher's carrier planes managed to sink the monster craft before it could do its nasty work.

"During the three-month campaign on Okinawa," writes Liddell Hart, "the Japanese made ten massed Kamikaze attacks—which they called 'Kikusui' (Floating Chrysanthemum). These totaled over 1,500 Kamikaze attacks, with almost as many suicidal attacks by other aircraft. Altogether thirty-four naval craft were sunk, and 368 damaged, mostly by Kamikazes." Still, Yankee perseverance won out at Okinawa.

Japanese forces held out until June 22 at staggering costs to themselves and the Americans. As in the case of Iwo Jima and the fighting in Germany, Americans at home were saturated with accounts of the slaughter as well as the heroics of individual GIs. Newsreels at local movie houses showed the Kamikazes in graphic detail, and *Newsweek* told its readers in May: "On Okinawa, 156 American marines and doughboys died each day last week. The shell-scarred, 5-mile-long no-man's-land stretching across the southern end of the island had, with the end of the European war, become the bloodiest battlefield in the world. This was the line the Japs had drawn for their final stand."

Before it ended, with American forces within striking distance of Tokyo, enemy losses reached 107,500 known dead, 7,000 prisoners, and an estimated 20,000 entombed in caves and underground bunkers. United States losses reached 12,000 dead and 36,000 wounded during combined operations. And as Southeast Asia forces under Lord Mountbatten marched toward Burma, Malaya, and Singapore, a strange irony occurred on Okinawa: General Simon Bolivar Buckner, commander of the American land forces, was killed on June 18 at a forward observation post by an enemy artillery burst; and four days later General Ushijimi committed Hara-Kiri to escape the dishonor of surrender.

As U.S. forces fought their way into Germany and across the Pacific, President Roosevelt was wheeled out on the White House portico for his record-setting fourth inauguration. Because of the continuing understanding among newsmen never to photograph the chief executive in the act of sitting down in or rising from his wheel chair, the public was not aware of his fast-deteriorating health. Because he was now unable to control his hands, a White House valet had to shave him prior to the January 20 ceremony; afterward, a nearly exhausted president, who had had to be lifted from his seat by his son, Colonel James Roosevelt, complained of chest pains.

It was a raw, snow-covered Washington as Harry Truman received the vice presidential oath before Roosevelt. About 7,800 people gathered on the White House lawn and another 3,000 on the ellipse across the street to watch in 30° weather. Although formal attire was not the order of the day—ambassadors were told to leave their long coats at home—at least two guests were seen in top hats: New Hampshire governor Charles M. Dale and comedian George Jessel. Chief Justice Harlan Stone administered the oath as FDR placed his hand upon a family Bible inscribed 1686; it was opened to the thirteenth chapter of First Corinthians: ". . . Beareth all things, believeth all things, hopeth all things, endureth all things. . . . And now abideth faith, hope, charity; but the greatest of these is charity."

With a clear voice, Roosevelt delivered the shortest of his four inaugural addresses, a scant 573 words. He did not mention the home front, nor domestic affairs, and made but one fleeting reference to the war: "We Americans of today, together with our Allies, are passing through a period of supreme test. It is a test of our courage—of our resolve—of our wisdom—of our essential democracy." Mostly his thoughts were on the future and the shape of the peace to come: ". . . So we pray to Him now and for the vision to see our way clearly—to see our way that leads to a better life for ourselves and for all our fellow men—and to the achievement of His will for peace on earth." Roosevelt would not live to enjoy that peace with his countrymen.

If Roosevelt said nothing about the home front at his swearing-in, it had surely been in his thoughts a week earlier. Surrounded by General George C. Marshall, Fleet Admiral Ernest King, and Byrnes, who had begun issuing his edicts on everything from nighttime revelries to defense workers, FDR called for greater civilian sacrifice. The armed forces, their joint statement said, would require 900,000 new recruits over the next six months. And, depending upon the fortunes of war, defense production would require increases in every category of weapons. Although WMC kept reassuring everyone that labor shortages were merely local difficulties, Roosevelt and his lieutenants called for 700,000 new civilian workers.

Washington's belt-tightening schemes subsided in the months ahead as the enemy war machines ground to a standstill. Although rationing and consumer shortages lingered, resources were found to undertake nonwar related ventures such as completion of New York's Lincoln Tunnel from Manhattan to Weehawken, New Jersey. The north tube, extending 7,500 feet under the Hudson River, was opened to automobile traffic on February 2. Because of increased use of the already completed south tube—New York Port officials said more than 5,750,000 vehicles passed through it during 1944—the north tunnel, which had an $80,000,000 price tag when completed under wartime conditions, was used to speed westbound traffic from the city. In spite of gasoline shortages and travel restrictions, enough people were riding around to keep the south tube, which had been used for two-way traffic, congested during the war.

Nor did the war deter one Michael Catan, who specialized in "firsts," from waiting at the head of the line to drive his automobile through the tunnel. "There was no rush," the press reported, "to test the riding quality of the new thoroughfare, and only a baker's dozen were waiting when the starting signal was given"; by nightfall, however, port authorities said

6,700 vehicles had driven through the new tunnel. Catan, with only an "A" rationing sticker and but two gallons of gasoline in his tank, had slept two days in his car; he had not run the engine to save fuel—coffee in his thermos turned cold during the wait. The "firster" told reporters he had undertaken the trip upon the suggestion of his brother, an enlisted man recuperating from battle injuries in an English hospital.

Spring 1945 also saw a thirteen-year-old beauty named Elizabeth Taylor gain recognition after Metro-Goldwyn-Mayer released her fourth movie, *National Velvet*. *Life* attributed her popularity to "a quiet, affectionate personality, which has an almost hypnotic effect on dogs and horses." The London-born Taylor—brought to this country before the war by her father, a Beverly Hills, California, art shop operator, had appeared in previous movies: *Lassie Come Home* (1943), *The White Cliffs of Dover* (1944), and *Jane Eyre* (1944). Starting with the Lassie film, a successful and idyllic picture built around a loyal Collie, Taylor quickly outdistanced other child actresses of the day: eight-year-old Margaret O'Brien, remembered for "the intensity and sensitivity of her emotional scenes in *Meet Me in St. Louis*"; and Peggy Ann Garner, another thirteen-year-old, from Canton, Ohio, best-known for her portrayal of Francie Nolan in the Hollywood version of Betty Smith's 1943 play, *A Tree Grows in Brooklyn*. While the others faded, a teenage Elizabeth Taylor continued upward following her 1945 appearance in *National Velvet*, "a story about a horse." Although first rejected by MGM because she was too small to manage the animal, the studio soon relented: "By eating steaks and going riding and roller-skating everyday she managed to grow three inches in four months and was given the part." The box office smash was no sooner released than MGM "loaned" her to RKO to make a screen adaption of Ernest Hemingway's novel about the Spanish Civil War, *For Whom the Bell Tolls*. The movie, which co-starred Ingrid Bergman and Gary Cooper, put her among the first rank of Hollywood performers.

Although it was downplayed by Washington bureaucrats anxious to court public opinion by paying lip service to a total war effort, the manpower dilemma improved during the first months of 1945. General Frank T. Hines, chief of the Veterans Administration indicated as much on February 27 before a House appropriations committee hearing despite calls from FDR and Byrnes for greater civilian participation in the war effort. Even though a watered-down public service bill had been given congressional approval, Hines made it clear that thousands of GIs were returning to the civilian work force. Hines, of course, was after funds for discharged servicemen "with disabilities," but he revealed war department plans to release 200,000–250,000 men per month after V-E day. And, he told the committee, "the present rate of discharges is running around 90,000 monthly." Approximately 700,000 of 1,600,000 men mustered out through November 30 had some form of physical or mental impairment.

Ex-GIs pouring into the domestic job market—and the rate of discharges accelerated as the fighting wound down—created problems for both management and labor. All of 1945, even the period after V-E day and victory over Japan, in August, was filled with labor discord. And the termination of contracts for defense production not only placed hardships on civilian workers but also dried up jobs for returning servicemen. An unresolved but thorny problem was job seniority for veterans, versus the job rights of civilians who had stayed at home. If economic conditions remained favorable there would be work for everyone; but a sagging economy spelled trouble. Veterans understandably demanded the jobs they had given up on entering the service. Accordingly, civilian workers who manned assembly lines during the war wanted job security as defense production faltered. Still, the number of unemployed at year's end was considerably less than government and labor leaders had anticipated.

A labor chief not afraid of Washington was John L. Lewis, who took his miners off the job one last time before the war ended. At the same time that Byrnes was ordering the midnight closing of nightclubs as well as a blackout of outdoor advertising and ornamental lights to save fuel, Lewis announced that bituminous coal miners would strike April 1 when their current contract expired. Although required to file advance notice under the Smith-Connally Act, his strike threat—and Lewis solidly enjoyed badgering Roosevelt—was announced at the same time that Interior Secretary Harold L. Ickes was returning seventy-two mines in Pennsylvania, West Virginia, and Kentucky to their owners. The pits had been seized in September, following widespread work stoppages in the Appalachian fields. Coal output for the shafts, which employed 25,000 miners, was 145,000 tons annually, a sizable percentage of the national total. Even with governmental intervention, the country used more coal than it produced in 1944; and, reported the Associated Press, "the general coal supply outlook for 1945 is as bad as it ever has been and probably the worst in recent years. Much of the bituminous shortage had been caused by cold weather, with manpower needs as an important factor."

Unabashed by the war, by public sentiment, or by a sick president, Lewis urged his negotiators to demand more benefits from the operators.

As the April 1 deadline neared, it became clear that the miners wanted contract concessions that included full pay for travel time to replace the two-thirds of the hourly rate then in effect. Lewis's gestures were the more threatening because the portal-to-portal issue had caused crippling work stoppages in 1943. Ickes and the government warned the miners that they faced military induction after Lewis met unsuccessfully with the bituminous operators on March 1 in a Washington hotel. Next, writes his biographer Saul Alinsky, "a familiar Lewis pattern began to emerge. At the last minute, Sunday, April 1, before the miners were to strike, he announced a thirty-day extention, to permit more time for negotiations."

Lewis called off the soft-coal strike on Easter Sunday, when New York City registered its largest Easter Day Parade ever, and he won a contract containing a "no-strike pledge" from the bituminous operators on April 11. But the wily union chief, who decided to worry Truman into acquiescence as he had done with Roosevelt, refused to settle with the anthracite operators. Then, May 1, the same day news arrived from Berlin of Hitler's death and Admiral Donitz's takeover in Germany, Lewis ordered 72,000 hard-coal miners off the job. Since anthracite is primarily Pennsylvania coal, the strike was confined to an area around Wilkes Barre and Scranton, where coal production dropped to zero. Immediately, WBP ordered the men back to work and Ickes seized the mines, but Lewis used a combination of luck and guile to evade back-to-work directives until May 21. During the interval, the Supreme Court unexpectedly came to Lewis's aid with a May 7 ruling that portal-to-portal pay was legal, and the anthracite operators agreed to underground travel plus other wage benefits.

Home-bound veterans could be seen everywhere during 1945 hurrying about looking for jobs and wives. The first part of the year, in fact, was a time of intense travel by every means, and, predictably, more accidents plagued the country. During February a navy transport plane bound for Cleveland, Ohio, from Oakland, California, plunged into San Francisco Bay, killing twenty-four navy men. A week later all but four passengers aboard an American Airlines flight were lost when it crashed into the Blue Ridge Mountains near Cedar Springs, Virginia. The nation's highways were just as dangerous; at the end of 1944, reported the Associated Press, traffic deaths had increased 53 percent over the previous year. The dramatic upsurge in automobile fatalities did not result from a sudden bonanza of derationed gasoline and tires, but from the use, by civilians and returning veterans alike, of "wornout cars."

For the men who braved battle duty and the perils of wartime travel, *Collier's* ran an article in May which told them "How to Get Married." After considerable hoopla about the responsibility of marriage, "the boy and girl" were urged to plan for the event: "We'd suggest you keep your plans as simple and constructive as possible, for a lavish display is out of order in wartime." Conservative weddings were the order of the day in 1945, but, "if a couple has very little time for tradition, then go down to City Hall and get married simply and quietly. It's just as appropriate —and as long lasting. . . ." So many returning GIs were bringing home wives from England, Australia, and New Zealand that the British journal, *Good Housekeeping*, offered the transplanted brides some practical advice on life in their new home: "Dress your smartest for first interviews, and remember that except in the smallest villages lipstick is expected. . . . In spite of many shortcomings America is a new country where past achievements are only a starting for the future. You will be welcome in America, for you too have taken a chance and embarked on a great adventure."

Not only war brides from overseas but all women, and men as well, faced a changed America after the war. No aspect of American life had altered more than the place of women in society. Eleanor Roosevelt added to the "female revolution" with her highly visible support of liberal and humanitarian causes; although she encountered great hostility across the South for her advocacy of civil rights and justice for blacks, she became the most visible of all First Ladies, before or since. WAVES, WACS, and other female services fell below their authorized enlistment levels throughout the war, but their collective roles in aiding the war effort helped bring about a new perception of American women; forty-five women were killed or wounded while on active duty during the hostilities and more than 250 were officially decorated. Women had been in and out of politics for several years—including a Georgia fireater named Rebecca Felton who became the first woman in the U.S. Senate during 1922—and their important committee work during 1942–1945, helped the cause of women everywhere.

The startling gains made by women caused *Life* to editorialize in January 1945: "The war has put about 1,000,000 women to work who otherwise would have stayed home. Though they are paid less than men in many industries, this is becoming less and less the rule." And besides their numbers in Congress, women were assuming an increased role in politics. For the first time, more women than men trekked to the polls in the 1944 presidential canvass; because of female political savvy, both parties inserted a proposed Equal Rights Amendment in their national platforms for the Roosevelt-Dewey canvass. "Nothing will be done about this amendment because it is largely nonsense," *Life* continued. Nonsense or not, women had played such a vital role in the war effort that Republicans and Democrats wanted their support; but Congress waited another four decades to approve the concept of equality for women.

12 APRIL-JULY 1945: TWO DICTATORS AND A PRESIDENT DIE

Traumatic times hit the home front during April–June 1945, although Allied armies throughout the world were pushing toward victory. April alone witnessed the death of three figures who had dominated the world stage for twenty-five years and more—Adolph Hitler, Benito Mussolini, and Franklin D. Roosevelt. In May, victory in Europe freed the nation to concentrate on the Pacific war. A continuing paradox was the development of serious meat and poultry shortages at the same time that Washington and OPA were moving to eliminate rationing and price controls of all kinds. Amid memories that failure to join the League of Nations at the end of World War I had helped fuel the present conflict, the first organizational meetings of the United Nations, with heavy United States participation, took place in San Francisco. But Roosevelt's death on April 12 had the greatest impact on the lives of millions from every political persuasion. Roosevelt, after all, had been at the center of American life since 1932, a period of thirteen years. Today, like memories of Pearl Harbor, there is scarcely a person alive that lived through the war who does not have vivid memories of FDR's passing and the days of mourning that followed.

The president's death stunned the nation for two reasons: despite occasional hints that the sixty-three-year-old Roosevelt was experiencing ill health, the public had no idea of his true physical state. By the first months of 1945, however, reporters and observers close to the White House were speculating privately about his worsening health. Still, his personal physician, Admiral Ross T. McIntire, termed his condition "excellent" two days after the inauguration when Roosevelt left for the Yalta Conference. He returned "looking tanned and refreshed" and drove to sleet-covered Arlington National Cemetery for the burial of General Edwin "Pa" Watson, a White House adviser who had died during the

Yalta trip. McIntire told reporters: "The president had a slight cold on the trip abroad, but despite long sessions of hard work, he stood up well under the strain, and the cold has disappeared."

But Roosevelt was not in good health and the illness that took his life had apparently started during October 1943 when he began losing weight. Press reports said that he had "the grippe." Although he was forced to spend New Year's Day 1944 in bed, McIntire, one day before Roosevelt's sixty-second birthday on January 28, issued a glowing diagnosis: "He is in better health than he has been since entering the White House and he is swimming five times a week." Sometime later he was in Bethesda Naval Hospital for removal of a twenty-year-old "wen" on the back of his head. Even then, speculation was rife that the skin disorder was symptomatic of a deeper, more dangerous problem.

Later, a few days before Roosevelt left Washington on April 4, 1944, for a month of rest at a South Carolina plantation owned by financier Bernard M. Baruch, the presidential physician gave out another report: "For a man 62-plus we have very little to argue about with the exception that we had to combat the influenza plus the respiratory complications that came along after." Upon his return to the Washington, Roosevelt's daughter, Mrs. John Boettinger, moved into the White House to help manage an obviously ill president. His public bravado notwithstanding, McIntire became increasingly alarmed. "Deeply disturbed," he related in his book about Roosevelt, he suggested complete rest at the presidential retreat in Georgia: "His heart, quite naturally, was our principal concern. Why not! Here was a man sixty-three, under terrific strain for years, who had been coughing heavily for more than two months in the spring of 1944. Time proved that our fears were groundless, for that stout heart of his never failed, but we could not foresee that this would be the case. As for the cerebral hemorrhage, it was and is unpredictable."

While posing for an artist, Elizabeth Shoumatoff, to paint his portrait at his Warm Springs desk as his longtime friend, Lucy Mercer Rutherfurd, looked on, Roosevelt suddenly grabbed his forehead. When Mrs. Shoumatoff asked if anything was wrong, he responded calmly, "I have a terrific headache," and slumped forward. Those were his last words. The president collapsed at 1:15 p.m., and within fifteen minutes Commander Howard G. Breunn, a navy doctor who accompanied him to Georgia, was at his side. Journalist Jim Bishop tells what happened next in his account of Roosevelt's death: "Breunn peeled the eyelids back one at a time. There appeared to be no dilation. Respiration was deep, stertorous. Wrist pulse was shallow and fast. The heart action was swift. Systolic blood pressure was 300 and probably more; the cuff only registered 300 at the top of the gauge." Quick action by Commander Bruenn, telephone calls to McIntire in Washington, and summoning of an Atlanta specialist, Dr. James Paullin, were not enough. With Mrs. Rutherfurd and the two medicos looking on, death came unobtrusively at 3:35 p.m. Dr. Paullin had injected adrenalin directly into the heart muscle with no result; he later issued a statement on the cause of death with Bruenn: "A massive intracerebral hemorrhage which, in all probability, had ruptured into the subarachnoid space."

As Mrs. Roosevelt traveled south to take charge, the president's confidants told Lucy Rutherfurd to leave Warm Springs quietly to avoid any embarrassment. Although the home front and the world were aghast at the news of Roosevelt's death, it was several years before his longstanding attachment to Mrs. Rutherfurd became widely known. Roosevelt even had two "maiden cousins," Margaret "Daisy" Suckley and Laura "Aunt Polly" Delano, join the Warm Springs party to gloss over her presence. Eleanor Roosevelt, notes her biographer, Joseph Lash, "might write to her old friend Esther Lape, as she did, that love for Franklin had died long ago, but by believing in his objectives she had rendered him a service of love in helping him achieve his purposes; but here melancholy and loneliness belied such protestations. She had been hurt anew by the discovery that Lucy Mercer Rutherfurd had been at Warm Springs at the time of Franklin's death, Lucy's presence having been kept a secret from her. . . ." The FDR-Rutherfurd tryst had been kept in the family closet, though, according to Lash, Eleanor Roosevelt became upset after the funeral when she learned from her daughter Anna that Rutherfurd had visited in the White House without her knowledge.

The loss of a national leader is always traumatic, but the outpouring for FDR was genuine. As the funeral cortege rolled toward the capital, grief-stricken crowds lined the railroads. The black community, because of the special chemistry its members felt with the Roosevelts, was particularly disturbed by his death. In Atlanta, *Newsweek* reported, "throngs jammed an overpass to watch the train go by. At the station it halted briefly as it did later at Greenville and Spartanburg, South Carolina, Charlotte and Salisbury, North Carolina, and Danville, Virginia. Each time fresh masses of flowers were put aboard the car where the casket rested." Word had gone ahead and whatever the hour—at Danville, it was 3 a.m.—people waited for the train. Blacks who felt a strong attachment to the president and Mrs. Roosevelt sang spirituals along the way, and "at Greenville, South Carolina, where thousands packed the station area, someone passed aboard a wreath from Mrs. Kate Finley, whose son had been killed in the war."

The body rested in the East Room of the White House, the same room where Lincoln's body had lain eighty years before in the closing days of the Civil War. Like the crowds that surged forward to catch a glimpse of the president traveling north, multitudes gathered in towns from Boston to San Francisco for his memorial services. At Newport, Rhode Island, Mayor Herbert E. McCauley placed Roosevelt's name "at the top of the city's roll of honor on the city hall lawn," while a navy bugler played taps. But in San Francisco, where retail stores and theaters closed for the day, defense workers in shipyards, anxious to win the war, paused briefly "with torches in hand" and returned to work. A service in New York City attracted 50,000 mourners; stores and businesses closed throughout the nation and radio networks observed periods of silence.

Following a twenty-three-minute ceremony at the White House led by the Right Reverend Angus Dun, Episcopal Bishop of Washington, and the singing of a grand old hymn, "Faith of Our Fathers," the funeral procession entrained for Hyde Park. Again, thousands gathered beside tracks long familiar to the Roosevelts: "Through Philadelphia, and into Manhattan; then across Hells Gate and up the New York Central's Hudson Division." At the New York graveside service, another Episcopal priest, the Reverend George W. Anthony, spoke briefly: "We commit his body to the ground, earth to earth, dust to dust . . . Blessed are the dead who die in the Lord. . . . Christ, have mercy on us." Cadets from nearby West Point fired a volley that echoed across the Hudson.

In the closing weeks of combat, as Allied armies penetrated deeper into Nazi territory, American prisoners of war released from German camps began to return home. Three days before Roosevelt's death, an army transport ship with 1,500 ex-POWs—the largest returning contingent yet—reached Boston. Although some were captured airmen who had been in captivity for a year or more, a majority had been in the stalags for only a short time. Earl Queen, a sergeant from Elkin, North Carolina, one of the 1,500, told reporters he had parachuted into Germany one day before the Normandy invasion. A member of the 82nd Airborn Infantry Division, he was "captured as the Americans stormed the beaches, and spent twenty-three days in a boxcar with about fifty other men with only two slices of bread to eat." Ranking officer aboard the ship was Lieutenant Colonel James Skeels from West Hartford, Connecticut, a POW since May 1944, when he had been captured in Italy following a reconnaissance mission. Queen and Skeels, like other homecoming POWs, were given back pay and sent to recuperation centers near their home towns. Some, particularly those returning from Japanese camps after long internments which had lasted from the fall of the Philippines, Guam, and Wake, received astronomical amounts of back pay. In the next months thousands of men came home to grateful families and a home front intrigued by the money paid for service time while in captivity.

At the same time, a home front that had always been protected from actual combat began to learn about the horrors of Nazi concentration-extermination camps during May and April. Photographs of starved, contorted, naked bodies bombarded American readers as the Allied armies uncovered the ghastly places. Nazi leaders, perhaps sensing impending collapse, had speeded their mass killings in the last days. Newsreels, magazines, and newspapers all carried accounts of the camps; and civilians for the first time got a firsthand view of German atrocities.

An indication of the enormity of the Holocaust came after the Russians broke into Oswiecim during March; Dr. Bela Fabian, author and onetime Hungarian politician with ties to the American Jewish community, freed by United States troops near Erfurt, gave out an interview through AP correspondents: 500,000 Jews had been killed at Oswiecim alone over the past year; Fabian, who "narrowly escaped" the crematorium himself, said the hurried executions had been performed over the past ten months and that every Jew "over age fifty had been automatically put to death." By early May, Jewish organizations in this country were saying that four to five million people had perished.

Official Washington had known about the killing camps long before our troops began to uncover them during 1944–1945. Since Hitler's *Mein Kampf* in the 1920s, the Nazis had made no secret about their aims for European Jewry. As early as 1940, writes historian Arthur Morse, Assistant Secretary of State Breckinridge Long, who was in charge of wartime refugees, "read diplomatic dispatches describing the murder of 250,000 in Poland, and he was shown accounts of refugees adrift among ice floes on the Danube." The American Jewish community, including Treasury Secretary Henry F. Morgenthau, repeatedly urged measures to relieve the unbelievable suffering. Yet the United States did nothing until January 1944, when the War Refugee Board was created to establish camps in Europe for Jews fortunate enough to escape the German death chambers. Earlier pleas to admit Jewish refugees in other than token numbers had gone unheeded. Aerial photographs and smuggled diagrams of the Auschwitz camp in occupied Poland failed to bring a response to the mass killings; suggestions that Allied planes bomb the camp were brushed aside as impractical. The United States had not only turned back ships laden with Jewish refugees until late in the war, but the State Department had discouraged private efforts to assist Holocaust victims.

The death camps remained hot news throughout the summer as dispatches came in of atrocity piled upon atrocity. The very day of Roosevelt's death, April 12, Generals Eisenhower, Bradley, and Patton toured recently captured Ohrdruf Nord near Gotha. Ike's biographer, Peter Lyon, describes the visit with telling prose: "The camp in question was not one of the spectacular pestholes, no showplace: but the routine stink of death emanating from three thousand or more corpses that lay, some buried in shallow graves, some exposed, lice crawling over them, scabbed black where they had been gutted to provide a meal for famished survivors. Bradley was revolted. Patton withdrew to vomit in a corner. Eisenhower, his face frozen white, forced himself to examine every last corner of the camp." And the truth about Auschwitz, Belsen, Dachau, Theresienstadt, Darcy, unsettled not only battle-hardened warriors but also a complacent America during 1945—perhaps an America that wanted to forget its past policies.

In this country, meanwhile, a frustrating meat shortage developed during the spring and summer. One "expert" in May figured that cattle traveled an average 1,100 miles from ranch or farm to the family table; and everyone from cattlemen to corner butcher had an explanation for the snafu. *Newsweek* branded it "the professors dance": the difficulty started during 1942 "when OPA was run by the economist Leon Henderson, and 60 percent of the key jobs in the agency were held by economists, college instructors, and lawyers, mostly in their thirties." Imbued with New Deal enthusiasum for bureaucratic engineering and caught up in wartime fervor, the professors had set a chain of events in motion that peaked in the spring of 1945.

By June meat shortages were real enough to cause hardships for individual housewives, although empty butcher lockers were located primarily in urban centers. Several shops in Salt Lake City were forced to close for lack of supplies and in Des Moines meat availability dropped 50 percent below normal, with stores forced to offer lesser cuts: spareribs, tongue, sweetbreads, kidney, pressed meats. On the West Coast, San Diego was termed "desperate" when meat in stores plunged below 55 percent of usual levels, and in San Francisco retailers could offer only lamb and sausage. Even in Dallas, within sight of huge cattle spreads, housewives had only "frankfurters, fish, and liver." Small towns and rural communities, on the other hand, had an abundance of meat. George Thiem, farm editor of the Chicago *Daily News*, toured several midwestern states in May and found no shortages: "At Austin, Minnesota, steaks, mutton, chops, and bacon; at Columbus, Nebraska, choice of tenderloin or sirloin steaks, grade AA roast beef."

While rural America found ample meat for the dinner table, much of it supplied from surrounding farms, lines of angry housewives could be seen in every urban area outside chain outlets, butcher shops, and groceries. There were plenty of places for the meat distribution chain to break down between range and neighborhood grocery—especially with the armed forces commandeering large chunks of processing plant output. Moreover, urban dwellers with defense money in their pockets inevitably turned to the black markets that flourished in many cities. In Louisville, for instance, an estimated 15 percent of all meat was controlled by under-the-counter operators. William H. Courtney, a writer for *Collier's* who studied the problem, encountered another way to get a pot roast for the family table—tipping: "A butcher in Houston told me he received from certain customers, from one to five dollars each in cash every week. He rates his customers, the amounts and grades they get, accordingly: 'Those who don't come across don't get!' he said. I know one large butcher in Queens, New York, who let his customers know he wanted liquor for Christmas. He got 500 bottles."

An Office of War Information release in February admitted that "organized black markets in sugar and meat are reappearing in dangerous proportions depending largely on counterfeit coupons." At the same time no formal market for cigarettes could be found in the country, although "petty chiselers constituted a real menace." Illicit trading in gasoline coupons and under-the-counter liquor sales had all but ceased. And, warned the report, which carried endorsements from the Secret Service and Alcohol Tax Unit of the Treasury: "If individual consumers would refuse to pay over-ceiling prices or accept rationed goods without giving valid coupons, all black markets would be completely wiped out in short order."

The average family could not purchase the items needed in every household—rubber galoshes, washing machines, radios, automobiles, phonographs, good liquors—and they were willing to get them on the black market until the end of the war. As criticism of OPA policy increased, President Truman after less than a month in the White House set the country straight. He spoke May 1, one day before New Mexico

Representative Clinton Anderson released a congressional report critical of OPA and continued price controls. Truman, who urged Congress to extend the agency's life, said that OPA under Chester Bowles had done good work in stabilizing prices and rationing vital supplies. Recognizing popular discontent, he added: "Our price control and rationing machinery extends into every home and affects directly the daily life of the housewife and her family. Naturally, things must be done which displease many people. No businessman, no farmer, no merchant likes to be told how much he can charge for his wares. No housewife likes to be told that she may have only a limited supply of meat, or sugar, or canned goods with which to feed her family." Wartime controls were necessary, and had it not been for OPA, the country would experience "runaway inflation," Truman concluded.

White House commitment to price controls and rationing extended into November 1946, when Republican victories in the off-year elections caused Truman to abandon the entire program. Shortly after V-J day, however, OPA, with Truman's blessing was able to end most rationing; and the agency held the wholesale price index to a comfortable 7 percent and the general cost of living index to 3 percent for the remainder of 1945. Even so, black market buying and selective inflation plagued the country after the New Year. Finally, a frightened Congress extended OPA for one year on July 26, 1945, in spite of conservative Democrat-Republican opposition to Truman's progressive programs that fitted the Rooseveltian mold. Opposition to OPA continued to mount, especially after victory over Japan, and on November 9, 1946—following the congressional elections—Truman terminated the remaining wage and price controls. Though a lid was kept on rents, sugar, and rice, OPA officially went out of business during December 1946, more than a year and a half after cessation of hostilities.

Amid the hassle over meat shortages and OPA meddling, the home front was jarred by news that Adolph Hitler had died in his Berlin bunker. Everyone realized an era had ended when Hitler and Mussolini died within hours of each other on Germany's collapse. Still, there was only a subdued outpouring and virtually no enthusiasm for rejoicing in the streets at the dictators' passing three weeks after Roosevelt's death. Many in this country were skeptical when word of Hitler's death first rolled over the airwaves, although scattered street celebrations erupted in the false belief that V-E day had arrived. Hitler entered his underground haven on January 16 as the Allies pushed closer to the city; for the next three-

and-a-half months he lived in a chamber with a sixteen-feet-thick concrete roof and walls six feet wide, constructed under tons of earth below the Reich Chancellery.

Monotony and fear trapped those around Hitler until life in the subterranean shelter became a living hell. James P. O'Donnell, a newspaperman in Berlin after the war, who penned a study of those last weeks, indicates that the führer, in steadily declining health, rarely went above ground except at night to walk his pet Alsatian, Blondi. Although scores of military, diplomatic, and civilian functionaries plodded in and out of the hideaway, Hitler's underground surroundings became "debilitating." And the fürher must have been the most pathetic of all. O'Donnell writes: "Hitler's eyes, once iceberg blue and lustrous, were now often glazed, the eyeballs sunken and bloodshot. His brown hair had suddenly turned gray. . . . Both hands trembled and he used the right hand to hold the left up close to the body. In the very last days, there was often spittle on his lips, and at times he simply drooled or whispered through his teeth. His complexion was sallow. Soup-slop and mustard spots now stained his once natty and spotless uniform jacket." Finally, with the Russians within sight, he married his longtime mistress Eva Braun, in a hurried midnight ceremony on Saturday, April 28. The next day, Hitler and his wife of less than twenty-four hours took their lives with poison and self-inflicted gunshot wounds.

The American home front seemed more stunned than joyous at Hitler's demise; although many thought it signaled an immediate end to the European war, V-E day waited until May 7. It was a false dawn; in New York, crowds in Times Square merely bought newspaper "extras" for the latest news and impromptu celebrations in a thousand other places petered out as well. While Paris prepared to light up again, and Moscow "went mad," people in this country remained indifferent. A Minneapolis cab driver said, "so what" when told about Hitler.

Thomas E. Dewey, still governor of New York, called on the country to forgo applauding the German collapse and urged a day of thanksgiving instead. General Eisenhower captured the national temper when he heard that his adversary of four years was dead; upon learning that Admiral Karl Doenitz, who had taken charge following the führer's suicide, had called it a hero's death, Ike issued a low-keyed statement from SHAPE headquarters: "It is a contradiction of the facts as we know them."

One American who crowed over Hitler's death was newswoman Dorothy Thompson. From Jerusalem, where she was reporting Zionist-Arab tensions when the war ended, Miss Thompson sent a blistering column to her American readers proclaiming that "the seeds of hatred that he sowed throughout the world still flourished." Since the early 1930s, she had carried on a one-woman crusade against Hitler and Nazism. During a 1931 interview in Berlin with the aspiring Reich Chancellor, a "violent" shouting match had taken place between the two. Afterwards she called him "inconsequential" and "the kind of character who crooks his little finger while holding a teacup." Hitler responded by kicking her out of Germany permanently when he came to power after 1933.

In a way Dorothy Thompson got the last laugh; in May 1945 the onetime wife of novelist Sinclair Lewis was writing a twice-weekly column that appeared in 125 newspapers and earning $80,000 a year. She remained unstinting in her blasts at Hitler until the end. During her stay in Berlin and Vienna, Thompson had cultivated a great love for pre-Nazi Germany—for the world of Beethoven, Schiller, and Goethe—and she saw brown-shirted storm troopers as destroyers of that genteel world. Nor were her anti-Hitler diatribes limited to the printed word; she was known to have punched people on Viennese streets for making Jewish slurs, and in 1938 "she invaded a German-American Bund rally in Madison-Square Garden and almost broke it up single-handed, laughing gustily at every statement until the Bundsters were livid." The incessant carping in the nation's newspapers and radio broadcasts by Thompson and others like her helped fuel United States determination to crush the Axis.

Richard C. Hottelett, CBS correspondent with the U.S. First Army in Europe, reported that most GIs were glad the führer was dead: "Hitler has become hated among the soldiers of our army, hated personally and violently, as the man who kept fighting a senseless war, kept the slaughter going for absolutely no reason." Yet even here, in Europe on the front line, fighting men took his death in stride. Just as no outcries of jubilation greeted the news from Berlin, our fighting men and the home front hardly noticed the sorrowful death of Benito Mussolini and his mistress, Clara Petacci, on April 29. El Duce's last days were dismal indeed from mounting pressure inside Italy to step down; after being propped up by Hitler, who told him, "once a dictator, always a dictator," he was abandoned by a crumbling wehrmacht racing to cross the Alps into Germany. Mussolini was speeding northward with a panzer unit when captured by Communist partisans.

Justice in the hands of his countrymen was swift: "They were taken out to a nearby quarry," writes A. P. J. Taylor, the British military historian: "Mussolini was stood against the wall. When Clara saw that they were going to shoot him, she stood in front of him. They were both shot dead. Their bodies were left there for some hours, and then taken down to Milan. The violence displayed against their bodies was so great that, to put them out of reach, they where hung upside down outside a garage." Initial press reports which reached this country said Mussolini "died badly—that when the guns were leveled at him, he cried, No! No!" A photograph showing the two suspended upside down soon appeared in every American newspaper and on every movie screen. It was a grisly picture of the grisly end to Italian Fascism. Taylor says the photograph seen by millions the world over, signified Mussolini's end: "Poor Mussolini, as someone said, always upside down, a man doomed to failure."

The deaths of Hitler and Mussolini within hours of each other climaxed the European war, although the official end waited another week. In those hectic last days several German leaders including Himmler sought to terminate the fighting and Sweden's Count Bernadotte agreed to act as go-between with the Allies. But Eisenhower and Montgomery, like the Russian generals flooding into Germany from the East, would accept nothing short of unconditional surrender. Their leader dead and the once proud panzer divisions reduced to ghosts, there was nothing left for the Reich but total capitulation.

Meanwhile, authorities in this country braced for an onslaught of joymaking on May 7—officially designated as V-E Day. Jonathan Daniels, Harry Truman's press secretary, gave out a May 1 statement from the president who asked that "no celebrations take place and he hoped Americans will continue in the job before them." Truman sent a letter to Fred M. Vinson, his Mobilization and Reconversion director, emphasizing a no-demonstration policy: "The debt is unpaid at least until we have finished the war and solved those urgent problems which war leaves in its aftermath."

Although General Marshall announced on May 4 that the army would not be reduced after V-E Day, but men in Europe would be sent to the Pacific, other Washington officials gave conflicting signals. James A. Krug, WPB chairman, said the nationwide "brownout" on outdoor billboards and window advertising [nighttime baseball had been exempted] would be lifted. Word from overseas about "wild demonstrations" in London, Paris, Copenhagen, and Moscow, led local police to ready themselves in this country. Finally, Vinson said on May 6 that federal authorities would not ban or interfere with V-E celebrations; but he asked "that there be no interruption of war production and no greater interruption of normal activity than the public's sense of rejoicing demands."

After a week or more of dramatic events in Europe coupled with the heavy fighting on Okinawa, the home front was more relieved and thankful than joyous over the German collapse. In New York's Times Square, still the war's domestic focal point, torn paper fluttered from skyscrappers and half a million New Yorkers milled around "waiting for the fun to start" before Mayor Fiorello LaGuardia asked everyone to go home "or return to your jobs." And in Atlanta the press reported more noise in one six-run inning of an Atlanta-Little Rock baseball game than could be found in the rest of the city. More than 800 police extras were called out in Chicago's Loop to prevent a repetition of the 1918 Armistice that resulted "in property damage of $1,000,000, injury to hundreds, and death for six." Chicago, like other cities from Boston to San Francisco, took little notice of the surrender. "Repressed excitement" was the order of the day in Philadelphia; and in Los Angeles, where the Japanese war was heavy on everyone's mind, shipyards and aircraft factories kept operating. Two and a half months later, however, when V-J Day arrived, the home front forgot the repressed excitement of May 7 as it pulled out the stops in a near orgy of celebration.

With the war fast approaching a climax in the Pacific, the country watched the private lives of Hollywood entertainers as intently as ever; the fascination with the make-believe of tinseltown did not vanish with the momentous events of April–August 1945. First, Cary Grant and his wife, Barbara Hutton, heiress to the Woolworth dime store fortune, were divorced in August, following a separation of several months. The marriage had taken place in July 1942 during a six-minute ceremony in the home of Frank Vincent, Grant's California manager. That was three weeks before the bridegroom officially became an American citizen and legally changed his name from Archibald Leach to Cary Grant; and at a time when he was preoccupied with his acting career. Grant was so busy filming *Once Upon a Honeymoon* that he failed to take one himself. "The groom went straight back to work," notes Grant biographer Lionel Godfrey, "though it was conceded that he might report on set an hour later than usual the day after his marriage."

But the marriage did not work and Godfrey assesses what happened: "If, however, one was to talk of mistakes in the partnership of Grant and Barbara Hutton, the first was the marriage itself. It held small promise of a happy future. As Grant came to realize, he and Barbara had little in common; being different in education, background and upbringing. Elegant living had brought them together, and as a shared interest, elegant living was not enough for partners in a marriage." Barbara Hutton was Grant's second wife, while the bride had been married twice before.

In order to counter rumors that he was a fortune hunter, Grant had signed a pre-marriage waiver to her money, an act neglected by her other six husbands: Alexis Mdivani, a Russian prince, and Count von Haugwitz-Reventlow, a Danish aristrocrat who gave Hutton her one child, Lance Reventlow, who became a racing driver and was killed in an airplane crash in 1972 at age thirty-six; Prince Igor Troubetzkoy, the playboy Porfirio Rubirosa, the tennis star Baron Gottfried von Cramm and Prince Raymond Doan Vinh Campack. Grant, who continued his filmmaking career after being rejected by the Army Air Force because of his age, stayed busy with countless USO and war bond drive appearances. Hutton, while she was not ungenerous with her pocketbook in behalf of relief causes, stayed at home writing poetry as her husband joined the Hollywood swirl boosting the war effort. Whatever the reason for their discord, the couple first separated in August 1944, a year before the divorce which was handled for Grant by Hollywood lawyer Jerry Giesler. Barbara Hutton obviously regarded Grant with some affection: "Cary Grant had no title, and of my husbands, he is the one I loved the most. He was so sweet, so gentle. It didn't work out, but I loved him," she said afterwards.

As the Grant-Hutton union dissolved, the storybook romance and marriage of Lauren Bacall and Humphrey Bogart was splashed across the country. The son of a New York physician and an artist mother, Bogart was a popular hero because of his top-drawing movies; and no matter that he had three ex-wives. "Seven sheriffs" were needed to keep curious fans from the May ceremony at the home of novelist Louis Bromfield near Mansfield, Ohio. *Life's* picture of the week for June 4 portrayed a forty-five-year-old Bogart and a twenty-year-old Bacall happily exchanging bites from their four-tiered wedding cake: "The ceremony was performed by Municipal Judge H. H. Shettler who read a service which he said contained a little of everything." Photographs and newsreel coverage of the wedding were seen by millions.

Bogart and his fashion-model-turned-actress bride had met several months before while filming Ernest Hemingway's *To Have and Have Not*. The marriage, which took place after Bogart divorced his third wife, Mayo Methot—they were known around Hollywood as the "Battling Bogarts"—lasted until "Bogie's" premature death from throat cancer twelve years later. Bogart and Bacall (she was born Betty Joan Perske) appeared in several movie productions, including the celebrated *Key Largo*, and their screen chemistry has become part of American folk culture. As late as the 1980s a popular country and western ballad compared a singer's love to "Bogie and Bacall in *Key Largo*." During one unforgettable scene in *To Have and Have Not*, Bacall drawls, "If you need anything, just whistle. . . . You know how to whistle, don't you?" The line nearly equals the famous, "Play it again, Sam," in the film Bogart made with Swedish actress Ingrid Bergman. That film, *Casablanca*, undoubtedly remains *the* movie classic of World War II.

"*To Have and Have Not* transformed me from a nothing to a combination of Garbo, Dietrich, Mae West, Katherine Hepburn," notes Bacall in her 1980 autobiography. Lauren Bacall, who has remained one of the country's most fascinating women throughout the 1980s, gained a place of her own in the American consciousness with the now-famous photograph of her lounging atop an upright piano played by Harry Truman. The widely-copied picture depicting "the sultry actress" and Truman was snapped in Washington's National Press Club Canteen during February 1945 when the vice president stopped by to entertain servicemen with his "old fashioned" piano playing.

Another couple in the news were socialite Gloria Vanderbilt and symphony conductor Leopold Stokowski. After a 1944 divorce from Pat di Cicco, whom she had married in 1942, the twenty-one-year-old Vanderbilt and the London-born Stokowski were married April 21, a few days after Roosevelt's death. The bride, who caught the eye of prying newsmen from the day of her birth, was not only a great-great-grand-daughter of railroad mogul Cornelius Vanderbilt and consequently heiress to a fabulous fortune, but also the subject of a notorious and long-running custody battle between her mother and an aunt. After her father's death, notes Vanderbilt biographer Edwin Hoyt, "Gloria Morgan Vanderbilt [her mother] was forced to live on an allowance from the inheritance of her daughter, little Gloria. Within a few years the the older Gloria's pleasant circumstances had become desperate by Vanderbilt standards. Gloria and her daughter were caught in a crossfire of emotions and court cases which involved Mother Morgan, the lawyers, and Gertrude Vanderbilt Whitney; and little Gloria grew up in an atmosphere of bickering that delighted Sunday supplements well into the 1940s."

Stokowski, thirty-six years older than his wife and a naturalized citizen since 1928, had conducted symphonies around the country: Cincinnati, Philadelphia, Los Angeles, San Francisco, the New York Philharmonic.

In 1945 he was conductor of the Hollywood Bowl Symphony; Stokowski was reportedly squiring screen actress Greta Garbo when he met his wife. Gloria Vanderbilt's wartime marriages to di Cicco and Stokowski were trumpeted to a home front long accustomed to watching her every move. The socialite/hostess and fashion setter divorced Stokowski ten years later in 1955.

The adventures and misadventures of "the pretty people" never ceased to amaze the public during the war years and serious battlefront news was frequently interspersed with their shenanigans. Opera singer Lily Pons and her conductor-husband, Andre Kostelanetz, attracted notice during April–May because of their near Herculean tours to entertain servicemen. Upon a return to New York on April 10, the Associated Press reported the couple had covered 38,000 miles since Christmas when their tour opened "in a park in Calcutta before 10,000 soldiers, most of whom were Americans." Pons and Kostelanetz gave sixty-three concerts on that jaunt alone to become "the only entertainers who have traveled the China, Burma, India, and European theaters during one continuous trip."

Lily Pons was beyond a doubt the country's foremost operatic singer during the 1940s and 1950s, with an enormous popular following. Unlike the customary huge-chested diva, she was something of a beauty, which greatly enhanced her stage appeal. "She actually fulfills Hollywood specifications," wrote musicologist David Ewen in 1949: "She is slight of build, weighing about 104 pounds and standing five feet two. . . . She is pert, attractive, as graceful in her movement as a dancer, at all times radiating charm. . . . Her face sparkles like a new coin. All this, and heaven too—the heaven of a voice that is, in the best traditions of an age of singing, now dead." The French-born Pons first sang in this country during 1930 at the Metropolitan and from that moment, her career was one continuous triumph.

Although Pons and Kostelanetz, a Russian-born musician-conductor who became a naturalized citizen in 1928, kept a low profile, Pons, who received medals and accolades from half the countries of Europe, became widely known. Two locomotives were named for her, to say nothing of Lilypons, Maryland; "numerous culinary dishes bear her name—a tribute, no doubt, to her reputation as a gourmet: at the Raleigh Hotel in Washington, D.C. they serve a 'Sole Lily Pons'; at the Madison Hotel in New York City, you can get a 'Soupe Lily Pons'; at the Carter Hotel in Cleveland, a specialty of the house is 'Chicken Lily Pons.' " With Kostelanetz, whom she married in 1938 at her side, Pons traveled more than 100,000 miles singing on the USO circuit besides giving regular operatic performances.

Mid-1945 also witnessed a steady literary outpouring. In spite of the war, veteran philosopher George Santayana and struggling playwright Tennessee Williams both received prestigious awards for their writings. Santayana was recipient of the Nicholas Murray Butler Gold Medal during April. Named in honor of longtime Columbia University president and William Howard Taft's vice presidential running mate in 1912, the award was handed out once every five years for "an outstanding work in education or philosophy." The eighty-two-year-old Santayana—then living in Rome—was recognized for his four-volume *Realms of Being*, which had been in progress since the 1920s.

Although born in Spain in 1863 during the American Civil War, Santayana had grown to manhood in a well-to-do Boston home. His parents, both Spanish nationals, had married while serving in the Philippine civil service before American seizure of the islands; but his mother had been married previously to a Boston merchant-banker with interests in Manila and had several older children. "In Boston," Santayana observes in his autobiography, "her three Sturgis children had numerous relations and a little property, and there she had promised their father to bring them up in case of his death. When this occurred in 1857, she therefore established herself in Boston; and this fact, by a sort of pre-natal or preestablished destiny, was the cause of my connections with the Sturgis family, with Boston, and with America." After his parents "agreed amicably" to live apart, Santayana from an early age made frequent trips to Spain and Europe to visit his father. His Spanish ancestry notwithstanding, the future philosopher became totally Americanized, setting a spectacular undergraduate record at Harvard, where he fell under the influence of William James and Josiah Royce. From 1889 until 1912 he taught philosophy himself at the Massachusetts citadel, besides turning out his first books.

Santayana abandoned his Harvard post during 1912 to become a European wanderer. He roamed from country to country and, according to his own account: "Fortune had become indifferent to me, except as fortune might allow me to despise fortune and to live simply in some beautiful place. . . . I have distributed my few possessions, eschewed chattels of every kind, a fixed residence, servants, carriages, or anything that would pin me down materially or engulf me in engagements." His extended sojourn in Europe started after publication of his opus, *The Life of Reason*, written during 1905–1906; it was a history of the human imagination, or the human mind. Once established as a philosophical thinker, Santayana turned out an endless stream of books. His *Realms of Being*, which appeared in four volumes beginning in 1927, was a further elaboration of his ideas, which included the belief that philosophical idealism was true yet useless in the real world.

If George Santayana was incomprehensible to the man on the street, Tennessee Williams was easy to appreciate—a homegrown product if ever there was one. Although rejected by the draft because of a heart condition and poor eyesight, Williams produced his *Glass Menagerie* in 1944. Born Thomas Lanier Williams in 1914 at Columbus, Mississippi, he thoroughly absorbed the culture of the South as he approached manhood in several southern locales—rural Mississippi, where a minister-grandfather held pastorates, Memphis, St. Louis, and later New Orleans. After the family moved to St. Louis, he was sent to the University of Missouri at Columbia by his shoe salesman father who wanted to distance him from a youthful romance. Here, notes Nancy Tischler, his biographer, "the southern accent that previously had evoked taunts delighted his college associates, who promptly nicknamed him 'Tennessee.' Tom was so pleased with the new name that he eventually assumed it."

Regarded as a failure, the literary-minded Williams withdrew from the university to spend three miserable years in a St. Louis shoe factory. Yet more study followed at Washington University in St. Louis during 1936–1937 where he had the good fortune to be a classmate of A. E. Hotchner, afterwards the dramatist of Hemingway's novels and biographer of the immortal "Papa." And Williams continued a steady writing output for local theater productions. "Writing always came easier to Tom than it does to most people," said Willard Holland, a newspaperman and fellow writer who knew him in St. Louis. "I call it literary diarrhea—it just poured out of him. His original manuscripts were the length of three full plays and you could throw out heaps of typewritten pages and still have more than enough left over for a full-length play." Next, Williams entered the drama program at the University of Iowa and finally received a Bachelor's Degree in 1938.

He soon found himself in New Orleans with his new diploma, struggling for literary recognition. In his own words: "I lived near the main street of the [French] quarter which is named Royal. Down this street, running on the same tracks, are two streetcars, one named Desire and the other named Cemetery. The indiscourageable progress up and down Royal struck me as having some symbolic bearing of a broad nature on life in the Vieux Carre—and everywhere else for that matter." Williams learned his craft well during the war years in New Orleans; his play *Streetcar Named Desire*, later made into a movie starring Marlon Brando, has become an American classic.

"When Williams arrived in New Orleans," Tischler continues, "he was a proper young man in a neat conservative suit, polished shoes, dress shirt and tie. When he left, he was headed for California with an ex-teacher-turned clarinet player in a decrepit Chevy. He was now Tennessee." In California during 1944, while waiting for a Hollywood studio to decide what to do with one of his earlier plays, he pounded out his now-famous *Glass Menagerie*. An earlier play, *Battle of Angels*, written in 1940 and produced by the New York Theater Group, enjoyed a limited success, although it was canceled before a scheduled Broadway opening; Williams thought it failed because of his treatment of "sex and religion," a combination he avoided ever after.

The coveted New York Drama Critics Award came Williams's way in April 1945; he received nine of the fourteen votes cast by New York magazine and newspaper reviewers for the award, which fixed him as a major American playwright. *Harvey* and *I Remember Mama*—other memorable plays of the war—also received a vote or two. But the *Glass Menagerie* swept the field. The play has only four characters: an aging woman, now impoverished, who looks back on a pleasant childhood before she married the wrong man, her son, her daughter, and her daughter's gentleman caller who visits the home. During his life Williams was to turn out a string of Broadway plays and books—many of them made into successful movies which have been seen by millions: *The Rose Tattoo, Cat on a Hot Tin Roof, Summer and Smoke, You Touched Me! The Roman Spring of Mrs. Stone*, and *Sweet Bird of Youth*.

Another book, *A Texan in England* by folklorist J. Frank Dobie, came out in May. Dobie, a true American original and sometime English professor at The University of Texas, spent 1943–1944 as visiting professor of American history at Cambridge.

For more than thirty-five years he had been a writer of southwestern folklore and a general debunker of American universities. Although he was a graduate of Columbia and a professor himself in Oklahoma and Texas, the crusty Dobie refused to earn his Ph.D; yet he became a full professor at Texas in spite of meager credentials. Besides his regular columns for Texas newspapers, he wrote such classics as *The Voice of the Coyote, Longhorns, Cow People, Tongues of the Monte, The Mustangs*, and *Apache Gold and Yaqui Silver*. "Dobie is by nature a maverick, and has always been so," wrote his friend and colleague, the frontier historian Walter Prescott Webb. "By maverick, I mean that he wears no man's brand. He runs free and easy with whatever crowd takes his fancy, or if the crowd gets too big or in any way objectionable, Dobie separates himself and runs in a herd by himself." Before his death in 1960, says his biographer Winston Bode, he "was sole author of eighteen books, a gifted and untiring folklore editor, a prolific preface writer and contributor to magazines and books. During his career Dobie wrote over 800 published articles, pamphlets, and books, not counting newspaper writings." Born on a south Texas ranch in 1888, he was no cloistered writer-scholar, but a man who took to horse and bedroll to collect his material.

As the home front watched entertainers cavort around Hollywood and writers produce new books, those devoted to the sports world remained as oblivious to the emergency as ever. That a president had worked himself into a premature grave and that thousands of GIs were dying in the far Pacific did not keep the country's golfers from the 1944–1945 professional tour. For the second straight season Toledo's Byron Nelson paced the prize winners. An Ohio umbrella manufacturer who had started as a Fort Worth caddy, Nelson won eight of eighteen tournaments on the circuit. In mid-April after he won the Iron Lung Tourney in Atlanta—used to boost fund raising for polio research—the Associated Press said he had picked up $22,615. Though most of his earnings came in war bonds, it was still a substantial sum. Nelson topped fellow golfer Jimmy Demaret's record of six victories in 1939–1940, by winning meets in Portland, Corpus Christi, New Orleans, Durham, Greensboro, and Charlotte before the Atlanta tournament.

The legendary Sam Snead—fresh from the navy and back on the pro-tour—came in second behind Nelson for the year. He managed to pick up $16,861 and six tournament titles in spite of a short season. "Mr. Golf," Samuel Jackson "Slammin Sammy" Snead, born at Ashwood, Virginia, in 1912, won a record eighty-four major tournaments during a career which reached to the 1970s. He played most of his time, nearly forty years in all, as club pro at the luxurious Greenbrier resort in West Virginia; and he started winning on the national circuit during 1936. Although Snead complained in later years about the low prize money during the 1940s compared to the fantastic winnings of the 1970s and 1980s, he stuck to the game. Byron Nelson, who also stayed active in golf circles, wrote later: "Sam has a God-given body that will never grow old. The thing that is amazing is that he still has the desire to compete. That is the really amazing thing." And compete he did, winning practically every major golf title over the next twenty-five years.

Likewise, baseball continued to draw huge crowds throughout 1945. After twenty-five years as baseball commissioner, Judge Kenesaw M. Landis died in 1945 and was replaced by Kentucky Senator Albert B. "Happy" Chandler. On May 3, when Chandler held his first news conference saying he was going to put "the gamblers and fixers out of baseball," the New York Yankees and crosstown Giants were leading the American and National leagues. Chandler, who was both United States senator and governor of Kentucky, bossed the game through the 1940s; and in May he told reporters that he had already complained to President Truman about the "unfair induction" of athletes into the service. In the aftermath of Byrnes's comments about professional players sidestepping military service, the War Department had begun a reexamination of all draft-exempt athletes.

An uproar started during the spring when Danny Litwhiler, an outfielder for the St. Louis Cardinals, was drafted with questionable ability to meet "minimum specifications." And representative Melvin Price of Illinois soon took up the fight; he joined Chandler in demanding a War Department investigation and urged that players inducted during April be deferred until it was concluded. Meanwhile, the new commissioner said he would continue to attend the Kentucky Derby—still attracting swarms of aficionados—but that he would not bet on the horses because he had asked his players not to gamble. When a reporter from the Chicago *Defender*, a Negro newspaper, asked when blacks would appear in major league uniforms, he answered: "I will invite Negro leaders to sit across the table and talk the problem over."

Although Jackie Robinson, the first black player to do so, did not break the major league color barrier for another two years, the *Defender's* question reemphasized a nagging dilemma—that ten years before the Brown decision outlawing racial segregation in the nation's schools, rank discrimination continued to plague an America fighting the horrors of Nazism. Nothing symbolized the plight of blacks more than the appearance of Richard Wright's *Black Boy* in April 1945. Published by Harpers, it was an autobiographical account of Wright's life in the South until age seventeen. Like Tennessee Williams, he grew up in the home of a religious grandmother in rural Mississippi, and while Williams stopped in St. Louis on his way North, Wright made Memphis his temporary home on his climb to literary fame. But Williams was white, and Wright was black, and thus, their paths diverged.

"*Black Boy* is a bitter, true story of a Negro boy's struggles against the life imposed on his race in the South," read *Life's* seven-page review in

June: "Some of the things that happened to him could have happened to many boys brought up in dire poverty anywhere. But Richard was more sensitive and articulate than most. He was also black and brought up in the south. This is what makes *Black Boy* not only a brilliant autobiography but a powerful indictment of a caste system which is one of America's biggest problems." And the review pulled no punches as it told home-front readers what Wright and millions of others had experienced.

Wright had attracted earlier attention with a novel, *Native Son*, that came out in 1940; on the eve of war it, too, was a work of racial protest—a work that not only identified him as a gifted writer but as a writer who could depict life in a northern ghetto. Shortly after he left Memphis in 1927 (he didn't return to the South for the next thirteen years) "he started producing proletarian poems, a number of which saw publication over a five-year period (1934–1939) in *New Masses* and other left-wing publications."

Thereupon, continues his biographer, Edward Margolies, "with the onset of the Depression—especially bitter for Negroes—he was persuaded to Marxism and joined the Communist Party sometime in late 1933. He remained a relatively active member for the next seven or eight years although he was undoubtedly restive under Party discipline." By 1935 he had landed a job with the New Deal-funded Federal Writers Project (Williams also worked for the same outfit) and by 1937 he was in New York as a writer for the *Daily Mirror*. Although Wright joined the party a few months after reaching Chicago from the South, he quickly became disenchanted with Communism, following publication of his 1936 novel, *Lawd Today*. Party bosses complained about his portrayal of working class whites and their attitudes toward blacks, though they remained publicly discrete.

In the beginning Wright had found Marxism appealing because of its call to the world's oppressed; but like other blacks who kept their protests within constitutional limits, he objected to demands for party obedience. Also, notes Wilson Record, an authority on American Communism, blacks have generally resented control from Moscow as well as the party's shifting stands on the importance of race relations. Although he never abandoned his protest against the lot of blacks in American life, Wright broke with the Communists in 1942 three years before publication of *Black Boy*.

But Negro equality was far from the mind of white America as the country waited for Japan to surrender once Hitler had been beaten. Homeward bound GIs, defense workers, and people in general wanted to get on with their lives; forty-three months of rationing, consumer shortages, and rearranged living were enough. And no pent-up desire was greater than the wish to buy a new family automobile. No new cars for the consumer market had rolled out of Detroit since the 1942 models, and they had been built in 1941. Even before the return of peace, car dealers from Maine to California were "taking lists" for new sedans once they did appear.

Everybody wanted a new car and with their bulging pockets buyers competed with each other to make sure local dealers put their names high on the list. The War Production Board announced in April 1945 that it was ready to release "$50 million of machine tools and equipment essential to the changeover of the automobile industry to civilian production" once the Pacific War ended. Detroit, moreover, found time to work on plans for new passenger cars as it turned out the last military vehicles; Ford announced its intention "to put cars on the assembly line sixty to ninety days after receiving permission to do so." The company said its "Post War Car Number 1" would resemble its 1942 models on the outside but improvements in the running gear were planned. Nash —a popular prewar make, now defunct—released drawings of a torpedo-shaped car it intended to build. Packard, General Motors, Chrysler, all started to whet the public appetite for new cars during late summer.

Although gasoline and tires were still rationed in 1945, the Society of Automotive Engineers released a survey it had conducted to see what drivers wanted on post-war automobiles. The results, gleaned from San Francisco, New Orleans, New York, and Chicago turned up a variety of speciality devices, including "clocks that really keep time." A universal demand was improved visibility from inside the car as well as better insulation from road noises. A generation that had grown to adulthood with the manual clutch and gear shift wanted automatic transmissions; and there were hopes for headlights that turned with the car—a suggestion that proved impractical when it was tried after the war—as well as built-in jacks to lift the car by pushing a button on the dash. Although improved tires and synthetic rubber blunted demands for easier tire changing, the public was ingenious in calling for sand-dispensing devices on new cars to improve traction on snow and ice.

13 AUGUST 1945: THE END: NEW BOMBS AND CELEBRATIONS

A ugust 1945 not only brought an end to the Japanese war machine, it also brought a release from the tensions of war to every American. A string of anxiety-producing events—the death of a revered president and the swearing in of an untried one, the last days of Hitler in his Berlin bunker, the terrible slaughter on Okinawa, a scant 300 miles from the home islands—added fuel to the jubilant celebrations which followed the final surrender. In every part of the country and wherever GIs were stationed around the world, news of the end was greeted with unrestrained cheering and rejoicing. From Bar Harbor to San Diego the entire population momentarily lost its balance in two or three days of gala merrymaking.

As the home front waited for Japan's capitulation—which did not come until the 15th—a bizarre mishap struck New York at the end of July. A two-engine B-25 bomber on a flight from New Bedford, Massachusetts, to New York's LaGuardia Field slammed into the north face of the Empire State Building, then the world's tallest structure. Crash survivors said the 102-story, 1,250 feet-high building "moved twice when hit by the bomber and then settled." Piloted by Lieutenant Colonel William F. Smith, deputy commander of the 457th Bomber Command and a decorated combat veteran, the B-25 struck the building between the seventy-ninth and the seventy-eighth floors, causing half a million dollars' worth of damage. Far worse, Smith and two crewmen, along with ten office workers inside the building, lost their lives. The 9:49 a.m. tragedy occurred in heavy fog after Smith told New York radio operators he was proceeding to Newark, New Jersey, in search of a better landing site.

Wire photos showing a gaping hole in the building saturated the press for days, although engineers said its basic structure was unharmed by the impact. They must have been right—the Empire State Building is still standing forty-four years after the crash. That day in July 1945, however, its occupants were terror stricken by the sound of the approaching aircraft's engines above fog-shrouded Manhattan. The plane, reported the New York *Times*, "crashed with a terrifying impact midway along the north or Thirty-Fourth Street wall of the building." Its wings were sheared off by the impact, but the motors and fuselage ripped a hole eighteen-feet-wide and twenty-feet-high in the outer wall. Brilliant orange flames shot as high as the observatory on the eighty-sixth floor, 1,050 feet above Fifth Avenue, as the plane's gasoline tanks exploded.

One engine shot across the seventy-ninth floor, tore a hole through the opposite wall and fell onto the roof of another building, destroying an artist's penthouse apartment; a propeller was found impaled in the side of the building. But the worst ruin came from burning gasoline which sped through several floors, literally engulfing clerks and secretaries at their desks. Luckily, the seventy-eighth floor was unoccupied except for storage of office supplies or the death count would have been higher.

Most miraculous of all was the escape of two young secretaries who fell seventy-five stories in a damaged elevator. The plane struck an I-beam between two elevator shafts on the north side of the building and one unoccupied car fell immediately to a sub-basement "with a plane engine on top of it." Cables on the other elevator snapped with its two occupants inside. Rescue workers were obliged to cut a hole through a foundation wall expecting to find tragedy; instead, continued the *Times*, "a 17-year-old Coast Guard hospital apprentice, selected to be the first through the hole because of his small stature, found the two women alive, although badly injured. Automatic devices evidently had slowed the falling car down enough to save their lives." As burning debris fell to the street below, Lieutenant Allen Aiman, a veteran of the south Pacific and his wife stood on the 102nd floor observatory-deck looking out at the fog-encased city. "The visibility was zero," he told reporters: "I was flabbergasted. I couldn't believe my own eyes when I saw the plane come out of the overcast. Then it hit the building with a force that sent a tremor through the entire structure."

Aiman was not the only returning serviceman enjoying the sights before his return to civilian life. Swarms of GIs, each with a yellow eagle insignia—the famed ruptured duck—signifying his discharge, could be seen wandering around the country during July and August. Both the *Queen Mary* and the *Queen Elizabeth*—running with full lights for the first time since 1940—were making regular troop-laden trips across the Atlantic. And when a reporter asked General "Vinegar Joe" Stilwell what the discharged veterans had most in mind, he replied: "It's a function of nature too elemental to describe." With the war coming to a close the FBI reported on August 6 that more than half a million draft evasion cases had been processed since 1940. After implementation of Selective Service, 12,550 men had been sent to prison for draft evasion and more than a million dollars in fines meted out; and, the FBI report said, "most of the evaders were made available to the armed forces." Every imaginable ruse and excuse was attempted to escape service, including that of one man who said, "Danged if I'm going to fight in any war I didn't start." Another told FBI agents he had been too busy running from his wife to report to his induction center. Agents in Alaska chased two draft dodgers across frozen backcountry "by aircraft and snowshoe before nabbing them at the base of McKinley."

Meanwhile, word filtered out of Detroit that "underwear-short men had been reduced to buying ladies' panties" because of clothing scarcities at the same time the first Ford sedans came off nearby assembly lines. OPA cut the number of ration coupons required to purchase butter, meat, and poultry products while the country marked time. The Ohio Legislature passed a law, promptly signed by Governor Frank Laushe, that required notification of both parents when state courts placed children for adoption. The law evolved out of a not-uncommon occurrence during the war—wives giving birth to illegitimate children while their husbands served overseas. Dubbed an "Anti-Concealment Bill," it resulted from an action by Columbus common pleas judge C. P. McClelland, who roused the ire of GIs everywhere when he placed one woman's four illegitimate children for adoption with a ruling that "it was not necessary to notify absent servicemen of their wives' unfaithfulness at home."

On August 6, California senator Hiram Johnson, an American political institution, passed away. The old-time political spoiler had just gained more notoriety in July by casting the only no vote on the Senate Foreign Relations Committee to ratification of the U.N. treaty. "No person, cause, or party ever fully controlled him," said *Time*'s obituary notice: "This obstinate independence cost him his father's love and the support of liberals who once adored him. It also cost him the Presidency of the U.S." Johnson, born in 1866 and a member of the California Bar from 1888, first shot to national prominence as an organizer of the Progressive or Bull Moose party; he was Theodore Roosevelt's running mate during the 1912 presidential race when the Bull Moosers, and Republicans under William Howard Taft went down to defeat at the hands of Woodrow Wilson.

Johnson had been elected governor in 1910 and 1914; to win in 1910 "He smashed the grip of the Southern Pacific Railroad on California politics. After his victory, his father, the railroad's attorney and a former congressman, refused to speak to him for ten years." Because of the same recalcitrance, he turned down the 1920 GOP vice presidential nomination under Warren G. Harding; had he accepted he would have entered the White House in 1923 instead of Calvin Coolidge. Johnson first entered the Senate in 1917 and remained there until his death at age seventy-nine.

Although Johnson spent most of the war years in and out of hospitals, his no vote on U.S. participation in the newly-created United Nations organization proved a futile gesture. American acceptance of the U.N. charter was a foregone conclusion, but a debate erupted among isolationists following adjournment of the international body's organizational meetings in San Francisco. From April 25, when the first plenary sessions opened, until their termination on June 26, the home front watched and read about a steady parade of foreign dignitaries as they worked to launch the United Nations. And the San Francisco meetings were marred by conflict between the United States and Russia. They might have dissolved completely had Truman at one point not made a direct appeal to Soviet premier Joseph Stalin. The completed charter, signed by representatives of fifty-odd countries on June 26, says historian Arthur S. Link, "was an American document with all its strengths and weaknesses—Wilson's League Covenant embellished and revised."

With Okinawa in American hands at last, the climax to forty-five months of war and the last anxious waiting for Tokyo's surrender began on August 6—the very day Hiram Johnson passed away—when news of mankind's first atomic bomb roared over the airwaves. Few Americans in 1945 had ever heard of nuclear energy and fewer still had the vaguest notion of the principles involved in exploding the bomb or of the Herculean efforts to make the new weapon. Yet people knew instinctively that a strange and awesome force had been unleashed on the world, and that an entirely new era had commenced. Overnight a new vocabulary was born as armchair physicists held forth at every crossroads on the atom and its power, whether understood or not.

The move toward the atomic age had been accelerated dramatically in the early twentieth century as a result of work by two intellectual giants, Max Planck and Albert Einstein. In 1900, ironically the first year of the new century, Planck unlocked the bond between energy and atomic structure with his famed quantum theory by advancing the revolutionary notion that energy emitted from vibrating electrons does not travel in a steady wave but radiates outward in "energy packets" of varying intensity which he called "quanta." Planck and his followers thus joined the on-going assault upon the fixed and ordered world formulated by Issac Newton two centuries earlier.

Einstein, on the other hand, hastened the journey toward a changing and nonfixed natural order, or a universe governed by the principles of relativity, with his earth-shaking theories of 1905 and 1915; he joined "light to time, and time to space, energy to matter, matter to space, and space to gravitation." And he suggested that the minuscule atom contained enormous reserves of energy because of its concentrated mass. The atomic mystery was further unraveled by the New Zealander Ernest Rutherford and his brilliant student Niels Bohr about the same time that Einstein published his trailblazing studies. In 1913, while only twenty-seven years of age, Bohr combined the ideas of Planck and Rutherford to explain the atom as a "miniature solar system."

Bohr's atom became fixed for all time in the layman's mind, the tiny but compact nucleus with equally minute electrons whizzing in orbits around it. And it spawned a debate among ivory-tower scientists that lasted for two decades: How to unleash the gargantuan amounts of power locked in the atom of Rutherford and Bohr. In short, could the atomic nucleus be bombarded with accelerated particles to make it fly apart and bombard other nuclei? Or could a chain reaction be sustained? That task was left for a Hungarian refugee from Nazi persecution named Leo Szilard, who worked first in England and then in the United States after 1933. Although Rutherford, now Lord Rutherford, did not think the atom had any real use and even dismissed a practical application of nuclear energy as "moonshine," Szilard was undeterred.

Let Jacob Bronowski, a colleague of Szilard and himself a participant in the bomb's development, describe how it happened: "He [Szilard] tells the story as all of us who knew him would picture it. He was living at the Strand Palace Hotel—he loved living in hotels. He was walking to work at Bart's Hospital and as he came to Southhampton Row he was stopped by a red light. . . . Before the light turned green, he had realized that if you hit an atom with one neutron, and it breaks and releases two, then you will have a chain reaction."

Meanwhile, Enrico Fermi, an escapee from Mussolini's Italy, who had already obtained chain reactions from the bombardment of uranium, the heaviest-known element in the 1930s, had arrived in the United States. He continued his experimentation at Columbia along with Szilard, who came from England. Certain that similar work was underway at Berlin's Kaiser Wilhelm Institute, it was these two—Szilard and Fermi—who encouraged Albert Einstein to send his famous letter to FDR in April 1940 saying an atomic weapon could be built. The father of relativity, also a refugee from European upheavals and then working at Princeton University, warned the president about ongoing scientific labors: ". . . . this new phenomenon would also lead to the construction of bombs, and it is conceivable—though much less certain—that extremely powerful bombs of a new type may thus be constructed."

Once roused to action, Roosevelt appointed another of his emergency agencies, the National Defense Research Committee, and charged it with the task of building the bomb suggested by Szilard and Einstein. Earlier, when he first got the letter, the president had hurriedly created something called the Briggs Committee, headed by Dr. Lyman J. Briggs, Director of the National Bureau of Standards, to examine the practical applications of nuclear fission. But government scientists like James Conant, a respected chemist and president of Harvard, and Vannevar Bush, who had taken over for an ailing Briggs, soon told Roosevelt the anticipated project was too large for the scientists alone to handle.

By mid-1942 these early efforts at atomic investigation had given way to formation of the Manhattan District that actually produced the atomic hardware dropped on Japan; it was a special "district" within the army corps of engineers to expedite and oversee the tremendous outlay of men and money. This far-flung organization headed by General Leslie R. Groves employed more than 100,000 people, with a budget exceeding $2 billion, in a crash program extending over the next three years. And its work was carried out in such secrecy that few Americans even knew the group existed. Most of the thousands of workers drawn to laboratories and production centers at Los Alamos, New Mexico, Hanford, Washington, and Oak Ridge, Tennessee, from every part of the country had no idea about the nature of their work.

At Oak Ridge, a specially constructed town on the Clinch River in the hills of east Tennessee, a giant sign greeted every worker:

WHAT YOU SEE HERE
WHAT YOU DO HERE
WHAT YOU HEAR HERE
WHAT YOU LEAVE HERE
LET IT STAY HERE

F.B.I. Agents checked into the background of every work applicant from ace physicist to handyman. *Life* reported after the destruction of

Hiroshima when details of the Manhattan District became known: "Names famous the world over arrived anonymously, advised and departed like shadows. Guardedly—for over their heads were always hung the threat of ten years in prison and a $10,000 fine—Oak Ridge's laboratory men, clerks, stenographers and scientists probed each other's information without result. Supremely careful planning had compartmentalized work and therefore knowledge." Not only Oak Ridge but the entire bomb search had a cloak and dagger flavor. "Outsiders were admitted," the *Life* account continued, "only when a resident obtained a pass for them. A resident's cameras and arms were all registered. Identification badges had to be worn at all times. Residents returning to the reservation were searched for firearms. Everywhere signs cautioned secrecy. To the curious, question-asking world Oak Ridge presented a united front. 'We're making the front end of horses,' it explained. 'We ship them to Washington, D.C. for final assembly.' "

Following a lengthy search through government bureaus and university departments, Groves picked J. Robert Oppenheimer, a forty-one-year-old physicist at Berkeley, to head his Manhattan Engineer District. Born in 1904 to Jewish immigrant parents, and reared in solid middle class surroundings on New York's Riverside Drive, Oppenheimer, who was something of a prodigy, had worked himself to the first rank among atomic physicists. A brilliant undergraduate career at Harvard had been followed by more study in the famed Cavendish Laboratory at Cambridge where he worked under J. J. Thompson and Ernest Rutherford, both Nobel Prize winners. During his stay abroad he had traveled widely on the continent absorbing not only its culture but also its latest scientific and intellectual breakthroughs.

In the fall of 1927 Oppenheimer joined the physics faculty at Berkeley, where he quickly established himself as a leading academic; although Robert Millikan, chairman of the department, a Nobel laureate, and one of the country's foremost scientists, took a strong dislike to him, Oppenheimer made lasting acquaintances with some of the biggest names in American and international physics—men who would help build the world's first A-bombs: Ernest O. Lawrence, developer of the cyclotron, Luis Alvarez, Robert Serber, and others. A joint appointment with the prestigious California Institute of Technology followed, and Oppenheimer maintained a professorship at both universities until 1947.

When he assumed command of the Manhattan Project during 1942, an immediate "chemistry" developed between Groves and Oppenheimer that stood the country in good stead. It led to a mutual partnership which produced a workable nuclear weapon; partly because of a need for secrecy and partly because Oppenheimer had vacationed in the area as a teenager and owned a ranch, *Perro Caliente* or Hot Dog, nearby, the Manhattan laboratories were established in isolated mesa country at Los Alamos, a few miles west of Santa Fe. Here, surrounded by "the biggest collection of eggheads ever," the first atomic weapons were conceived, designed from scratch, and made ready for use by Oppenheimer's researchers. Los Alamos, chosen in part because of its isolated and therefore safe location, was visited by many of the world's leading scientists—Neils Bohr, Sir James Chadwick, Philip Morrison, Hans Bethe, Enrico Fermi, Edward Teller, among others—from 1942 through 1945.

Although he was able to recognize and recruit the best scientific talent in the world, Oppenheimer's researchers relied on others to supply the raw materials needed for an atomic detonation. As early as July 1941 an "atomic pile" had been put into operation at Columbia University in New York, and five months later the first sustaining pile was created in the "Metallurgical Laboratory" of Arthur Holly Compton under the famed football stadium at the University of Chicago. The practical manufacture of uranium and plutonium—the basic stuff of nuclear weapons—was thereby established. These early piles in university labs led to the construction of plants at Oak Ridge and Hanford, Washington, for the large-scale production of both materials. After a gas separation method devised by chemist Harold Urey had been deemed impractical, the Oak Ridge facility was built to utilize a process worked out by Ernest O. Lawrence to obtain U-235 used in the bomb from ordinary uranium.

Lawrence, a colleague of Oppenheimer at Berkeley and recipient of the 1937 Nobel Prize in physics, played a premier role in the bomb's development and remained a fixture in the atomic establishment until his death. Like Oppenheimer he had joined the physics department at Berkeley in the 1920s during the heyday of modern atomic development; and while Oppenheimer concentrated on theoretical physics, Lawrence charged headlong into the world of practical applications. Almost single-handedly he had designed and built ever-larger cyclotrons in his California laboratories—"atom smashers" or huge devices to electromagnetically accelerate subatomic particles to high speeds thereby creating new elements.

Edward Teller, developer of the hydrogen bomb, was also a member of Oppenheimer's Los Alamos team. Although the possible use of deuterium (a heavy form of hydrogen) had first been suggested by the Italian Fermi as raw material for a "super" or thermonuclear device, it was Teller who molded the idea into a workable bomb. Teller had wanted the country to build a hydrogen weapon instead of an uranium bomb before creation of the Manhattan Project. But when invited to join the Los Alamos team, the Hungarian-born scientist grew disenchanted with work on Oppenheimer's bomb and went his own way. The thirty-seven-year-old Teller, who received a doctorate at Leipiz in 1930, had arrived in this country during 1935 from the University of London to teach at several institutions including the University of Chicago; afterward, as director of the Livermore Laboratories in California, he developed the hydrogen bomb tested at Eniwetok in the Pacific after the war.

The uranium and plutonium bombs assembled by the Manhattan Project were ready for use by the first part of 1945; using raw materials from Hanford and Oak Ridge, the first bomb was detonated, July 16, 1945, at an air force bombing range 200 miles south of Los Alamos near Alamogordo, also in the New Mexico desert. And the secrecy surrounding manufacture of the bomb nearly exploded with it; the initial nuclear blast was seen by hundreds of people over a 300-mile radius. Residents of two adjoining states felt three distinct aftershocks and thousands more saw the atomic flash. A correspondent for the El Paso *Herald-Post* stationed at Silver City, New Mexico, reported to his editor 150 miles to the southeast that local inhabitants had noticed the sudden bursts. The press in several parts of the country went into a frenzy after picking up on the story. Phone calls flooded police and newsroom switchboards throughout the Southwest. In response to persistent inquiries, air force officials at Alamogordo issued a statement that claimed that the discharges had been caused by accidental explosion of an ammunition dump. The country had to wait another full month to learn the truth about the New Mexico fireworks.

Development of the A-bomb was carried out in such concealment that most high-ranking military and civilian leaders were unaware of its existence. Even General MacArthur, supreme commander of the war against Japan, did not learn about the bomb until the latter part of July. A war department official called at his Manila headquarters to explain the bomb that was in the works "only a couple of weeks before one was dropped." When Karl Compton, president of M.I.T., detailed the new application of atomic power for him on August 7, MacArthur did not think the bomb necessary for Japan's capitulation. Unlike most Allied leaders privy to the bomb's potential, he felt that the Rising Sun was already beaten and would surrender without its use. Nor did Eisenhower, who had led the Allies to victory in Germany, think the use of nuclear energy advisable on war targets. Like MacArthur he was slow in learning about the Manhattan Project. Ike was at the Potsdam Conference as adviser to Truman when Secretary of War Henry L. Stimson quietly told him about the atomic cudgel. Eisenhower was horrified at the use of such explosives on human beings and counseled Truman not to make his "Great Decision."

Truman had joined Churchill, shortly replaced by Laborite Clement Attlee, and Stalin for the Potsdam meeting on July 17 in occupied Europe. As the American public was being prepared to expect a climactic assault on Japan itself, it awaited news of the last wartime gathering of the Allied chiefs at a former palace of the German emperors outside Berlin to decide the fate of the Axis nations. Word of the successful blasts at Los Alamos first reached Truman at Potsdam by secret code. An already burdened president was thus forced into making his decision to use the A-bomb against a faltering enemy at the same time he was joining in the Potsdam Declaration to demand Japan's immediate and unconditional surrender.

The home front was unaware that a new age had arrived as Truman and Stimson, along with Generals George C. Marshall and Hap Arnold, debated how best to proceed after word from Los Alamos. Although he was surrounded by top counselors in Europe, it was Truman's decision alone to make. And make it he did. With his military planners predicting the loss of a million men during landings on the Japanese homeland, he considered use of the bomb mandatory. Many leading scientists, including Leo Szilard, who had first conceived the weapon, joined with Eisenhower, MacArthur, and other military brass in opposing the drop. Most were terrified by the awesome destruction unfurled on the New Mexico desert when the earth at ground zero had been turned into glass.

Ironically, Truman had been one of the last men in Washington to learn about the Manhattan Project. In fact he did not know the bomb existed until he entered the White House. Though he had been in the Senate since Pearl Harbor and vice president since January, Truman like his countrymen, had been in the dark. Stimson, the same man who broke the news to Eisenhower, told him about the ongoing nuclear research on the day of Roosevelt's death. On receiving the presidential oath, Truman had called a cabinet meeting at the White House where he told department heads that the new administration would continue the foreign and domestic policies of his predecessor. As the assemblage filed out of the executive mansion, the Secretary of State lingered behind. It was Truman's first inkling that America had a workable super weapon. The hours-old president also realized immediately that he would have to make the decision to use the bomb on Japan or to leave it in the laboratory.

Later, as the presidential entourage headed home from Potsdam, feverish preparations rushed forward on Tinian Island, a pinpoint in the Pacific. Here Colonel Paul W. Tibbets, Jr., and the crew of the *Enola Gay*, named for his mother, prepared to not only open the atomic age but also to bring the war to a speedy climax. General Hap Arnold had personally picked the twenty-nine-year-old native of Quincy, Illinois, to drop the bomb. Following a top-notch flying and engineering record in North Africa and Europe, he had been tapped to form and train the 509th Composite Bomber Command to deliver the first atomic hardware. Truman's momentous order finally arrived at Spaatz's Guam headquarters July 29: "The 509 Composite Group, 20th Air Force will deliver its first special bomb as soon as weather will permit visual bombing after about 3 August 1945 on one of the targets: Hiroshima, Kokura, Niigata, and Nagasaki."

Eight days later Tibbets and the *Enola Gay*, using an airfield built by the Japanese, lifted off the runway on Tinian, at 2:35 a.m. August 6. Five hours and forty minutes later the first "little boy" was released through a momentary break in otherwise heavy cloud cover over Hiroshima, a city of 245,000. Actually two kinds of bombs had been built by Oppenheimer's scientists; the "little boy," made from uranium, and the "fat boy," fueled with plutonium. Wags said they were called after Roosevelt and Churchill but the weapons were really named for their respective sizes. And the Japanese just awakening and preparing for the activities of August 6 were unaware that an unbelievable hell was about to descend on them from the sky. Nor were they particularly alarmed at the presence of enemy bombers overhead since conventional bombing of the home islands had been underway for months.

News reports reaching the United States reported enemy counterstrokes as our fleet neared the home islands in the aftermath of Okinawa. A feeble defense against high-flying B-29s and Halsey's Hellcats stemmed from a dwindling reserve of gasoline and matériel after years of war making. Unlike the fathomless American war chest, imperial Japan's fighting machine was scraping bottom in 1945. Still, the enemy was hording precious fuel and planes for last-ditch Kamikaze attacks on the circling armada. The dreaded suicide missions by Japanese fliers committed to glory and a desperate defense of their homeland did not stop with the Okinawa fighting. On Sunday, August 12, three days after the second A-bomb devastated Nagasaki, the wire services reported that Kamakazes sank twenty U.S. warships and damaged another thirty. An estimated 2,200 Kamakazi missions were flown during the war and when MacArthur landed on the home islands in 1945 another 5,300 fully-armed planes were found. Enemy submarines, like the German wolf packs that wreaked havoc in the North Atlantic until the final collapse of Hitler, also operated against our ships until the very end. Japan had more than a million men under arms and even more ready reserves, a fact that caused a war-weary America to applaud Truman's order to use the bomb.

Last efforts to keep MacArthur at bay halted when the *Enola Gay* opened her bomb doors over Hiroshima. The destruction defied description, with upwards of 80,000 people killed in the initial blast. Countless thousands who escaped instant death were burned and maimed, adding to the misery at ground zero. Among the first accounts to reach this country was a New York *Times* article with a massive headline: "FIRST ATOMIC BOMB DROPPED ON JAPAN . . . FORCE OF 20,000 TONS OF TNT." As the giant fireball—the hallmark of nuclear blasts fixed for all time in the popular mind—rose hundreds of feet into the air, city sidewalks, and thoroughfares glowed red hot from the intense heat. Even the colorful patterns of kimonos worn by Hiroshima women were imprinted upon the skins of victims, and bodies found more than two miles from ground zero were horribly burned. The subsequent tales of carnage and death soon became legend.

News of the bomb was greeted with subdued disbelief on this side of the Pacific. And pride that our country had made the bomb first. But little or no rejoicing followed the staggering death reports that began filtering in, only a long-sought relief that the war would end before long and that loved ones would soon return from far-flung battlefields. There were few people in the United States or indeed in the world who did not see the billowing mushroom of the atomic blast in local movie houses or in magazine photos. While some in 1945 may have known vaguely that radium on watch dials or phosphorescent lightbulbs had some connection with radioactivity, news of the bomb's impact drove the new science home to every American. It produced what amounted to national awe.

Word of the Japanese inferno did not reach the outside world for some time. American military men announced it would be delayed because "enormous clouds of dust and smoke covered Hiroshima." The city remained hidden from reconnaissance planes for hours. Shortly after news of the explosion reached the United States at 10 a.m., Monday, August 6, Truman issued a public statement: "That bomb had more than 2,000 times the blast power of the British 'Grand Slam' which is the largest bomb ever used in the history of warfare." And, he continued as a wonder-struck population waited, "it is an atomic bomb. It is the harnessing of the basic power of the universe. The force from which the sun draws its power has been loosed against those who brought war to the Far East." Three days later the nation was again jolted when American fliers dropped a second nuclear payload on Japan—this time on Nagasaki, one of the original cities targeted for atomic ruin. Although Nagasaki was a coastal city with four Mitsubishi aircraft factories, it escaped the death spilled on Hiroshima. The "fat boy" used for this second drop missed its target point by three miles; and a crisscross pattern of hills and valleys running through the city blunted the impact. But enough carnage resulted to electrify a world reeling from the first detonation. An estimated 35,000 people were killed outright and 60,000 injured, including Dutch and American prisoners of war interned in the city.

As the country tried to digest the meaning of Hiroshima and Nagasaki Truman hurled down the gauntlet. Reported *Newsweek*: "Millions of Americans heard him warn Japan to quit or suffer more atomic attacks." And the radio waves carried news that the Russians had entered the fray by opening a Manchurian front on a pledge given at Potsdam before the bombs had been used. "By implication, the President sought to dispel rumors that Russia's price for making war on Japan was the secret of the new weapon." But international ramifications of nuclear warfare would have to await the cold war of the 1950s. In August 1945 the feeling of astonishment that swept the country over the new power at its command became interwoven with a pent-up jubilation that the war was nearly done. Premature celebrations erupted all over the country the minute word about Nagasaki reached home-front America. The rejoicing, how-ever, stopped momentarily when Japan refused immediate capitulation.

In Tokyo the imperial cabinet was in session with Emperor Hirohito, searching for an honorable path out when Nagasaki was bombed. But the gloom gripping the home islands was also manifesting itself as joy in the United States. "Congress," reported the Associated Press, "was con-fident and jubilant that the bombs and Russian intervention would shorten the war materially." So was every American whether at home or on the battlefield. After what seemed an eternity, the Japanese agreed to capitulate under terms set forth in the Potsdam Ultimatium. During the early hours of August 10 Japanese envoys at Berne and Stockholm were told to seek accommodation, provided the emperor was allowed to remain on the imperial throne. The White House issued a statement which disclosed that Truman was in communication with London, Moscow, and the Chinese regarding the offer.

Although negotiations between Washington and Tokyo dragged on for another four or five days, an extravaganza of celebration and street rejoicing had already started; and the merrymaking, surely the wildest in the nation's history, lasted for days. Practically every American alive at that time knows where he or she happened to be when they found out that the war was over. Former President Richard M. Nixon relates in his *Memoirs* how he and Mrs. Nixon were eating in a Philadelphia restaurant when a waiter walked over to his table with word that the war had ended. Ex-servicemen who fought in Europe recall their joy at not having to enter the Pacific war. And this author has vivid memories of watching hell-raising servicemen and civilians alike in downtown Seattle as a twelve-year-old. The nationwide party that started sporadically picked up steam when the Japanese said they were willing to capitulate. Anxious callers seeking information jammed switchboards at police stations, newspaper desks, and radio stations in countless cities and towns. Hastily, impromptu crowds gathered to cheer the end. The New York garment district put on a "riotious show" as thousands swirled in its narrow streets. "The first big break had come at last," a national magazine reported, "and with it optimism too buoyant to be drowned."

But the partying spirit slowed when Washington announced it had responded to Japanese feelers with a counter declaration, known as the Byrnes Note. Hirohito could stay, but, said the American reply, his authority "to rule the state shall be subject to the supreme commander of the Allied powers who shall take such steps as he deems proper to effectuate the surrender terms." While the home front waited for the enemy to accept the inevitable, Truman appointed MacArthur as overseer of Japan, following the surrender. And the men in Tokyo began issuing statements designed to prepare their proud countrymen for the end.

As the war cabinet pondered its reply, this country heated up following a false radio dispatch that the surrender was complete. It came on Sunday, August 12, when most of the nation was at home from work and anxiously awaiting the final signal. Shortly after 9:30 p.m., as the radio networks —NBC, ABC, CBS and the Mutual Broadcasting System—picked up on an earlier United Press release, the celebrations started anew. Although the war was not over, the commotion developed when UP sent a "flash" over its mammoth teleprinter hookup: "Japan accepts surrender terms of the Allies." Then, recognizing the error, a correction was sent on the same wire two minutes later: "Hold up that Flash." Four minutes afterward, but not before it was made public by eager broadcasters, a red-faced UP crew attempted to backtrack: "Our Washington Bureau advised they did not send the flash just transmitted on our leased wires. We are investigating to ascertain the origin."

Try as they might, the damage could not be undone as the merrymaking gathered steam. In Canada a pre-recorded peace message from Prime Minister MacKenzie King was broadcast that touched off a series of demonstrations. As radio and press networks worked to correct their mistake, a two-hour celebration gripped downtown Miami; and a cheering throng in Worcester, Massachusetts, ignited a bonfire on downtown streets which firemen were powerless to quench. In New York police estimated that more than 100,000 people had gathered in Times Square by 11:00 p.m., while firecrackers and street dancing erupted in the narrow streets of Greenwich Village. Shavery Lee, the "unofficial mayor" of New York's Chinatown, reported that "every man, woman, and child was in the streets." Although the opening euphoria had cooled by midnight, authorities at most army and navy bases found it necessary to call out extra patrols to contain nearly hysterical servicemen.

The nation had settled down to more waiting while other news services jumped with joy over UP's mistake. The United States held its breath in unbelievable anticipation as the Japanese warlords debated their fate. Finally in the early hours of Tuesday, August 13, the world heard the answer: the Japanese empire was ready to accept the demands in the Byrnes Note. For the first time in forty-five months—since the bombing of Pearl Harbor—the fighting had really ceased.

Perhaps the first to hear about the surrender on this side of the Pacific was D. Reginald Tibbetts, a San Francisco radio buff. While listening to high-speed Morse code transmissions on equipment in the bedroom of his home, Tibbetts overheard a communiqué passing from Japan to Switzerland. It was a dispatch from Domei, official news agency of the Japanese government. Also recorded by FCC engineers "in a white frame house in Portland, Oregon," the message contained Japan's notice of surrender and instructed her envoys in Europe to open final negotiations for an American occupation.

Since official word came in the small hours of August 15, spokesmen at the White House said President Truman was sleeping and would not be disturbed. But after more checking to make certain the notes from

Tokyo were valid, Truman announced at 7:00 p.m., Washington time, that a reply to the Byrnes Note had been received and that the war had ended. MacArthur, he added, would accept the official surrender. The president issued orders for military commanders to halt offensive operations and he said the proclamation for V-J day would be delayed until after the signing of peace documents.

The home front had heard enough! A great spontaneous spree that lasted for the next three or four days commenced the moment Truman confirmed the capitulation. Churchbells tolled, horns blared, whistles howled as a wave of madcap antics swept the country. Nothing like it had taken place since the 1919 celebrations commemorating Germany's surrender in World War I when perfect strangers had made love on London streets. While most of the funmaking in America was innocent enough, the festivities were marred by scattered incidents of looting, molestation of women, and rioting. Much of the boisterous demonstrating was done by exuberant GIs. In Washington masses of army and navy men joined government workers outside the White House as guards struggled to keep the crowds from surging onto the lawn. And Chicago's Loop was a scene of bonfires and shouting by servicemen from nearby bases. A group of soldiers sped through downtown Los Angeles perched atop a swerving jeep; that city, reported *Life*, "rocked with joy as impromptu pedestrian parades and motor calvacades whirled along, hindered only by the whiskey bottles, amorous drunks and collisions." In San Francisco two shapely young blonds—subjects of a widely-circulated photograph—splashed about completely nude in a ceremonial pool near the city's civic center. Also in San Francisco potted plants were hurled by joyous civilians at servicemen carousing through downtown streets shouting, breaking into liquor stores, and smacking girls.

Yet for countless millions peace was a time for sober reflection and thanksgiving. In Skaneattles, New York, the wife of General Wainwright told reporters she was too excited and happy to speak. She had received no definite word about her husband since the fall of Corregidor four years earlier, and like mothers and wives everywhere Mrs. Wainwright was anxious about her husband's whereabouts. Twenty-one-year-old Margaret Truman, who had watched her father wrestle with earth-shaking decisions, was "thrilled to death with the news." She celebrated the surrender with a phone call to her parents at the White House from the Missouri home of her grandmother, Mrs. W. C. Wallace. Joe Louis, who was stationed at Camp Shanks, New York, was just as happy to see the end.

"We sure landed a knockout punch on Japan," the reigning heavyweight champion told newsmen.

And no Americans received the news more eagerly than the long-suffering Nisei. Though the harsh restrictions imposed upon Japanese-Americans had been relaxed since January, several thousand remained at detention centers along the East Coast. George Watanbe a San Diego merchant seaman before the war, and thirty-two other Nisei were living at a "Relocation Hostel" in downtown Brooklyn when the war ended. Unable to return home because of federal edict, Watanbe and his companions, including eight women, listened to radio accounts of the final negotiations. "With saki, the traditional wine of Japan, they drank toasts to the end of the war." Like their much maligned comrades in similiar "hostels," Watanbe and the others were prayerful that peace would bring jobs and a normal life. Mostly they hoped for an end to the prejudice that had darkened their lives since Pearl Harbor.

Additional fire was added to the partying spirit when Truman released all nonessential government workers for a two-day national holiday. State and federal employees joined with workers in defense plants, food markets, and department stores as businesses of every kind closed their doors. Virtually all economic activity in the country halted momentarily as the peace celebrations gained momentum. The New York Stock Exchange also shut down for the two-day period but not before its president, Emil Schram, declared that "the occasion should be more of thanksgiving than of exultation."

Many took time to offer prayers and hosannas for victory and national deliverance amid the revelry. Thousands gathered for special services in churches and synagogues to hear ministers and rabbis lead their flocks in calls for divine guidance as the world groped for lasting peace. New York's St. Patrick's Cathedral was jammed for a hastily called service in which hundreds of uniformed servicemen could be seen in the crowd. And many others unable to enter the venerable old church worshiped on the steps outside. A poem penned by Archbishop, later Cardinal, Francis J. Spellman was read in Roman Catholic services across the nation: ". . . . help us to gain the greater triumph of the spirit, that out of victory true peace may come to all mankind, that the wounds of war may be speedily healed and life may be renewed again."

Victory also found the largest radio audience in the twenty-five year history of broadcasting. "The continuous fluctuations in the tenor of the news kept persons close to their sets," one radio executive announced.

Literally everyone was eager for news as the networks carried steady flashes about the war's termination. One public opinion group estimated that not even Pearl Harbor attracted more listeners.

But the central focus lay with the good-time throngs in the streets. Everywhere people seemed possessed with devouring as many spirits as humanly possible; it became a basic feature of the celebrations. Businesses that handled liquor of any kind were fair game for the surging crowds. The minute Truman issued the peace proclamation liquor store windows were smashed and their shelves looted in many areas. In every part of the country liquor concerns boarded up windows and doors in an effort to protect their supplies. In New Jersey the State Alcoholic Beverage Commissioner ordered all taverns to close down; restaurants and hotels were likewise told to cease dispensing spirits. Night spots and cabarets from Maine to the Pacific were packed to overflowing with heavy-drinking celebrants.

The grand hoopla also had its share of pain and injury. In Philadelphia medical authorities reported the city's hospitals treated 200 emergency cases during the first twenty-four hours. At least ten people had been struck by stray bullets; but most celebration-related injuries in the City of Brotherly Love were from sheer exhaustion and fatigue. People had been slashed by broken glass, bruised in the street rough-and-tumble, or burned by exploding fireworks. In Muskegon, Michigan, a twenty-three-year-old housewife was shot and killed when her husband fired a revolver to celebrate the Japanese surrender. And in New York City an estimated 800 injuries were reported during the first few hours of merrymaking. The entire metropolis was filled with pandemonium; police said 1,200,000 persons formed a human sea "in the area bounded by Fortieth and Fifty-second Streets, between Sixth and Eighth Avenues." Chinatown, like Times Square, kept up its raucous demonstrations during the first hours of peace. Throughout the city fifty felony arrests and numerous lesser ones were made stemming from the festivities; seventy-eight automobiles were reported stolen; 377 fire alarms were set off; a twelve-year-old boy died after falling from a parading truck. And while New York was letting go, a band of Eskimos at Barrow, Alaska, greeted the surrender with a dance accompanied by music from "drums made of walrus linings stretched over driftwood hoops."

Around military installations the uproar was overpowering; in several areas celebrations by exuberant servicemen gave way to outright riot. Rear Admiral Carleton H. Wright, Commandant of the Twelfth Naval District, was forced to cancel liberty for all naval personnel, including coast guardsmen, marines, and WAVES, within 100 miles of San Francisco after three days of uninterrupted mayhem. His order came after club-swinging police joined beleaguered shore patrolmen when a mass brawl on Market Street started to get out of hand. Women were not only molested and their escorts roughed up by marauding servicemen but automobiles were driven through storefronts to get at liquor supplies. Bottles were thrown through display windows throughout the downtown area and before the melée ended, ten people were killed and more than one thousand treated at hospital emergency rooms.

At the other end of the country state guardsmen with fixed bayonets helped naval police subdue rampaging sailors in New Bedford, Massachusetts. A riot had erupted during "an impromptu parade through the city's business section." The trouble started when a group of sailors from a nearby naval base threatened local policemen about to take a recently-discharged seaman into custody. Nine arrests resulted when a jeering crowd interceded to save the hapless sailor after police asked him to get out of an automobile because he was blocking the driver's vision. Yet all of the carousing was not ill-tempered; in Milwaukee a woman who "weighed 300 pounds" got caught up in the jubilation and grabbed a passerby, kissing him so hard it knocked three teeth from his lower denture.

As the good times subsided and the world returned to normal, the country knew the war was over when OPA moved to lift the nettling rationing restrictions. On August 15 rationing was ended for gasoline. Immediately great lines of fuel-starved automobiles lined up at neighborhood filling stations for the first fill-up in more than three years. A good portion of the country simply took an old-fashioned joyride for the first time since Pearl Harbor. Then, as controls were lifted on every conceivable item from baby carriages to nylon hose, a number of "enthusiastic townsmen at Joliet, Illinois," demonstrated their distaste for OPA's wartime moratorium on civilian driving; gasoline-ration coupons were thrown into an open casket outside city hall. "An undertaker had promised a caisson and two black horses to carry the casket through the streets; then there would be a big bonfire," Newsweek reported. But the shenanigan was called off by the mayor after Ethel Heinselman, an OPA-rationing clerk objected. "I don't see anything funny about it," she told reporters.

Mostly late August 1945 was a time for going home; jam-packed trains and buses, in addition to bustling highways once gasoline became plentiful, carried millions of servicemen and civilians to homes of loved ones and to new jobs and to peacetime lives. Among the localities that attracted masses of people for the duration was southern California where people from the rural South had flocked since 1941. Droves of "Oakies" and "Arkies" had come to its burgeoning defense factories and shipyards to escape the draft as well as the monotony of farm life. With Japan beaten they had only one thing in mind—to go home, although millions remained in the promised land. Ernest Hall, an inspector with the Arizona Department of Agriculture at Ehrenberg on the California border, also knew the war had ended one day after V-J Day. He counted 417 passenger cars passing his checkpoint in a single day—most of them loaded with families headed for Texas and Oklahoma.

Servicemen and civilians returned to every part of the country with the certain knowledge they had served a just cause. Evil men had attacked a peace-loving America and the national temper had demanded that they be crushed. Although great changes lay on the horizon as the country struggled to right festering social injustices and to meet the challenge of international Communism during the Cold War era, the United States in August 1945 had the assurance that it was the number one power on earth. It possessed the world's only atomic weapons as well as great economic and military superiority. Unlike the peoples of Europe and Asia, America herself had escaped the horrors of war; the killing and destruction had taken place elsewhere, far removed from these shores. Moreover, the absence of any real dissent had made the nation a happy place to live and work. And since it had confronted a clearly defined enemy there was nothing to nag at the collective conscience. Americans had simply enjoyed themselves as they closed ranks against the common foe.

The United States came out of the war in better shape than when it started. So, 1941–1945 were happy years for the millions who took part in the unprecedented prosperity and patriotic fervor that gripped the country. Men and women of every station knew they had helped the war effort. Total war meant that each individual could think he or she had shared in the common triumph. That sureness of spirit had enabled people to think well of themselves during the conflict. For nearly every person, especially the impressionable young who had courted and waited for sweethearts or merely watched the parade of wartime activity, the conflict had a special appeal. But the excitement of participation was not confined to any one group. Paper drives, war bond rallies, victory garden campaigns, mock air raid drills, the constant outpouring of new films and catchy dance tunes, rationing sign-ups, and sporting events of every description engulfed the entire population. The forty-five months from December 1941 and the Japanese attack on Pearl Harbor until the closing hoopla of August 1945 were filled with unceasing movement; the good times rolled as the country joined in the crusade to beat Hitler and Tojo, and for those Americans who did not suffer in combat or lose loved ones, World War II was nothing short of wonderful.

Index

Abbott and Costello, 128, 130-31
Acuff, Roy, 150-53
Adams, Ben, 68
Adoption, 240
After the Fall, 193
Agriculture Department, U.S., 80-81
Airplane crashes, 93-94, 213
Aimen, Allen, 239
Alabama Dry Dock and Shipbuilding
    Company, 106-107
Alaska Highway, 67-68
Algeria, 91
Alinsky, Saul, 101, 213
Allen, James S., 102
Allen, William R., 16
All My Sons, 193
Allwright, S. E., 150
Alpert, Mickey, 75
Alvarez, Luis, 244
America First Committee, 18
America Has No Enemies in Asia, 11
American Automobile Association, 16
American Bund, 159, 160, 225
American Civil Liberties Union, 28,
    116
American Federation of Labor
    (AFL), 99, 183
American Federation of Musicians, 100
American Institute of Public
    Opinion, 78
American Newsreel, 22
American Radio Relay League, 12
AmeriKaland (tanker), 24

Anderson, Clinton, 223
Anderson, Karen, 167
Andreyeff, Nicolai Ivanovitch, 203
Anthony, Reverend George W., 219
Archiquette, Floyd, 89-90
Aries, Robert S., 69
Arnall, Ellis Gibbs, 64
Arnold, Eddie, 154
Arnold, Hap, 142, 183, 247, 248
Arnold, Thurston, 42
*Arsenal of Democracy: The Story of
    American War Production*
    (Nelson), 38
Associated Grocery Manufacturers of
    America, 13
Associated Press, 55, 163, 186, 212,
    213, 220, 230, 234, 250
Atkinson, Brooks, 132
Atomic Bomb, 241-50, 257
Aurand, Henry S., 112
Auschwitz, 220-21
Australia, 89, 90, 146
Automobiles, 14-15, 16, 43, 237,
    240; accidents, 213; gasoline for,
    see Gasoline rationing; tires, 13,
    14-15, 41, 55, 120, 192, 237
Autry, Gene, 154
Avery, Sewell Lee, 58-59
Ayres, Lou, 190

Bacall, Lauren, 36, 228-29
Baer, Buddy, 28
Baesell, Norman F., 200, 201

Baker, Josephine, 108-109
Baltimore Orioles, 164
Barkley, Alben, 173, 183
Barnette family, 115
Barnum, P. T., 96
Barnum and Bailey, 164
Barr, John A., 58
Barretts of Wimpole Street, The, 132
Barry, Joan, 129-30
Barrymore, Lionel, 183
Baruch, Bernard, 171, 217
Baseball, 17, 48-49, 109-10, 113,
    164, 185-87, 235
Bass, Eva, 158
Bass, William, 198
Bataan, 45-46
Bataan Death March, 23-24
Battle of Angels, 233
Battle of Britain, 24, 38, 140
Battle of the Bulge, 145, 196, 197,
    198, 202
Baugh, Samuel Adrian, 133
BBC, 200
Beaumont, Texas, 105-106
Beaverbrook, Lord, 39
Bedroom-bath practices, survey of,
    156-57
Bell for Adano, A (Hersey), 73, 179-
    80
Bell Telephone System, 18
Benét, Stephen Vincent, 95
Bennett, John J., 62-63
Benson, Jackson, 142
Berger, Ernest Peter, 50
Bergman, Ingrid, 129, 211, 229
Berlin, Irving, 36
Berlin, Germany, 204, 205
Bernadotte, Count, 226
Bethe, Hans, 245
Biddle, Francis, 10-11, 51, 58, 59
Big Inch Pipeline, 68-69
Billiards, 188
Bishop, Jim, 217-18
Black Boy (Wright), 235-36
Black market, 70-72, 126-27, 222, 223
"Blackouts," 8, 9, 10, 20
Blacks, 20, 21, 174, 218-19; in

armed services, 113, 161-62;
    famous, 28-33, 108-10, 235-36;
    population shift, 167-68; racism,
    discrimination and segregation, 29,
    30-32, 64, 98, 102-103, 105-108,
    110-13, 121-22, 161-62, 168, 235-
    36; voting by, 64, 150;
    unemployment, 167
Blaine, Buck, 34
Blamey, Thomas, 90
Blanchard, Felix "Doc," 188
Blesse, Frederick, 141
Blum, John Morton, 35
Bode, Winston, 234
Boeing Aircraft, 43, 140
Boettinger, Mrs. John, 217
Bogart, Humphrey, 128-29, 131,
    228-29
Bohr, Niels, 242, 245
Boire (destroyer), 165
Boise City, Oklahoma, 120-21
Boldson, C. M., 112-13
Bon Marché, 83
Bookweek, 194
Borden Company, 176-77
Boston Red Sox, 48, 185, 186
Bowles, Chester, 71, 72, 120, 223
Boxing, 28-30
Boy Scouts, 6
Bracken, Eddie, 183
Braddock, Jimmy, 29
Bradley, Omar, 144, 203, 221
Brando, Marlon, 233
Brassfield, Rod, 154
Braun, Eva, 224
Brethren, 190
Breunn, Howard G., 217, 218
Brice, Fanny, 184
Bricker, John, 147, 148, 149, 161,
    162, 163, 181, 184, 191
Bridges, Harry, 103
Briggs, Dr. Lyman J., 243
Broadway productions, 131-32, 142,
    193-94
Bromfield, Louis, 78
Bronowski, Jacob, 242
Brooklyn Dodgers, 49, 109

Brooks, Van Wyck, 180
Brotherhood of Sleeping Car
    Porters, 30
Browder, Earl, 101, 102, 103, 182,
    184
Brown, Harry, 180
Brown, Herbert, 8-9
Brown, J. Douglas, 44
Brown, Jimmy, 49
Brown, Prentiss M., 62
B-17, 140
B-29, 140
Buckner, Simon Bolivar, 209
Budd Manufacturing, 165
Bull Moose party, 240
Bureau of Economic Welfare
    (BEW), 123, 124-25
Bureau of Labor Statistics, 169
Burke-Wadsworth Act, 3
Bush, George, 97
Bush, Vannevar, 243
Bushnell, Robert T., 96-97
Business Week, 16, 53, 57
Byrd, Harry F., 174
Byrnes, James F., 56-57, 125, 166,
    178, 179, 197, 198, 199, 205,
    210, 211, 235
Byrnes Note, 251, 252, 253

Cagney, James, 128
California, 65, 257
"Camel Caravan," 154
Canada, 202, 203-204, 252
Cannery Row (Steinbeck), 143
Carlson, John Roy, 160
Carmen Jones, 132
Carnegie-Illinois Steel Corpora-
    tion, 113
Carter, Jimmy, 97
Casablanca, 129, 229
Casey, Joseph E., 64
Casualties, war, 4
Catan, Michael, 210-11
Cat on a Hot Tin Roof, 233
CBS, 80, 194
Chadwick, Sir James, 245
Chandler, Albert B. "Happy," 235

Chaplin, Charlie, 129-30
Chaplin, Oona, 130
Charleston Gazette, 3
Chemical Industries, 69
Chiang Kai-Shek, 12
Chicago Bears, 133, 134
Chicago Cubs, 186
Chicago Daily News, 181
Chicago Defender, 235
Chicago Tribune, 160
Chicago White Sox, 185
China, 12, 25, 166
Chinese-Americans, 25-26
Christian Century, 189
Chrysler Corporation, 41, 237
Chungking Radio, 12
Churchill, Winston, 18, 24, 92,
    141, 178, 182, 247
Cigarette smoking, 126, 178, 222
Civil defense organizations, 10
Clark, Mark, 104, 113, 142, 204
Clark, Zeke, 143, 144
Clarke, Carter C., 184
Cleveland Indians, 113
Cleveland Rams, 134
Clothing shortages, 179, 240
Coal miners, see United Mine
    Workers of America
Coca Cola, 13
Cochran, Weller, 188
Coconut Grove, 75, 96-97
Coleman, Ronald, 177
Collier's, 126-27, 187, 214, 222
Columbia Broadcasting System, 80,
    194
Comic books, 127
Communist Party of America, 102,
    103, 236
Communist Political Association, 182
Communists, 101-103, 236;
    organized labor and, 101-102
Compton, Karl, 246
Conant, James, 243
Concentration camps, German,
    220-21
Congress, U.S., 60; counter-
    declaration of war on Germany

Congress, U.S. (*cont.*)
  and Italy, 4-5; declaration of war
  on Japan, 3, 5; elections, 61-66,
  193; House Committee on
  UnAmerican Activities, 194-95
Congress of Industrial Organizations
  (CIO), 98, 102, 174
Connally, Tom Terry, 64, 100-101
Conn, Billy, 30
Conrad, Earl, 67
Conscientious objectors, 189-91
Consumer goods, production of,
  166, 199
Cooke, Alistair, 129
Coolidge, Calvin, 102, 241
Cooper, Gary, 1, 128, 177-78, 183,
  211
Cooper, Prentice, 152
Coos Bay, U.S.S., 169-70
Copas, Cowboy, 154
Coral Sea, Battle of, 22, 25
Cornell, Katharine, 132
Corregidor, 46
Costello, Lou, 128, 130-31
Costello, Lou, Jr., 130, 131
Cotez, Ricardo, 177
Coughlin, Father Charles E., 50-52
Country and western music, 150-54
Courtney, William H., 222
Cousins, Norman, 179
Coxey, Jacob S., 161
Crosby, Bing, 28, 128, 201
Crowley, Leo T., 125
Crucible, The, 193
Crump, Ed, 152

Dale, Charles M., 209
Daniels, Jonathan, 226
Daniels, Josephus, 95, 173
Darden, Colgate W., 111
Dasch, George J., 50
Davies, Ralph K., 138
Davis, Benjamin O., 32
Davis, Betty, 184
Davis, B. O., Jr., 113
Davis, Elmer, 79, 80

Davis, James Houston "Jimmy,"
  150, 151, 153
Davis, Oscar, 110
Davis, William H., 43, 45, 53
Deatherage, George, 159
Death of a Salesman, 193
Debs, Eugene V., 102
de Cortova, Arturo, 177
Defense Communications Board, 12
Defense workers, 4, 7, 8, 16, 17, 37,
  42, 44, 48, 79, 86, 199-200, 212;
  black, 31; strikes by, 169-70; as the
  war was ending, 165-66, 169-70,
  218; women, 33, 85-86
de Gaulle, Charles, 109, 144-45
de Havilland, Olivia, 184
Demaret, Jimmy, 234
DeMille, Cecil B., 182
Democratic National Committee, 18
Demographics, 21
Dempsey, Jack, 30
Dempsey, Miles, 144
De Rochemont, Louis de, 23
Detroit, Michigan, 107, 111-13
Detroit Lions, 134
Detroit Tigers, 113, 185, 186
Dewey, Thomas E., 59, 62-63, 65,
  147, 148-49, 150, 175, 178, 224;
  campaign of, 180-85, 191-93;
  nomination of, 161, 162-63
DeWitt, John Lessesne, 21, 26
de Cicco, Pasquale, 16-17
Dies, Martin, 113
Dilling, Elizabeth, 160
DiMaggio, Joe, 28, 48-49
Dirksen, Everett McKinley, 162
Disney, Walt, 183
Dobbs, R. D., 121
Dobie, J. Frank, 233-34
Doenitz, Karl, 213, 224
Domei, 137, 252
Donald, David, 14
Donovan, Joseph M., 81
Doolittle, James H., 25
Dorsey, Jimmy, 200
Dorsey, Tommy, 35, 200
Douglas, Emily Taft, 193

Douglas, Helen Gahagan, 193
Douglas, William O., 174
Draft, the, see Selective service
    system
Duffy, Edmund, 25
Dun, Right Reverend Angus, 219
Dunkley, Charles, 186
Dunning, Jack, 131
Dupuy, Ernst, 204
Dupuy, Trevor, 204
Durante, Jimmy, 131
Durbin, Deanna, 178

Economic Defense Board, 124
Eichelberger, Clark M., 161
Eichler, Edward C., 161
Einstein, Albert, 241, 242, 243
Eisenhower, Dwight D., 28, 59, 91-
    92, 97, 100, 103, 141, 143, 197,
    221, 224, 226; nuclear weapons
    and, 246-47; Normandy Invasion,
    144, 161
Eisenhower, Milton, 27
Eisenstein, Sergei, 32
El Alamein, 92
Elsie-the-Cow, 176-77
Emancipation Proclamation, 20
Emerson, Ralph Waldo, 180
Empire State Building, 238-39
Eniwetok, 145, 246
Enlistment into the armed services,
    5, 92-93
Enola Gay, 248, 249
Equal Rights Amendment, 214-15
Esquire, 75-76
Ewen, David, 230

Fabian, Dr. Bela, 220
Fadiman, Clifton, 142
Fair Employment Practices
    Commission (FEPC), 31, 167
Family, 240; changes in the, 7, 79,
    87
Far Eastern Affairs, 11
Farley, Jim, 172
Fashions, teenage, 156
FBI, 10, 49, 240, 243

Federal Communications
    Commission, 12
Federal Shipbuilding and Dry Dock,
    165
Federal Writers Project, 236
Feller, Bob, 5
Felton, Rebecca, 214
Ferguson, Homer, 62
Fermi, Enrico, 242-43, 245
Ferrer, Jose, 32
Fields, Gracie, 132
Firestone, 60
Fleischman, Harry, 192
Flowering of New England, The
    (Emerson), 180
Flynn, Edward J., 18, 61-62, 172
Flynn, Errol, 66-67
Focus (Miller), 194
Fohl, Leo A., 185-86
Fonda, Henry, 143
Fontaine, Lynn, 36, 132
Food rationing, 12-13, 71, 73, 77,
    79-82, 119-20, 127, 136; meat
    shortages of 1945, 221-22;
    preparations for end of, 178-79,
    216, 240
Football, 21, 28, 60-61, 77, 132-34,
    187, 188, 197, 198-99
Ford, Gerald R., 97
Ford, Henry, 14
Ford, James W., 102, 103
Ford Motor Company, 237, 240
Foreign nationals, 10-11, 26-28; see
    also individual groups
"For the duration," 3, 4
Forrestal, James V., 165
For Whom the Bell Tolls, 211
Foster, William Z., 101, 102, 103
Fox Movietone, 22
France, 92; invasion of, 139, 144
Francis, Kay, 177
Freeman, Douglas Southall, 67
Fuchida, Mitsuo, 2

Gable, Clark, 34, 104, 128, 129,
    177
Galbraith, John Kenneth, 72-73

Gallup polls, 78-79, 82, 136
Garbo, Greta, 230
Gard, Wayne, 65
Garner, Elmer J., 160-61
Garner, John Nance, 125
Garner, Peggy Ann, 211
Garrett, Frank, 121
Garson, Greer, 128
Gasoline rationing, 46-48, 55, 60, 69-70, 72, 120, 126-27, 136, 138, 222, 237, 256
Gavin, John T., 208
General Cable Company, 53
General Motors, 237
General's Life, A (Bradley), 203
Georgia, 64
German-Americans, 10-11, 27-28
Germany: defeat of, 178-79, 204-205, 216, 226; development of atomic bomb in, 243; V-E day, 212, 224, 226-27; war against, 4-5, 24, 88-89, 91-92, 136, 139-45, 165, 170, 197, 198, 202-205; see also Hitler, Adolf
Gibson, Joshua "Josh," 109
Giesler, Gerry, 66, 67, 228
GI Hamlet, 132
Gilbert, John, 177
Glass Menagerie, 232, 233
Godfrey, Lionel, 227
Goebbels, Joseph, 51
Golf, 17, 234
Gompers, Samuel, 99
Gone With the Wind, 34, 104, 129
Good Housekeeping, 214
Goodman, Benny, 34
Goodyear Rubber, 60
Gorham, Ethel, 87
Goring, Reichmarshal, 140
Grable, Betty, 128
Graham, Otis L., 171, 191
Grandma Moses, American Primitive (Bromfield and Kallir), 78
Grand Ole Opry, 153-54
Grant, Cary, 66, 227-28
Grapes of Wrath, The (Steinbeck), 143

Gray, Wyshner, 186-87
Great Britain, 18, 24, 39, 92, 139-40, 144, 202-204, 205, 207
Green, Dr. Charles E., 71
Green Bay Packers, 134
Greenberg, Hank, 5
Greenwood, Don, 21
Griffith, Samuel B., 91
Grimes, Oscar, 186
Griswold, Dwight Parker, 162
Groves, Leslie R., 243, 244-45
Grumman Aircraft, 165
Guadalcanal, battle for, 73, 75, 90-91
Guam, 23, 146, 206
Guderian, Heinz, 204

Hagan, Uta, 32
Hager, Carl, 1
Hahesalza, East Prussia, 89
Hall, Ernest, 257
Hallelujah (Hurst), 138
Halsey, William F. "Bull," 146, 161
Hamilton, Ian, 191
Hamilton, John H., 9-10
Hamilton, Virginia, 32
"Ham" radios, 12
Hannegan, Robert, 171, 173, 182
Hansen, Betty, 66-67
Harding, Warren G., 241
Harlem, New York, 20, 121, 122
Harlow, Jean, 177
Harrodsburg, Kentucky, 45-46
Hart, Liddell, 141, 202, 208
Haruma (battleship), 19, 23
Harvey, 233
Hassett, Buddy, 49
Hastie, William H., 32
Haupt, Hans, 50
Hayden, Frank, 138
Hayes, Helen, 132
Hayes, Philip, 168
Haynes, Dick, 35
Haynes, Don, 201
Hayworth, Rita, 184
Hearst newspapers, 22
Hecht, Ben, 34

Heinselmen, Ethel, 256
Hemingway, Ernest, 211, 228, 232
Henderson, Leon, 14, 15, 57, 69, 70, 71, 72, 73, 120
Henry, Thomas F., 16
Hepburn, Katherine, 184
Hersey, John, 73, 179-80
Hershey, Lewis B., 4, 87, 189, 199
Higham, Charles, 34
High Noon, 177
Hildegarde, 36
Hillman, Sidney, 40, 174, 182, 184, 185
Himmler, Heinrich, 226
Hines, Frank T., 211-12
Hirohito, Emperor, 250-51
Hiroshima, 248, 249
Hispanics, discrimination and racial conflicts, 104-105
History of the Communist Party in the United States (Foster), 102
History of the Standard Oil Company (Tarbell), 137-38
Hitler, Adolf, 137, 204, 205; attempt on life of, 170; death of, 213, 216, 223-25, 226; declaration of war on U.S., 4-5
Hit Parade, 35
H. J. Heinz Company, 42
Hobby, Oveta Culp, 52
Hodges, Courtney, 202-203
Hohenlohe-Waldenburg-Schillinsfurst, Princess Stefanie, 11
Holland, Willard, 232
Holocaust, 220-21
Homma, General, 24
Hong Kong, 24
Hoopes, Darlington, 192
Hoover, Mrs. Herbert, 137
Hoover, Herbert, 124, 137
Hoover, J. Edgar, 16, 159
Hope, Bob, 128, 131
Hoppe, Willie, 188
Hopper, Hedda, 183
Horne, Lena, 108
Horseracing, 45, 187-88, 197, 199, 235

Hosiery, women's, 57-58, 256
Hotchner, A. E., 232
Houston *Chronicle*, 59
Hoyt, Edwin, 229
Hurst, Fanny, 138
Huston, Walter, 184
Hutton, Barbara, 66, 227-28
Hydrogen bomb, 245-46

Ickes, Harold L., 59, 69, 100, 101, 123, 212, 213
Incident at Vichy, 193-94
Indianapolis, Indiana, 107
Indochina, 24
Inflation, 56-57, 206, 223
International Longshoremen's and Warehousemen's Union, 103
International News Service, 160
I Remember Mama, 233
Irving, Washington, 180
Italian-Americans, 10-11, 27-28
Italy, 92, 104, 113, 204, 225-26; Allied drive in, 141-44; counterdeclaration of war with, 4-5
Ives, Burl, 36
Iwo Jima, Japan, 205, 206-207

Jackson, Sam, 174
Jacobs, Mike, 30
James, Henry, 35
James, William, 231
Jane Eyre, 211
Japan, 9, 136, 137, 165; battles against, 22, 23-24, 25, 45-46, 73, 75, 89-91, 145-46, 205-209; Pearl Harbor attack, 1-3; submarine attacks by, 8; U.S. declares war against, 3, 5; use of nuclear weapons against, 246-50; victory against, 223, 227, 238, 241, 250-53
Japanese-Americans, 25-26; internment of, 10, 25, 26-27, 116, 196, 254
Japanese Times and Mail, 11
J. B. Pierce Foundation, 156-57
Jeffers, William M., 59, 69, 70

Jehovah's Witnesses, 98, 114-16, 190
Jessel, George, 209
Jews, 157-58; Holocaust, 220-21
Johnson, Hiram, 240-41
Johnson, Jed Joseph, 72
Johnson, J. Morgan, 197
Johnson, Lyndon B., 65, 97
Jolson, Al, 132
Jones, Buck, 75
Jones, Coleen, 121
Jones, Jesse Holman, 59, 123, 124, 125
Justice Department, U.S., 11, 42, 50, 51, 150
Juvenile delinquency, 6, 7

Kaiser, Henry J., 40-41
Kalinchok, George, 103-104
Kallir, Otto, 78
Kaltenborn, Hans V., 23, 80
Kamikazes, 206, 208-209, 248-49
Keller, Helen, 184
Kelly, Colin P., Jr., 19, 23
Kelly, Ed, 191
Kelly, Francis E., 63
Kelly, Grace, 177
Kelly, Harry F., 62, 112, 113
Kennedy, John F., 91, 97
Kerr, Bob, 173
Kesselring, Albert, 142, 143, 203
Key Largo, 229
Kharkov, Soviet Union, 89
Kilgore, Harley M., 174
Kinder, Beulah, 178
King, Ernest J., 164-65, 210
King, MacKenzie, 252
King George V, H.M.S., 207
Knights of Columbus, 6
Knights of the White Camellia, 159
Knox, Frank, 2
Knudsen, William S., 40
Konev, Marshal, 204
Kostelanetz, Andre, 230-31
Kotzebue, Albert K., 203
Krammer, Arnold, 74-75
Krug, James A., 179, 226
Ku Klux Klan, 159

Kuribaysashi, Tadamichi, 207
Kwajalein, 145

Labor, organized, 4, 31, 44-45, 53-54, 56, 57, 98-104, 122-23, 136, 139, 168-70, 212-13
Labor market: ex-GIs in, 212; shortages, 55-56, 210
Lafayette, U.S.S. (ship), 33
La Guardia, Fiorello, 9, 10, 120, 227; race riots and, 122
Lamont, Thomas W., 96
Landis, Kenesaw M., 235
Landon, Alf, 162
Langtry, Lily, 36
Lape, Esther, 218
LaSalle Motor Company, 14-15
Lash, Joseph, 218
Lassie Come Home, 211
Lausche, Frank, 240
Lawrence, Ernest O., 244, 245
Layden, Elmer, 134
Lee, Shavery, 252
Lee's Lieutenants (Freeman), 67
LeMay, Curtis, 207
Lend Lease, 39, 88
Leningrad, battle for, 89, 204
Lepke (murderer), 191
Leuders, Henry, 159
Lewis, John L., 98-102, 103-104, 111, 113, 122-23, 212-13
Lewis, Sinclair, 184
Lexington, U.S.S. (ship), 25
Leyte Gulf, Battle of, 146
Lieb, Frederick G., 49
Life, 6, 23, 26, 46, 73, 108, 117, 156, 173, 178, 195, 201, 203, 211, 214-15, 228, 235-35, 243-44, 253
Life in Our Times, A (Galbraith), 73
Life of Reason, The (Santayana), 231-32
Lincoln Tunnel, 210-11
Lindbergh, Charles, 18
Liquor, 127, 137, 179, 180, 222,255
Little Steel decision, 53, 56, 57, 58, 98, 123, 136, 139

Liuzza, James E., 150
Lockheed, 140
Lodge, Henry Cabot, 63-64
Lombard, Carole, 34, 177
London, England, 139
Long, Breckinridge, 220
Long, Huey, 62, 151
Longstreet, Helen Dortch, 137
Los Angeles, California, 8-9, 104-105, 253
Louis, Joe, 28-30, 168, 253-54
Lowell, Robert, 190-91
Luce, Henry R., 117
Luckman, Sid, 133
Luftwaffe, 24, 139-41
Lunt, Alfred, 36, 132

MacArthur, Douglas, 19, 23, 35, 90, 147, 149, 162, 206, 249, 253; nuclear weapons and, 246, 247; as overseer of Japan, 251; recapture of Philippines, 146
McAuliffe, Anthony, 145
McCarthy, Joe, 48, 49
McCauley, Herbert E., 219
McClelland, C. P., 240
McCrae, Joel, 183
McIntyre, Ross T., 192, 216, 217, 218
McMillan, G. G., 23
McNary-Haugen Farm Bill, 124
McNear, George, 53
McNutt, Paul V., 43-44, 58
McQuinn, George, 186
MacWilliams, Joe, 160
Maine, 62
Makin, 145
Malone, Bill C., 152, 153
Manchester, William, 178
Manhattan Project, 243-47
Man Who Had All the Luck, The, 193, 194
Maras, Johnny, 92-93
March, Frederic, 132
March of Time, The, 22, 24
Margolies, Edward, 236
Marianas, 146

Marquart, E. J., 55
Marriages: boom in, 17; GI, to foreign brides, 157, 214; returning troops and, 188-89, 214
Marsh, Frederick, 184
Marshall, George C., 132, 184, 210, 226, 247
Marshall, Thurgood, 110
Martin, Joseph W., Jr., 18, 61, 62
Marx, Harpo, 184
Massachusetts, 62, 63-64
Massey, Raymond, 132
Meet Me in St. Louis, 211
Menjou, Adolphe, 183
Mennonites, 190
Mercer, Dillard, 9
Metropolitan Life Insurance Company, 188
Mexico, 104
Meyer, Dutch, 133
Miami, Florida, 134-35, 199, 206, 252
Michener, James, 205
Michigan, 61
Midway Island, Battle of, 22, 25
Migration, internal, 6-7, 117-19, 153, 167-68, 257
Mikolich, John J., 94
Miller, Arthur, 142, 193-95
Miller, Glenn, 200-202
Miller, Johnny, 29
Miller, Mark, 126
Millikan, Robert, 244
Milwaukee Journal, 149
"Miracle, The," 11
Misfits, The, 193
Mize, Johnny, 17
Montebello, 8
Monte Cassino, attack on, 143
Montgomery, Field Marshal, 41, 92, 141, 142, 144, 197, 202, 203, 226
Montgomery Wards, 41, 58-59
Moody, "Big Train," 199
Moon is Down, The (Steinbeck), 142
Moore, Terry, 49
Moran, Lord, 171
Moran, Lewis L., 151

Morgan, F. O., 200-201
Morgan J. Pierpont, 95-96
Morgentau, Henry, 17, 165, 220
Morison, Samuel Eliot, 91, 206-207
Morocco, 91, 92
Morris, Edwin, 5
Morrison, Herbert, 25
Morrison Philip, 245
Morse, Arthur, 220
Morse, Wayne L., 58
Moscow, Soviet Union, 89, 204
Moses, Grandma, 77-78
Moss, Leonard, 194
Motion Picture Herald, The, 128
Mountbatten, Lord, 209
Movies, 128-31, 143, 177-78, 211,
    227-29; popularity of, 34, 128;
    war-flavored, 35, 142; *see also*
    names of actors and actresses
Murray, Philip, 174
Murrow, Edward R., 77
Mussolini, Benito, 216, 223, 225-26
Mutual Broadcasting Company, 9
My Wicked, Wicked Ways (Flynn), 67

Nagasaki, 248, 250
Nation, The, 59
National Aeronautics and Space
    Administration (NASA), 205
National Association for the
    Advancement of Colored People
    (NAACP), 31, 150
National Broadcasting Company, 2,
    152, 194
National Defense Advisory
    Committee, 37, 38
National Defense Research
    Committee, 243
National Football League, 132-34
National Labor Relations Board
    (NLRB), 123
National Opinion Research Center,
    190
National Recovery Administration, 38
National Velvet, 211
National War Labor Board (NWLB),
    44-45, 53-54, 99, 100, 103

National Youth Administration, 5
Native Son (Wright), 236
NBC, 2, 152, 194
Nellis, Richard W., 93
Nelson, Byron, 234
Nelson, Donald Marr, 37-38, 40,
    59, 69, 82, 83, 100, 125, 166, 179
Netherlands, 24
New Guinea, 89-90, 146
Newhall, Arthur B., 60
New Hampshire, 62
New Jersey, 62, 255
New Masses, 236
News of the Day, 22
Newsreels, 22-23, 145, 209, 220,
    228
Newsweek, 41, 46, 48, 66, 79, 85,
    86, 103, 104, 111, 122, 125, 127,
    138, 146, 177-78, 187, 189, 203,
    205, 209, 218, 221, 250, 256
New York, New York, 9, 10, 20,
    149, 210-11, 219, 252, 255
New Yorker, 142
New York Giants (baseball), 17, 185,
    235
New York Giants (football), 133, 134
New York *Herald Tribune*, 148
New York State, 62
New York *Times, The*, 18, 26, 48,
    55, 61, 119, 132, 176, 180, 190,
    193, 194, 239, 249
New York Yankess, 48-49, 185, 186,
    235
Nimitz, Chester A., 90, 145, 206,
    207
Niven, David, 66
Nixon, Richard M., 97, 251
Normandie (ship), 33
Normandy invasion, 139, 144, 161
Norris, George, 63
North Africa, fighting in, 91-92,
    100, 114
Nuclear weapons, 241-50, 257

O'Brien, Margaret, 211
O'Daniel, Wilbert Lee "Pappy," 64-
    65, 151, 153

O'Donnell, James P., 224
Office of Civilian Defense, 9, 10
Office of Civilian Supply (OCS), 82-83
Office of Defense Transportation (ODT), 119, 120, 197-98
Office of Economic Stabilization (OES), 56-57
Office of Price Administration (OPA), 14, 15, 46, 47-48, 57-58, 69-72, 80-81, 120, 123, 125, 159, 179, 195, 221, 240, 256; criticism of, 222-23; end of, 223
Office of Production Management (OPM), 9, 15
Office of War Information (OWI), 35, 80, 88, 169, 222
Office of War Mobilization, 125
Ohrdruf Nord, 221
Okinawa, Japan, 208-209, 229, 241
Oklahoma, 132
Olson, Culbert L., 65
Once There Was a War (Steinbeck), 143
One World (Willkie), 148
Operation Barbarossa, 88-89, 101
Operation Iceberg, 208
Operation Torch, 91-92
Oppenheimer, J. Robert, 244-45
Oswiecim, 220
Othello, 32-33
Ouija board, 163

Packard, 237
Paige, Satchel, 110
Paper and paper products, 158-159, 179
Papert, Kate, 33
Paris, France, 144-45
Pathe's Weekly, 22
Patterson, Robert, 166
Patton, George S., 92, 141, 144, 203, 204, 221
Paullin, Dr. James, 218
Paulus, Friedrich, 88
Pearl, Minnie, 154
Pearl Harbor, Japanese raid on, 10;

news of, 1-3; lack of preparedness, charges of, 183, 184, 191
Pearson, Drew, 144
Pecora Investigating Committee, 96
Pelley, William, 159-60
Pendergast, Tom, 174
Pennsylvania Railroad, 118-19
Pepper, Claude, 150
Pepsi Cola, 13
Perkins, Milo, 124, 125
Perrett, Geoffrey, 70
Petacci, Clara, 225-26
Petrillo, James C., 100
Petrochemical industry, 59, 60
P-47 Thunderbolts, 140, 207
P-51 Mustangs, 140, 158, 207
Philadelphia, Pennsylvania, 117-18, 168, 255
Philadelphia Athletics, 49, 186
Philadelphia Eagles, 134
Philippines, 23-24, 25, 35, 45-46, 206; recapture of, 146
Philippine Sea, Battle of the, 145
Pittsburgh Steelers, 134
Pius XII, Pope, 18
Planck, Max, 241-42
Pledge of allegiance to the flag, 114-16
Political Action Committees (PACs), 174, 182
Politics, domestic: in 1942, 61-66; in 1944, 146-51, 161-63, 170-75, 180-85, 191-93; in 1946, 223; unity, 18
Pollet, Howie, 49
Pons, Lily, 230-31
Port Moresby, 90
Postal Telegraph, 23
Post Office, U.S., 58
Potsdam Conference, 247, 250
Powell, Adam Clayton, Jr., 20
Powell, William, 34
POWs, 250; American, 219-20, 250; Germany and Italian, 73-75, 141
Price, Melvin, 235
Price controls, see Office of Price Administration

Prince of Wales (battleship), 24
Prisoners-of-war, *see* POWs
Prostitution, 6, 84-85
Psychological Corporation, 177
Putnam, Roger L., 63
Pyle, Ernie, 113-114, 142, 194

Quakers, 190
Quantum theory, 241-42
Queen, Earl, 219-20

Racial problems, *see* Blacks;
    Hispanics
Radio, 80, 131, 153-56, 219; news of
    the war, 251-52, 254-55; news of
    Pearl Harbor attack, 2; shortwave, 12
Railroads: accidents, 118-19, 163-64,
    180-81, introduction of diesel-
    powered locomotives, 119; strike,
    139; travel by, 6, 55, 117-19, 120,
    197-98
Raleigh *News and Observer*, 95
Rand McNally, 9
Randolph, A. Philip, 30, 31
Rankin, Jeanette, 5
Rascoe, Burton, 194
Rationing, 8, 12-13, 43, 70-73, 77,
    79-82, 119-20, 136, 178, 256;
    gasoline, 46-48, 55, 60, 69-70,
    72, 120, 126-27, 136, 138, 222,
    237, 256; preparation for end of,
    178-79, 216, 240
Reagan, Ronald, 97
Real estate values, 206
Realms of Being (Santayana), 231,
    232
Reconstruction Finance Corporation,
    59, 123, 124
Record, Wilson, 236
Red Cross, 6
Reece, B. Carroll, 153
Refugees, 157-58
Remagen, bridge at, 202-203
Remington Arms Company, 42
Republican National Committee, 18
Repulse (battleship), 24
Rice, Harry R., 16

Rickey, Branch, 109
Ritter, Grant A., 162
Rizzuto, Phil, 49
Robertson, William, 203
Robeson, Paul, 30, 32-33, 108, 110
Robinson, Jackie, 109, 235
Robinson, Sugar Ray, 29
Rogers, Ginger, 183
Rogers, Will, Jr., 65
Roman Spring of Mrs. Stone, The,
    233
Rome, Italy, 143
Rommel, Erwin, 91, 92, 170
Rooney, Mickey, 128, 131
Roosevelt, Anna, 218
Roosevelt, Eleanor, 10, 111, 214,
    218
Roosevelt, Franklin D., 19, 26, 35,
    48, 50, 58, 60, 65, 95, 103, 110,
    112, 148, 162-63; building of
    atomic bomb and, 243;
    Casablanca meeting with
    Churchill, 92, 141; civil rights
    and, 31; death of, 216-19;
    declaration of war against Japan, 3;
    fireside chats, 3; fourth inaugural,
    209-10; labor relations and, 4,
    100, 101, 123, 139, 168, 212;
    midterm elections and, 63, 64;
    1944 elections, 146-47, 161, 170-
    75, 180, 181, 183-85, 191, 93;
    Pearl Harbor attack and, 2;
    rationing and, 69; sons of,
    enlistment of, 5; split in inner
    circle of, 123-25; State of the
    Union addresses, 199; wage
    ceilings and, 56; war production
    and, 37-40
Roosevelt, James, 209
Roosevelt, Theodore, 240
Roper poll, Elmo, 172
Rose, Billy, 205
Rose Tattoo, The, 233
Royal Air Force (RAF), 139, 140
Royce, Josiah, 231
Rubber, 13, 14-16, 59-60, 69; *see
    also* Tires

Rubber Reserve Corporation, 59
Ruffing, Red, 49
Russia, *see* Soviet Union
Rutherford, Ernest, 242, 244
Rutherford, Lucy Mercer, 217, 218

St. Louis, Missouri, 121-22
St. Louis Browns, 185-86, 187
St. Louis Cardinals (baseball team),
    17, 49, 185, 186, 187, 235
St. Louis Cardinals (football team),
    134
St. Louis *Globe-Democrat*, 180, 185
Saipan, 206, 207
Salerno, Italy, 142
Saltonstall, Leverett, 63, 96
Salvation Army, 6
Sanford, Herb, 201
San Francisco, California, 9, 253
San Gil (freighter), 25
Santayana, George, 231-32
Santilli, Alex, 21
Saratago (ship), 206
Satterlee, Peggy, 66-67
Saturday Review, 179
Schleppi, Francis, 93-94
Schmeling, Max, 29
Schoeinger, Carl S., 193
Schram, Emil, 254
Schwarz, E. Perrin, 51
Scott, Joseph, 130
Scott, Randolph, 17
Scottsboro Boys, 102
Sears catalog, 41
Seaton, Albert, 205
Sedition, trial for, 159-61
"See It Now," 77
Selective service system, 3-4, 39, 44,
    60, 86-87, 138-39, 197, 198, 199,
    210, 235; conscientious objectors,
    189-91; draft resisters, 164, 189, 240
Selkirk, George, 49
Sellers, Grover, 150
Serber, Robert, 244
Sexual promiscuity, 7, 84-86
Shenango Personnel Replacement
    Center, 106

Sheppard, Morris, 65
Sheridan, Ann, 66
Sherwood, Robert E., 37
Shettler, H. H., 228
Shipbuilding, 55, 165
Shostakovich, Dimitri, 89
Shoumatoff, Elizabeth, 217
Sicily, 141
Silver Shirts, 160
Simmons, Richard O., 93
Simon, Abe, 29, 30
Simon, George T., 200
Sinatra, Frank, 28, 35, 156, 177
Singapore, 24
Situation Normal (Miller), 194
Skeels, James, 219-20
Skelton, Red, 131
Slaughter, Enos, 49
Smith, Al, 124, 173
Smith, Betty, 211
Smith, Gerald L. K., 62, 161
Smith, Howard W., 100-101
Smith, Dr. Lonnie E., 150
Smith, Robert N., 182
Smith, Walter "Beetle," 144
Smith, William F., 238
Smith-Connally Anti-Strike Act,
    100, 123, 168, 212
Smoking, 126, 178
Smythe, Edward, 159
Snead, Sam, 234
Sobel, Robert, 43
Socialist Party, 192
Social Justice, 50-52
Society of Automotive Engineers,
    237
Solomon Islands, 90, 91
Southern Pacific Railroad, 241
Southern Worker, The, 102
Soviet Union, 88, 101, 103, 140,
    203-204, 241, 250; battles in the,
    88-89, 204
So Your Husband's Gone to War
    (Gorham), 87
Spaatz, Carl, 139, 140
Space (Michener), 205
Spangler, Harrison, 147, 148

Spellman, Cardinal Francis J., 254
Spies, 49-50
Sports, 28-29, 45, 185-88, 197-99,
    234-35; baseball, 17, 48-49, 109-
    10, 113, 164, 185-87, 235;
    football, 21, 28, 60-61, 77, 132-
    34, 187, 188, 197, 198-99
Spruance, Raymond A., 145, 206
Stage Door Canteen, 35-36, 132,
    201
Stalin, Joseph, 88, 89, 92, 101, 182,
    241, 247
Stalingrad, fighting at, 88, 89, 204
Standard Oil, 137-38
Stars and Stripes, 100
Stassen, Harold, 149, 161, 162
Steinbeck, John, 142-43
Stevenson, Coke R., 65
Stewart, James, 177
Stilwell, "Vinegar Joe," 239-40
Stimson, Henry L., 30, 32, 139, 247
Stock market, 42-43, 254
Stokowski, Leopold, 229-30
Stone, Harlan, 209
Stoops, Tod, 70
Story of GI Joe, The (Pyle), 194
Stover, John F., 119
Streetcar Named Desire, A, 233
Sullivan brothers, 5
Sulzberger, C. L., 139-40
Summer and Smoke, 233
Summers, Hatton W., 72
Supreme Court, U.S., 50, 64, 65,
    134, 150, 213; Jehovah Witnesses
    case, 114, 115-16
Sweet Bird of Youth, 233
Sylvashko, Alexander, 203
Syndicalist League of North
    America, 102
Szilard, Leo, 242-43, 247

Taft, Robert A., 147, 161, 193
Taft, William Howard, 240
Talmadge, Eugene, 64
Tarawa, 145
Tarbell, Ida Mae, 137-38
Taylor, A. J. P., 225-26

Teller, Edward, 245-46
Texan in England, A (Dobie), 233
Texas, 64-65
Theil, Werner, 50
This is the Army, Mr. Jones, 36, 132
Thomas, Lowell, 22-23
Thomas, Mary, 176
Thomas, Norman, 192
Thomas, R. J., 170
Thompson, Dorothy, 224-25
Thompson, J. J., 244
Tibbets, Paul W., Jr., 248
Tibbetts, D. Reginald, 252
Tierney, Gene, 183
Time, 1, 23, 33, 49-50, 52, 55-56,
    63, 96, 114, 127, 149, 150, 160,
    168, 175, 179, 195-96, 207
Time for Decision, A (Welles), 180
Timulty, Joseph F., 97
Tinian Island, 146, 206, 248
Tires, 13, 14-16, 41, 55, 59, 120,
    197, 237
Tischler, Nancy, 232, 233
To Have and Have Not, 228, 229
Tojo, Premier, 137
Tokyo, bombing raids on, 25, 207,
    208
Toledo, Peoria, and Western
    Railroad, 53
Toronto, Canada, 105
Townsend, Ralph, 11
Toys, 195
Tracy, Spencer, 177
Trains, *see* Railroads
Tree Grows in Brooklyn, A, 211
True, James, 159, 161
Truman, Harry S, 39, 65, 97, 209,
    229; decision to use nuclear
    weapons, 247-48; John L. Lewis
    and, 213; as President, 222-23,
    226, 235, 241, 247, 249-55; the
    railroads and, 119; as Vice
    Presidential candidate, 174-75,
    182, 187, 191
Truman, Margaret, 253
Tubb, Ernest, 154
Tull, Charles J., 51

Tunisia, 91, 92, 114
Turner, Lana, 184

U-boat, German, 8, 24-25
Union Carbide Chemicals, 60
United Auto Workers (UAW), 170
United Mine Workers and America
  (UMWA), 98, 99-101, 103-104,
  111, 113, 122-23, 212-13
United Nations, 216, 240, 241
United Press, 160, 251-52
U.S. Army, 5, 141, 142, 144, 188,
  202-204, 208; Air Force, 113,
  139-40, 247
U.S. Coast Guard, 5, 30
U.S. Marine Corps., 5, 145, 206,
  207, 208
U.S. Navy, 5, 25, 33, 90, 188, 206,
  207
U.S. Steel, 56
United States vs. Joseph E.
  MacWilliams, et al., 160
Ushijimi, M., 208, 209
USO, 6, 49, 132, 201, 228, 231

Vandenberg, Arthur H., 72
Vanderbilt, Gloria, 16-17, 229-30
Vandergrift, Alexander A., 90
Van Gelder, Robert, 190
Van Zandt, James, 47
V-E day, 212, 224, 226-27
Velez, Lupe, 177-78
Venereal diseases, 85
Verrett, Emile, 151
Veterans Administration, 211-12
Veterans of Foreign Wars, 193
Victory gardens, 82, 127
Viereck, George Sylvester, 160
Vinson, Fred M., 126-26, 226-27
V-J day, 227, 253
Vollmoelier, Karl, 11
von Bock, Fedor, 89
Von Braun, Wernher, 205
von Leeb, Wilhelm, 89
von Mannerheim, Carl, 89

von Rundstedt, Gerd, 89, 145, 196,
  203
Von Stauffenburg, Claus, 170

Wage freeze, 56, 57, 98, 139; end
  of, 223
Wainwright, Mrs. Jonathan, 253
Wainwright, Jonathan, 23, 253
Wake Island, 23
Walker, Frank A., 52
Walk in the Sun, A (Brown), 180
Wallace, George, 102
Wallace, Henry, 39, 123-25, 147,
  172-73, 174, 182, 183-84
Wallace's Farmer, 124
Waller, Odell, 110-11
War bond drives, 17-18, 34, 43,
  165, 195, 228
War Department, 9, 74, 196, 235
War Food Administration, 127
"War is Hell," 155
War Labor Board, 43, 56, 57, 58-59,
  123, 139
War Manpower Commission, 43-44,
  133, 166, 199, 200, 205, 210
Warner Brothers, 36
War Powers Act, 124
War Production Board, 4, 13, 37-40,
  59, 82, 83, 112, 125, 159, 166,
  197, 199, 213, 237; railroads and,
  119
War Relief Charities, 133
War Refugee Board, 220
War Relocation Authority, 27, 157
Warren, Earl, 28, 65, 105
Washburn, Lois de Lafayette, 160,
  161
Washington Redskins, 133, 134
Washington Senators, 186
Washington Star, 160
Watanabe, George, 254
Waters, Ethel, 132
Watson, Edwin "Pa," 216-17
Wayne, John, 131, 177
Webb, Walter Prescott, 233-34
Weidemann, Fritz, 11
Weissmuller, Johnny, 177

Welansky, Barnett, 96
Welles, E. A., 181
Welles, Orson, 3, 184
Welles, Sumner, 180
Western Defense Command, 21
Western Union, 22-23
West Virginia State Board of Education vs. Barnette, 115-16
"We the People," 137
White, Byron "Whizzer," 134
White, Walter, 31
White Cliffs of Dover, The, 211
Wickard, Claude R., 79-80, 81, 82
Williams, Aubrey W., 5-6
Williams, Frederick (Wiggy), 11
Williams, Tennessee, 231, 232-33, 236
Willis, Paul S., 13
Wilkie, Wendell, 28, 39, 98, 147, 148, 149, 150, 161
Wills, Bob, 151
Wills, Raymond E., 70
Wilson, Margaret, 94-95
Wilson, Woodrow, 63, 240, 241
Winters, Shelly, 83-84
Wisconsin, 62
W. L. Sneed (merchantman), 24-25
Woman's Army Auxiliary Corps (WACs), 52-53

Women, 137-38, 214-15; in the armed services, 52-53, 214; in Congress, 193, 214; in labor force, 6, 33, 85-86, 167, 214; "lonely wife," 87-88; movement of, 6-7
W₁AW, 12
Wood, Robert E., 18
Woodhouse, Chase G., 193
Woodruff, E. N., 72
Workers' Defense League, 110
Works Progress Administration (WPA), 40
World of Washington Irving, The (Brooks), 180
WOR radio, 2, 9
Wright, Carleton H., 255-56
Wright, Cleo, 30-31
Wright, Richard, 235-36
Wright Aircraft, 169-70

Yamamoto, Isoroku, 3, 25, 91
Yamata (warship), 208
Ying Ong, 12
You Touched Me!, 233

Zhukov, Marshal, 89, 204
Zoot suit riots, 104-105

ABOUT THE AUTHOR

Paul Douglas Casdorph, Ed.D., was born in Appalachia where his family has resided for six generations; after receiving two degrees from The University of Texas at Austin, he earned a doctorate at the University of Kentucky in 1970. He has been a chemical plant worker, a social welfare officer, a college professor, and is currently chairman of the history faculty at West Virginia State College; he is also adjunct professor of history in the West Virginia College of Graduate Studies and has been a visiting professor at the University of Charleston.

In addition to his interest in World War II, the author has been a longtime student of southern politics; his previous books include A *History of the Republican Party in Texas, 1865–1965* (with an Introduction by Dwight D. Eisenhower), *Republicans, Negroes, and Progressives in the South, 1912–1916*, and more than seventy articles and reviews in professional journals that deal with various phases of American history. He has also been an active radio ham operator (W8HXX) for more than forty years.

He is married and lives with his wife, Patricia, in Charleston, West Virginia.